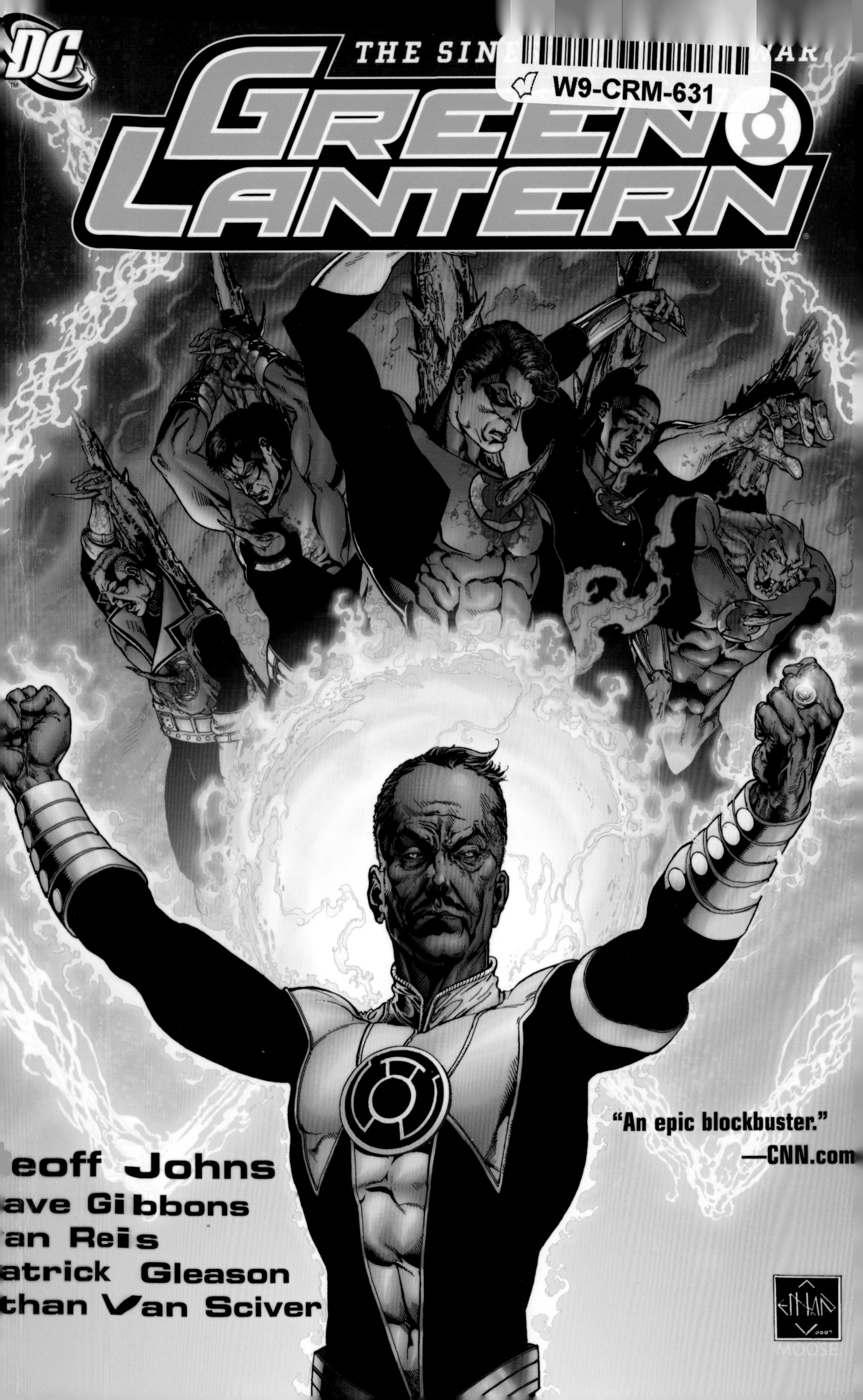
DC
THE SINE
WAR
GREEN LANTERN
"An epic blockbuster."
—CNN.com
eoff Johns
ave Gibbons
an Reis
atrick Gleason
than Van Sciver

GREEN LANTERN

THE SINESTRO CORPS WAR

volume one

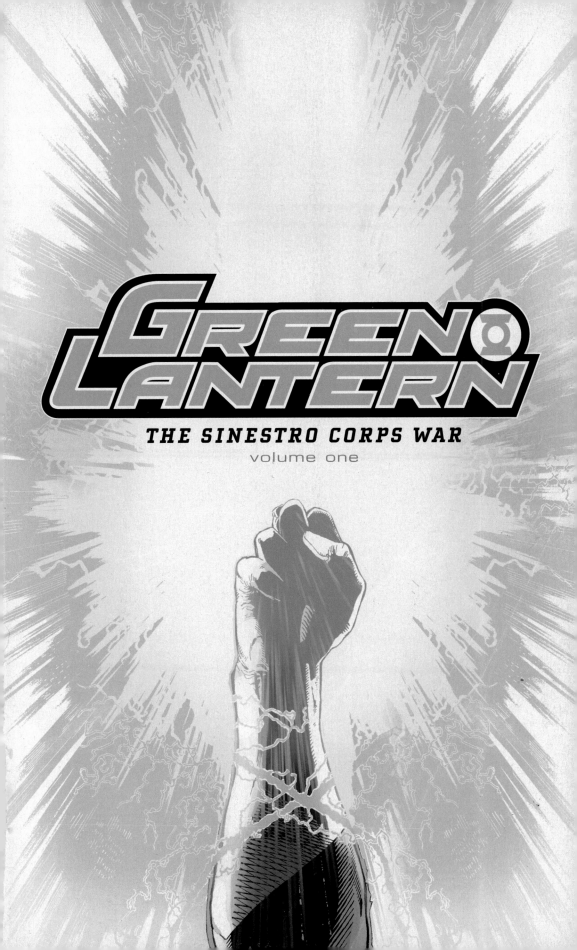

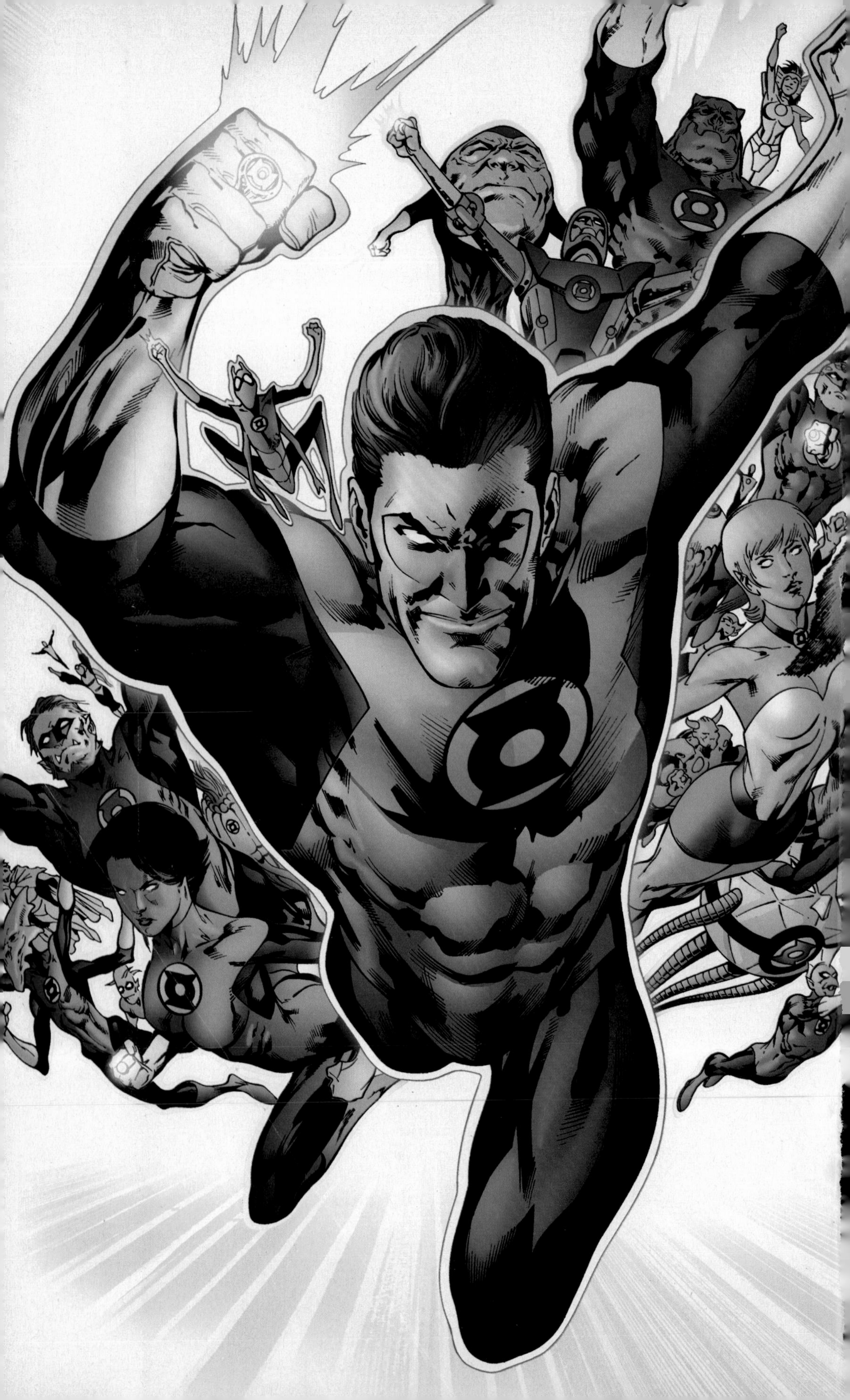

GREEN LANTERN

THE SINESTRO CORPS WAR

Geoff Johns   Dave Gibbons
Writers

Ethan Van Sciver   Ivan Reis   Patrick Gleason   Angel Unzeta
Pencillers

Ethan Van Sciver   Oclair Albert   Prentis Rollins   Drew Geraci
Inkers

Moose Baumann   Guy Major
Colorists

Rob Leigh   Phil Balsman
Letterers

DC COMICS

Dan DiDio Senior VP-Executive Editor
Peter Tomasi Eddie Berganza
Editors-original series
Elisabeth V. Gehrlein Adam Schlagman
Assistant Editors-original series
Bob Joy Editor-collected edition
Robbin Brosterman Senior Art Director
Paul Levitz President & Publisher
Georg Brewer VP-Design & DC Direct Creative
Richard Bruning Senior VP-Creative Director
Patrick Caldon Executive VP-Finance & Operations
Chris Caramalis VP-Finance
John Cunningham VP-Marketing
Terri Cunningham VP-Managing Editor
Stephanie Fierman Senior VP-Sales & Marketing
Alison Gill VP-Manufacturing
David Hyde VP-Publicity
Hank Kanalz VP-General Manager, WildStorm
Jim Lee Editorial Director-WildStorm
Paula Lowitt Senior VP-Business & Legal Affairs
MaryEllen McLaughlin VP-Advertising &
Custom Publishing
John Nee VP-Business Development
Gregory Noveck Senior VP-Creative Affairs
Sue Pohja VP-Book Trade Sales
Steve Rotterdam Senior VP-Sales & Marketing
Cheryl Rubin Senior VP-Brand Management
Jeff Trojan VP-Business Development, DC Direct
Bob Wayne VP-Sales

Cover art by Ethan Van Sciver and Moose Baumann

GREEN LANTERN: THE SINESTRO CORPS WAR
Volume 1
Published by DC Comics. Cover and compilation Copyright © 2008
DC Comics. All Rights Reserved.

Originally published in single magazine form in GREEN LANTERN 21-23,
GREEN LANTERN CORPS 14-15, GREEN LANTERN: SINESTRO CORPS
SPECIAL. Copyright © 2007 DC Comics. All Rights Reserved.
All characters, their distinctive likenesses and related elements featured
in this publication are trademarks of DC Comics. The stories,
characters and incidents featured in this publication are entirely
fictional. DC Comics does not read or accept unsolicited submissions
of ideas, stories or artwork.

DC Comics, 1700 Broadway, New York, NY 10019
A Warner Bros. Entertainment Company
Printed in Canada. First Printing.

ISBN: 978-1-4012-1870-6

SUSTAINABLE FORESTRY INITIATIVE
Certified Fiber Sourcing
www.sfiprogram.org

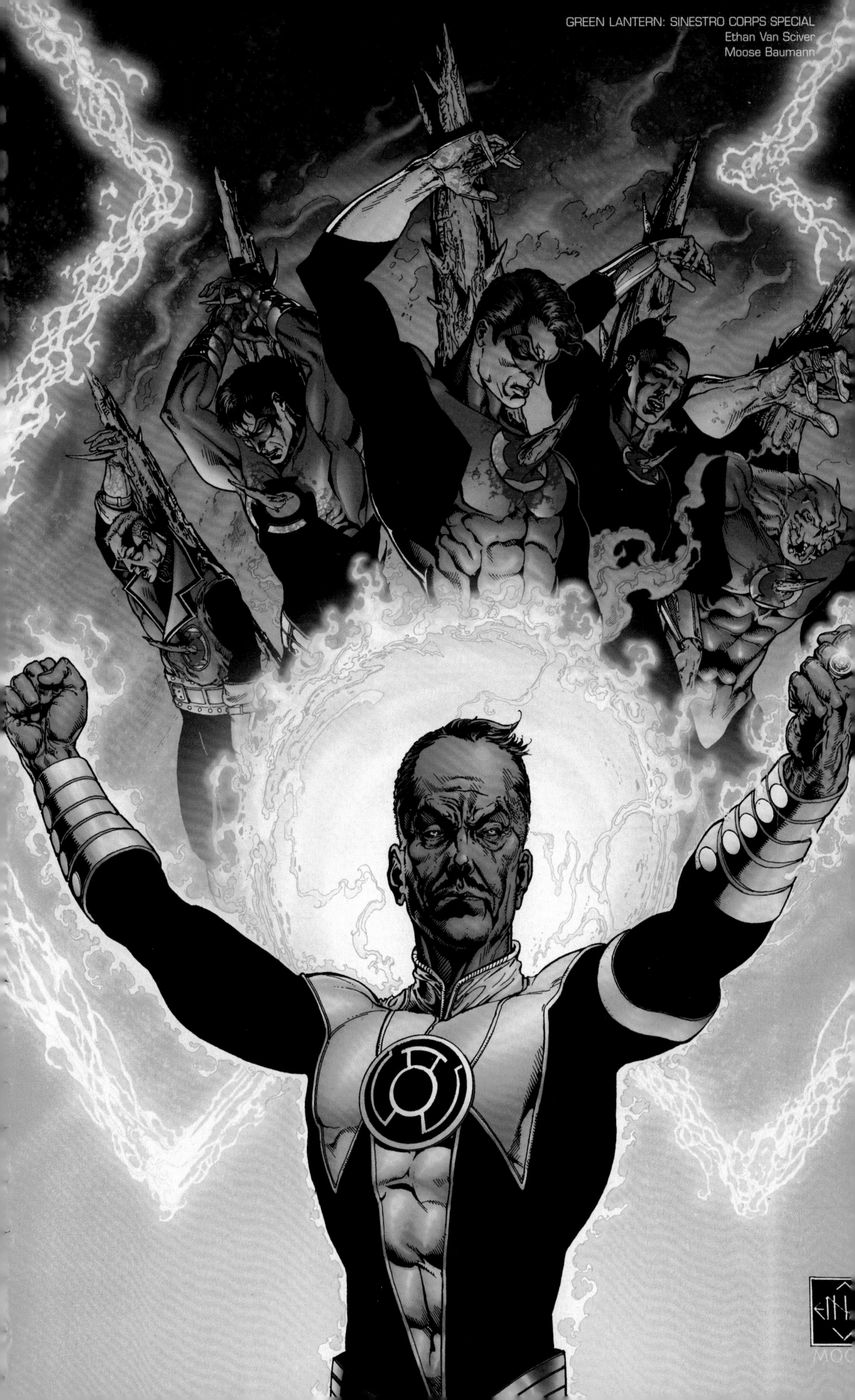

GREEN LANTERN: SINESTRO CORPS SPECIAL
Ethan Van Sciver
Moose Baumann

THE SINESTRO CORPS WAR
Prologue
THE SECOND REBIRTH
Writer: **Geoff Johns**
Artist: **Ethan Van Sciver**
Colorist: **Moose Baumann**

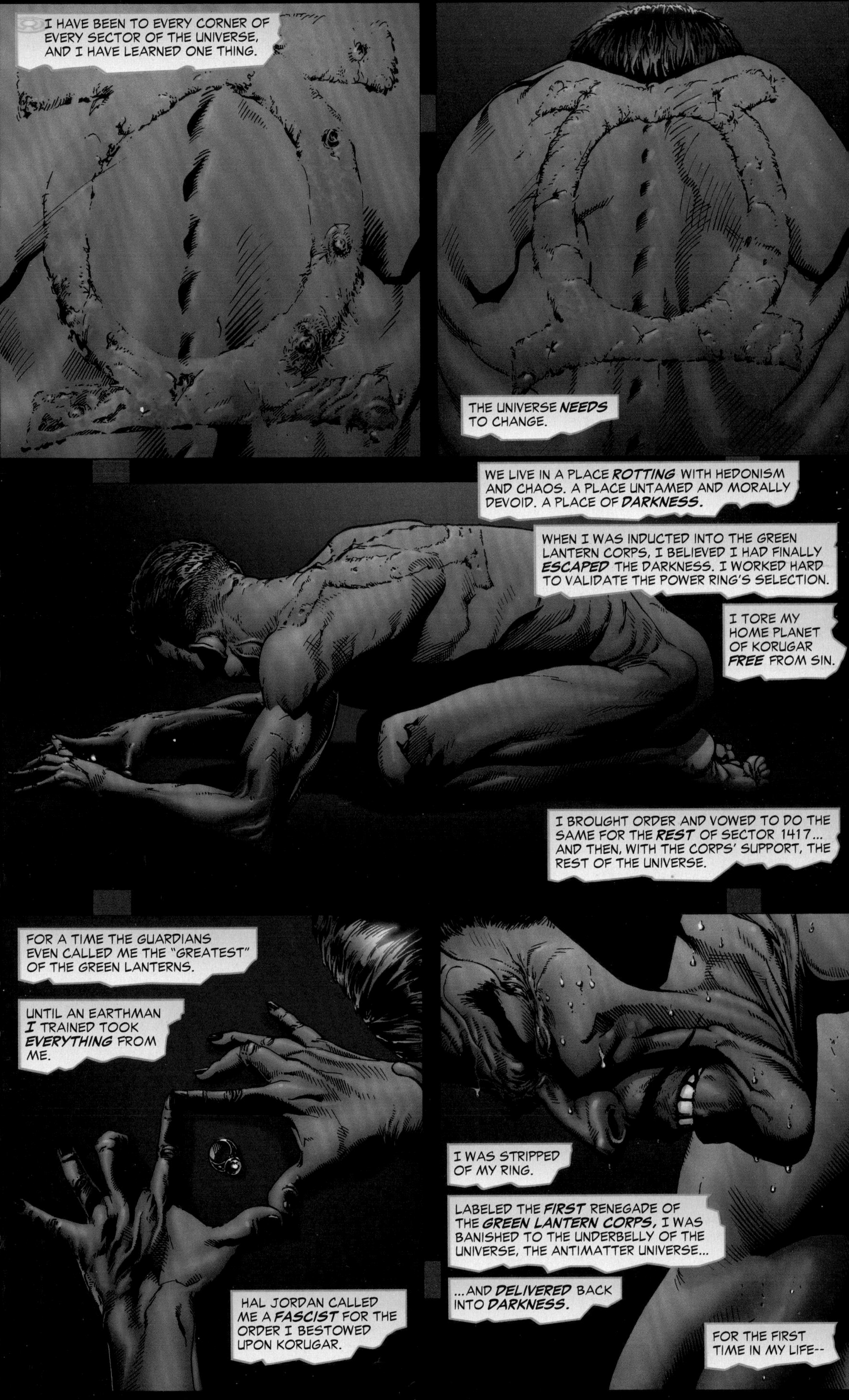
I HAVE BEEN TO EVERY CORNER OF EVERY SECTOR OF THE UNIVERSE, AND I HAVE LEARNED ONE THING.
THE UNIVERSE NEEDS TO CHANGE.
WE LIVE IN A PLACE ROTTING WITH HEDONISM AND CHAOS. A PLACE UNTAMED AND MORALLY DEVOID. A PLACE OF DARKNESS.
WHEN I WAS INDUCTED INTO THE GREEN LANTERN CORPS, I BELIEVED I HAD FINALLY ESCAPED THE DARKNESS. I WORKED HARD TO VALIDATE THE POWER RING'S SELECTION.
I TORE MY HOME PLANET OF KORUGAR FREE FROM SIN.
I BROUGHT ORDER AND VOWED TO DO THE SAME FOR THE REST OF SECTOR 1417... AND THEN, WITH THE CORPS' SUPPORT, THE REST OF THE UNIVERSE.
FOR A TIME THE GUARDIANS EVEN CALLED ME THE "GREATEST" OF THE GREEN LANTERNS.
UNTIL AN EARTHMAN I TRAINED TOOK EVERYTHING FROM ME.
HAL JORDAN CALLED ME A FASCIST FOR THE ORDER I BESTOWED UPON KORUGAR.
I WAS STRIPPED OF MY RING.
LABELED THE FIRST RENEGADE OF THE GREEN LANTERN CORPS, I WAS BANISHED TO THE UNDERBELLY OF THE UNIVERSE, THE ANTIMATTER UNIVERSE...
...AND DELIVERED BACK INTO DARKNESS.
FOR THE FIRST TIME IN MY LIFE--

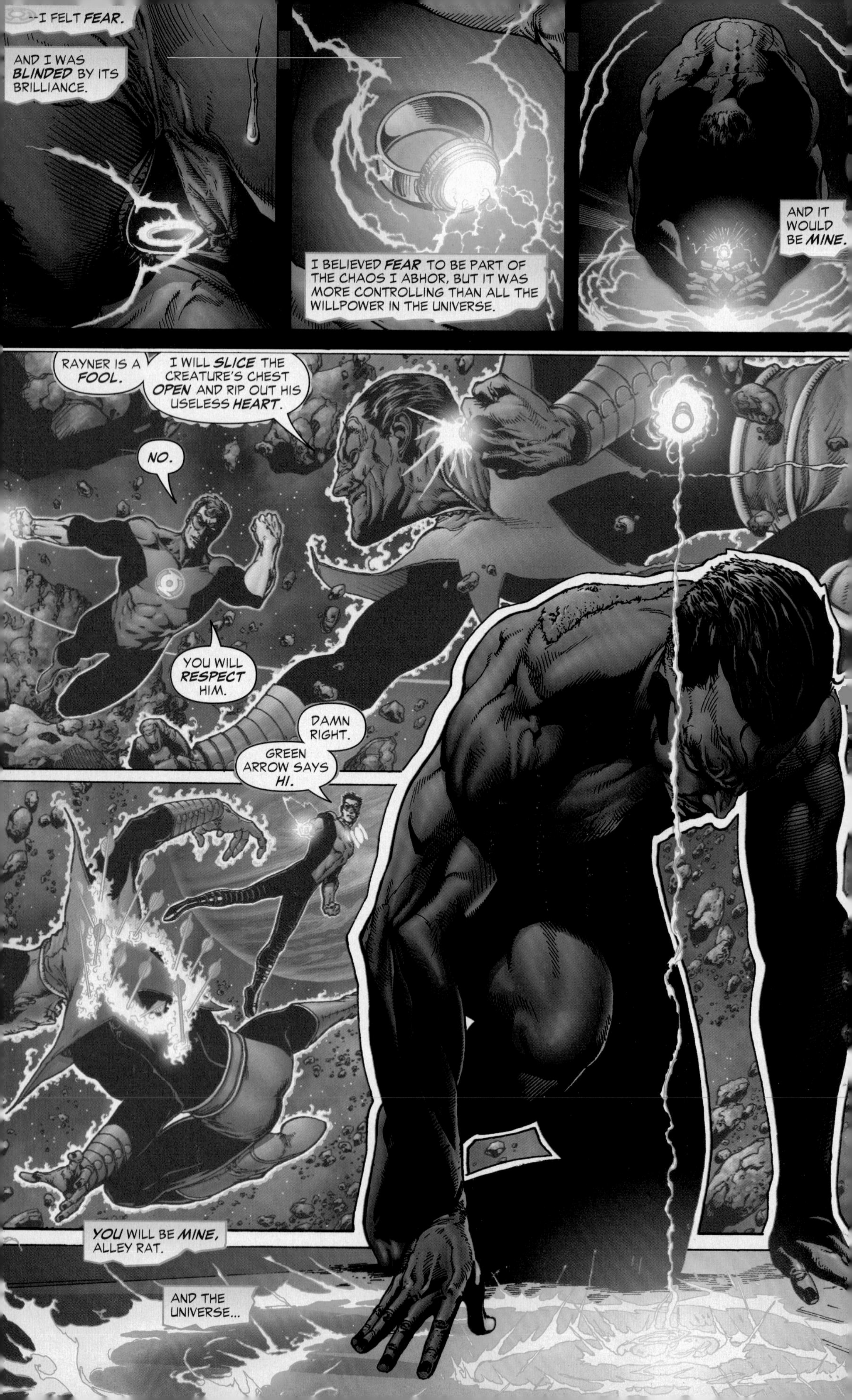
--I FELT FEAR.
AND I WAS BLINDED BY ITS BRILLIANCE.
I BELIEVED FEAR TO BE PART OF THE CHAOS I ABHOR, BUT IT WAS MORE CONTROLLING THAN ALL THE WILLPOWER IN THE UNIVERSE.
AND IT WOULD BE MINE.
RAYNER IS A FOOL.
I WILL SLICE THE CREATURE'S CHEST OPEN AND RIP OUT HIS USELESS HEART.
NO.
YOU WILL RESPECT HIM.
DAMN RIGHT.
GREEN ARROW SAYS HI.
YOU WILL BE MINE, ALLEY RAT.
AND THE UNIVERSE...

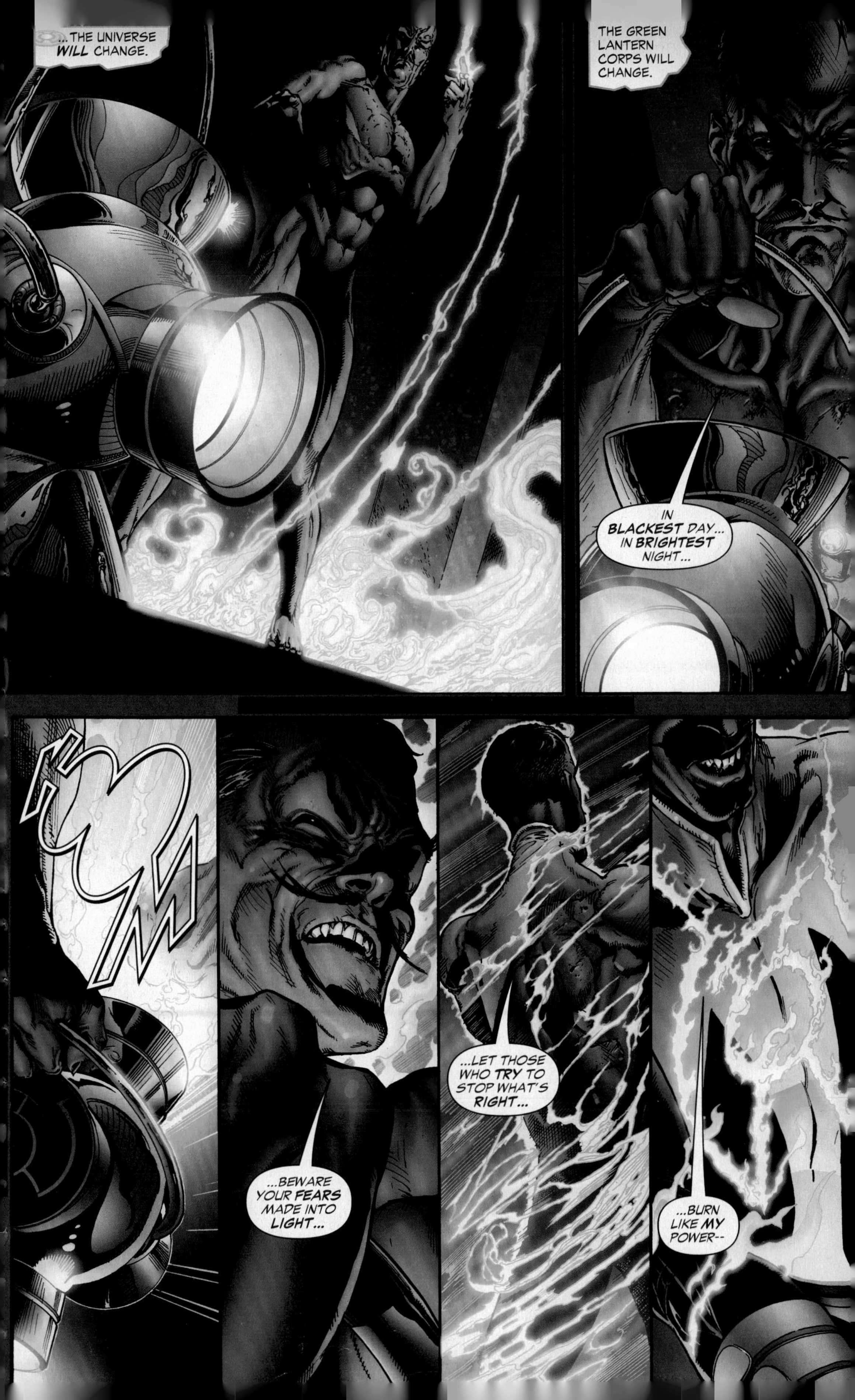
...THE UNIVERSE WILL CHANGE.
THE GREEN LANTERN CORPS WILL CHANGE.
IN BLACKEST DAY... IN BRIGHTEST NIGHT...
...BEWARE YOUR FEARS MADE INTO LIGHT...
...LET THOSE WHO TRY TO STOP WHAT'S RIGHT...
...BURN LIKE MY POWER--

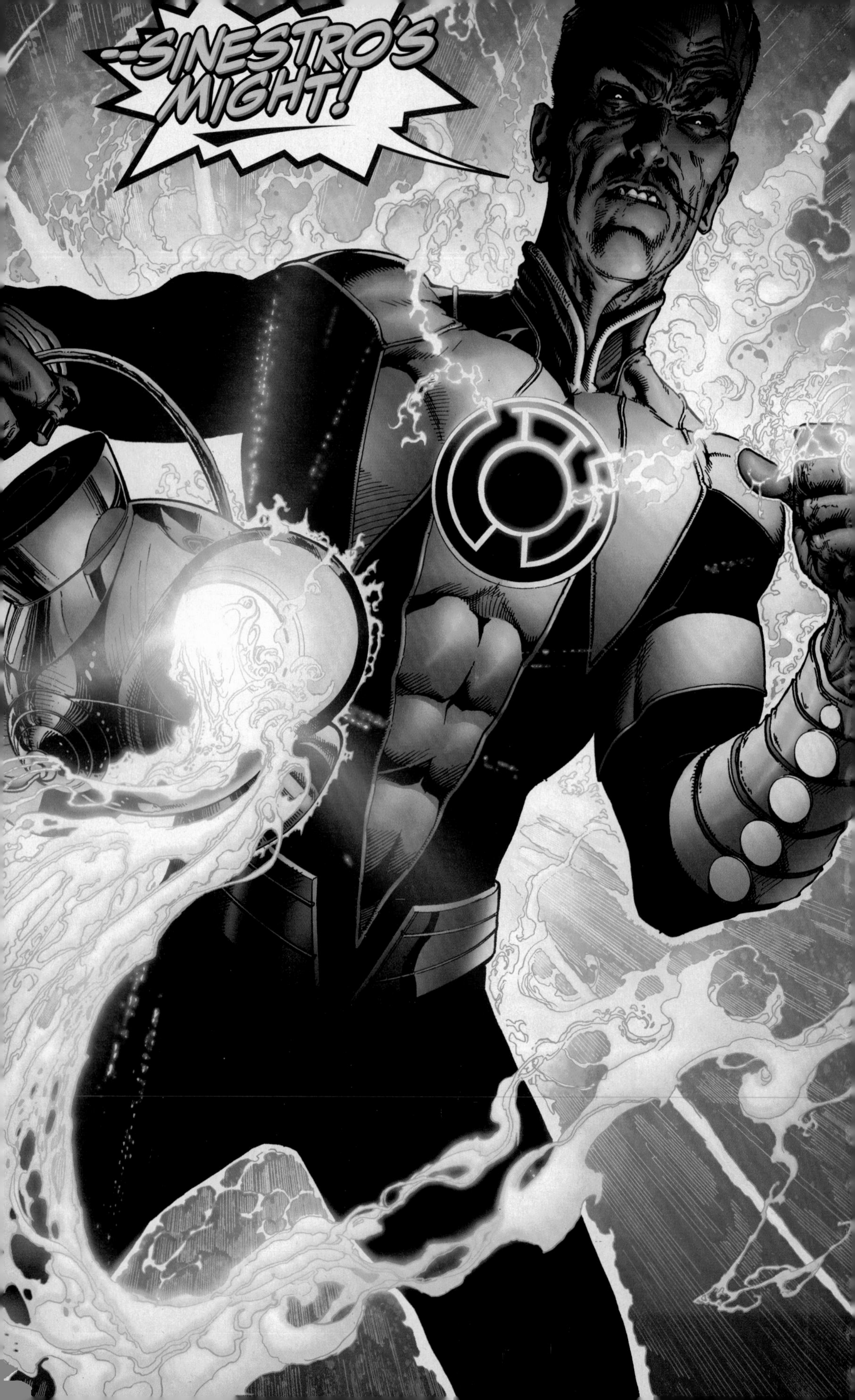
--SINESTRO'S MIGHT!

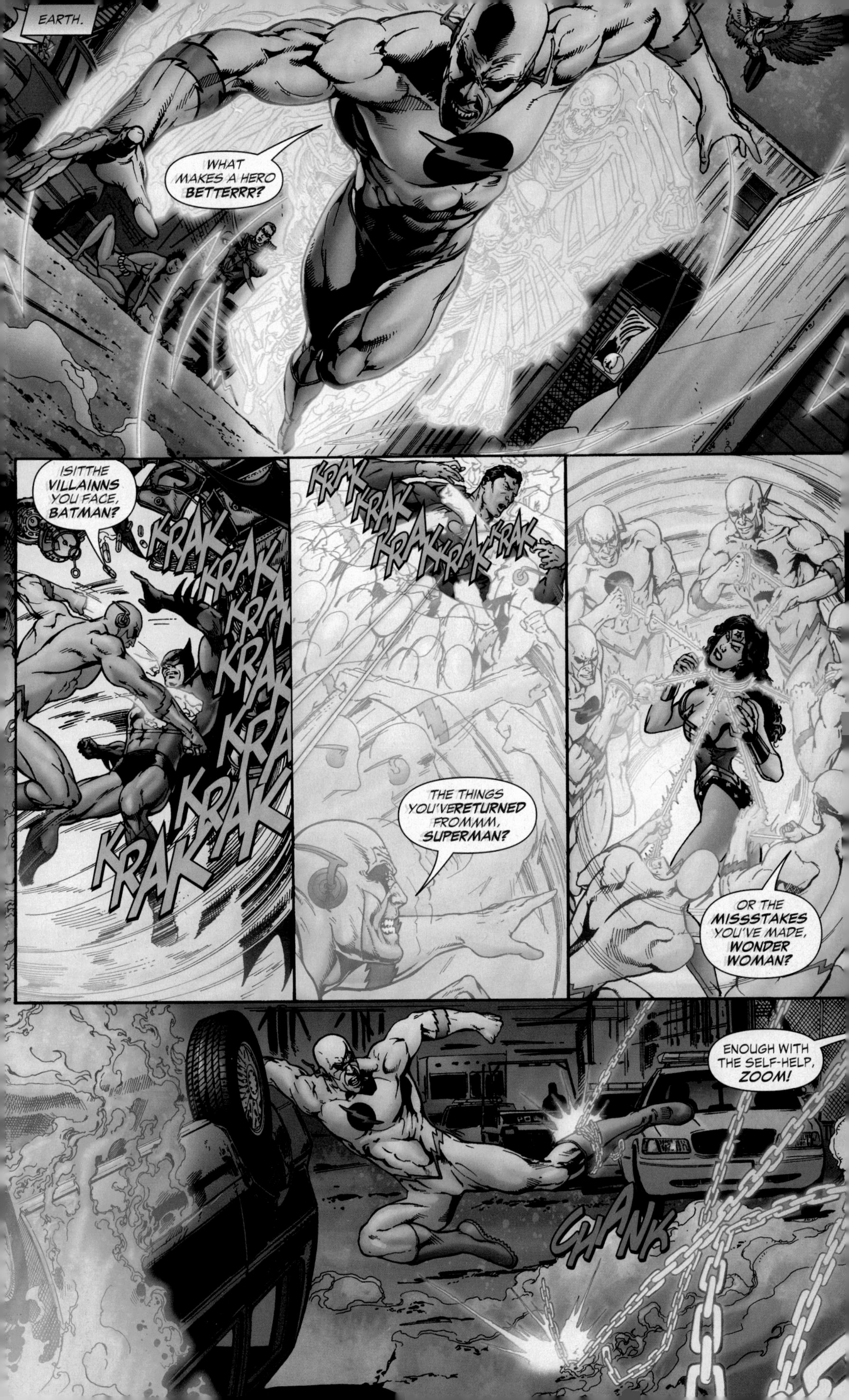
EARTH.
WHAT MAKES A HERO BETTERRR?
ISITTHE VILLAINNS YOU FACE, BATMAN?
KRAK KRAK KRAK KRAK KRAK KRAK KRAK KRAK KRAK
KRAK KRAK KRAK KRAK KRAK
THE THINGS YOU'VERETURNED FROMMM, SUPERMAN?
OR THE MISSSTAKES YOU'VE MADE, WONDER WOMAN?
ENOUGH WITH THE SELF-HELP, ZOOM!
CHANK

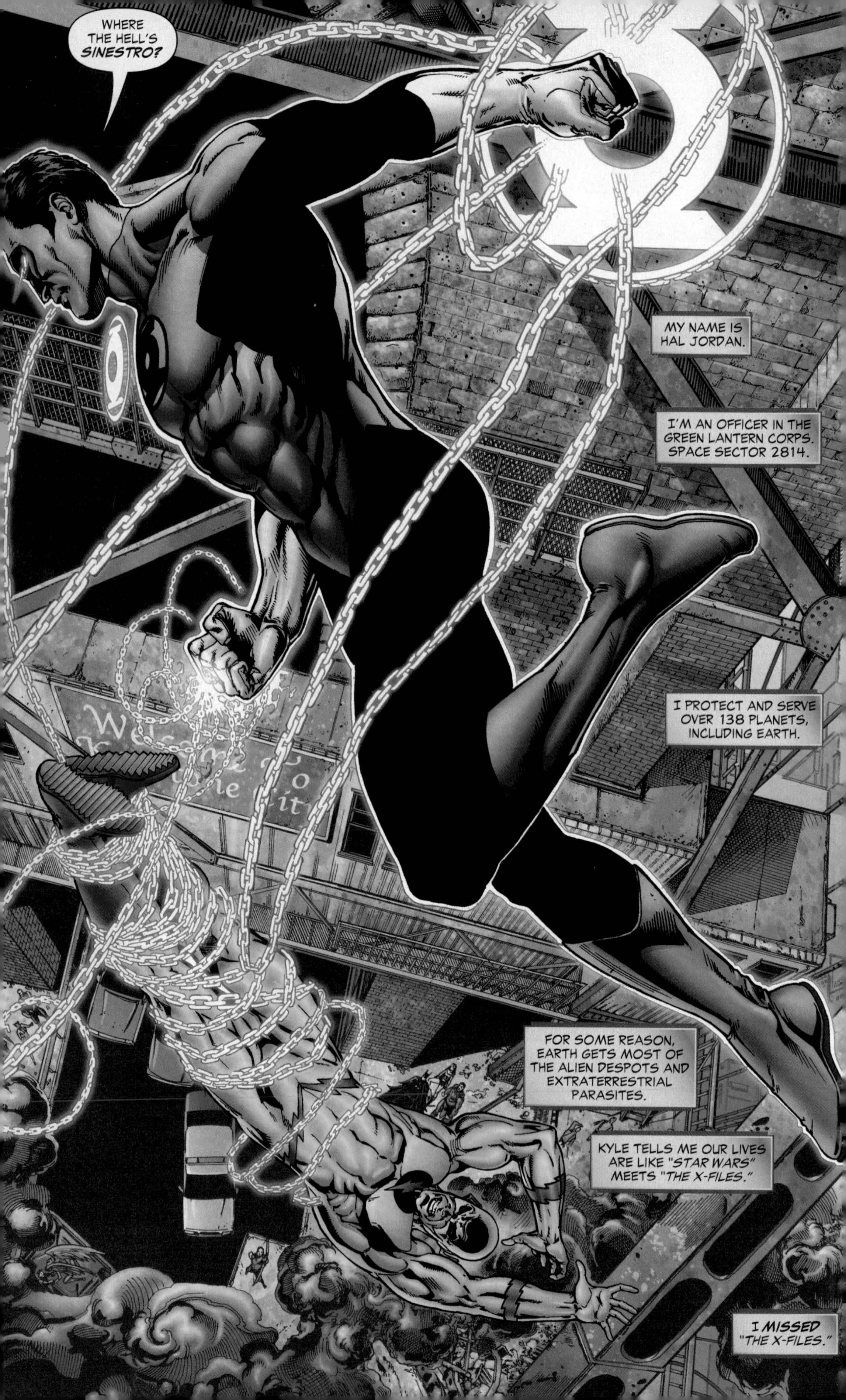
WHERE THE HELL'S *SINESTRO?*
MY NAME IS HAL JORDAN.
I'M AN OFFICER IN THE GREEN LANTERN CORPS. SPACE SECTOR 2814.
I PROTECT AND SERVE OVER 138 PLANETS, INCLUDING EARTH.
FOR SOME REASON, EARTH GETS MOST OF THE ALIEN DESPOTS AND EXTRATERRESTRIAL PARASITES.
KYLE TELLS ME OUR LIVES ARE LIKE "*STAR WARS*" MEETS "*THE X-FILES.*"
I *MISSED* "*THE X-FILES.*"

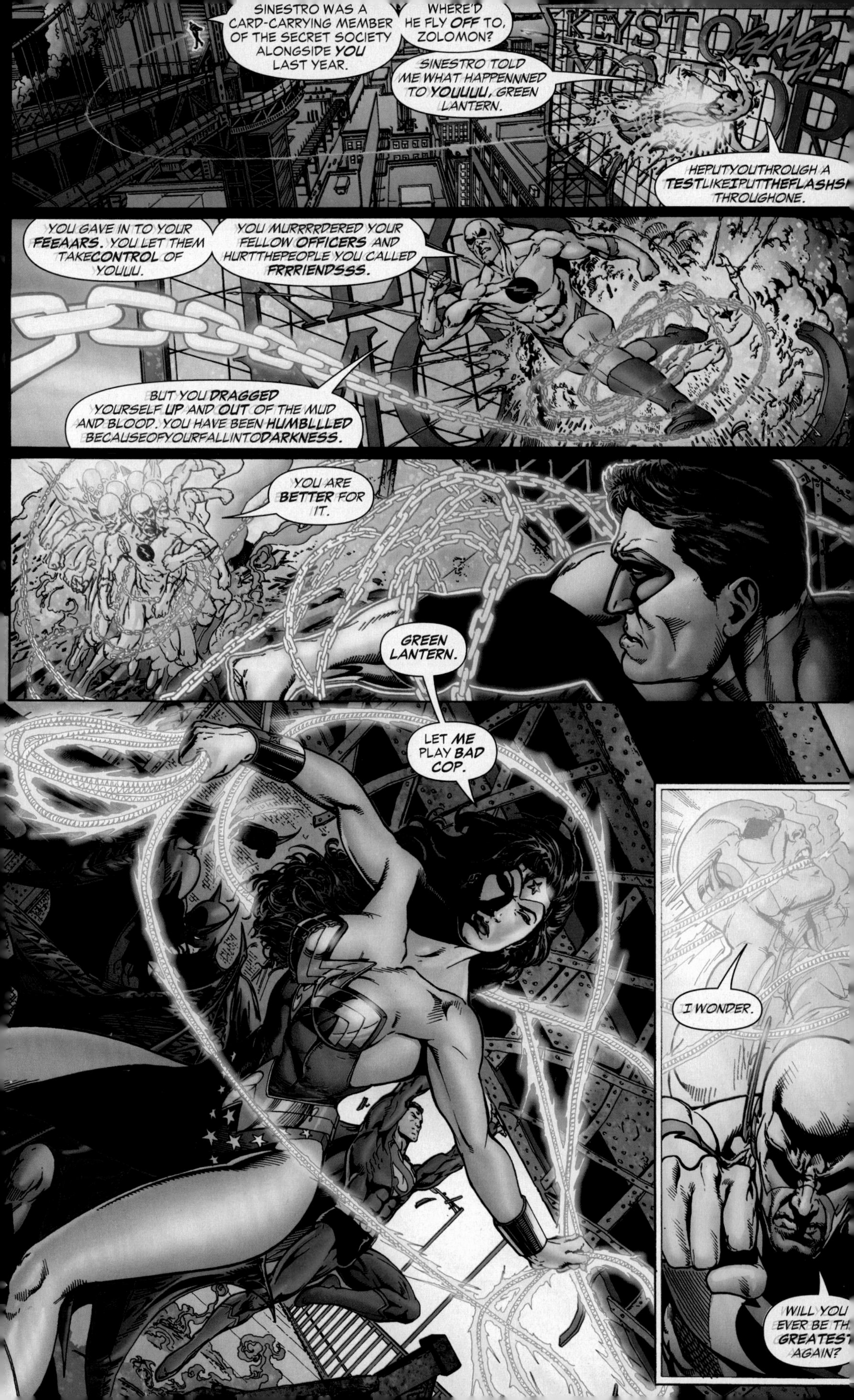
SINESTRO WAS A CARD-CARRYING MEMBER OF THE SECRET SOCIETY ALONGSIDE YOU LAST YEAR.
WHERE'D HE FLY OFF TO, ZOLOMON?
SINESTRO TOLD ME WHAT HAPPENNNED TO YOUUUU, GREEN LANTERN.
HEPUTYOUTHROUGH A TESTLIKEIPUTTHEFLASHS THROUGHONE.
YOU GAVE IN TO YOUR FEEAARS. YOU LET THEM TAKECONTROL OF YOUUU.
YOU MURRRRDERED YOUR FELLOW OFFICERS AND HURTTHEPEOPLE YOU CALLED FRRRIENDSSS.
BUT YOU DRAGGED YOURSELF UP AND OUT OF THE MUD AND BLOOD. YOU HAVE BEEN HUMBLLLED BECAUSEOFYOURFALLINTODARKNESS.
YOU ARE BETTER FOR IT.
GREEN LANTERN.
LET ME PLAY BAD COP.
I WONDER.
WILL YOU EVER BE THE GREATEST AGAIN?

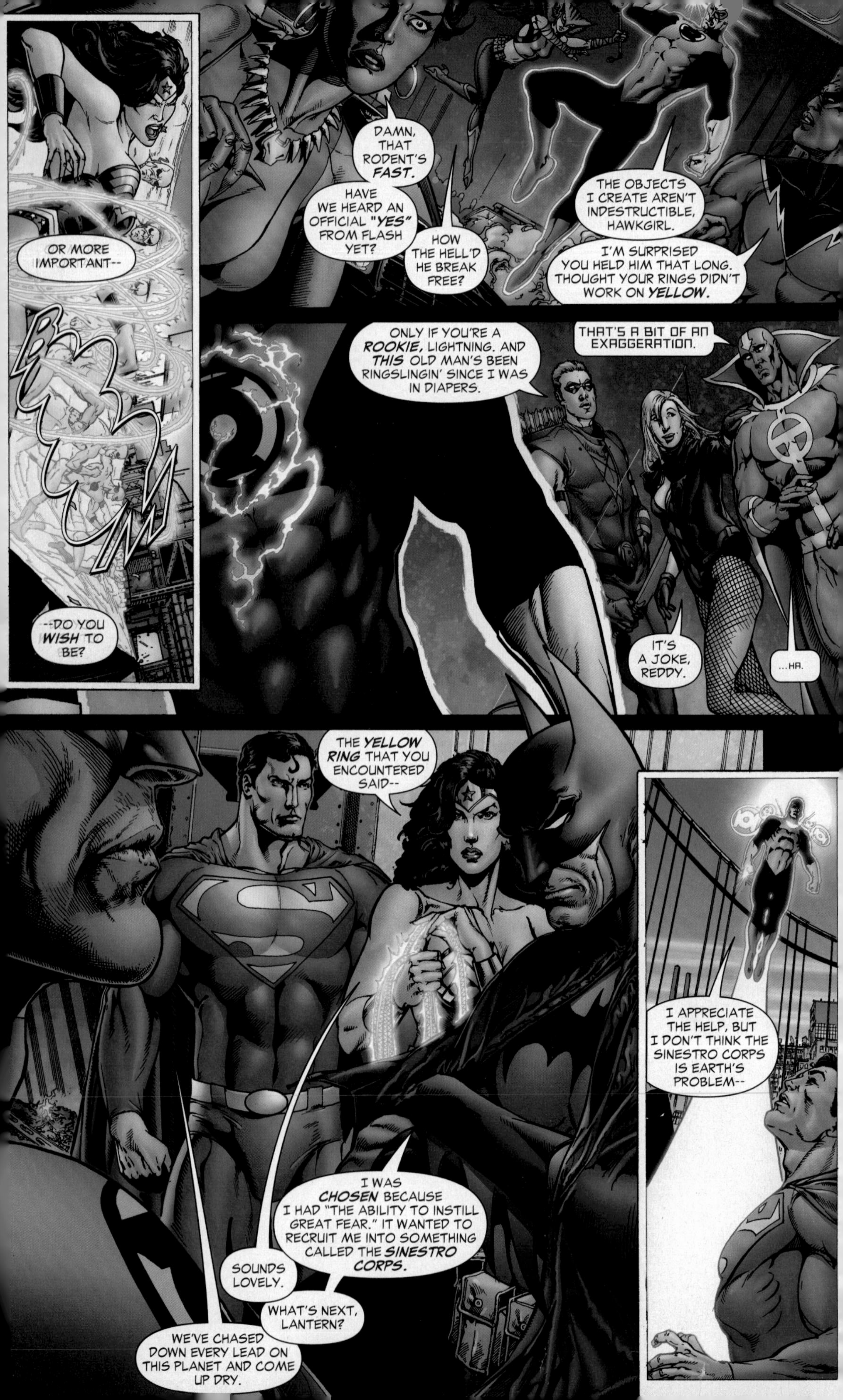
DAMN, THAT RODENT'S FAST.
HAVE WE HEARD AN OFFICIAL "YES" FROM FLASH YET?
HOW THE HELL'D HE BREAK FREE?
THE OBJECTS I CREATE AREN'T INDESTRUCTIBLE, HAWKGIRL.
I'M SURPRISED YOU HELD HIM THAT LONG. THOUGHT YOUR RINGS DIDN'T WORK ON YELLOW.
OR MORE IMPORTANT--
BOOM
--DO YOU WISH TO BE?
ONLY IF YOU'RE A ROOKIE, LIGHTNING. AND THIS OLD MAN'S BEEN RINGSLINGIN' SINCE I WAS IN DIAPERS.
THAT'S A BIT OF AN EXAGGERATION.
IT'S A JOKE, REDDY.
...HA.
THE YELLOW RING THAT YOU ENCOUNTERED SAID--
I WAS CHOSEN BECAUSE I HAD "THE ABILITY TO INSTILL GREAT FEAR." IT WANTED TO RECRUIT ME INTO SOMETHING CALLED THE SINESTRO CORPS.
SOUNDS LOVELY.
WHAT'S NEXT, LANTERN?
WE'VE CHASED DOWN EVERY LEAD ON THIS PLANET AND COME UP DRY.
I APPRECIATE THE HELP, BUT I DON'T THINK THE SINESTRO CORPS IS EARTH'S PROBLEM--

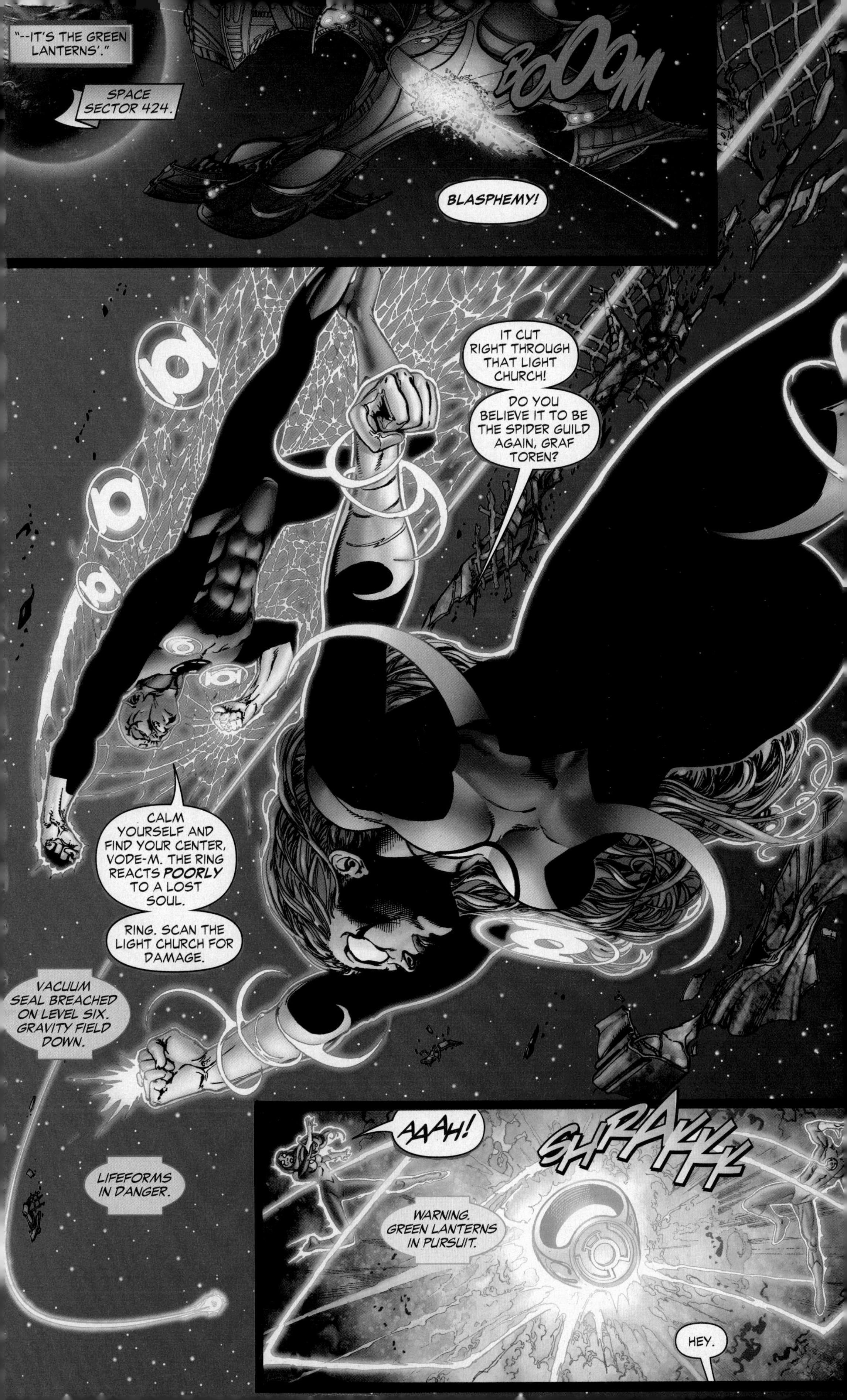
"--IT'S THE GREEN LANTERNS'."
SPACE SECTOR 424.
BOOOOM
BLASPHEMY!
IT CUT RIGHT THROUGH THAT LIGHT CHURCH!
DO YOU BELIEVE IT TO BE THE SPIDER GUILD AGAIN, GRAF TOREN?
CALM YOURSELF AND FIND YOUR CENTER, VODE-M. THE RING REACTS POORLY TO A LOST SOUL.
RING. SCAN THE LIGHT CHURCH FOR DAMAGE.
VACUUM SEAL BREACHED ON LEVEL SIX. GRAVITY FIELD DOWN.
LIFEFORMS IN DANGER.
AAAH!
SHRAKKK
WARNING. GREEN LANTERNS IN PURSUIT.
HEY.

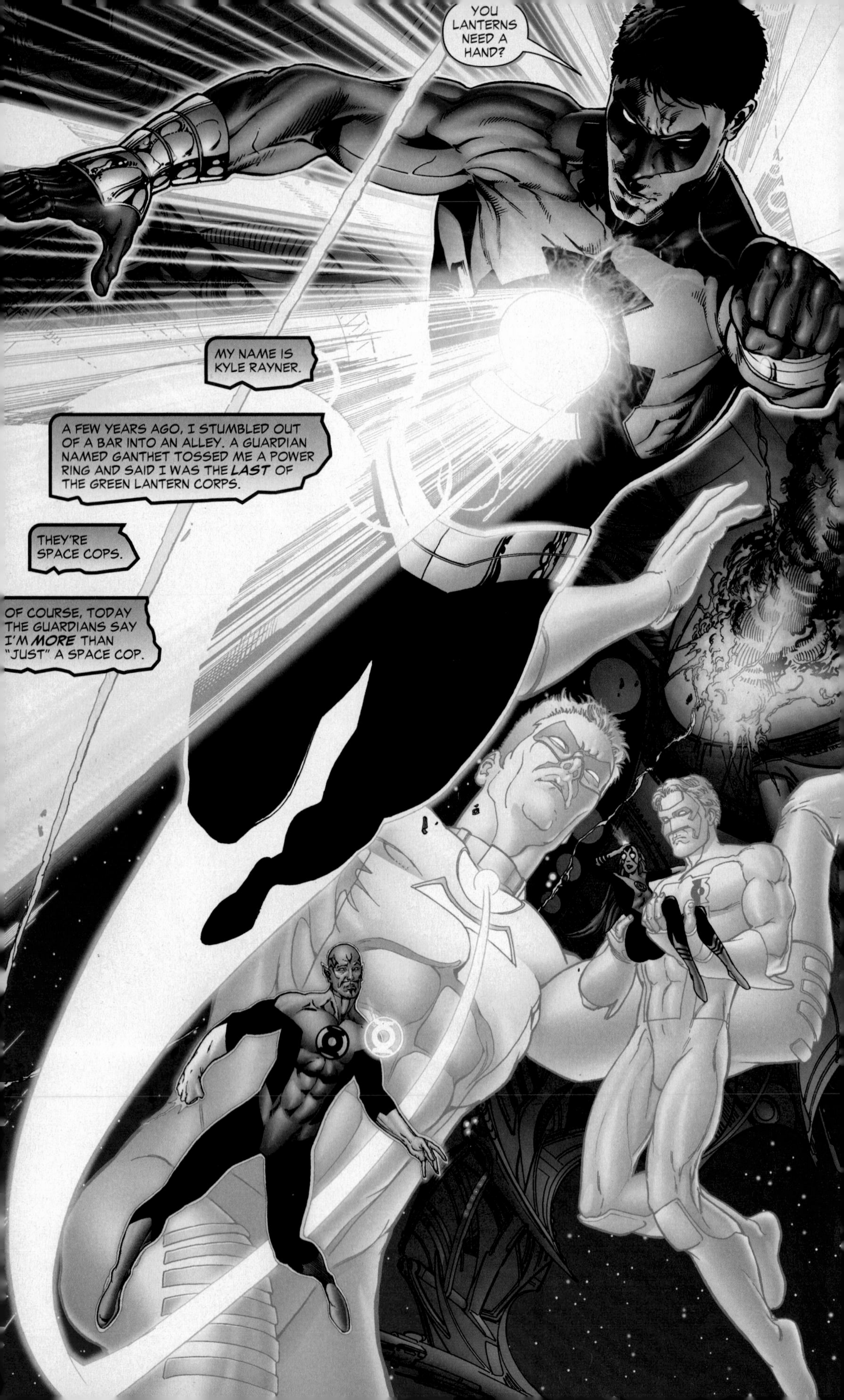
YOU LANTERNS NEED A HAND?
MY NAME IS KYLE RAYNER.
A FEW YEARS AGO, I STUMBLED OUT OF A BAR INTO AN ALLEY. A GUARDIAN NAMED GANTHET TOSSED ME A POWER RING AND SAID I WAS THE LAST OF THE GREEN LANTERN CORPS.
THEY'RE SPACE COPS.
OF COURSE, TODAY THE GUARDIANS SAY I'M MORE THAN "JUST" A SPACE COP.

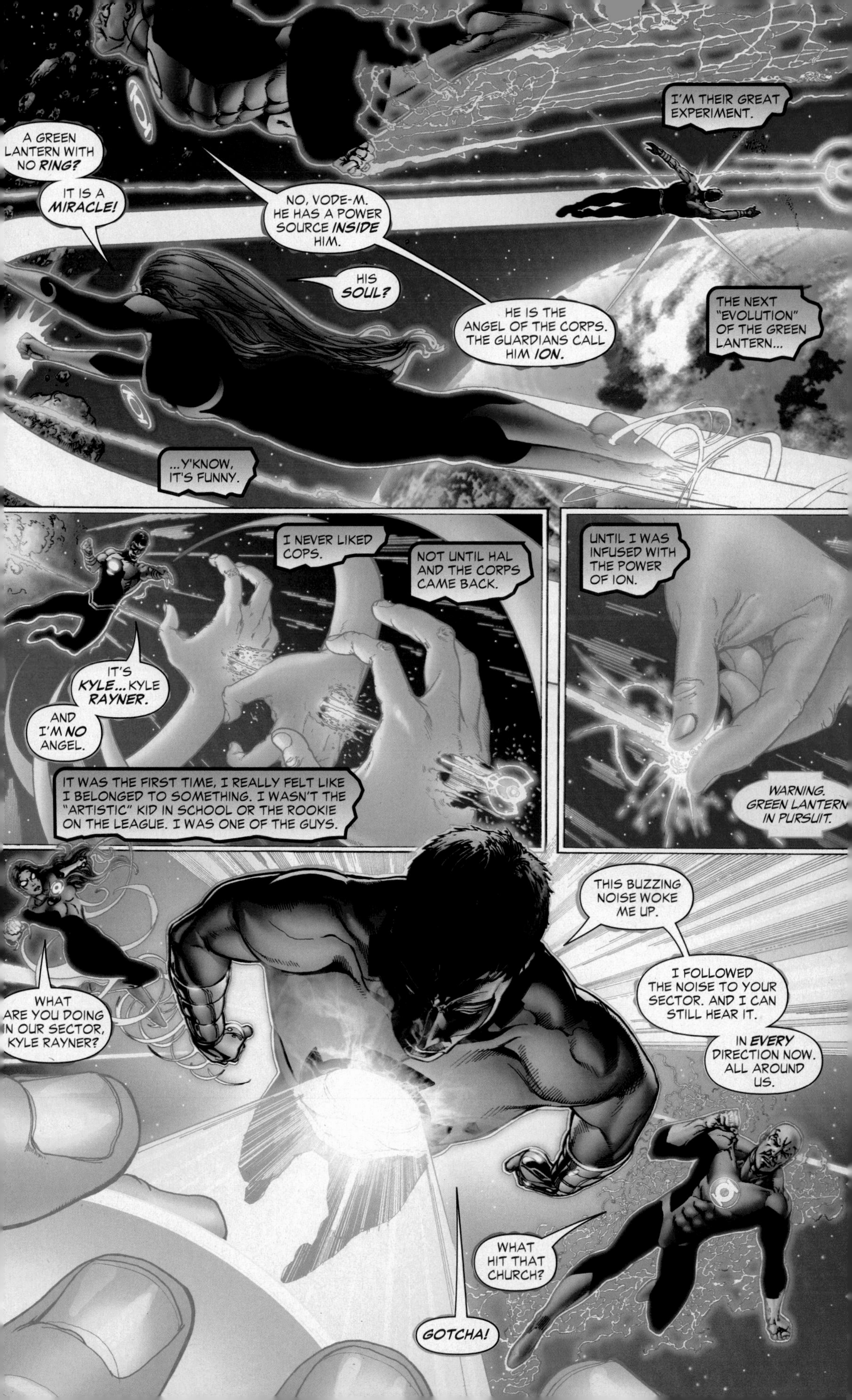
A GREEN LANTERN WITH NO RING?
IT IS A MIRACLE!
NO, VODE-M. HE HAS A POWER SOURCE INSIDE HIM.
HIS SOUL?
HE IS THE ANGEL OF THE CORPS. THE GUARDIANS CALL HIM ION.
I'M THEIR GREAT EXPERIMENT.
THE NEXT "EVOLUTION" OF THE GREEN LANTERN...
...Y'KNOW, IT'S FUNNY.
I NEVER LIKED COPS.
NOT UNTIL HAL AND THE CORPS CAME BACK.
IT'S KYLE... KYLE RAYNER.
AND I'M NO ANGEL.
IT WAS THE FIRST TIME, I REALLY FELT LIKE I BELONGED TO SOMETHING. I WASN'T THE "ARTISTIC" KID IN SCHOOL OR THE ROOKIE ON THE LEAGUE. I WAS ONE OF THE GUYS.
UNTIL I WAS INFUSED WITH THE POWER OF ION.
WARNING. GREEN LANTERN IN PURSUIT.
WHAT ARE YOU DOING IN OUR SECTOR, KYLE RAYNER?
THIS BUZZING NOISE WOKE ME UP.
I FOLLOWED THE NOISE TO YOUR SECTOR. AND I CAN STILL HEAR IT.
IN EVERY DIRECTION NOW. ALL AROUND US.
WHAT HIT THAT CHURCH?
GOTCHA!

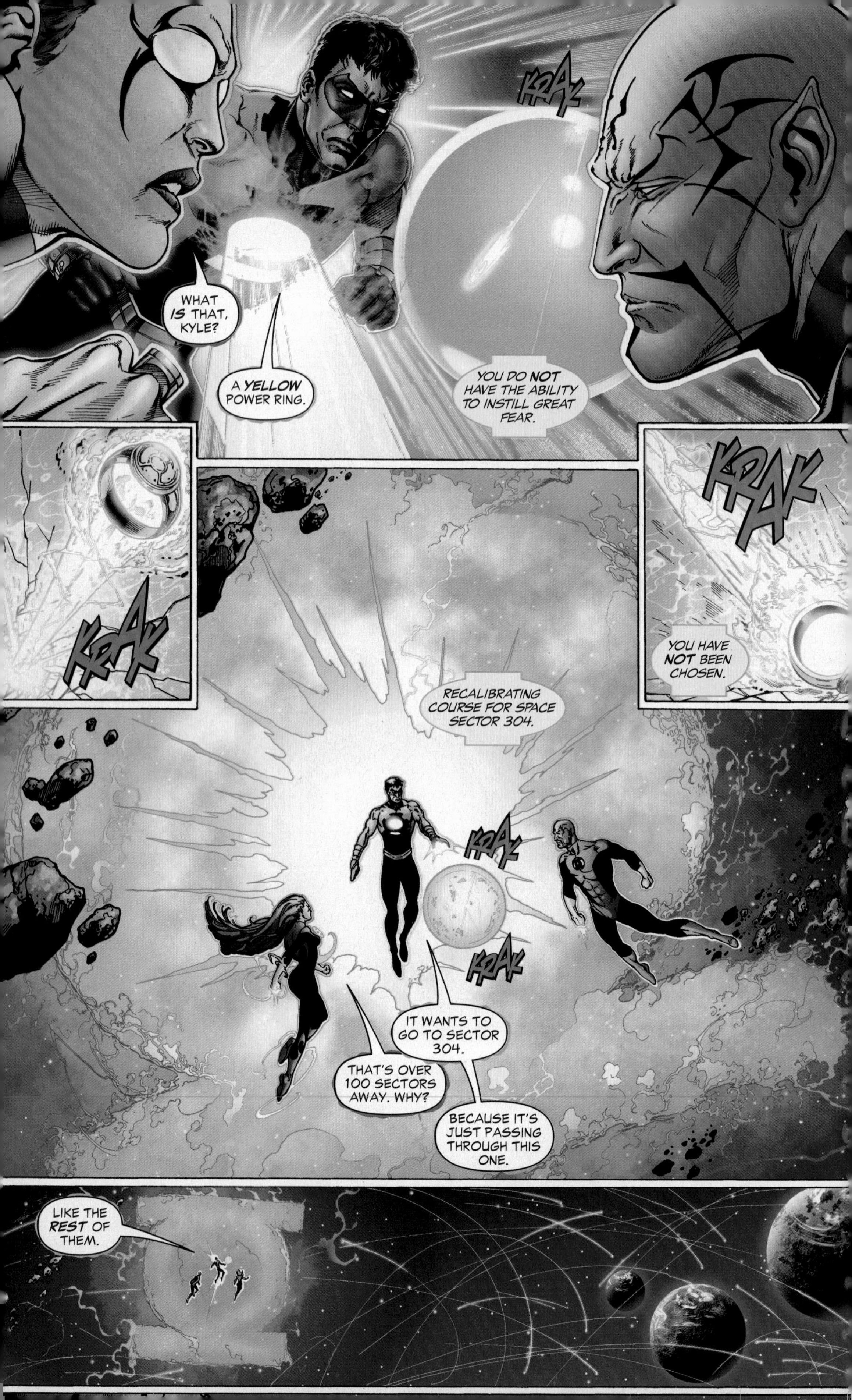
KRAK
WHAT IS THAT, KYLE?
A YELLOW POWER RING.
YOU DO NOT HAVE THE ABILITY TO INSTILL GREAT FEAR.
KRAK
KRAK
YOU HAVE NOT BEEN CHOSEN.
RECALIBRATING COURSE FOR SPACE SECTOR 304.
KRAK
KRAK
IT WANTS TO GO TO SECTOR 304.
THAT'S OVER 100 SECTORS AWAY. WHY?
BECAUSE IT'S JUST PASSING THROUGH THIS ONE.
LIKE THE REST OF THEM.

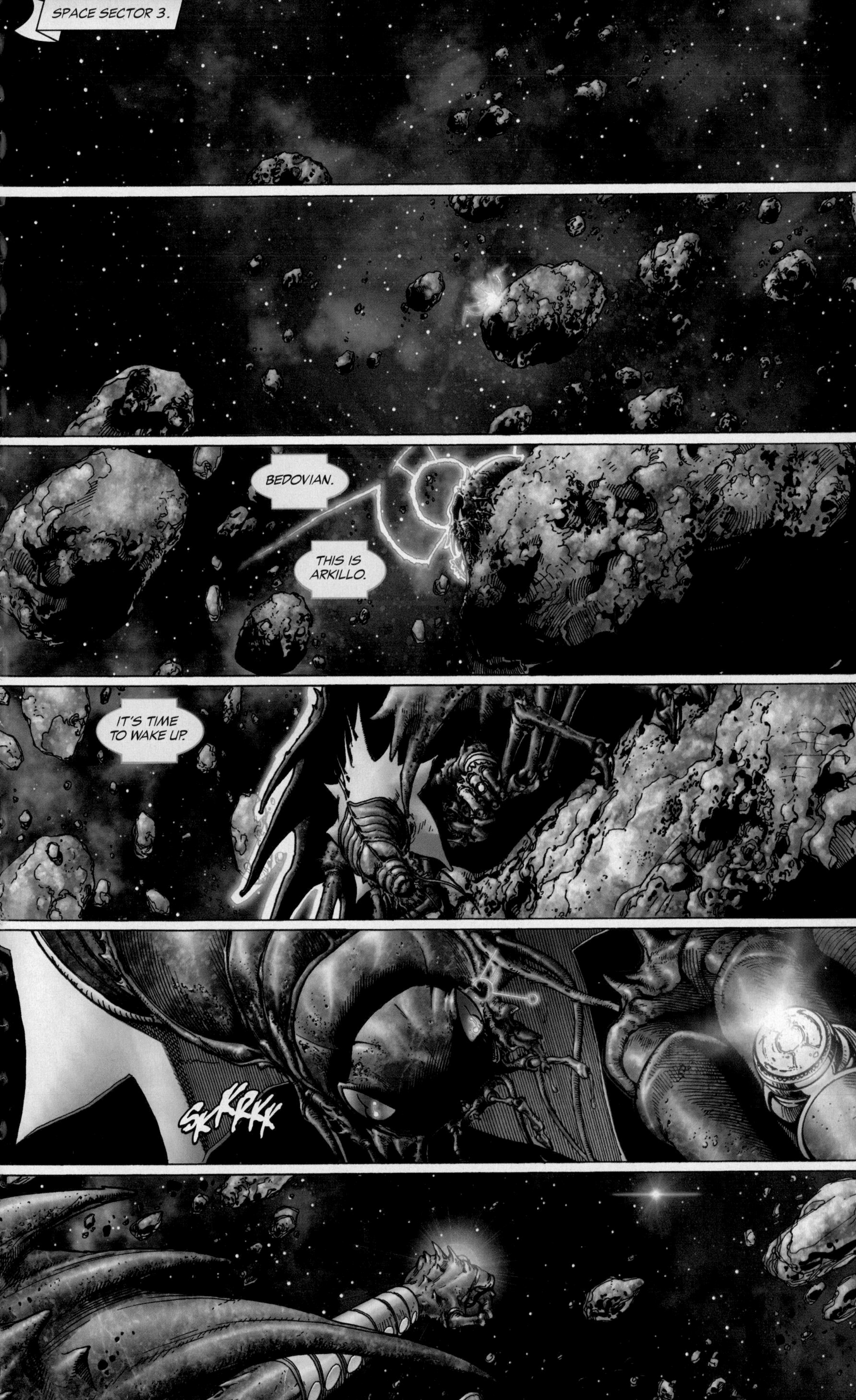
SPACE SECTOR 3.
BEDOVIAN.
THIS IS ARKILLO.
IT'S TIME TO WAKE UP.
SKKRKK

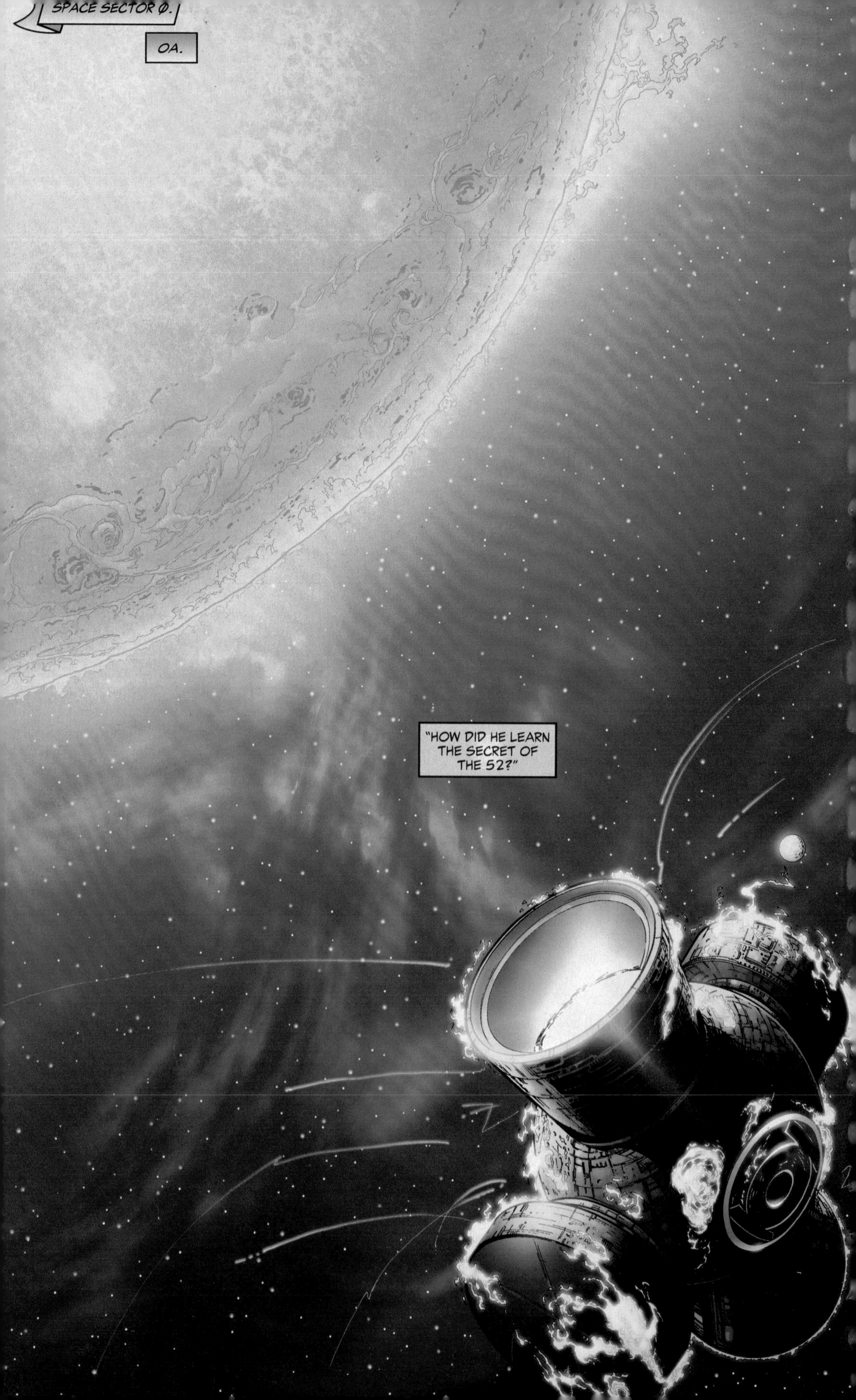
SPACE SECTOR Ø.
OA.
"HOW DID HE LEARN THE SECRET OF THE 52?"

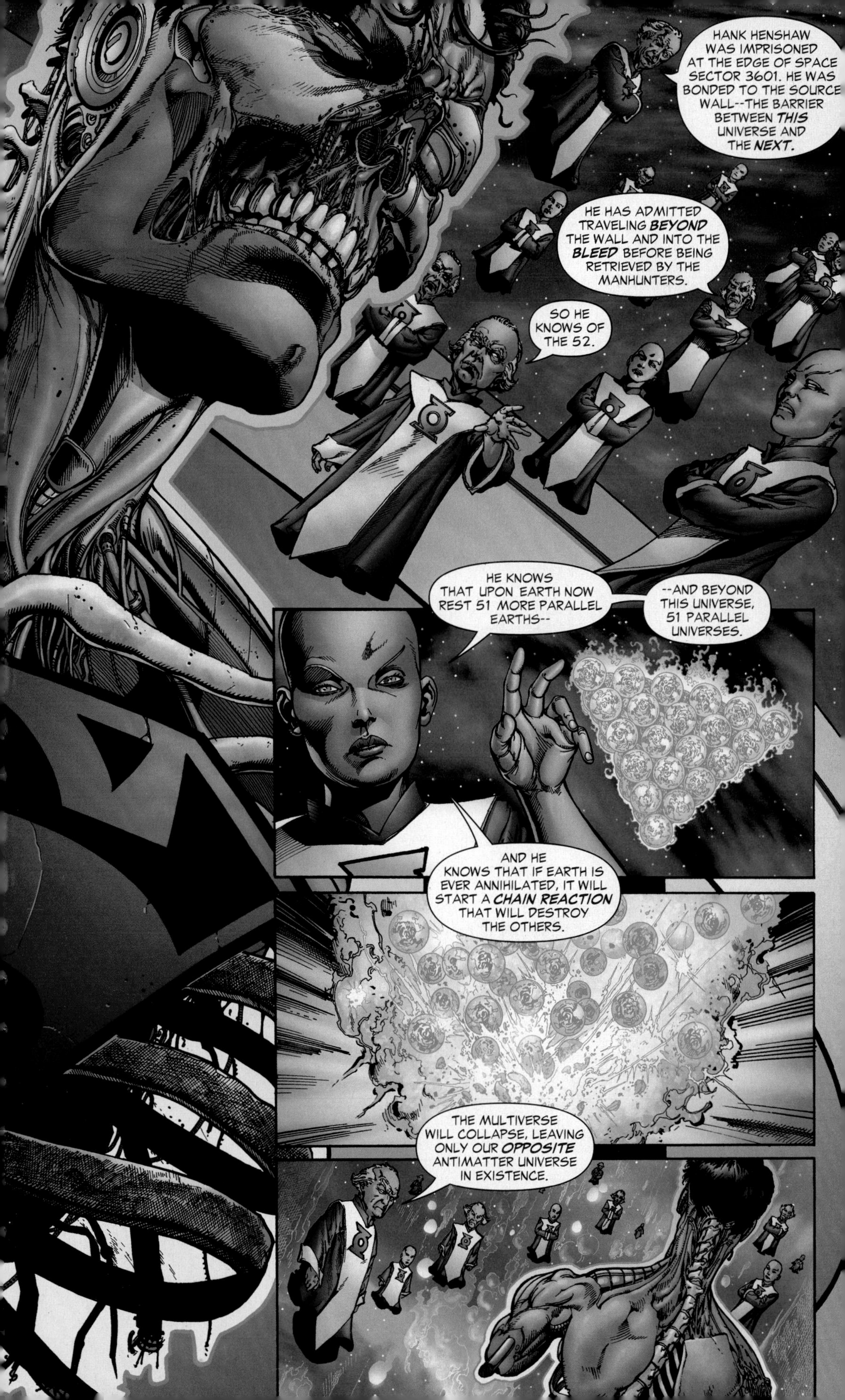
HANK HENSHAW WAS IMPRISONED AT THE EDGE OF SPACE SECTOR 3601. HE WAS BONDED TO THE SOURCE WALL--THE BARRIER BETWEEN THIS UNIVERSE AND THE NEXT.
HE HAS ADMITTED TRAVELING BEYOND THE WALL AND INTO THE BLEED BEFORE BEING RETRIEVED BY THE MANHUNTERS.
SO HE KNOWS OF THE 52.
HE KNOWS THAT UPON EARTH NOW REST 51 MORE PARALLEL EARTHS--
--AND BEYOND THIS UNIVERSE, 51 PARALLEL UNIVERSES.
AND HE KNOWS THAT IF EARTH IS EVER ANNIHILATED, IT WILL START A CHAIN REACTION THAT WILL DESTROY THE OTHERS.
THE MULTIVERSE WILL COLLAPSE, LEAVING ONLY OUR OPPOSITE ANTIMATTER UNIVERSE IN EXISTENCE.

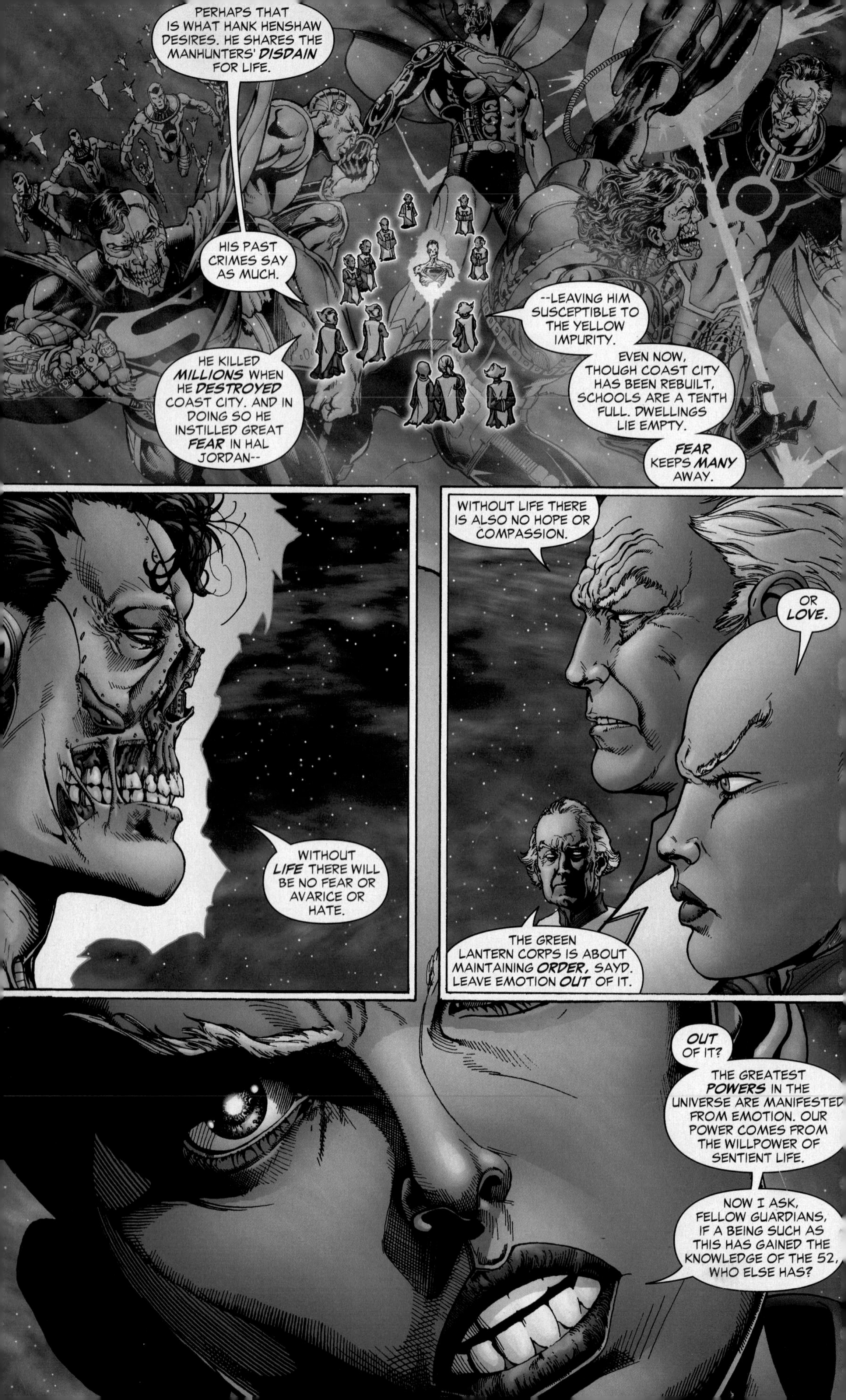
PERHAPS THAT IS WHAT HANK HENSHAW DESIRES. HE SHARES THE MANHUNTERS' DISDAIN FOR LIFE.
HIS PAST CRIMES SAY AS MUCH.
HE KILLED MILLIONS WHEN HE DESTROYED COAST CITY. AND IN DOING SO HE INSTILLED GREAT FEAR IN HAL JORDAN--
--LEAVING HIM SUSCEPTIBLE TO THE YELLOW IMPURITY.
EVEN NOW, THOUGH COAST CITY HAS BEEN REBUILT, SCHOOLS ARE A TENTH FULL. DWELLINGS LIE EMPTY.
FEAR KEEPS MANY AWAY.
WITHOUT LIFE THERE WILL BE NO FEAR OR AVARICE OR HATE.
WITHOUT LIFE THERE IS ALSO NO HOPE OR COMPASSION.
OR LOVE.
THE GREEN LANTERN CORPS IS ABOUT MAINTAINING ORDER, SAYD. LEAVE EMOTION OUT OF IT.
OUT OF IT?
THE GREATEST POWERS IN THE UNIVERSE ARE MANIFESTED FROM EMOTION. OUR POWER COMES FROM THE WILLPOWER OF SENTIENT LIFE.
NOW I ASK, FELLOW GUARDIANS, IF A BEING SUCH AS THIS HAS GAINED THE KNOWLEDGE OF THE 52, WHO ELSE HAS?

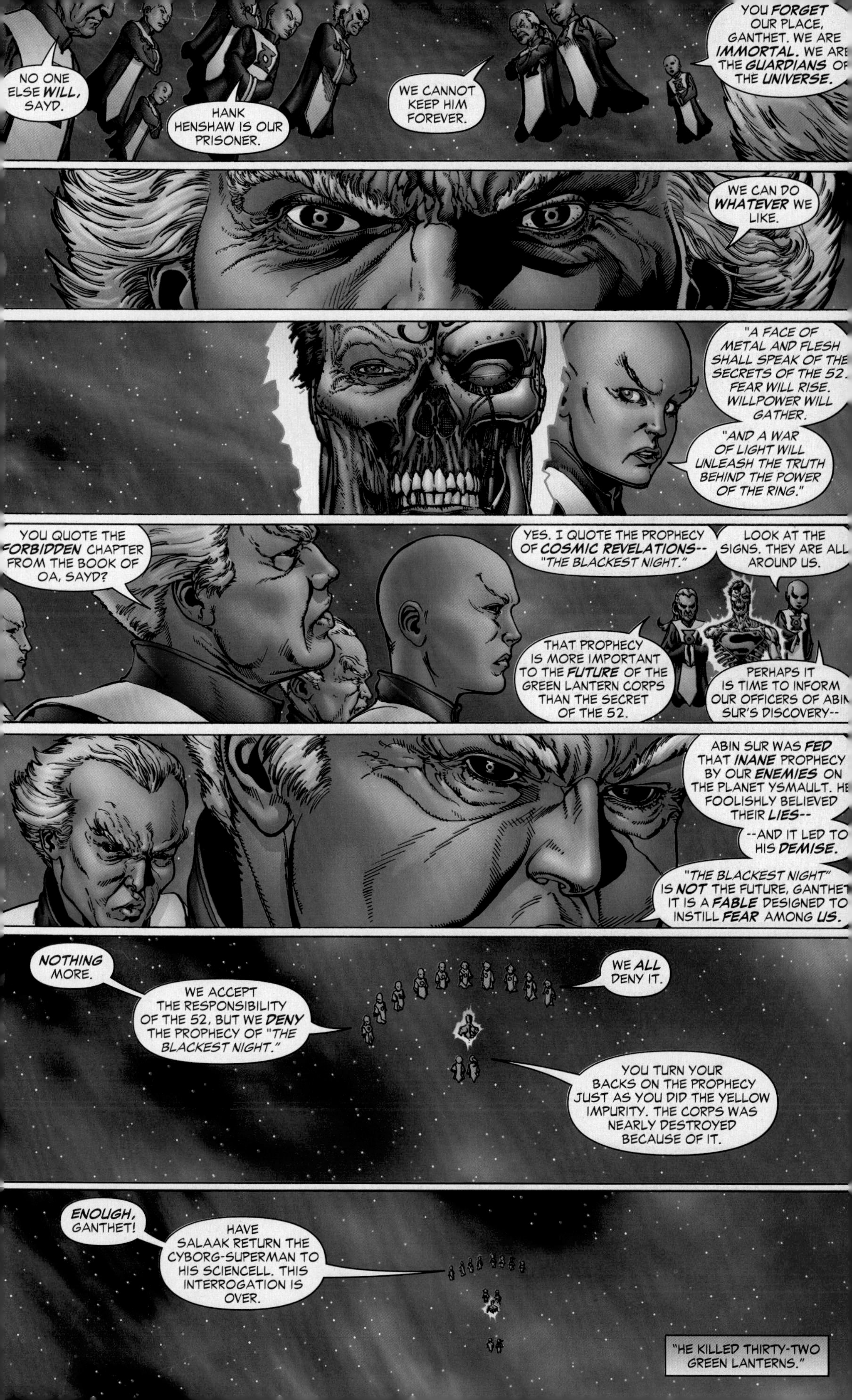
NO ONE ELSE WILL, SAYD.
HANK HENSHAW IS OUR PRISONER.
WE CANNOT KEEP HIM FOREVER.
YOU FORGET OUR PLACE, GANTHET. WE ARE IMMORTAL. WE ARE THE GUARDIANS OF THE UNIVERSE.
WE CAN DO WHATEVER WE LIKE.
"A FACE OF METAL AND FLESH SHALL SPEAK OF THE SECRETS OF THE 52. FEAR WILL RISE. WILLPOWER WILL GATHER.
"AND A WAR OF LIGHT WILL UNLEASH THE TRUTH BEHIND THE POWER OF THE RING."
YOU QUOTE THE FORBIDDEN CHAPTER FROM THE BOOK OF OA, SAYD?
YES. I QUOTE THE PROPHECY OF COSMIC REVELATIONS-- "THE BLACKEST NIGHT."
LOOK AT THE SIGNS. THEY ARE ALL AROUND US.
THAT PROPHECY IS MORE IMPORTANT TO THE FUTURE OF THE GREEN LANTERN CORPS THAN THE SECRET OF THE 52.
PERHAPS IT IS TIME TO INFORM OUR OFFICERS OF ABIN SUR'S DISCOVERY--
ABIN SUR WAS FED THAT INANE PROPHECY BY OUR ENEMIES ON THE PLANET YSMAULT. HE FOOLISHLY BELIEVED THEIR LIES--
--AND IT LED TO HIS DEMISE.
"THE BLACKEST NIGHT" IS NOT THE FUTURE, GANTHET. IT IS A FABLE DESIGNED TO INSTILL FEAR AMONG US.
NOTHING MORE.
WE ACCEPT THE RESPONSIBILITY OF THE 52, BUT WE DENY THE PROPHECY OF "THE BLACKEST NIGHT."
WE ALL DENY IT.
YOU TURN YOUR BACKS ON THE PROPHECY JUST AS YOU DID THE YELLOW IMPURITY. THE CORPS WAS NEARLY DESTROYED BECAUSE OF IT.
ENOUGH, GANTHET!
HAVE SALAAK RETURN THE CYBORG-SUPERMAN TO HIS SCIENCELL. THIS INTERROGATION IS OVER.
"HE KILLED THIRTY-TWO GREEN LANTERNS."

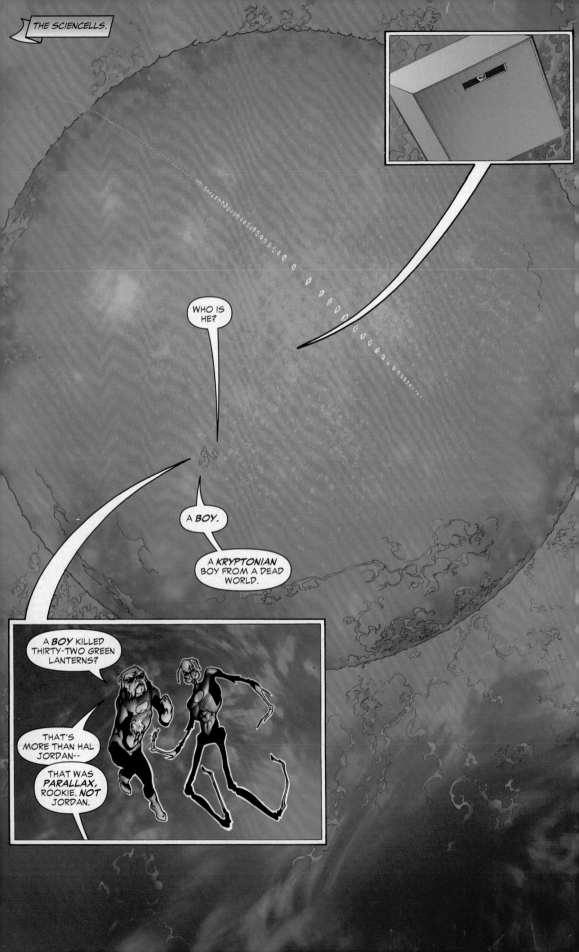

THE SCIENCELLS.

WHO IS HE?

A *BOY.*

A *KRYPTONIAN* BOY FROM A DEAD WORLD.

A *BOY* KILLED THIRTY-TWO GREEN LANTERNS?

THAT'S MORE THAN HAL JORDAN--

THAT WAS *PARALLAX*, ROOKIE. *NOT* JORDAN.

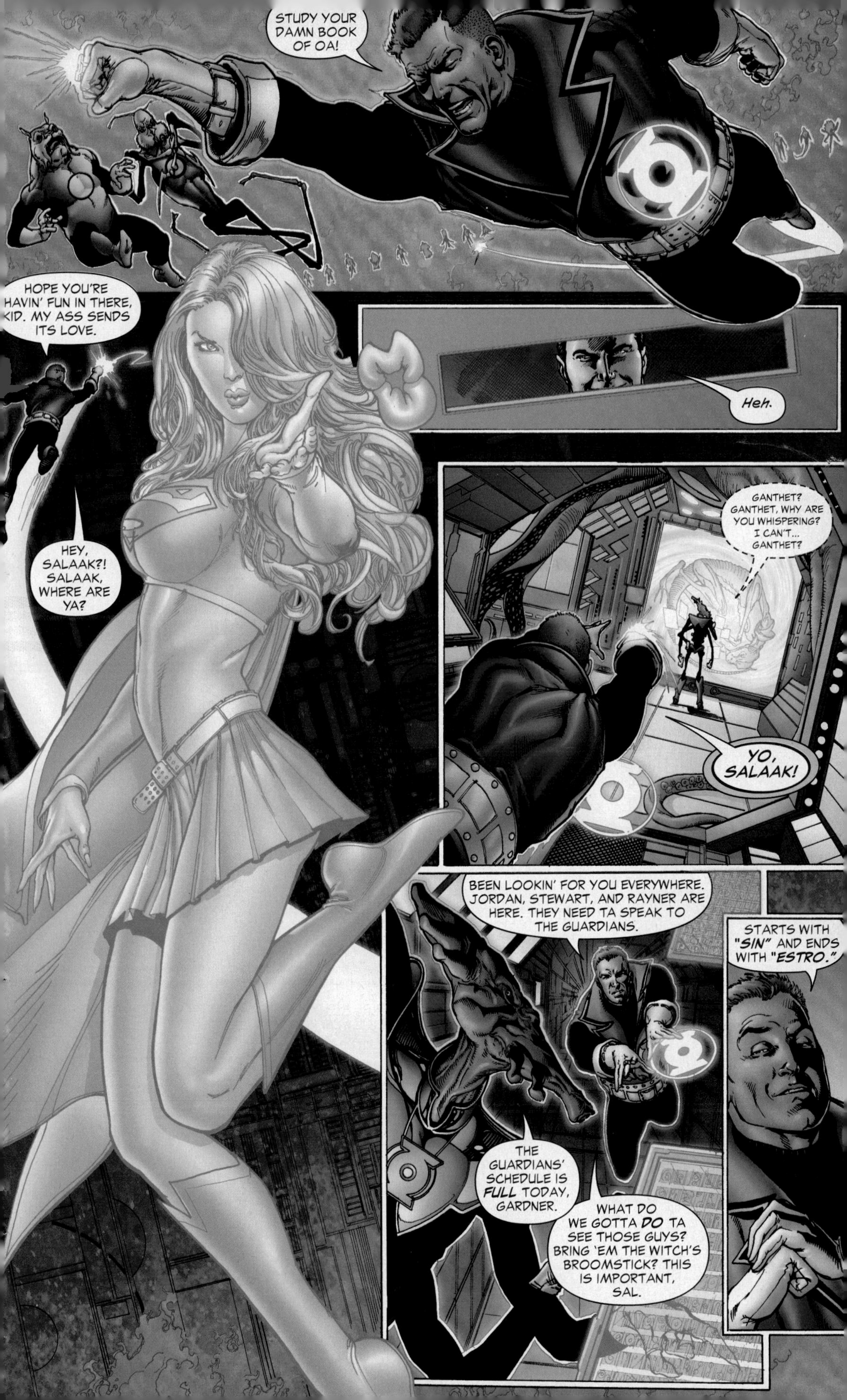
STUDY YOUR DAMN BOOK OF OA!
HOPE YOU'RE HAVIN' FUN IN THERE, KID. MY ASS SENDS ITS LOVE.
Heh.
HEY, SALAAK?! SALAAK, WHERE ARE YA?
GANTHET? GANTHET, WHY ARE YOU WHISPERING? I CAN'T... GANTHET?
YO, SALAAK!
BEEN LOOKIN' FOR YOU EVERYWHERE. JORDAN, STEWART, AND RAYNER ARE HERE. THEY NEED TA SPEAK TO THE GUARDIANS.
THE GUARDIANS' SCHEDULE IS FULL TODAY, GARDNER.
WHAT DO WE GOTTA DO TA SEE THOSE GUYS? BRING 'EM THE WITCH'S BROOMSTICK? THIS IS IMPORTANT, SAL.
STARTS WITH "SIN" AND ENDS WITH "ESTRO."

...DON'T CARE WHAT KILOWOG SAYS, I WOULDN'T TURN MY BACK TO JORDAN...

...ION ON OUR TEAM, THE CORPS AIN'T EVER GONNA GO DIM...

...STEWART COULDN'T BEAT *YELLOW*, LIKE A SPROCKIN' *ROOKIE*, AND XANSHI WENT *BOOM*...

KEEP THAT YELLOW RING *HIDDEN*, KYLE. WE DON'T WANT TO START A PANIC.

BRRP

WHEN'S THE LAST TIME YOU SAW A GROUP OF GREEN LANTERNS *PANIC*, HAL?

JUST THE SAME, LET'S--

OH, GOODY, I'M HAL JORDAN'S FRIEND.

ANY LUCK WITH SALAAK?

HE'S TRYIN' TA GET US IN, THOUGH TRUTH BE TOLD, WE SHOULD JUST BYPASS THE RED TAPE. WE ALREADY GOT THE *ONE GUY* THE GUARDIANS WILL CRACK THEIR DOOR OPEN FOR RIGHT HERE.

THEIR *PRECIOUS* TORCHBEARER.

HELL, LET'S JUST HAVE THE GREAT AND POWERFUL ION BEND OVER WHILE THE GUARDIANS PUCKER UP AND KISS HIS GLOWIN' GREEN BUTT--

I DIDN'T EXPECT OR WANT ANYTHING. BUT I REMEMBERED ON THE WAY...THERE WAS THIS PAINTING SHE HAD HANGING IN THE LIVING ROOM WHEN I WAS GROWING UP.

IT WAS THE ONLY COLOR IN THE HOUSE. I USED TO STARE AT IT FOR HOURS.

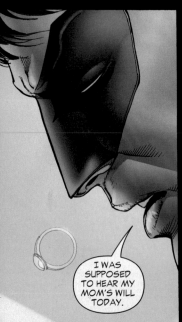

I WAS SUPPOSED TO HEAR MY MOM'S WILL TODAY.

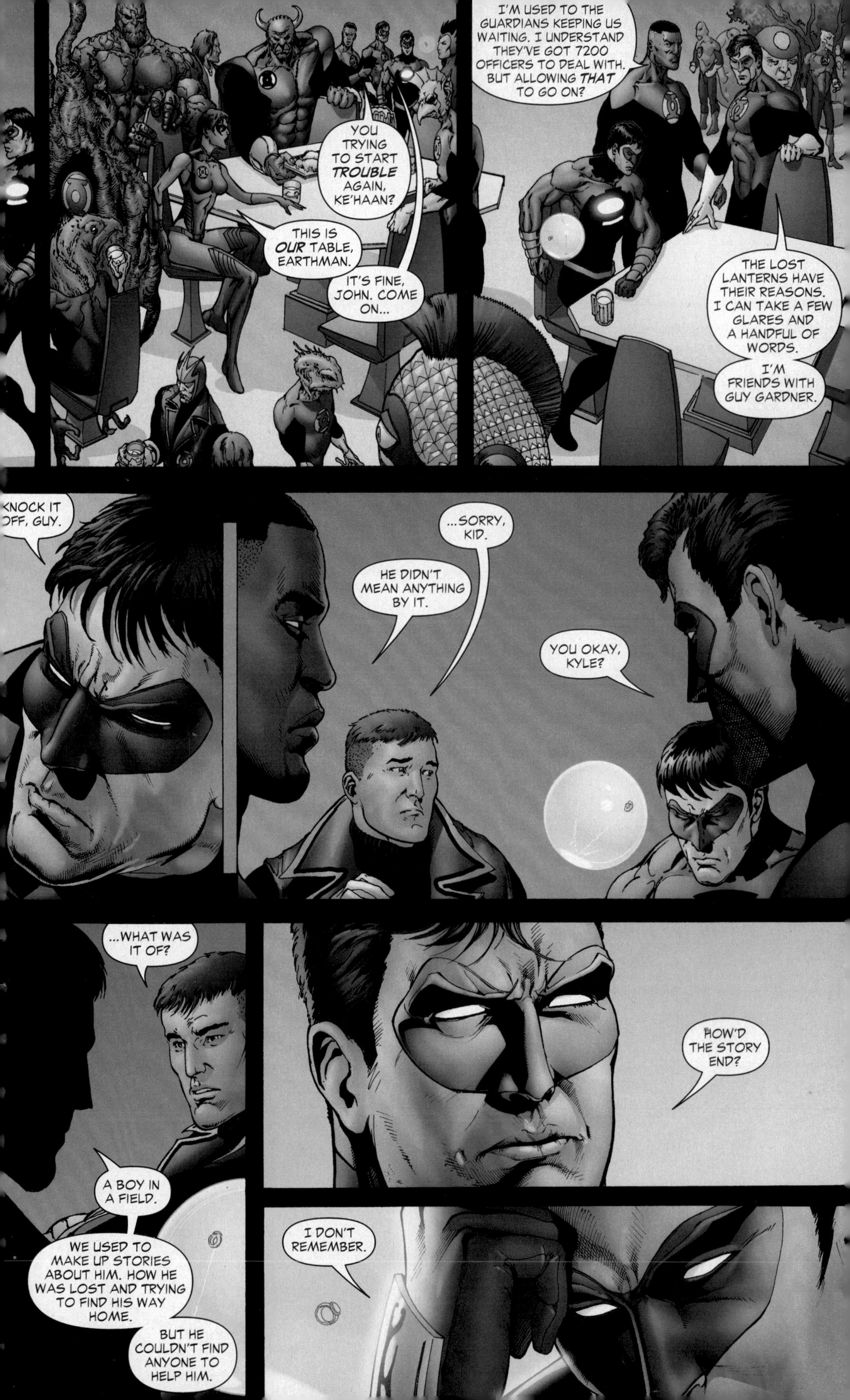
YOU TRYING TO START TROUBLE AGAIN, KE'HAAN?
THIS IS OUR TABLE, EARTHMAN.
IT'S FINE, JOHN. COME ON...
I'M USED TO THE GUARDIANS KEEPING US WAITING. I UNDERSTAND THEY'VE GOT 7200 OFFICERS TO DEAL WITH. BUT ALLOWING THAT TO GO ON?
THE LOST LANTERNS HAVE THEIR REASONS. I CAN TAKE A FEW GLARES AND A HANDFUL OF WORDS.
I'M FRIENDS WITH GUY GARDNER.
KNOCK IT OFF, GUY.
...SORRY, KID.
HE DIDN'T MEAN ANYTHING BY IT.
YOU OKAY, KYLE?
...WHAT WAS IT OF?
A BOY IN A FIELD.
WE USED TO MAKE UP STORIES ABOUT HIM. HOW HE WAS LOST AND TRYING TO FIND HIS WAY HOME.
BUT HE COULDN'T FIND ANYONE TO HELP HIM.
HOW'D THE STORY END?
I DON'T REMEMBER.

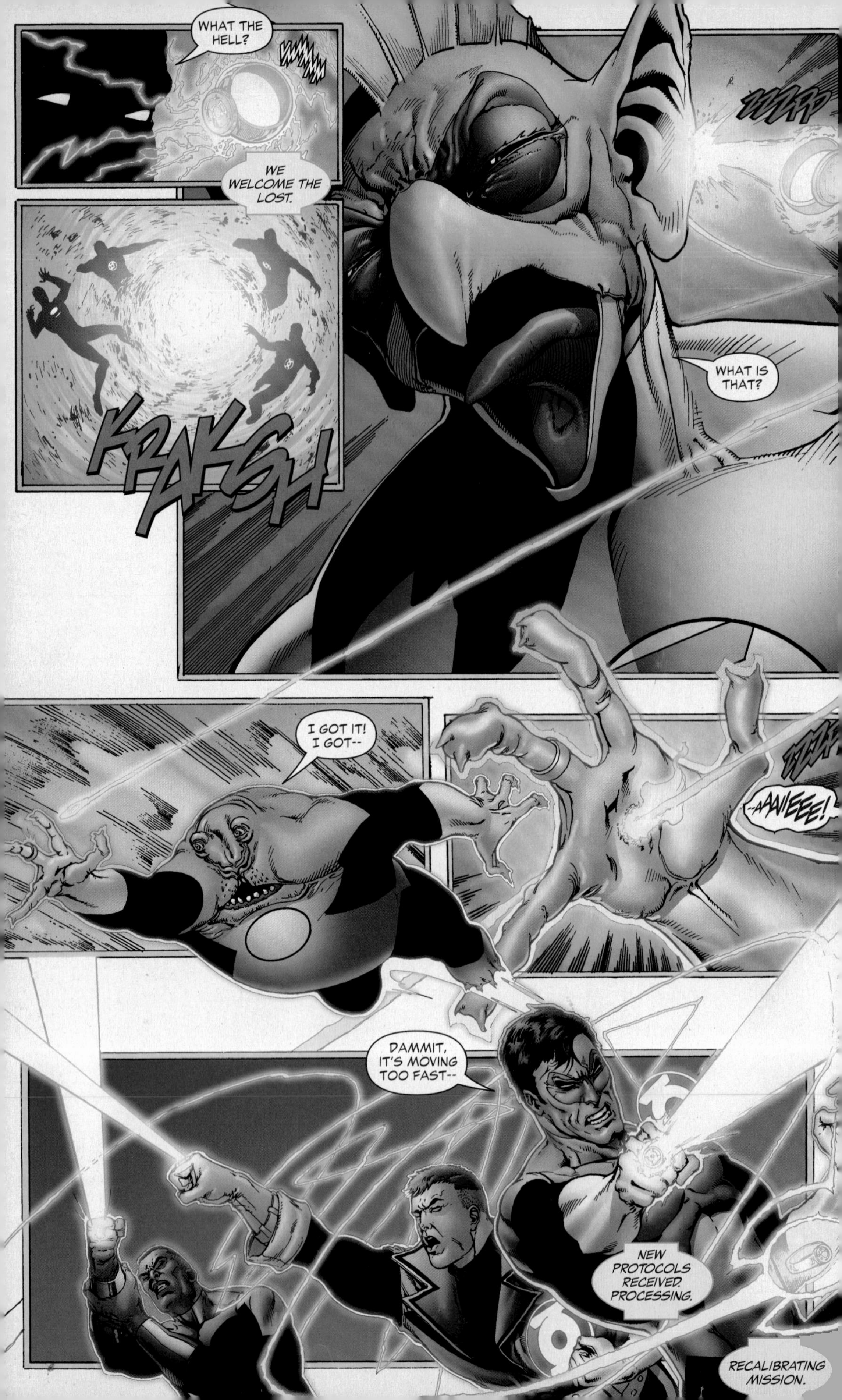
WHAT THE HELL?
VMMMM
WE WELCOME THE LOST.
KRAKSH
ZZZAPP
WHAT IS THAT?
I GOT IT! I GOT--
--AAIIEEE!
DAMMIT, IT'S MOVING TOO FAST--
NEW PROTOCOLS RECEIVED. PROCESSING.
RECALIBRATING MISSION.

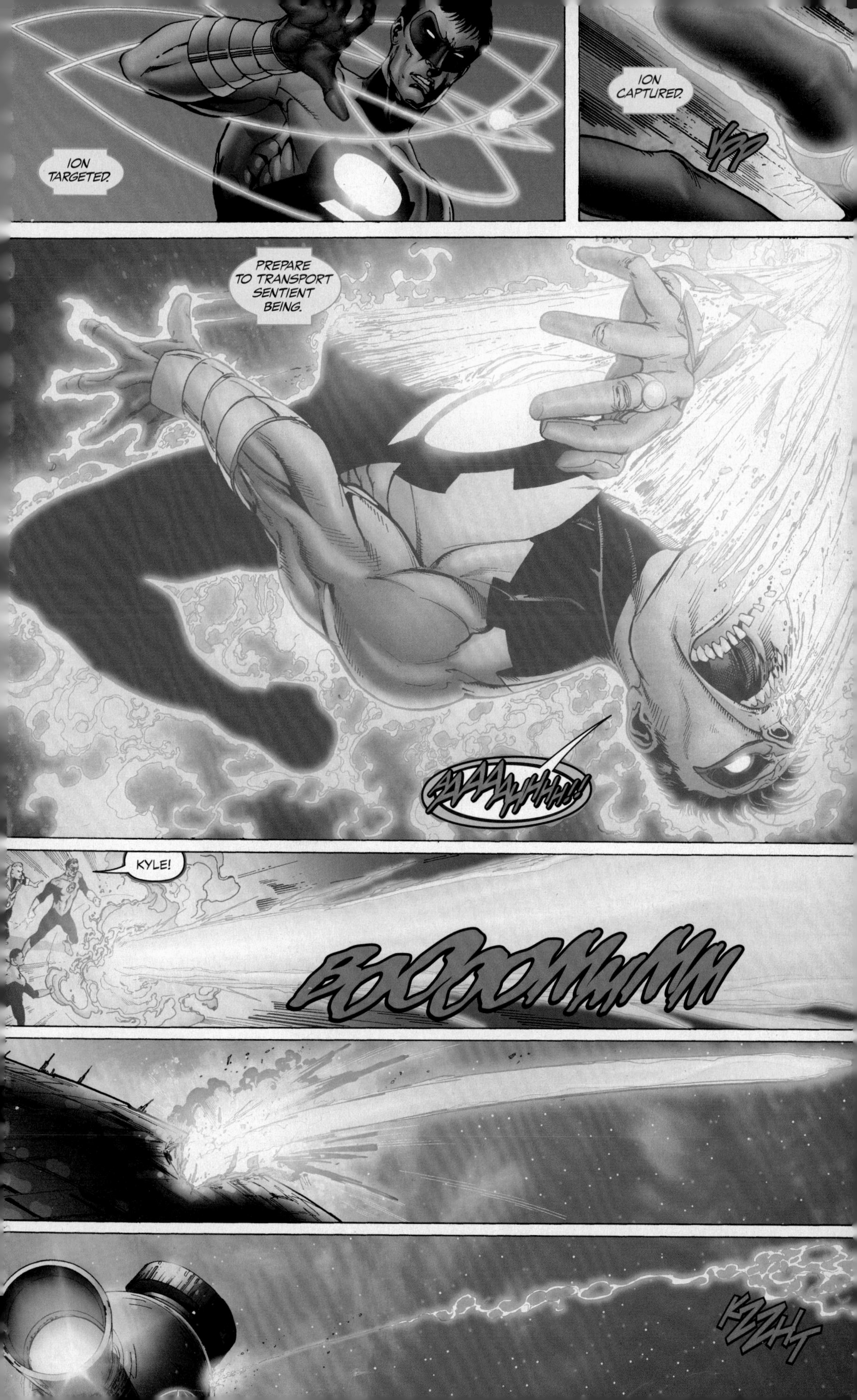
ION TARGETED.
ION CAPTURED.
VZZP
PREPARE TO TRANSPORT SENTIENT BEING.
AAAAAHHHH!!
KYLE!
BOOOOMMMM
KZZHT

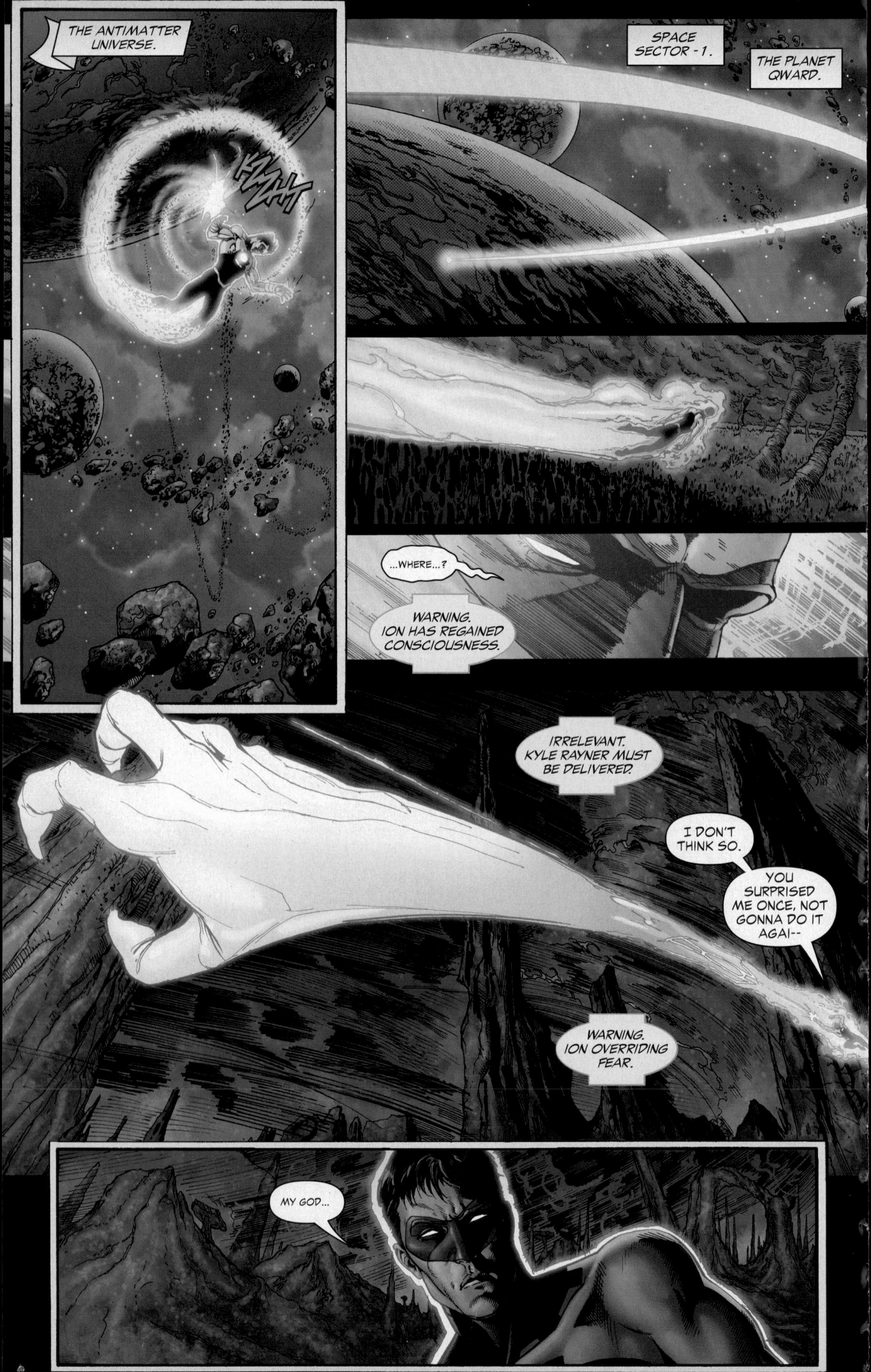
THE ANTIMATTER UNIVERSE.
KZZAKT
SPACE SECTOR -1.
THE PLANET QWARD.
...WHERE...?
WARNING. ION HAS REGAINED CONSCIOUSNESS.
IRRELEVANT. KYLE RAYNER MUST BE DELIVERED.
I DON'T THINK SO.
YOU SURPRISED ME ONCE, NOT GONNA DO IT AGAI--
WARNING. ION OVERRIDING FEAR.
MY GOD...

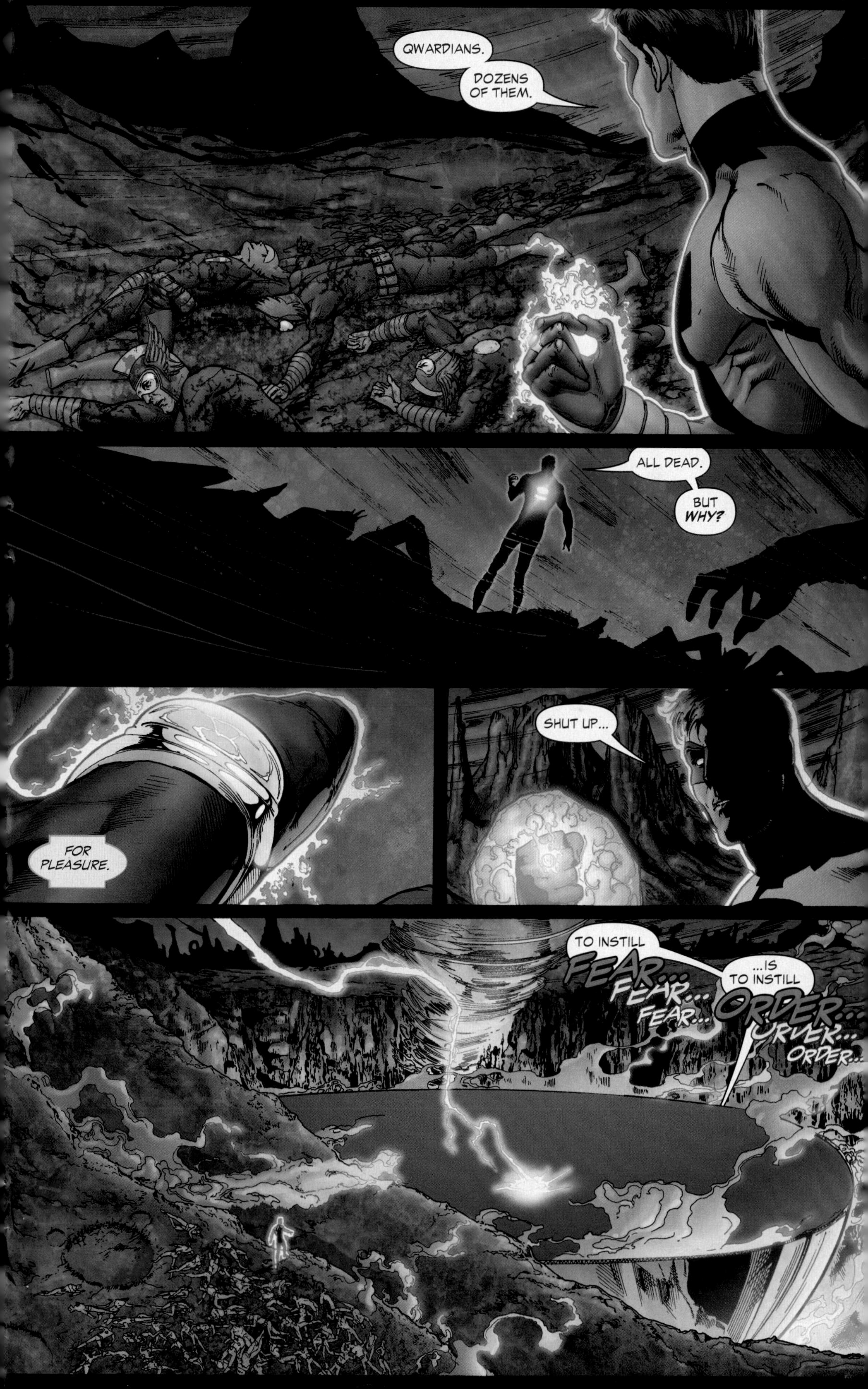
QWARDIANS.
DOZENS OF THEM.
ALL DEAD.
BUT *WHY?*
FOR PLEASURE.
SHUT UP...
TO INSTILL FEAR... FEAR... FEAR...
...IS TO INSTILL ORDER... ORDER... ORDER...

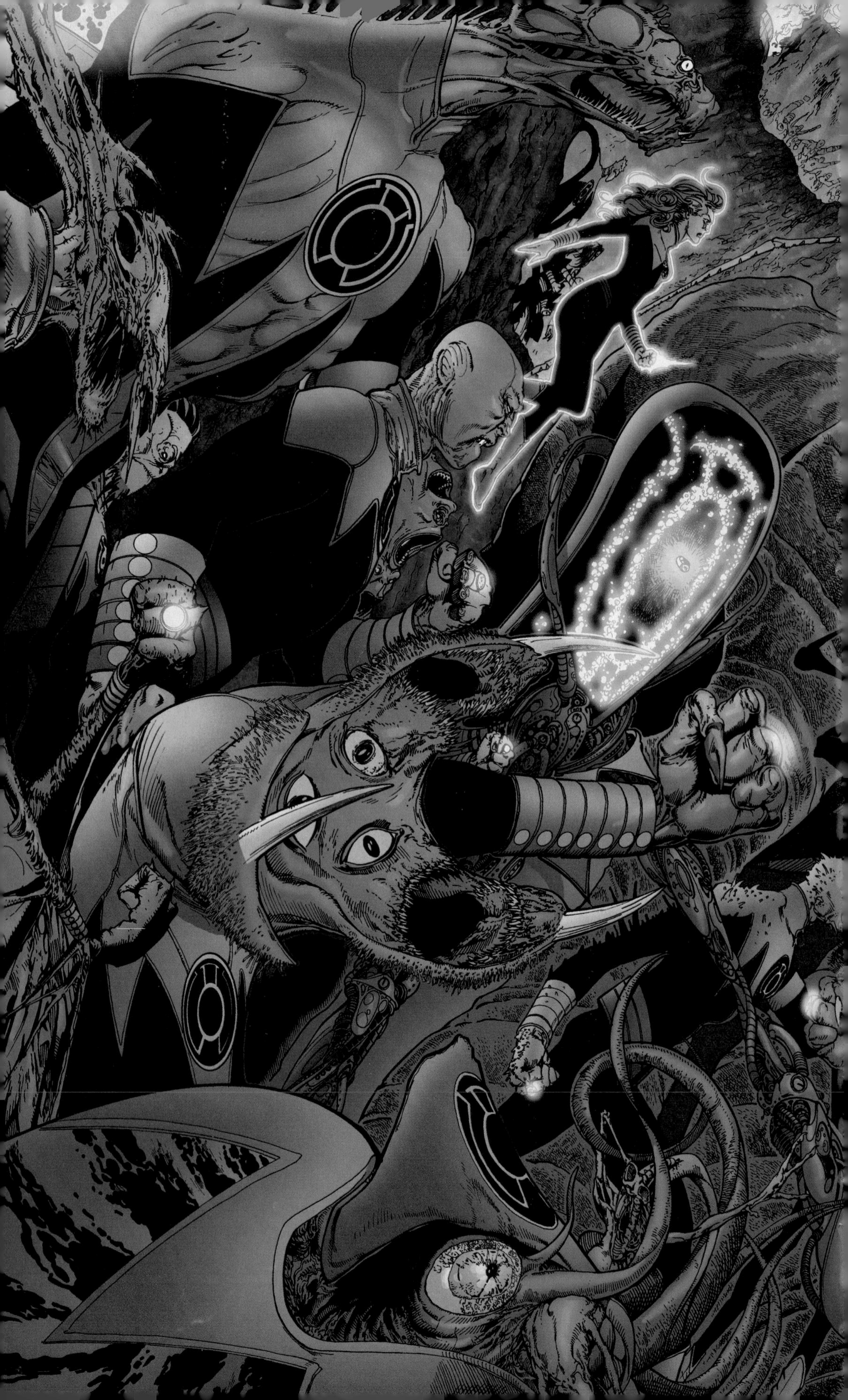

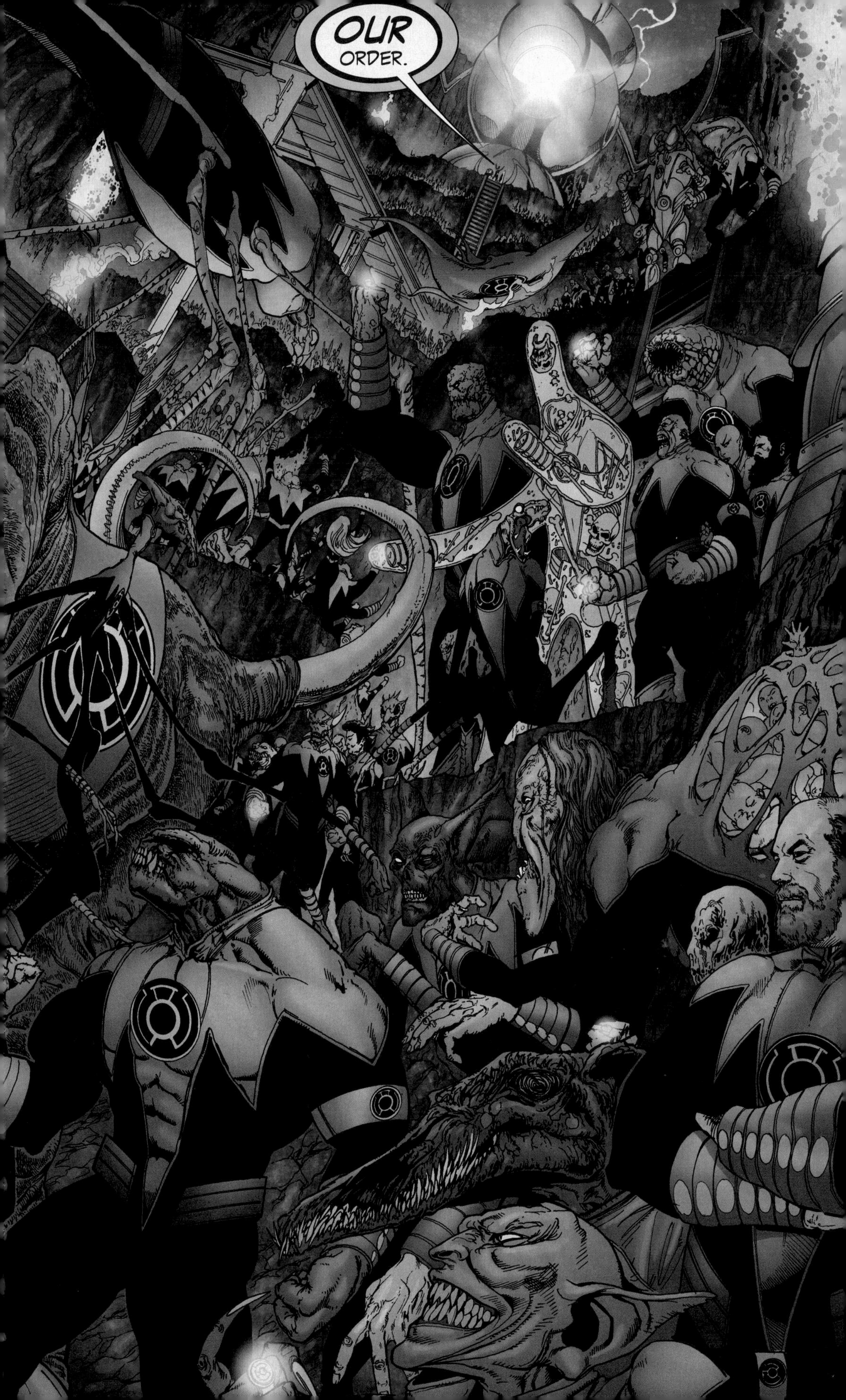
OUR ORDER.

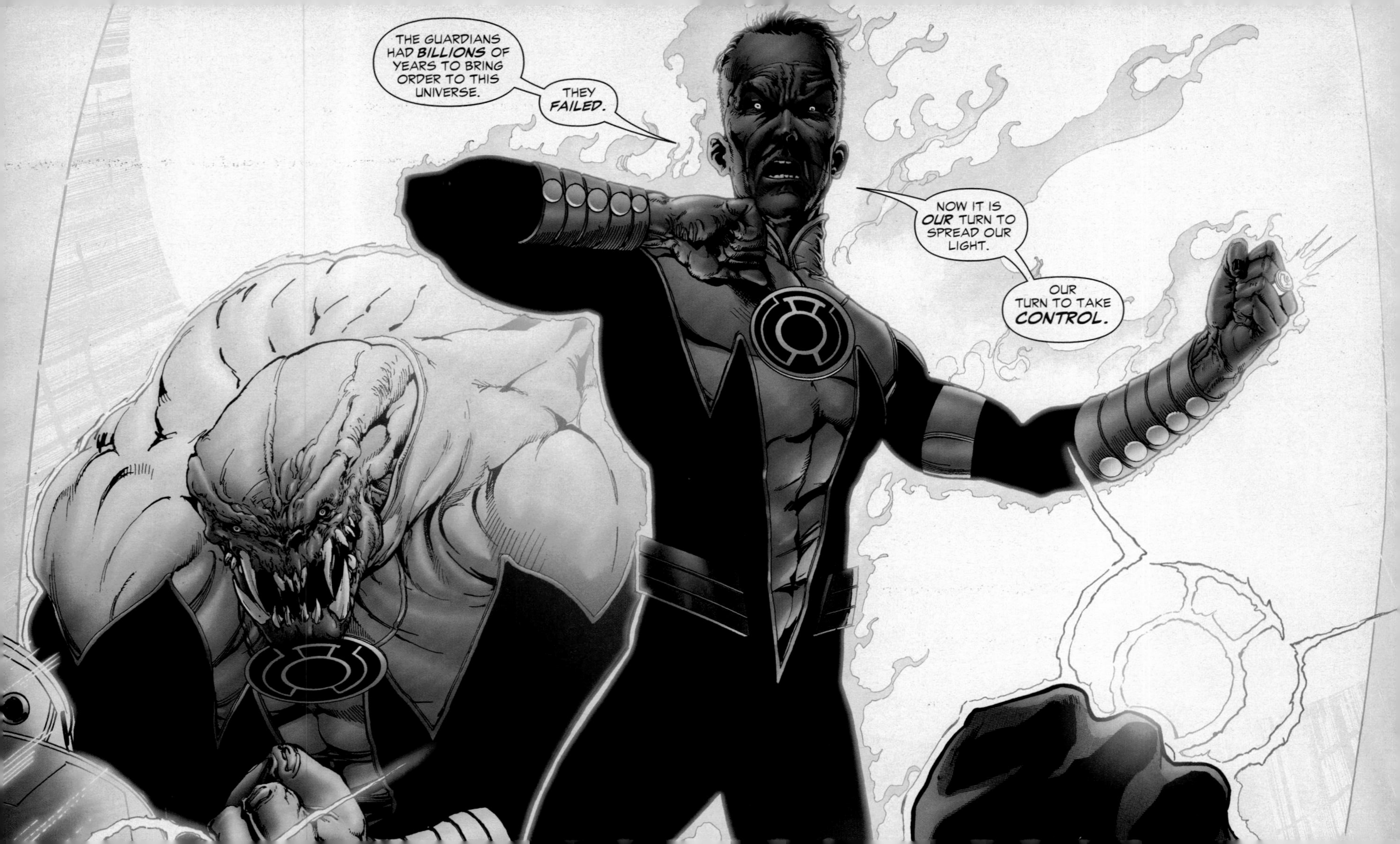
THE GUARDIANS HAD *BILLIONS* OF YEARS TO BRING ORDER TO THIS UNIVERSE.
THEY *FAILED*.
NOW IT IS *OUR* TURN TO SPREAD OUR LIGHT.
OUR TURN TO TAKE **CONTROL**.

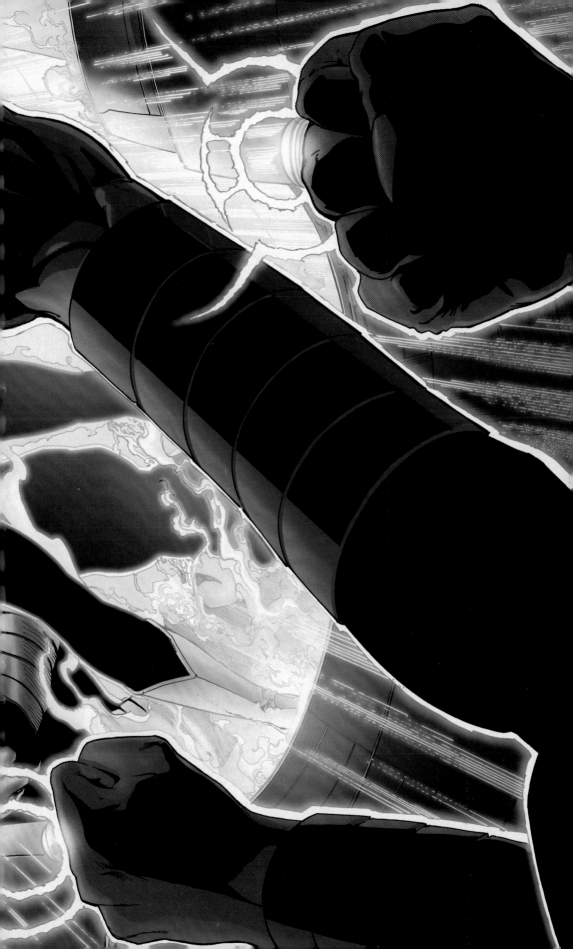

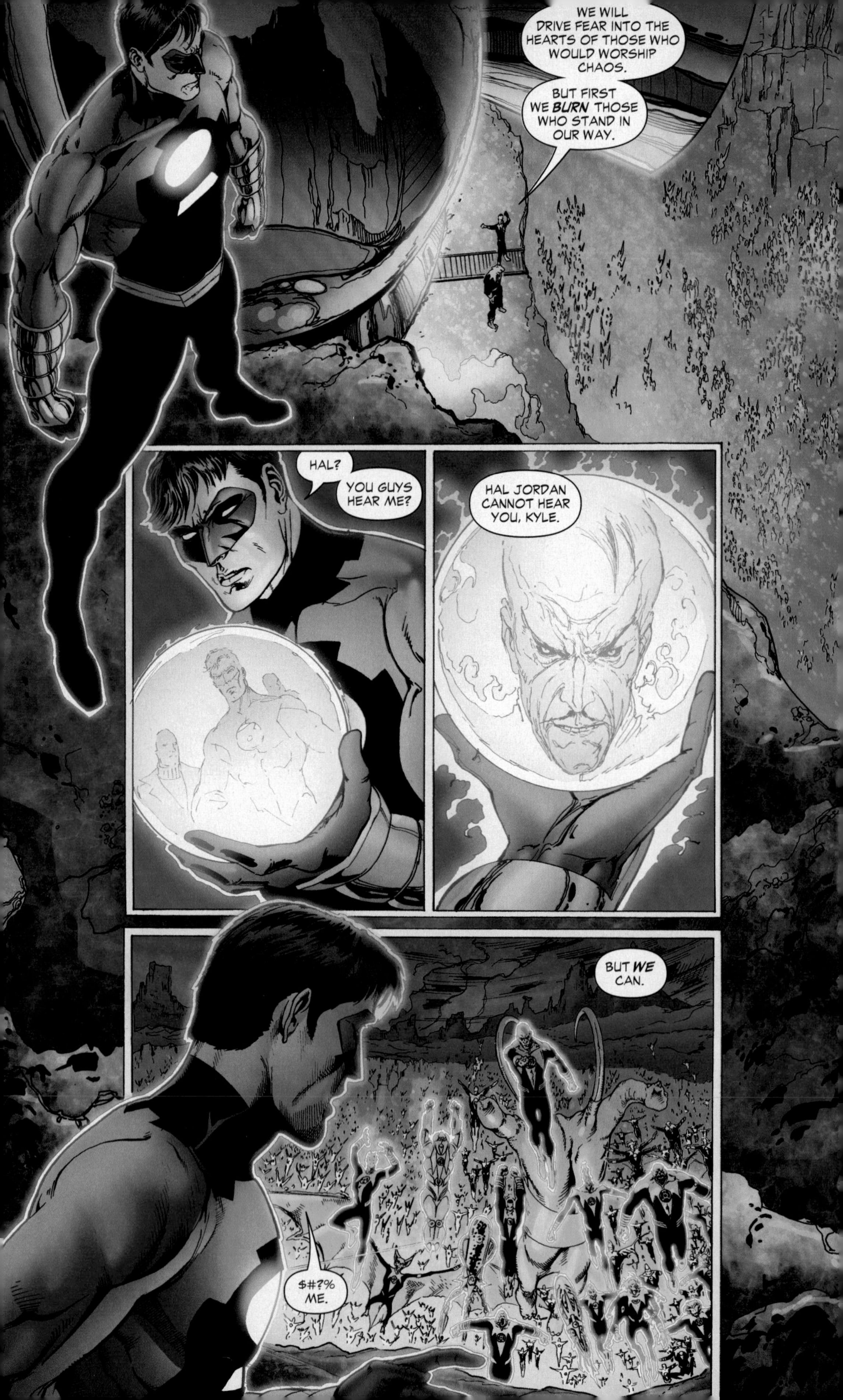
WE WILL DRIVE FEAR INTO THE HEARTS OF THOSE WHO WOULD WORSHIP CHAOS.
BUT FIRST WE BURN THOSE WHO STAND IN OUR WAY.
HAL?
YOU GUYS HEAR ME?
HAL JORDAN CANNOT HEAR YOU, KYLE.
BUT WE CAN.
$#?% ME.

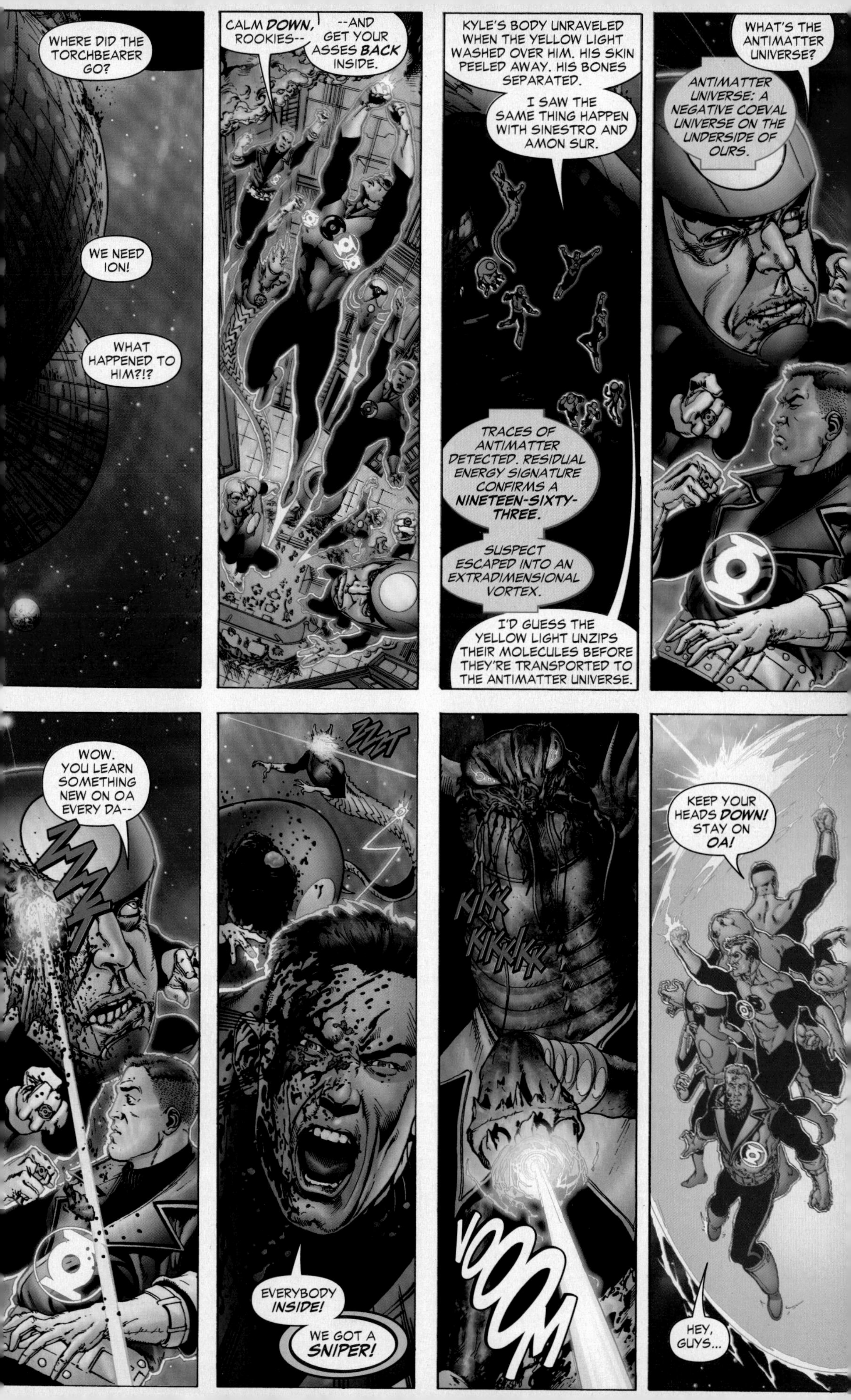
WHERE DID THE TORCHBEARER GO?
WE NEED ION!
WHAT HAPPENED TO HIM?!?
CALM DOWN, ROOKIES--
--AND GET YOUR ASSES BACK INSIDE.
KYLE'S BODY UNRAVELED WHEN THE YELLOW LIGHT WASHED OVER HIM. HIS SKIN PEELED AWAY. HIS BONES SEPARATED.
I SAW THE SAME THING HAPPEN WITH SINESTRO AND AMON SUR.
TRACES OF ANTIMATTER DETECTED. RESIDUAL ENERGY SIGNATURE CONFIRMS A NINETEEN-SIXTY-THREE.
SUSPECT ESCAPED INTO AN EXTRADIMENSIONAL VORTEX.
I'D GUESS THE YELLOW LIGHT UNZIPS THEIR MOLECULES BEFORE THEY'RE TRANSPORTED TO THE ANTIMATTER UNIVERSE.
WHAT'S THE ANTIMATTER UNIVERSE?
ANTIMATTER UNIVERSE: A NEGATIVE COEVAL UNIVERSE ON THE UNDERSIDE OF OURS.
WOW. YOU LEARN SOMETHING NEW ON OA EVERY DA--
EVERYBODY INSIDE!
WE GOT A SNIPER!
VOOOM
KEEP YOUR HEADS DOWN! STAY ON OA!
HEY, GUYS...

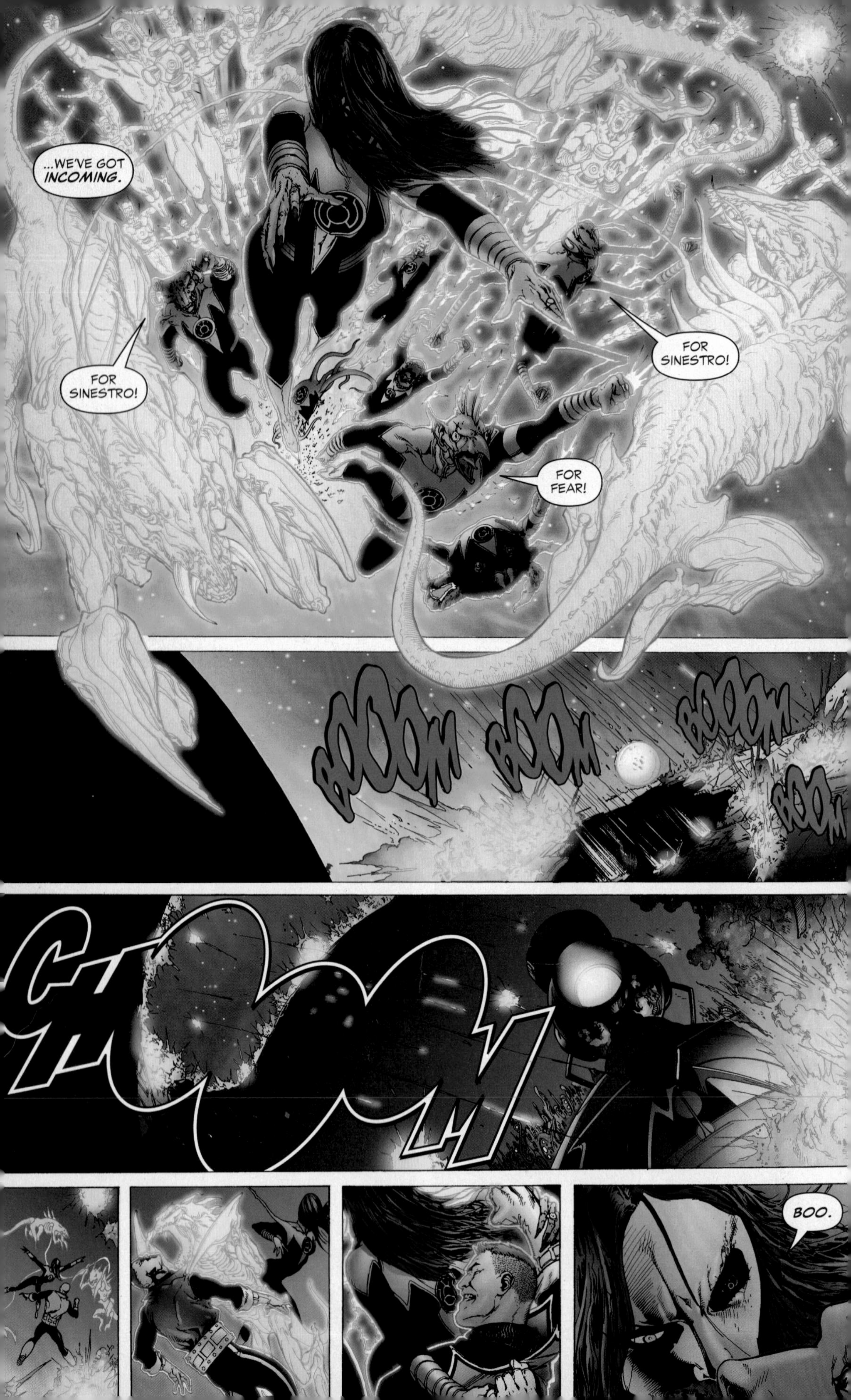
...WE'VE GOT INCOMING.
FOR SINESTRO!
FOR SINESTRO!
FOR FEAR!
BOOOM
BOOM
BOOOM
BOOM
CHOOM
BOO.

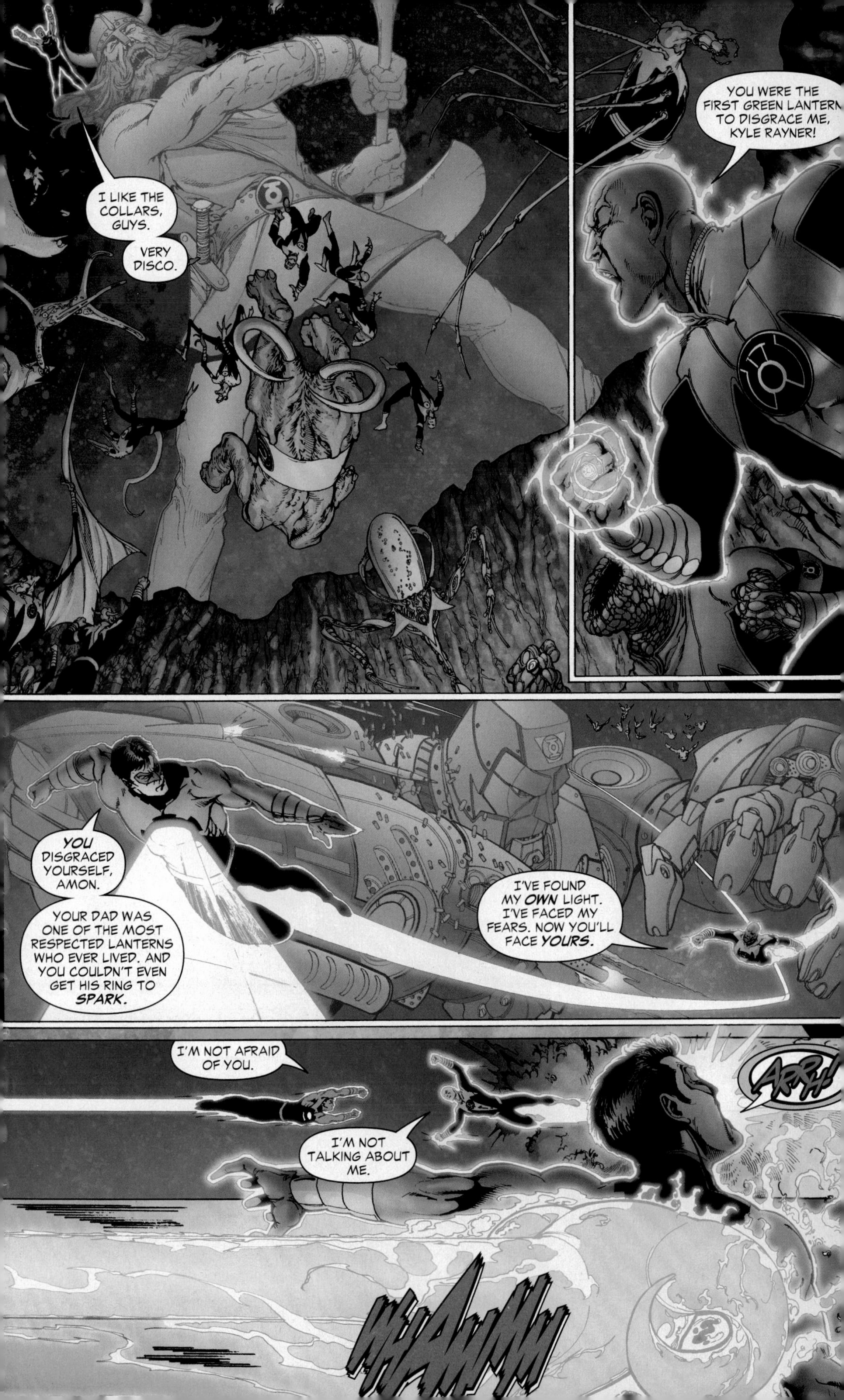
I LIKE THE COLLARS, GUYS.
VERY DISCO.
YOU WERE THE FIRST GREEN LANTERN TO DISGRACE ME, KYLE RAYNER!
YOU DISGRACED YOURSELF, AMON.
YOUR DAD WAS ONE OF THE MOST RESPECTED LANTERNS WHO EVER LIVED. AND YOU COULDN'T EVEN GET HIS RING TO SPARK.
I'VE FOUND MY OWN LIGHT. I'VE FACED MY FEARS. NOW YOU'LL FACE YOURS.
I'M NOT AFRAID OF YOU.
I'M NOT TALKING ABOUT ME.
ARRH!

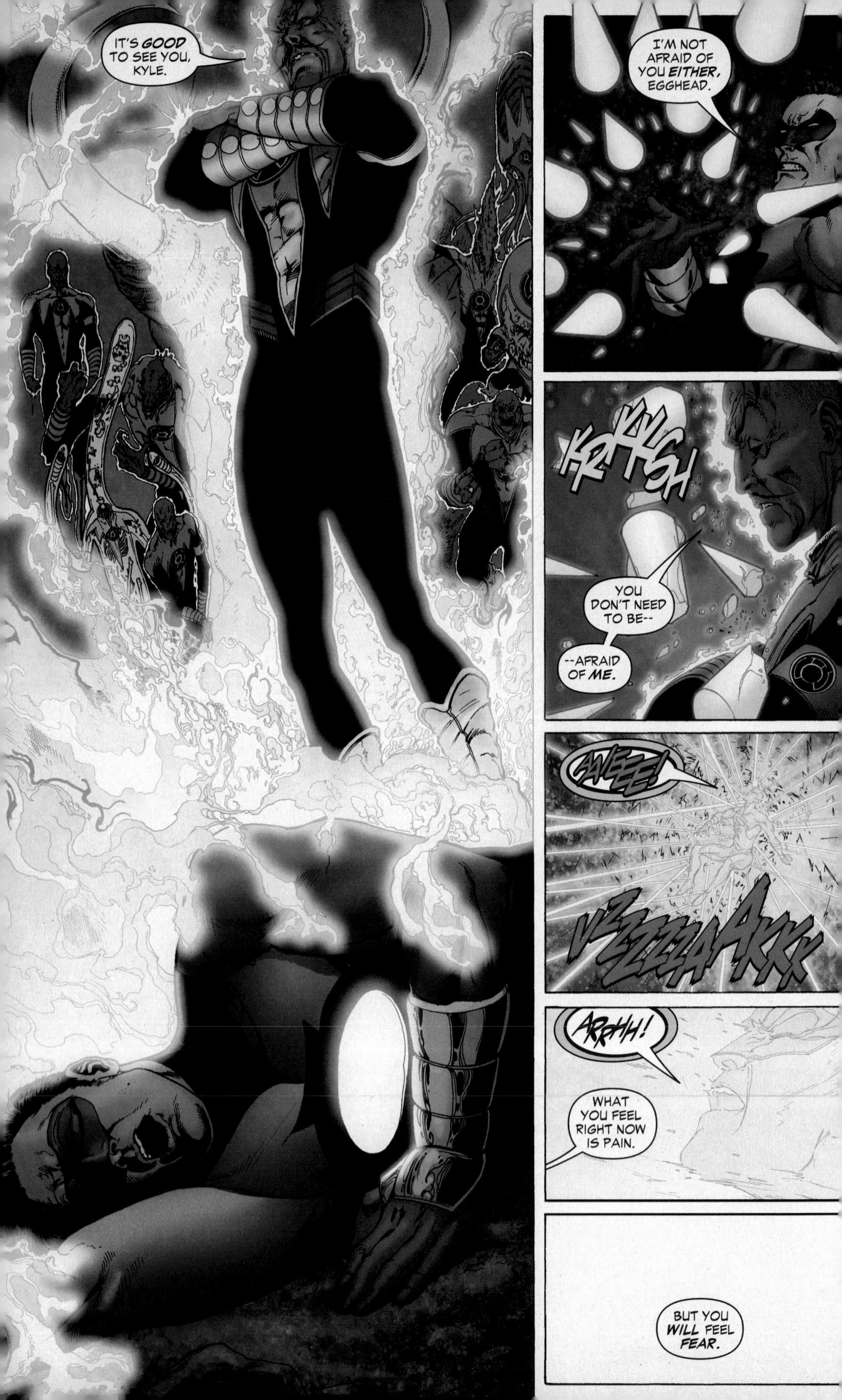
IT'S GOOD TO SEE YOU, KYLE.
I'M NOT AFRAID OF YOU EITHER, EGGHEAD.
KRKKSH
YOU DON'T NEED TO BE--
--AFRAID OF ME.
AVEEEE!
VZZZZAAKKK
ARRHH!
WHAT YOU FEEL RIGHT NOW IS PAIN.
BUT YOU WILL FEEL FEAR.

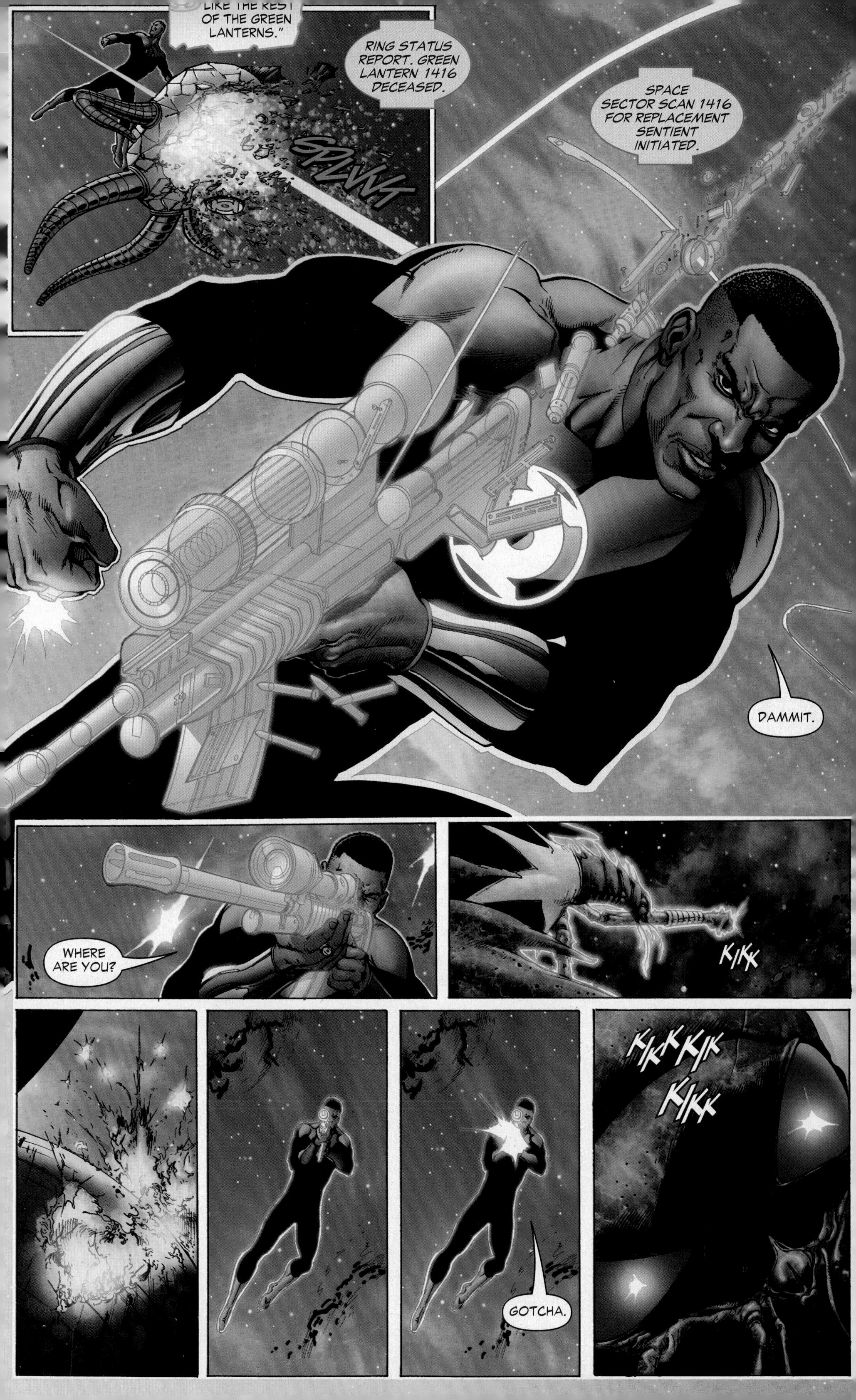
LIKE THE REST OF THE GREEN LANTERNS."
RING STATUS REPORT. GREEN LANTERN 1416 DECEASED.
SPLVVK
SPACE SECTOR SCAN 1416 FOR REPLACEMENT SENTIENT INITIATED.
DAMMIT.
WHERE ARE YOU?
KIKK
KIKK KIK
KIKK
GOTCHA.

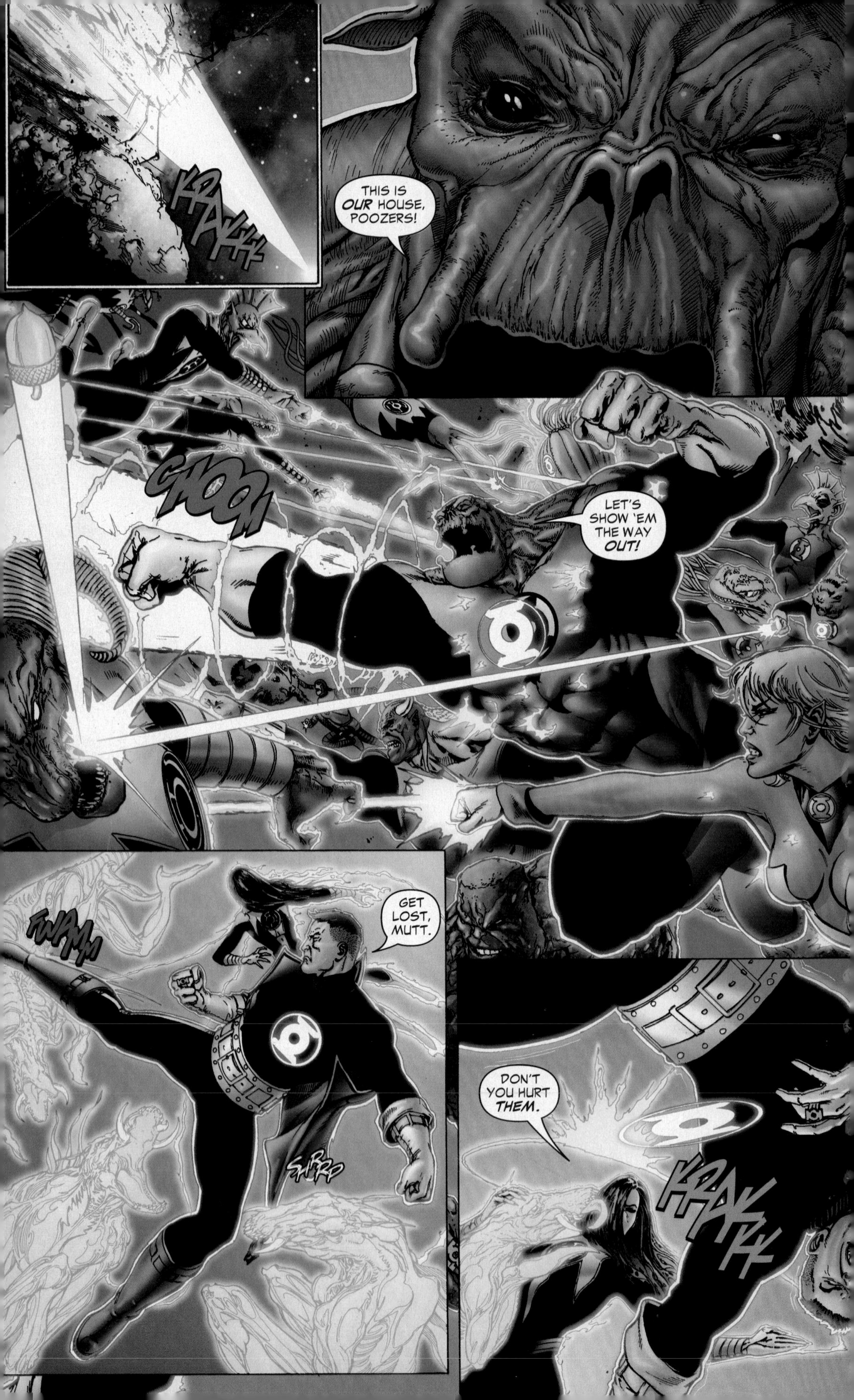
KRAKKK
THIS IS OUR HOUSE, POOZERS!
CHOOOM
LET'S SHOW 'EM THE WAY OUT!
FWAMM
GET LOST, MUTT.
SHRRP
DON'T YOU HURT THEM.
KRAKKK

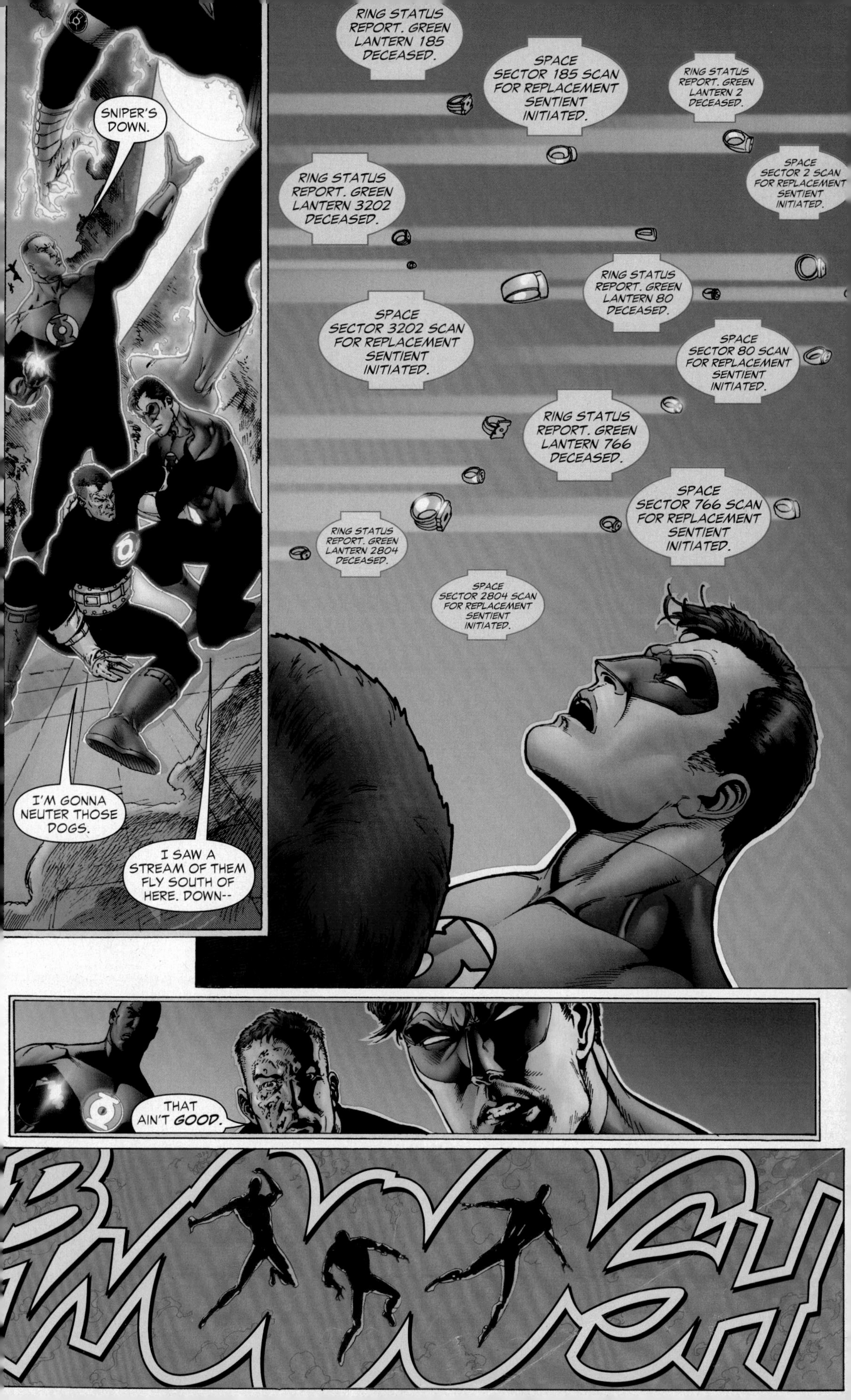
SNIPER'S DOWN.
I'M GONNA NEUTER THOSE DOGS.
I SAW A STREAM OF THEM FLY SOUTH OF HERE. DOWN--
RING STATUS REPORT. GREEN LANTERN 185 DECEASED.
SPACE SECTOR 185 SCAN FOR REPLACEMENT SENTIENT INITIATED.
RING STATUS REPORT. GREEN LANTERN 2 DECEASED.
SPACE SECTOR 2 SCAN FOR REPLACEMENT SENTIENT INITIATED.
RING STATUS REPORT. GREEN LANTERN 3202 DECEASED.
RING STATUS REPORT. GREEN LANTERN 80 DECEASED.
SPACE SECTOR 3202 SCAN FOR REPLACEMENT SENTIENT INITIATED.
SPACE SECTOR 80 SCAN FOR REPLACEMENT SENTIENT INITIATED.
RING STATUS REPORT. GREEN LANTERN 766 DECEASED.
SPACE SECTOR 766 SCAN FOR REPLACEMENT SENTIENT INITIATED.
RING STATUS REPORT. GREEN LANTERN 2804 DECEASED.
SPACE SECTOR 2804 SCAN FOR REPLACEMENT SENTIENT INITIATED.
THAT AIN'T GOOD.

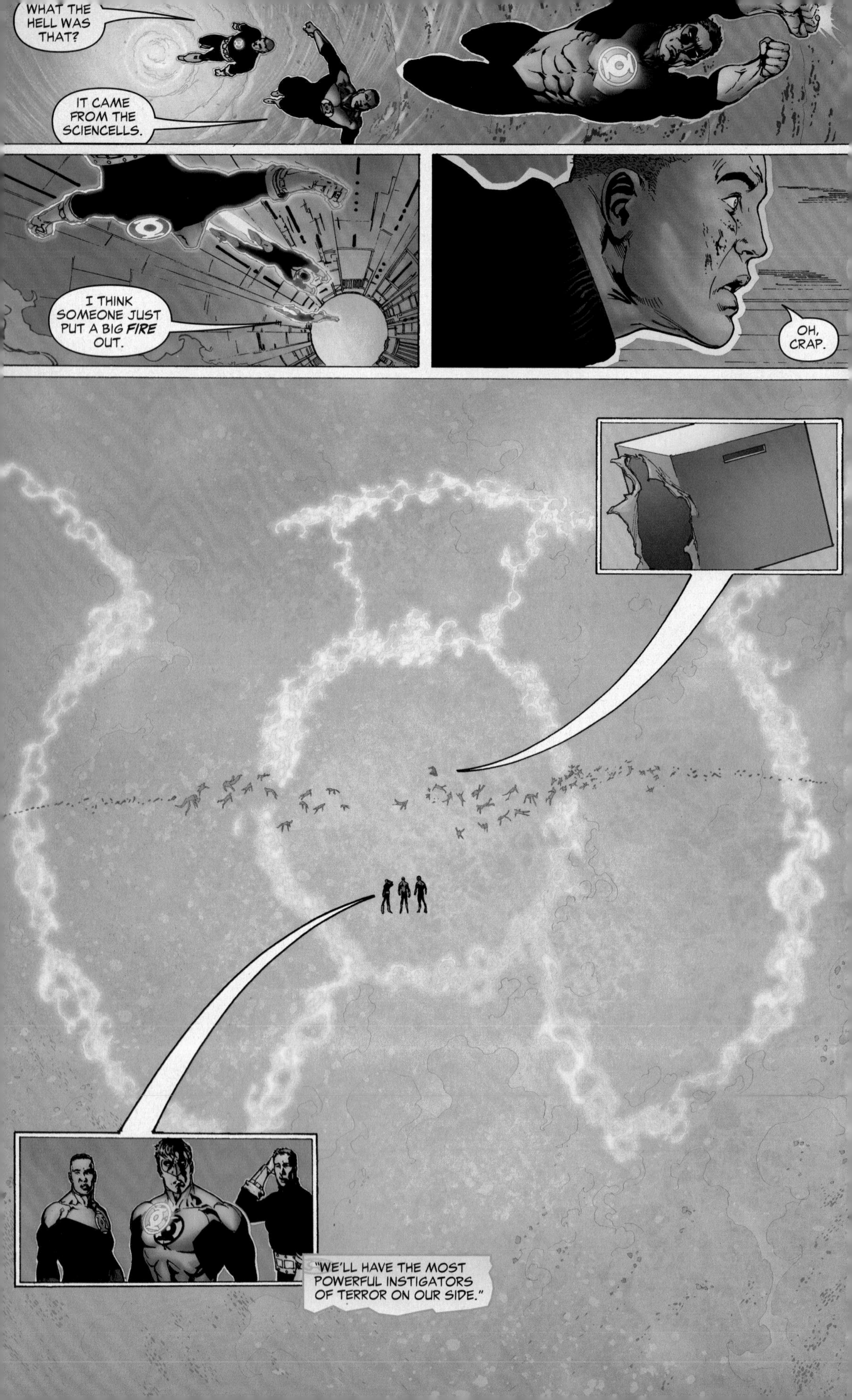
WHAT THE HELL WAS THAT?
IT CAME FROM THE SCIENCELLS.
I THINK SOMEONE JUST PUT A BIG FIRE OUT.
OH, CRAP.
"WE'LL HAVE THE MOST POWERFUL INSTIGATORS OF TERROR ON OUR SIDE."

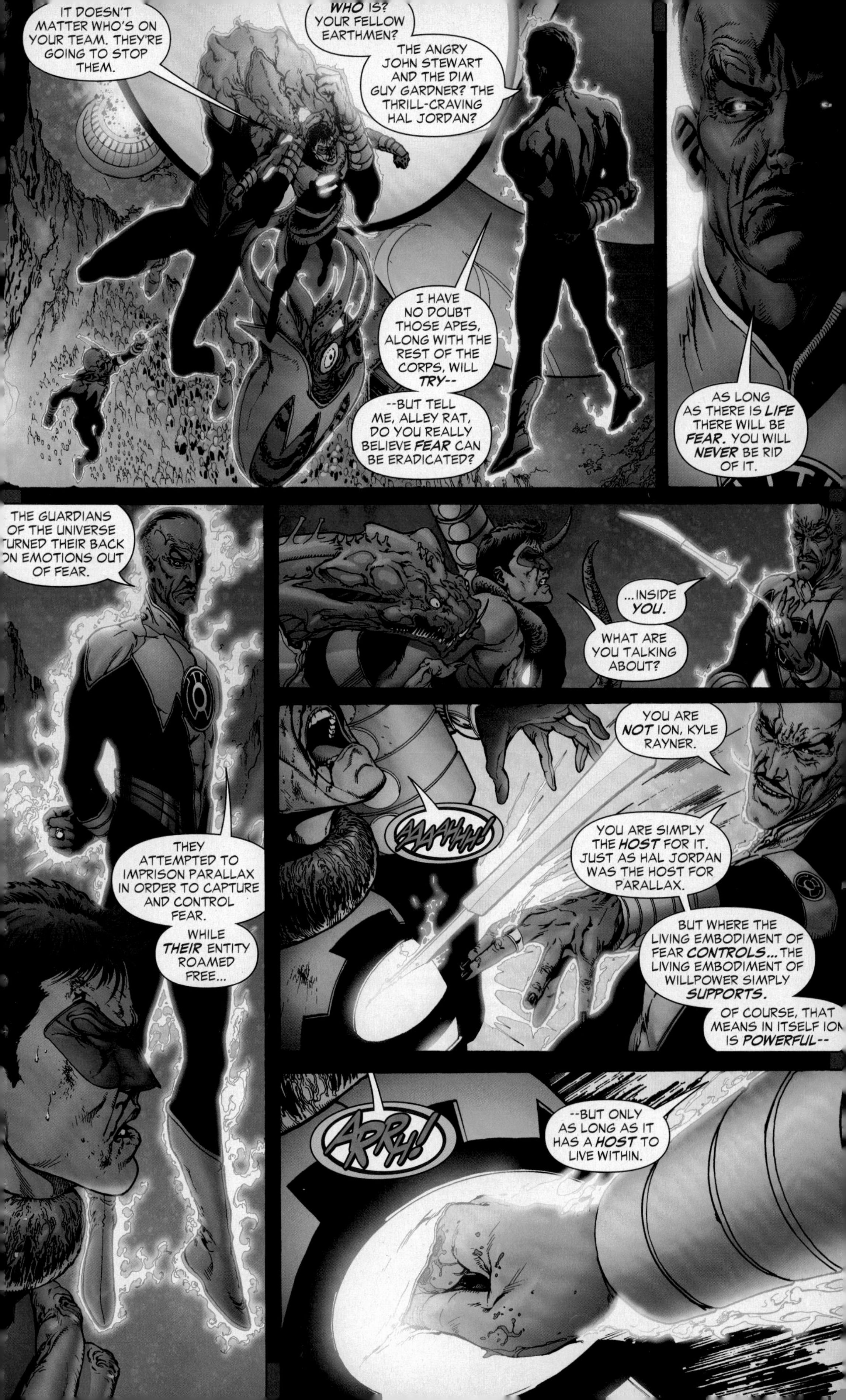
IT DOESN'T MATTER WHO'S ON YOUR TEAM. THEY'RE GOING TO STOP THEM.
WHO IS? YOUR FELLOW EARTHMEN?
THE ANGRY JOHN STEWART AND THE DIM GUY GARDNER? THE THRILL-CRAVING HAL JORDAN?
I HAVE NO DOUBT THOSE APES, ALONG WITH THE REST OF THE CORPS, WILL TRY--
--BUT TELL ME, ALLEY RAT, DO YOU REALLY BELIEVE FEAR CAN BE ERADICATED?
AS LONG AS THERE IS LIFE THERE WILL BE FEAR. YOU WILL NEVER BE RID OF IT.
THE GUARDIANS OF THE UNIVERSE TURNED THEIR BACK ON EMOTIONS OUT OF FEAR.
THEY ATTEMPTED TO IMPRISON PARALLAX IN ORDER TO CAPTURE AND CONTROL FEAR.
WHILE THEIR ENTITY ROAMED FREE...
...INSIDE YOU.
WHAT ARE YOU TALKING ABOUT?
YOU ARE NOT ION, KYLE RAYNER.
AAAHHH!
YOU ARE SIMPLY THE HOST FOR IT. JUST AS HAL JORDAN WAS THE HOST FOR PARALLAX.
BUT WHERE THE LIVING EMBODIMENT OF FEAR CONTROLS... THE LIVING EMBODIMENT OF WILLPOWER SIMPLY SUPPORTS.
OF COURSE, THAT MEANS IN ITSELF ION IS POWERFUL--
ARRH!
--BUT ONLY AS LONG AS IT HAS A HOST TO LIVE WITHIN.

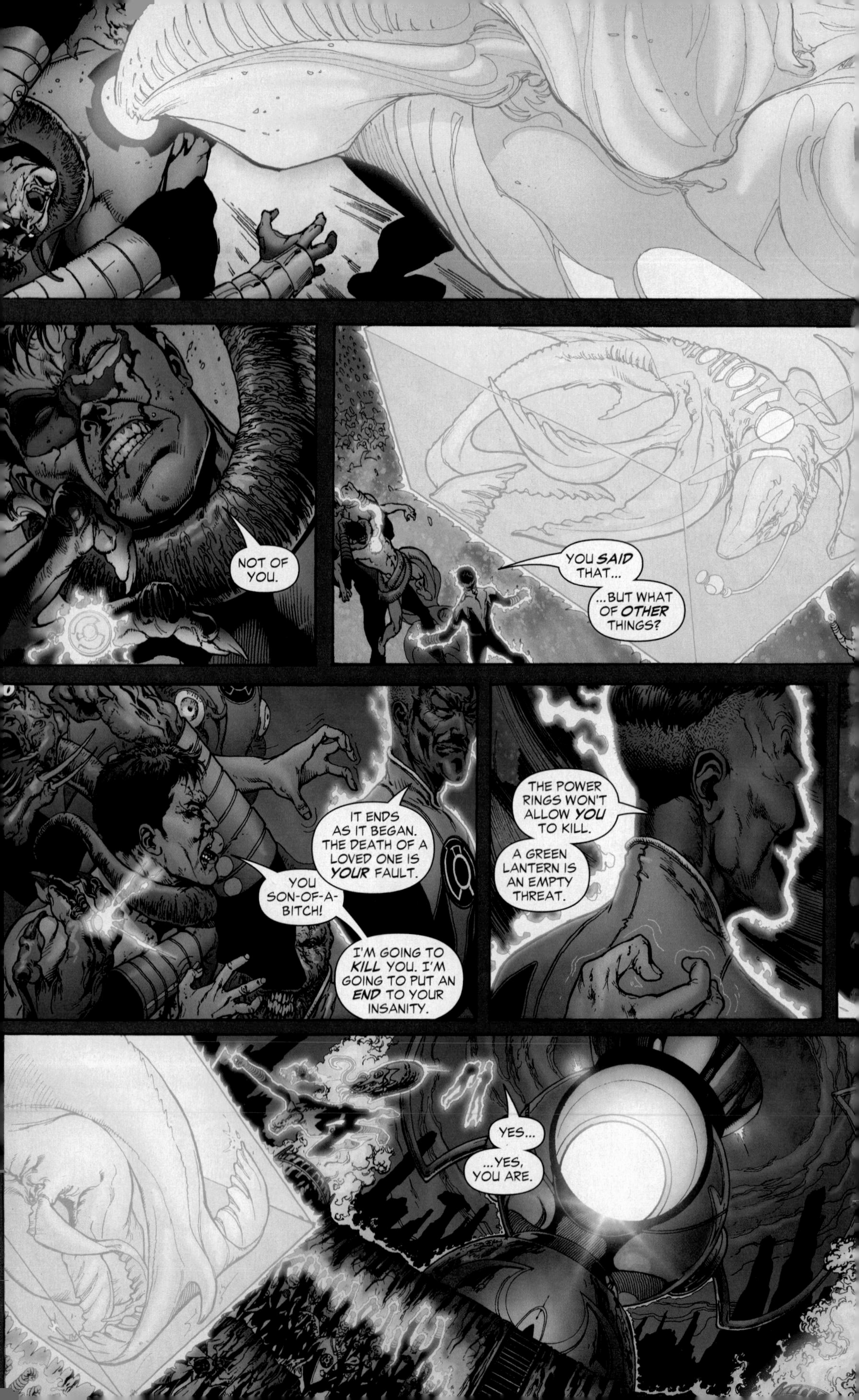
NOT OF YOU.
YOU *SAID* THAT...
...BUT WHAT OF *OTHER* THINGS?
IT ENDS AS IT BEGAN. THE DEATH OF A LOVED ONE IS *YOUR* FAULT.
YOU SON-OF-A-BITCH!
I'M GOING TO *KILL* YOU. I'M GOING TO PUT AN *END* TO YOUR INSANITY.
THE POWER RINGS WON'T ALLOW *YOU* TO KILL.
A GREEN LANTERN IS AN EMPTY THREAT.
YES...
...YES, YOU ARE.

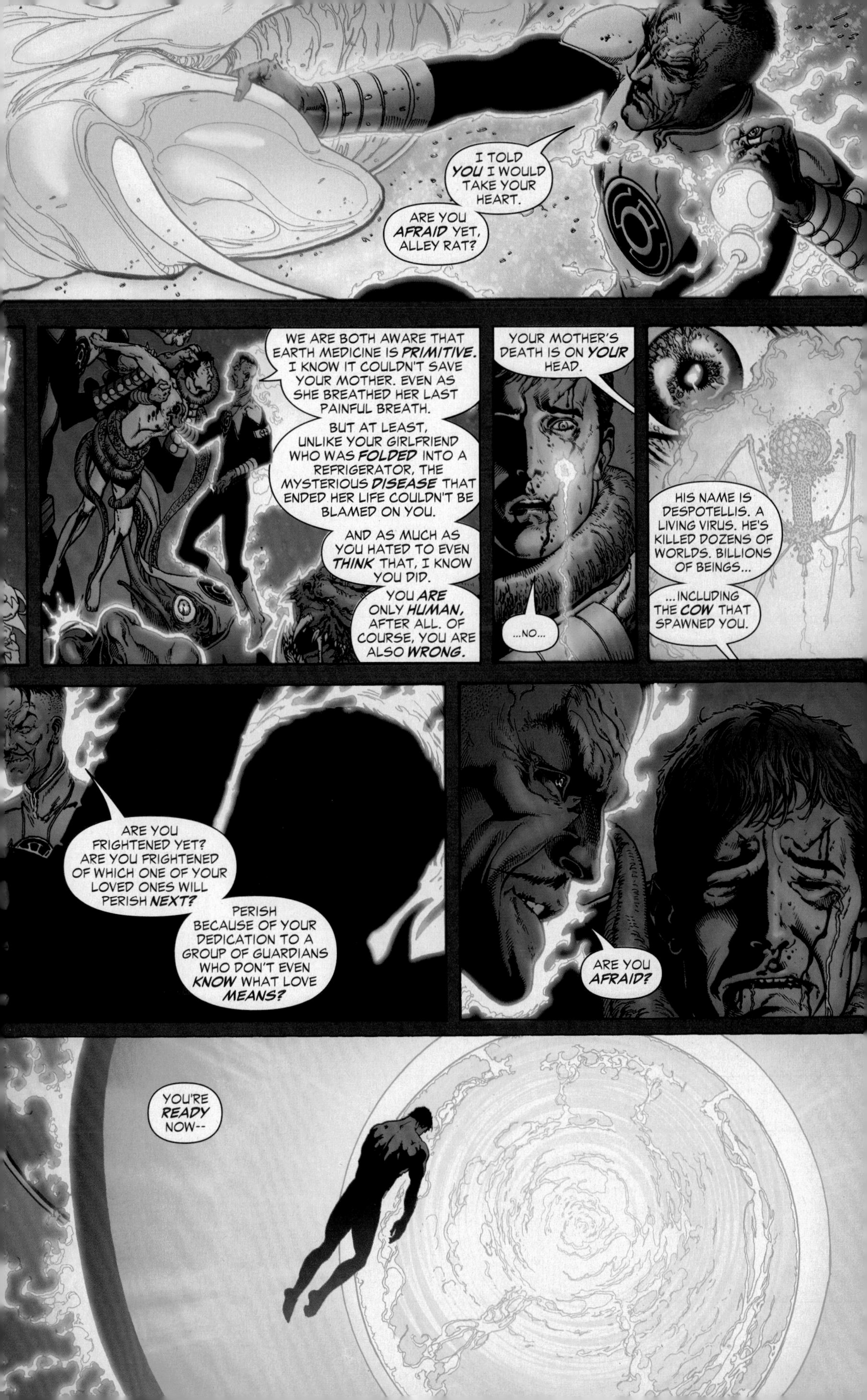
I TOLD *YOU* I WOULD TAKE YOUR HEART.
ARE YOU *AFRAID* YET, ALLEY RAT?
WE ARE BOTH AWARE THAT EARTH MEDICINE IS *PRIMITIVE*. I KNOW IT COULDN'T SAVE YOUR MOTHER. EVEN AS SHE BREATHED HER LAST PAINFUL BREATH.
BUT AT LEAST, UNLIKE YOUR GIRLFRIEND WHO WAS *FOLDED* INTO A REFRIGERATOR, THE MYSTERIOUS *DISEASE* THAT ENDED HER LIFE COULDN'T BE BLAMED ON YOU.
AND AS MUCH AS YOU HATED TO EVEN *THINK* THAT, I KNOW YOU DID.
YOU *ARE* ONLY *HUMAN*, AFTER ALL. OF COURSE, YOU ARE ALSO *WRONG*.
YOUR MOTHER'S DEATH IS ON *YOUR* HEAD.
...NO...
HIS NAME IS DESPOTELLIS. A LIVING VIRUS. HE'S KILLED DOZENS OF WORLDS. BILLIONS OF BEINGS...
...INCLUDING THE *COW* THAT SPAWNED YOU.
ARE YOU FRIGHTENED YET? ARE YOU FRIGHTENED OF WHICH ONE OF YOUR LOVED ONES WILL PERISH *NEXT?*
PERISH BECAUSE OF YOUR DEDICATION TO A GROUP OF GUARDIANS WHO DON'T EVEN *KNOW* WHAT LOVE *MEANS?*
ARE YOU *AFRAID?*
YOU'RE *READY* NOW--

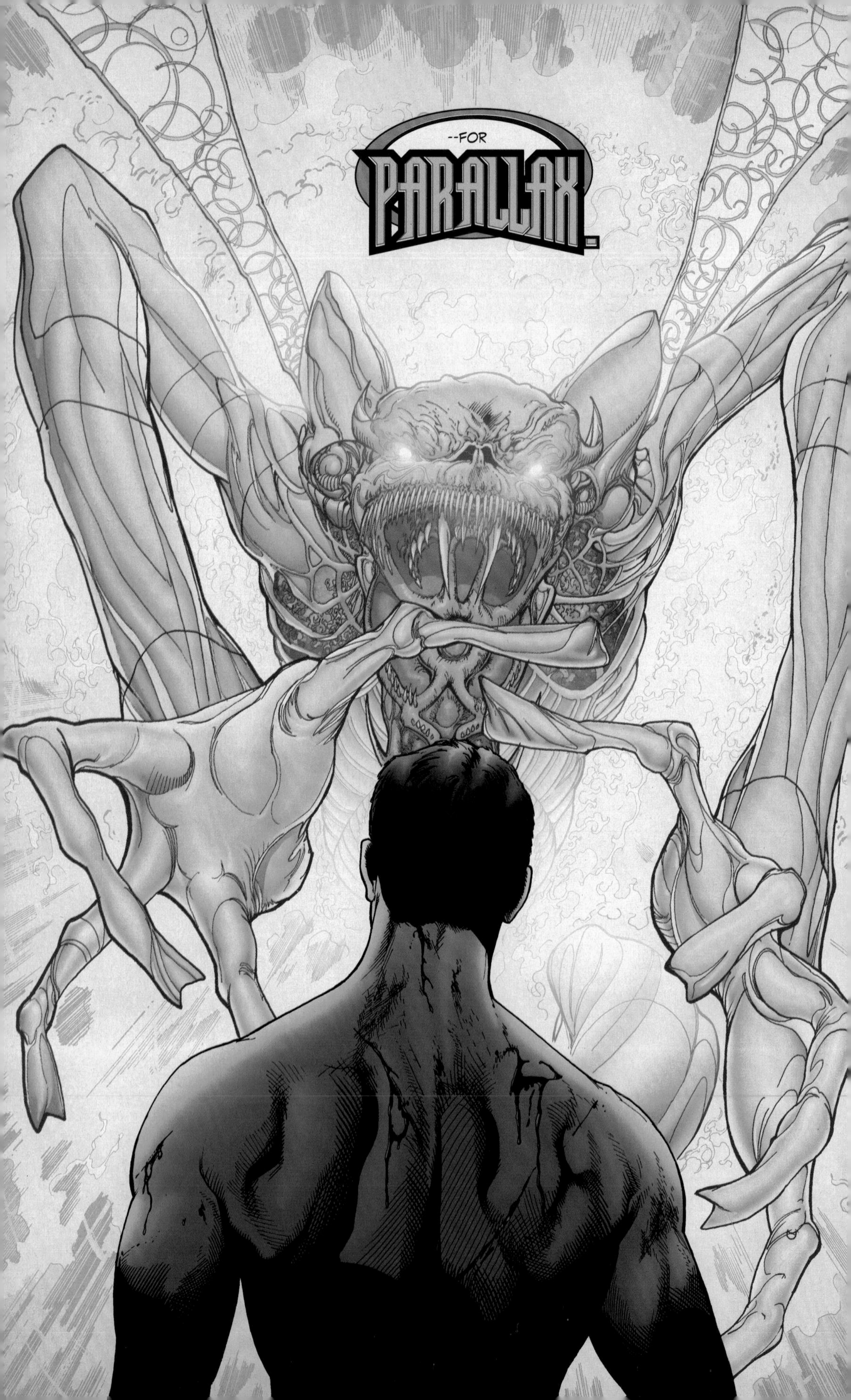
--FOR
PARALLAX.

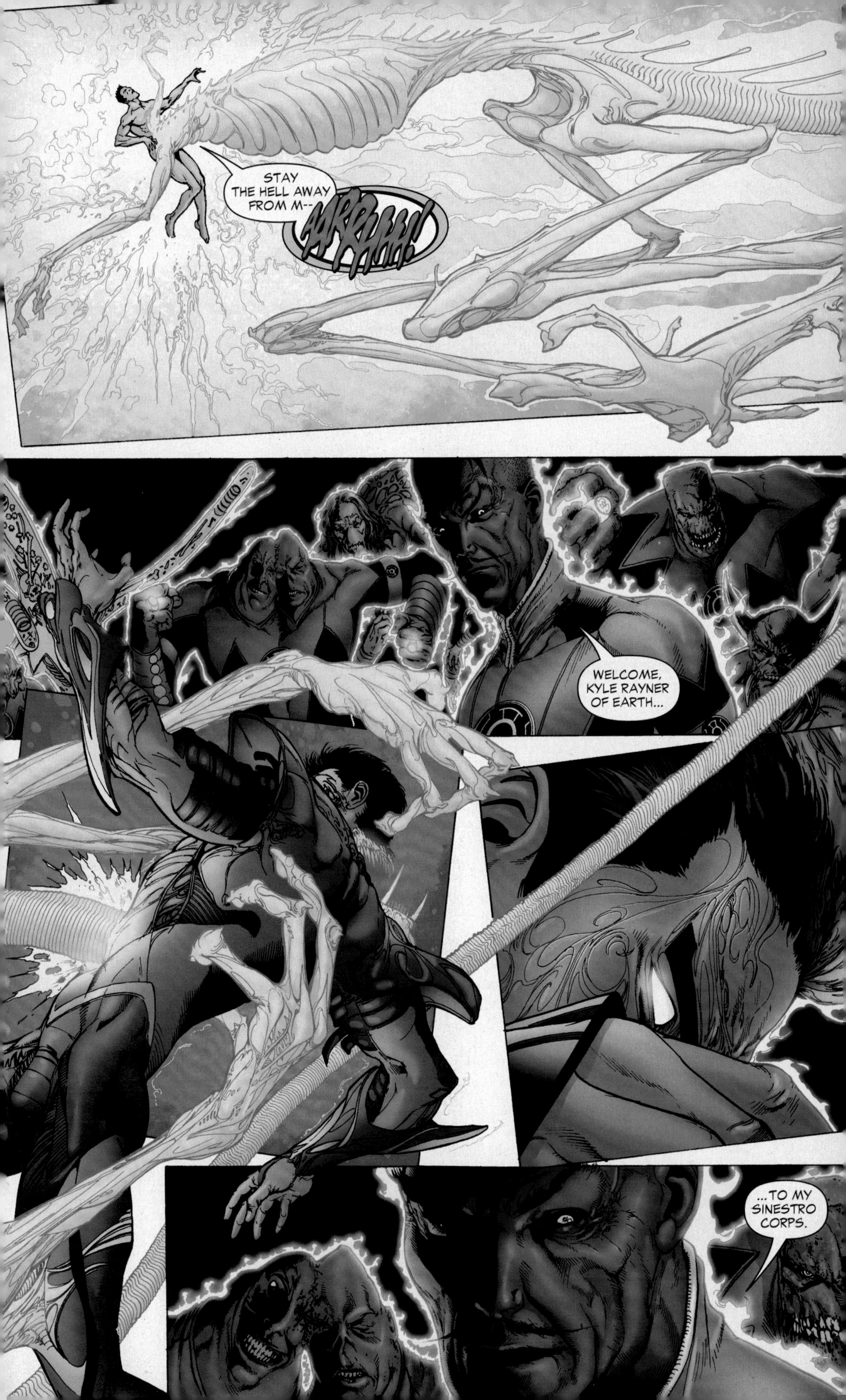
STAY THE HELL AWAY FROM M--
AARRAAAA!
WELCOME, KYLE RAYNER OF EARTH...
...TO MY SINESTRO CORPS.

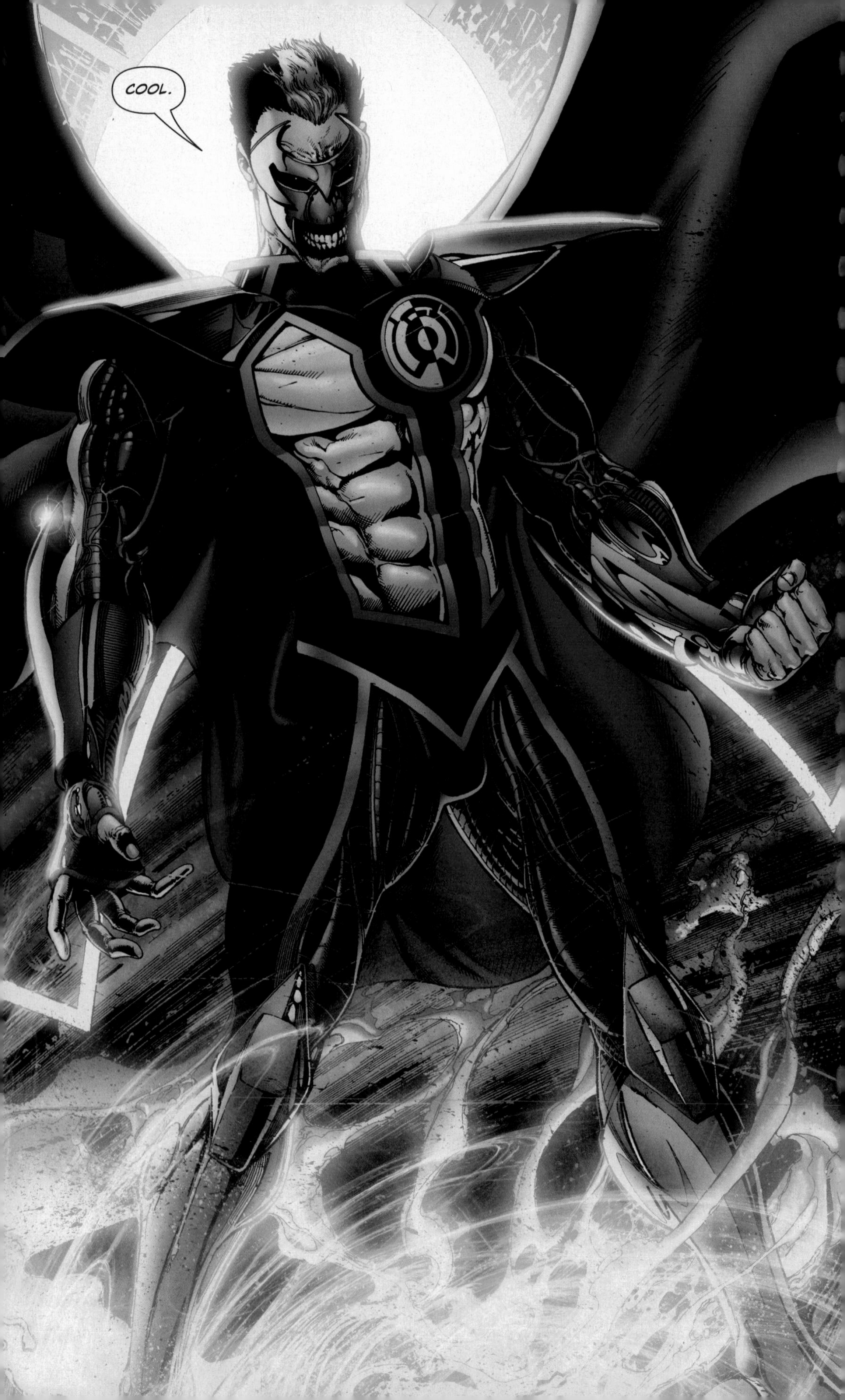
COOL.

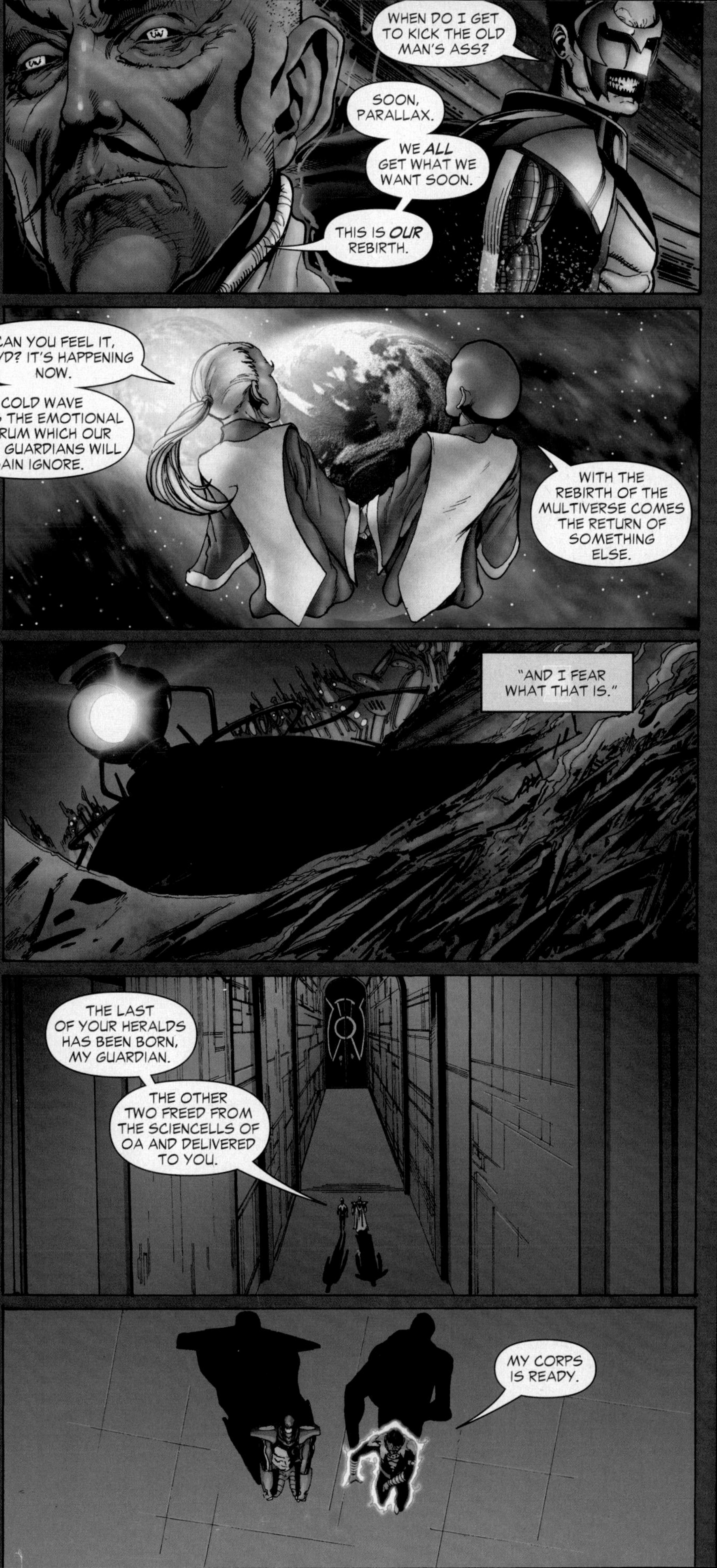
WHEN DO I GET TO KICK THE OLD MAN'S ASS?
SOON, PARALLAX.
WE ALL GET WHAT WE WANT SOON.
THIS IS OUR REBIRTH.
CAN YOU FEEL IT, SAYD? IT'S HAPPENING NOW.
A COLD WAVE ACROSS THE EMOTIONAL SPECTRUM WHICH OUR FELLOW GUARDIANS WILL AGAIN IGNORE.
WITH THE REBIRTH OF THE MULTIVERSE COMES THE RETURN OF SOMETHING ELSE.
"AND I FEAR WHAT THAT IS."
THE LAST OF YOUR HERALDS HAS BEEN BORN, MY GUARDIAN.
THE OTHER TWO FREED FROM THE SCIENCELLS OF OA AND DELIVERED TO YOU.
MY CORPS IS READY.

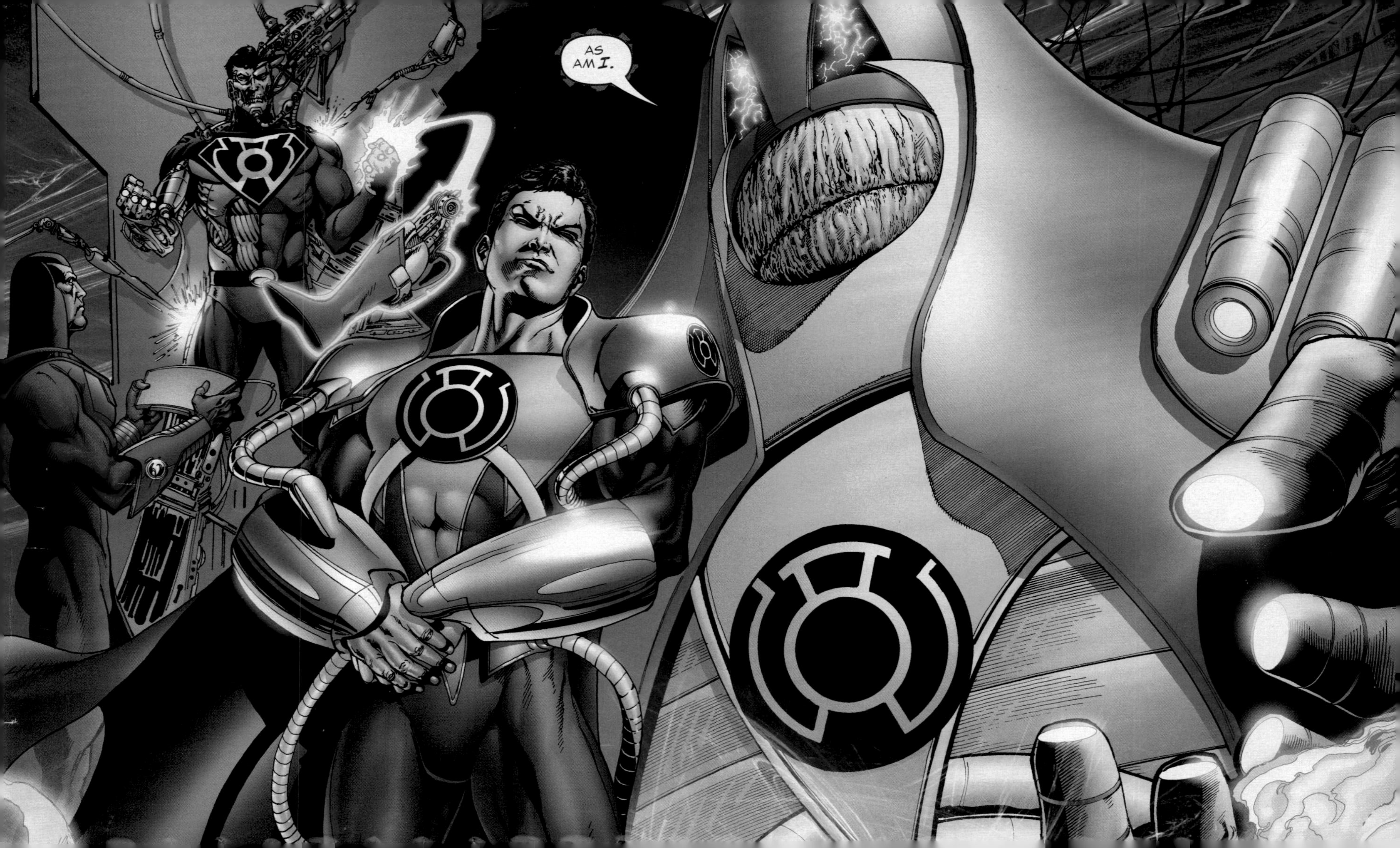
AS AM I.

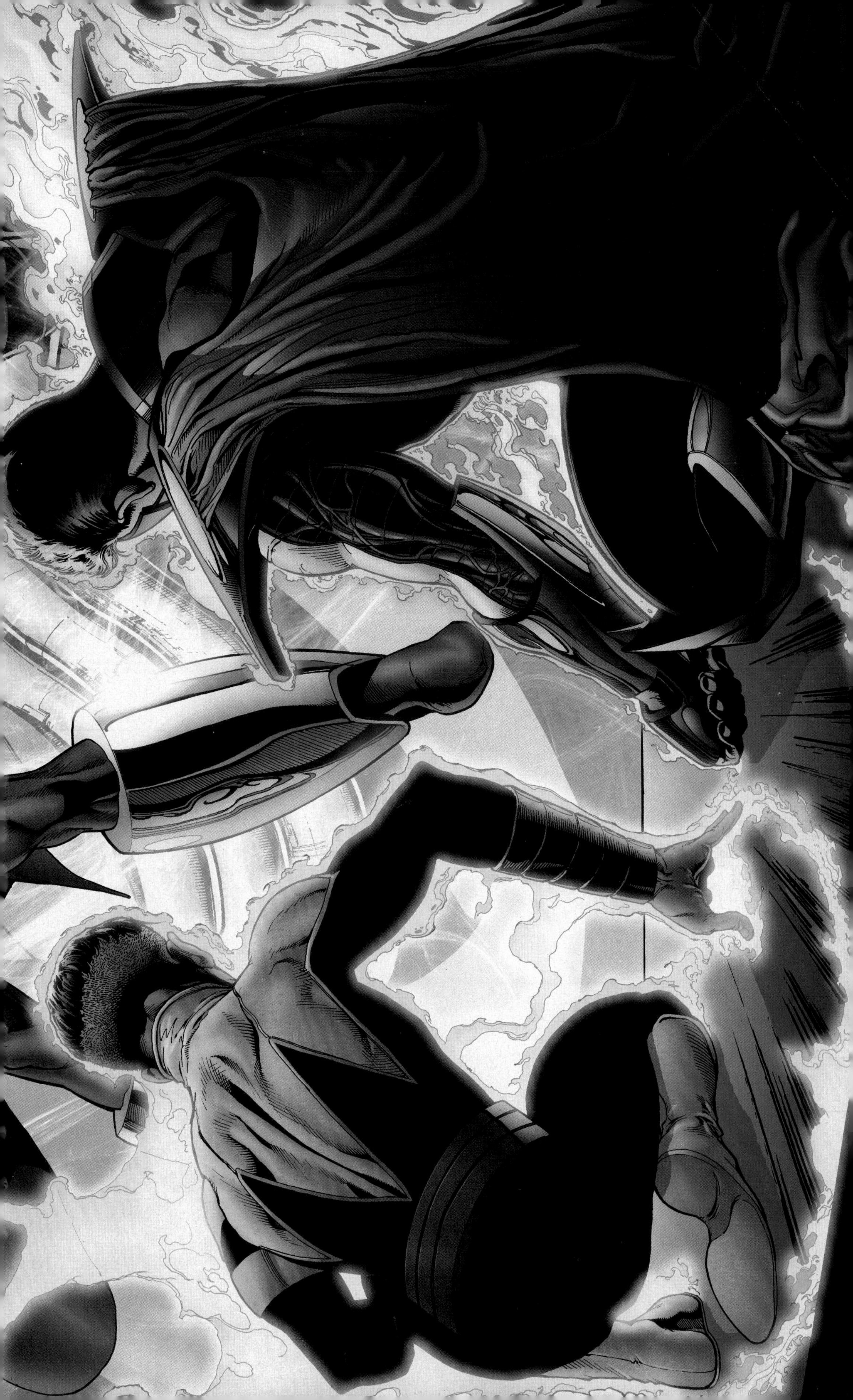

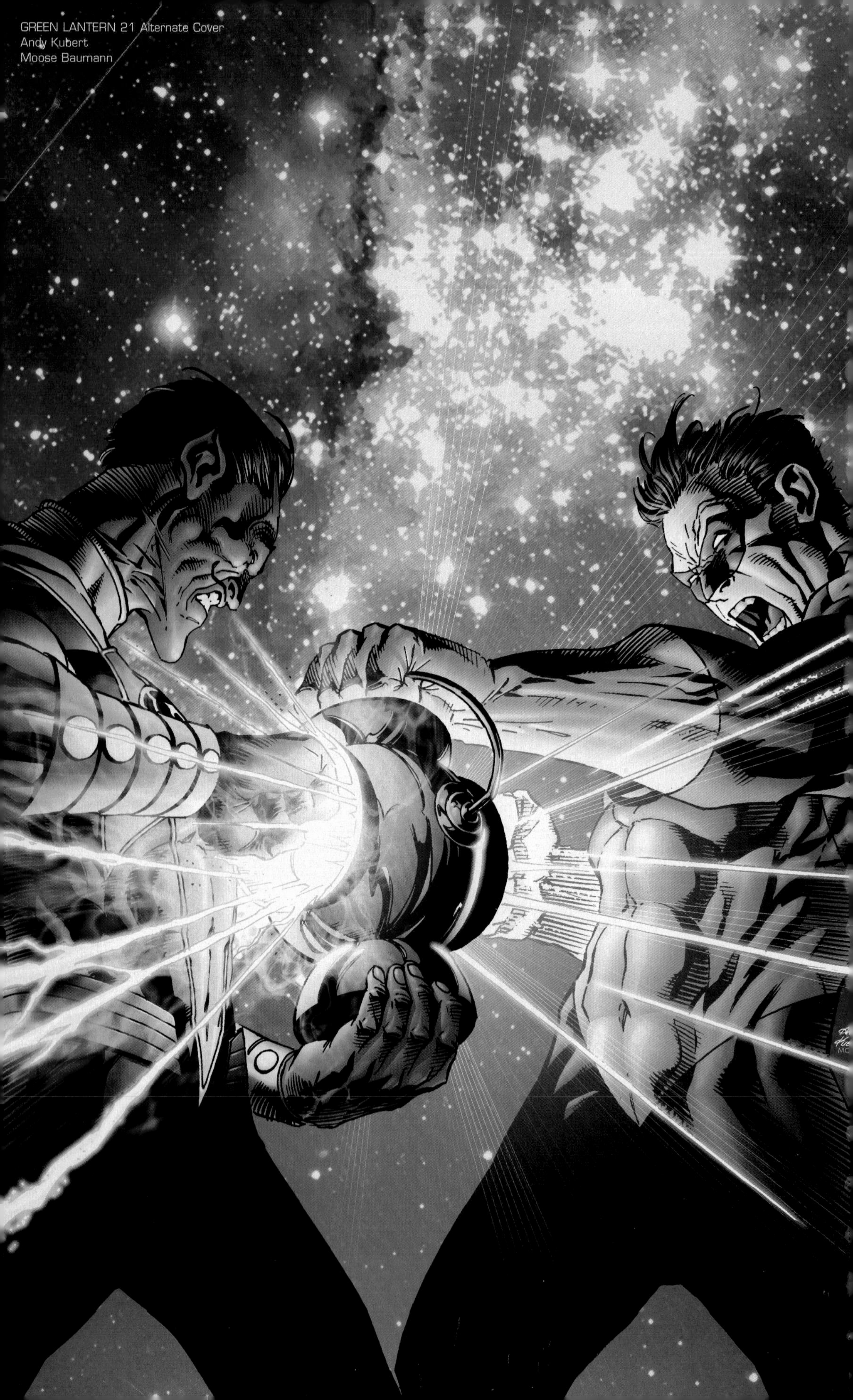

GREEN LANTERN 21 Alternate Cover
Andy Kubert
Moose Baumann

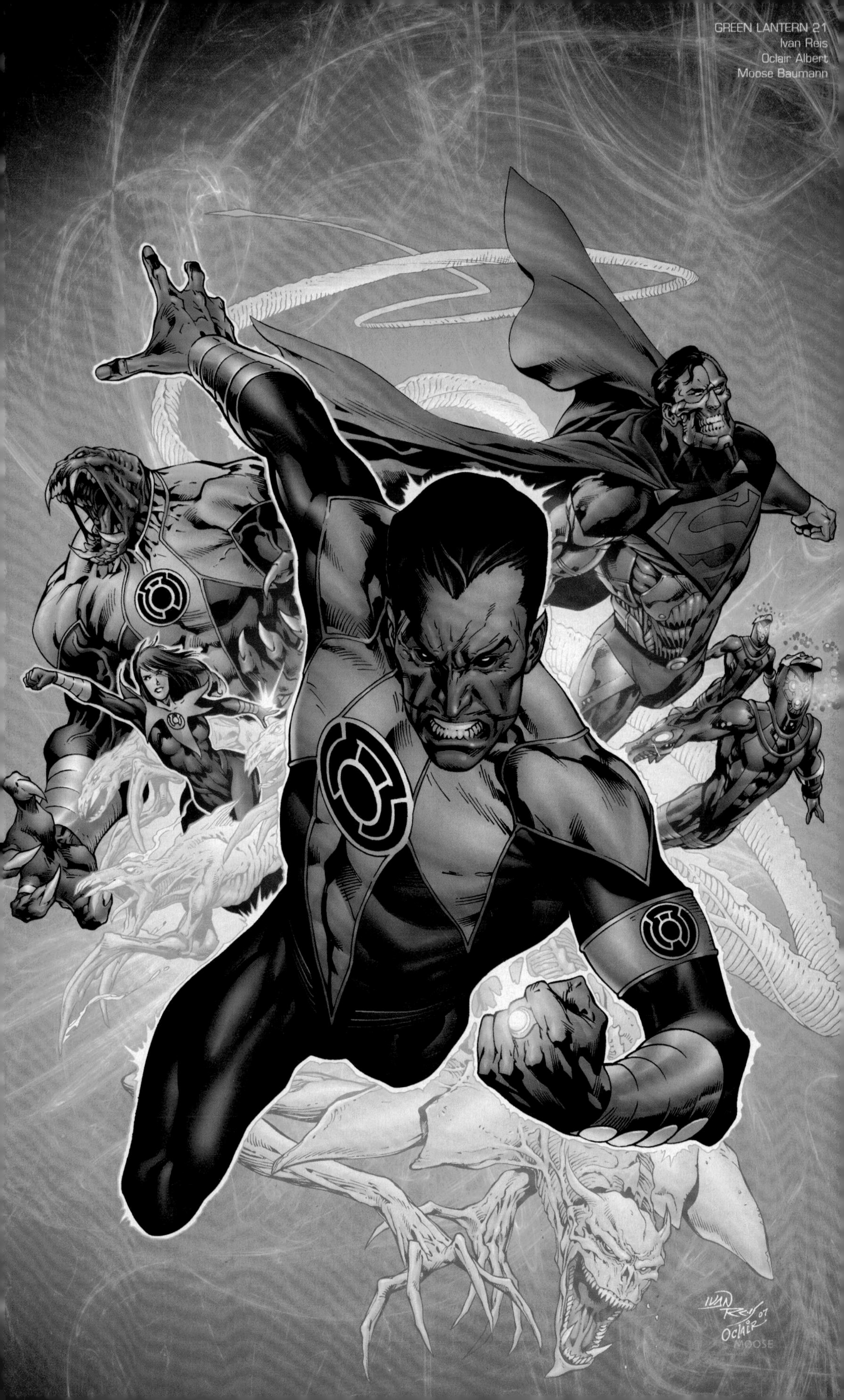
GREEN LANTERN 21
Ivan Reis
Oclair Albert
Moose Baumann

THE SINESTRO CORPS WAR
Chapter One
FEAR & LOATHING
Writer: **Geoff Johns**
Penciller: **Ivan Reis**
Inker: **Oclair Albert**
Colorist: **Moose Baumann**
Letterer: **Rob Leigh**

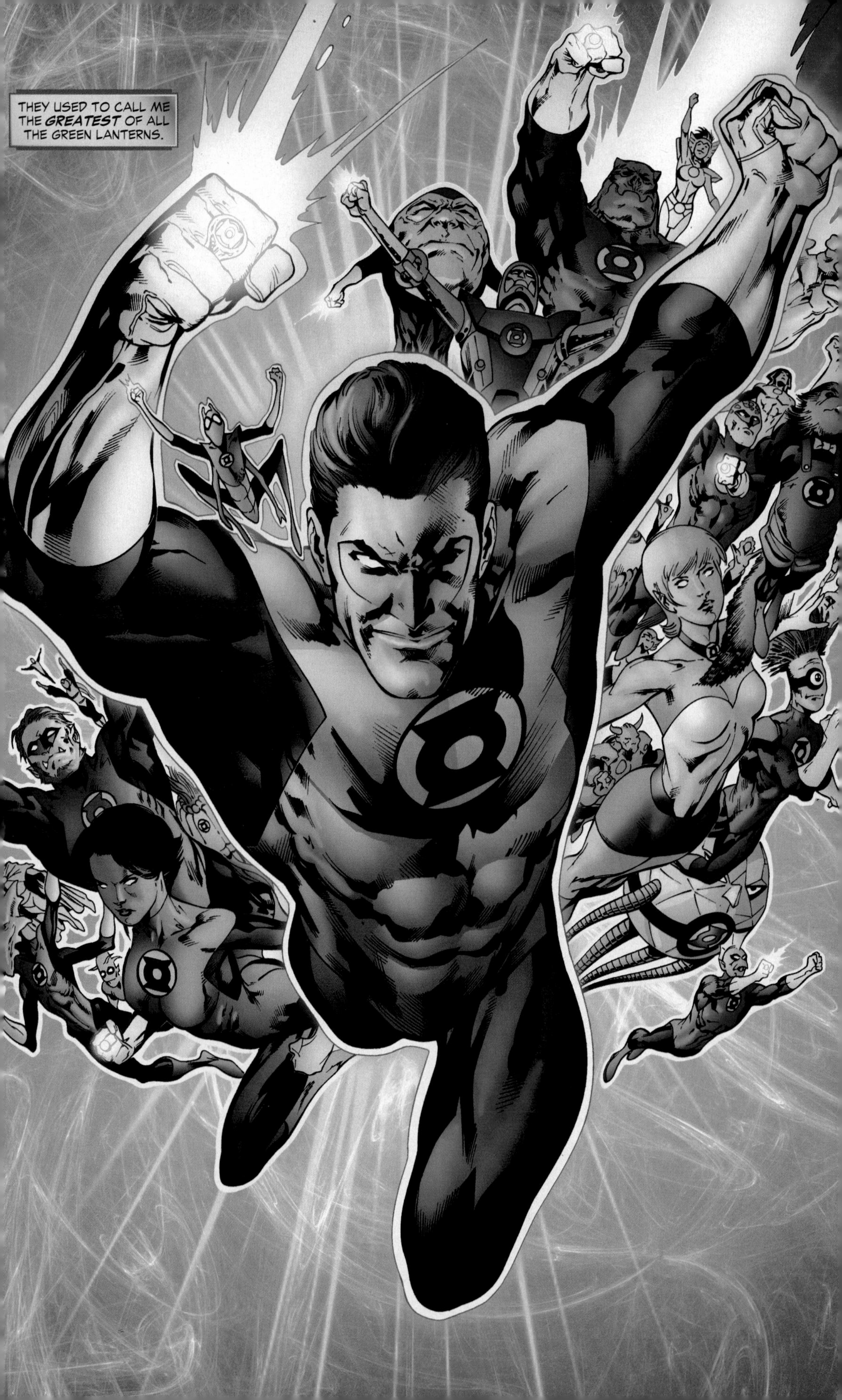
THEY USED TO CALL ME THE GREATEST OF ALL THE GREEN LANTERNS.

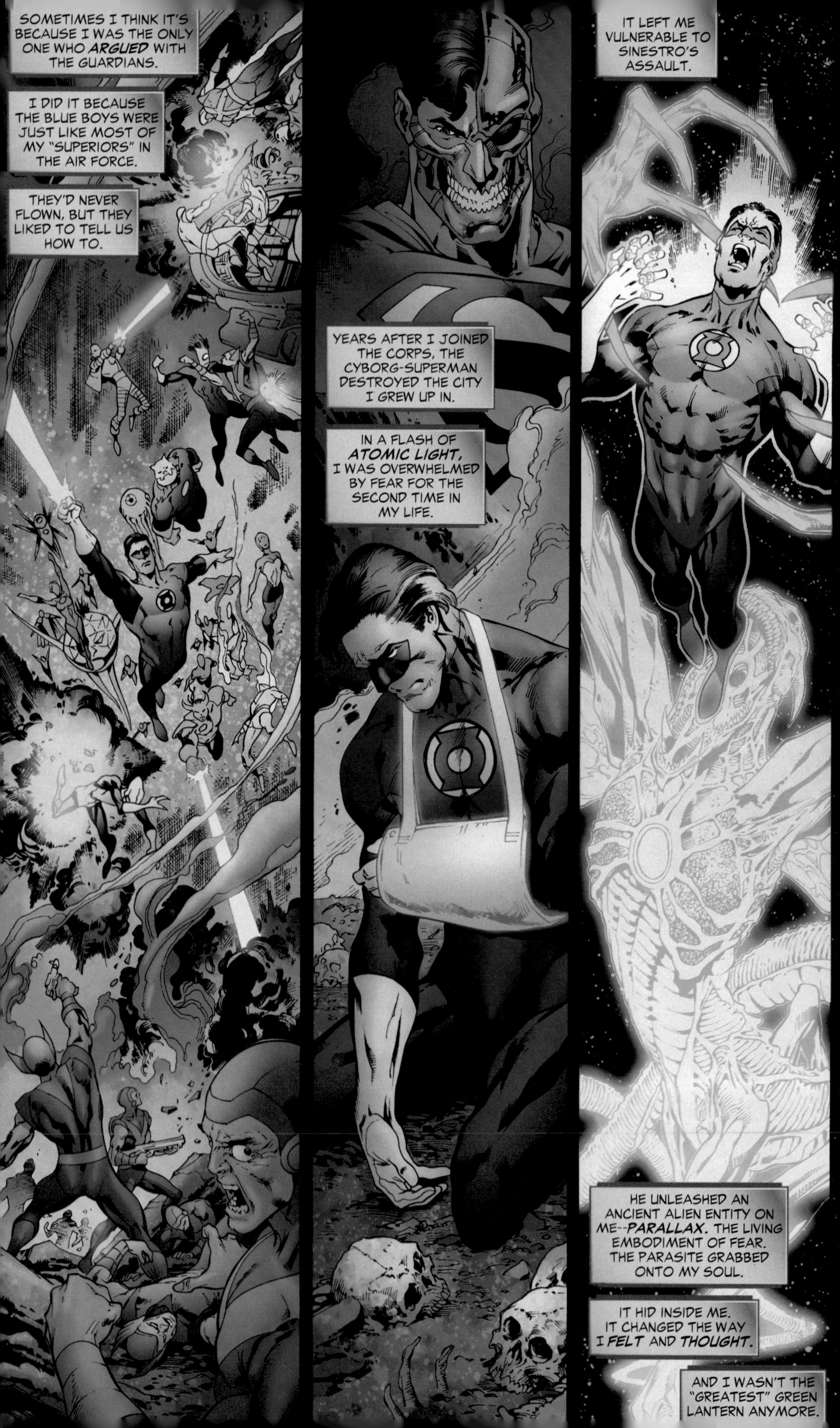
SOMETIMES I THINK IT'S BECAUSE I WAS THE ONLY ONE WHO ARGUED WITH THE GUARDIANS.
I DID IT BECAUSE THE BLUE BOYS WERE JUST LIKE MOST OF MY "SUPERIORS" IN THE AIR FORCE.
THEY'D NEVER FLOWN, BUT THEY LIKED TO TELL US HOW TO.
YEARS AFTER I JOINED THE CORPS, THE CYBORG-SUPERMAN DESTROYED THE CITY I GREW UP IN.
IN A FLASH OF ATOMIC LIGHT, I WAS OVERWHELMED BY FEAR FOR THE SECOND TIME IN MY LIFE.
IT LEFT ME VULNERABLE TO SINESTRO'S ASSAULT.
HE UNLEASHED AN ANCIENT ALIEN ENTITY ON ME--PARALLAX. THE LIVING EMBODIMENT OF FEAR. THE PARASITE GRABBED ONTO MY SOUL.
IT HID INSIDE ME. IT CHANGED THE WAY I FELT AND THOUGHT.
AND I WASN'T THE "GREATEST" GREEN LANTERN ANYMORE.

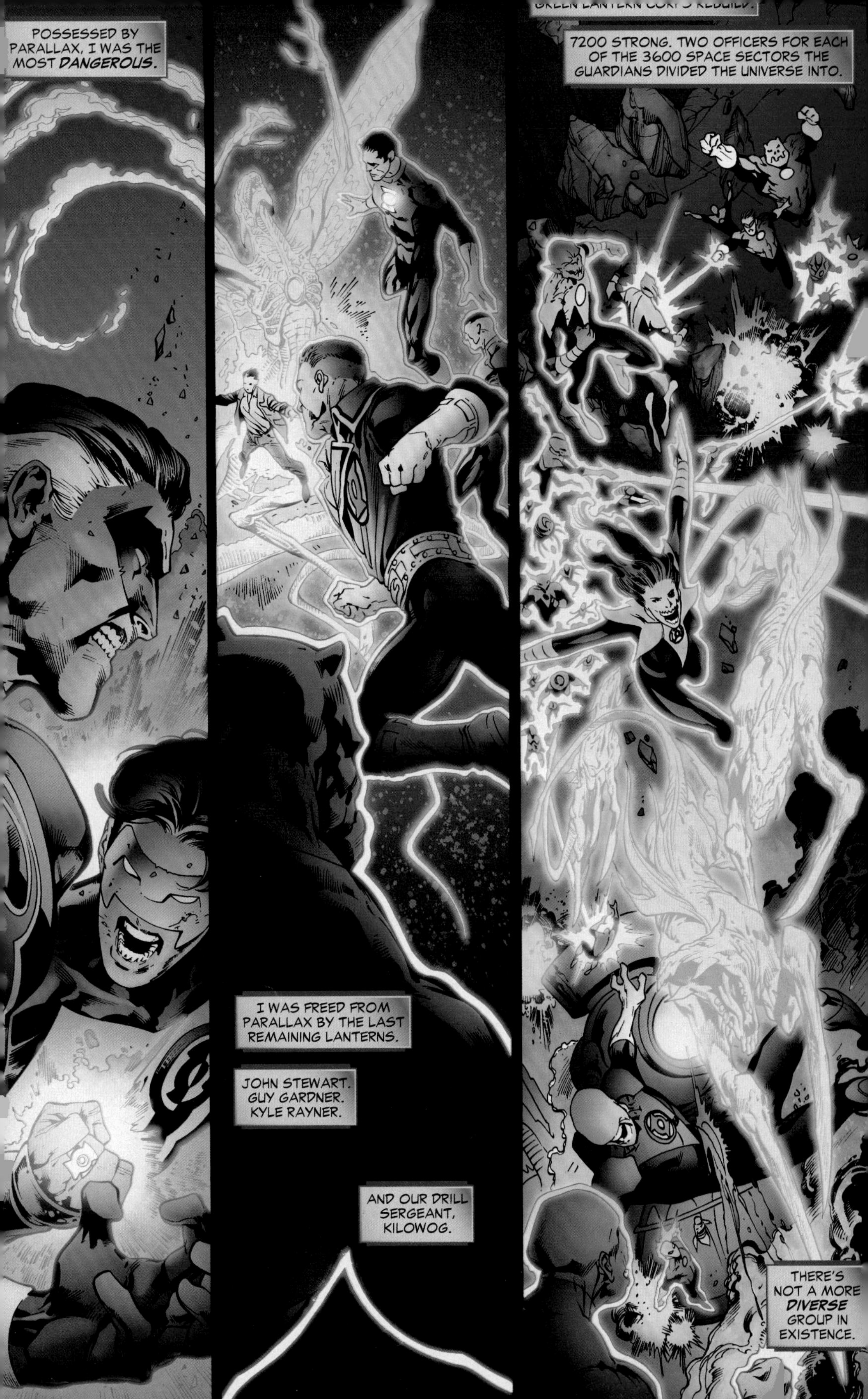
POSSESSED BY PARALLAX, I WAS THE MOST DANGEROUS.
I WAS FREED FROM PARALLAX BY THE LAST REMAINING LANTERNS.
JOHN STEWART. GUY GARDNER. KYLE RAYNER.
AND OUR DRILL SERGEANT, KILOWOG.
7200 STRONG. TWO OFFICERS FOR EACH OF THE 3600 SPACE SECTORS THE GUARDIANS DIVIDED THE UNIVERSE INTO.
THERE'S NOT A MORE DIVERSE GROUP IN EXISTENCE.

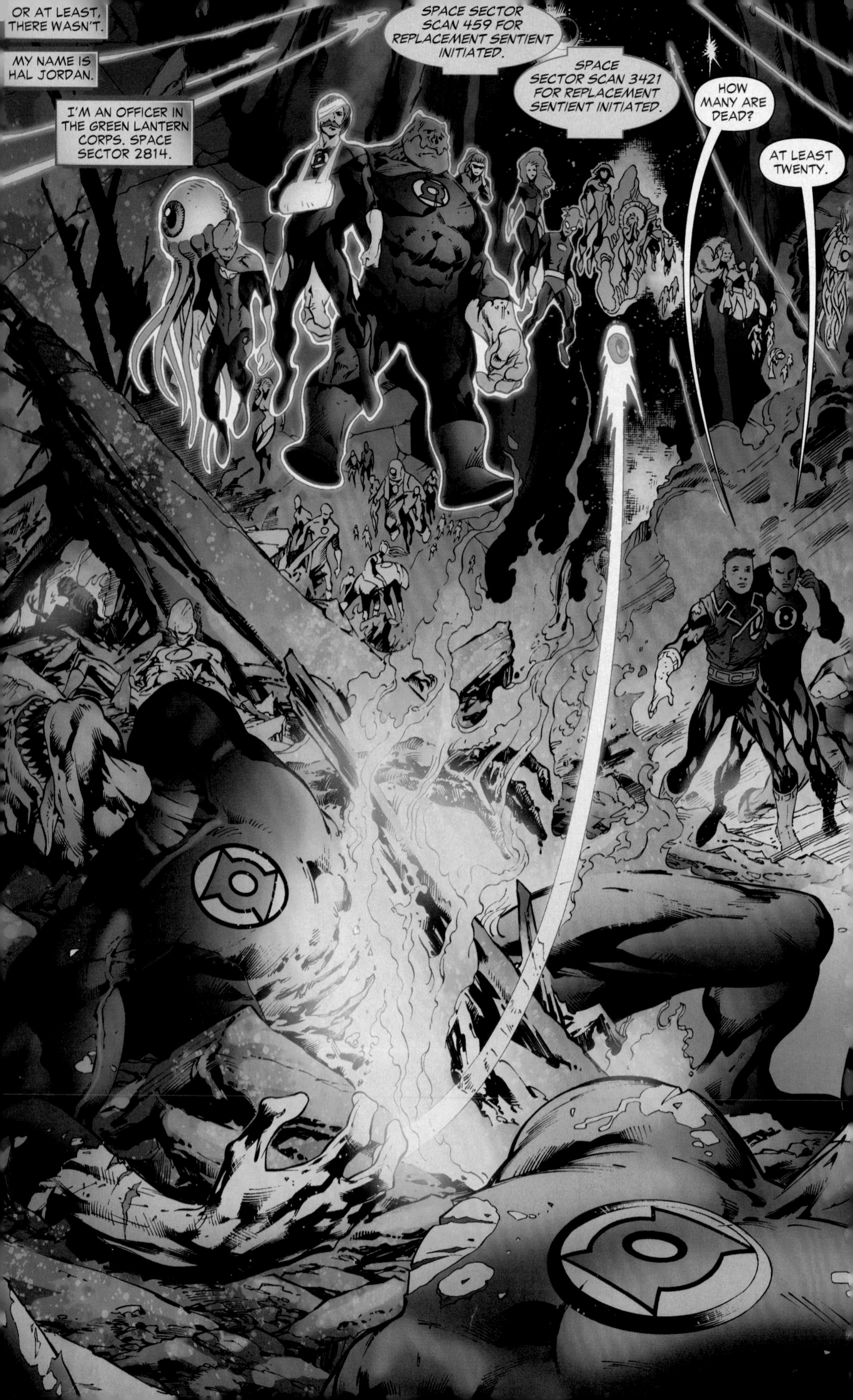
OR AT LEAST, THERE WASN'T.
MY NAME IS HAL JORDAN.
I'M AN OFFICER IN THE GREEN LANTERN CORPS. SPACE SECTOR 2814.
SPACE SECTOR SCAN 459 FOR REPLACEMENT SENTIENT INITIATED.
SPACE SECTOR SCAN 3421 FOR REPLACEMENT SENTIENT INITIATED.
HOW MANY ARE DEAD?
AT LEAST TWENTY.

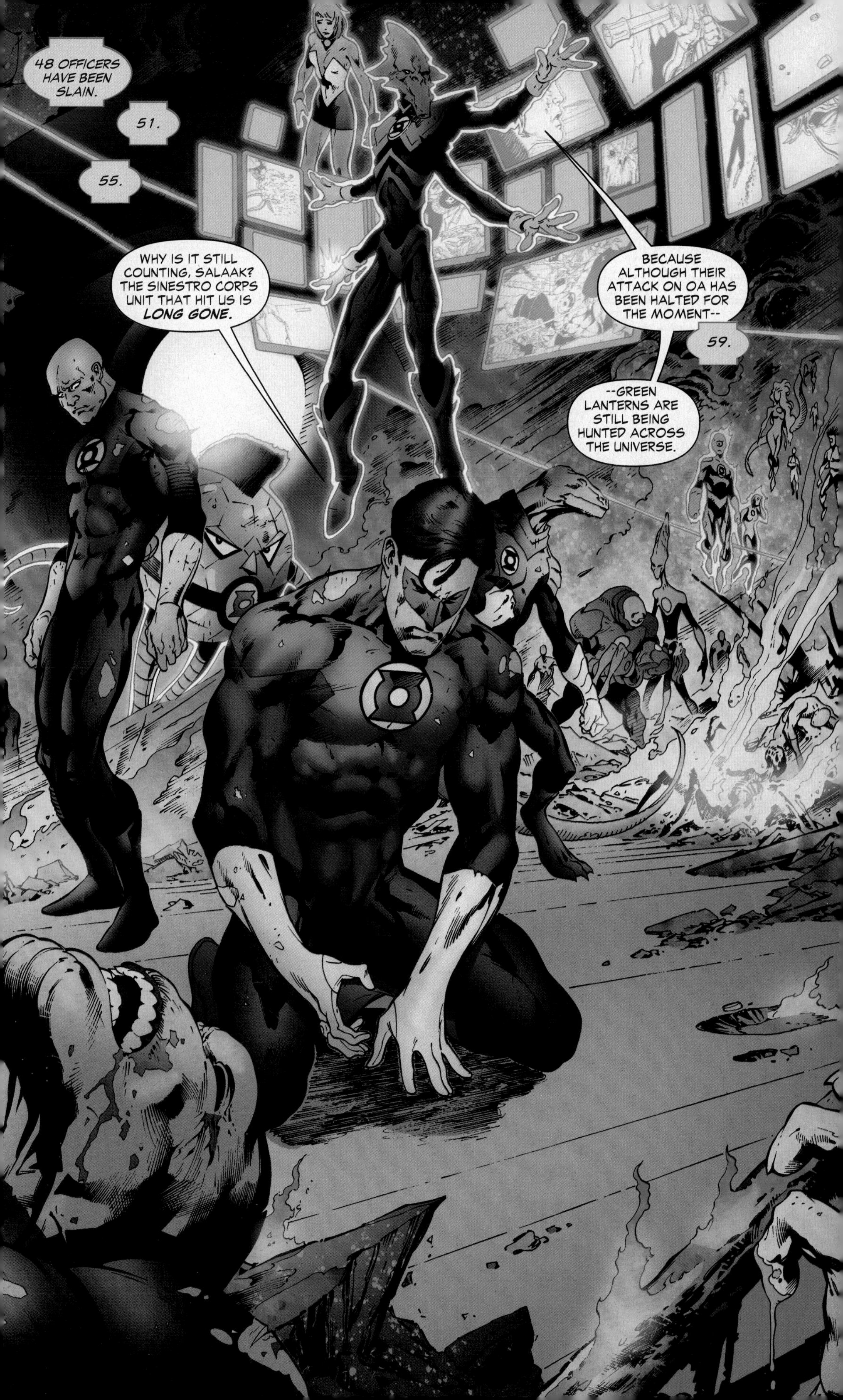
48 OFFICERS HAVE BEEN SLAIN.
51.
55.
WHY IS IT STILL COUNTING, SALAAK? THE SINESTRO CORPS UNIT THAT HIT US IS **LONG GONE.**
BECAUSE ALTHOUGH THEIR ATTACK ON OA HAS BEEN HALTED FOR THE MOMENT--
59.
--GREEN LANTERNS ARE STILL BEING HUNTED ACROSS THE UNIVERSE.

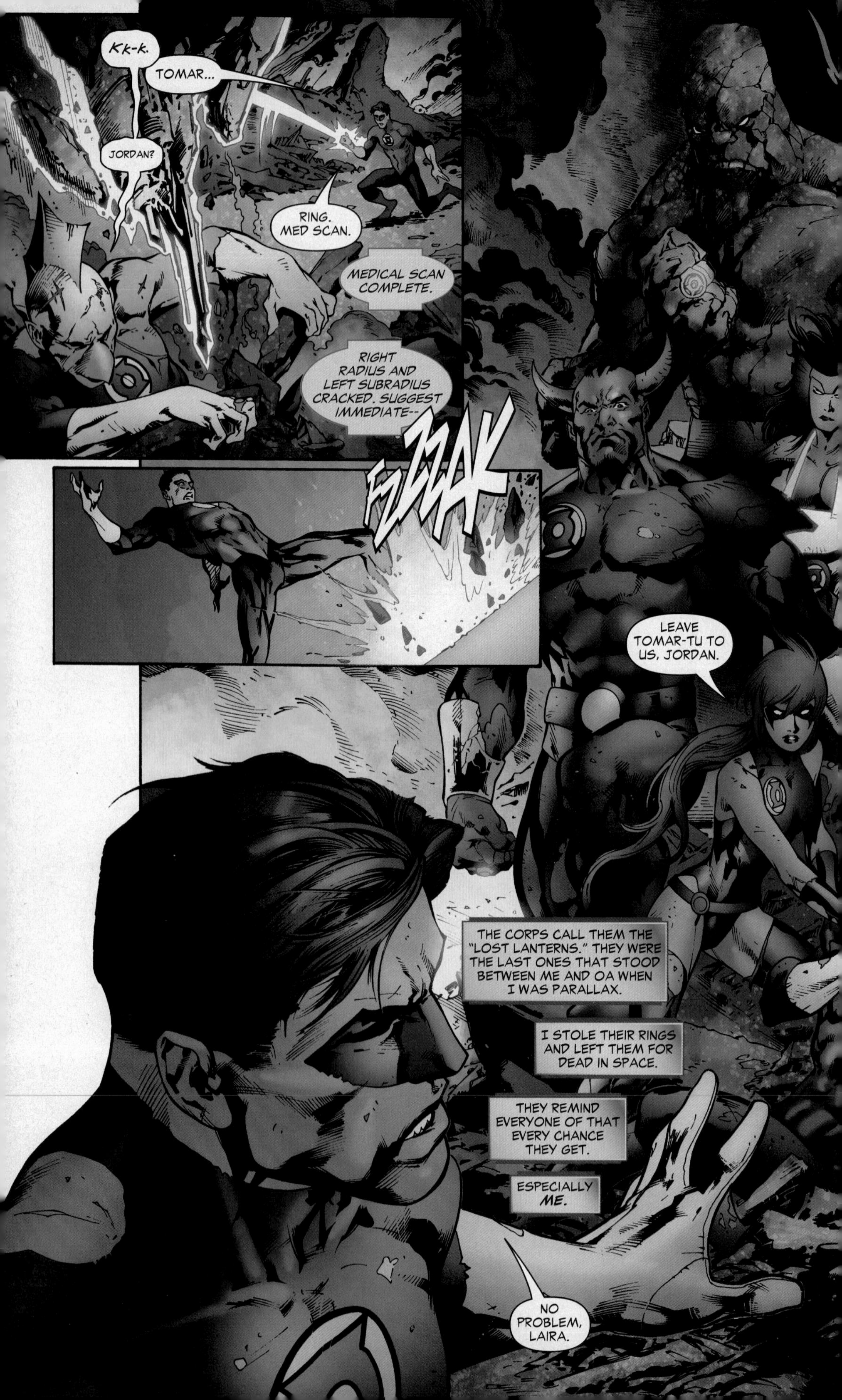
Kk-k.
TOMAR...
JORDAN?
RING. MED SCAN.
MEDICAL SCAN COMPLETE.
RIGHT RADIUS AND LEFT SUBRADIUS CRACKED. SUGGEST IMMEDIATE--
FZZZAK
LEAVE TOMAR-TU TO US, JORDAN.
THE CORPS CALL THEM THE "LOST LANTERNS." THEY WERE THE LAST ONES THAT STOOD BETWEEN ME AND OA WHEN I WAS PARALLAX.
I STOLE THEIR RINGS AND LEFT THEM FOR DEAD IN SPACE.
THEY REMIND EVERYONE OF THAT EVERY CHANCE THEY GET.
ESPECIALLY ME.
NO PROBLEM, LAIRA.

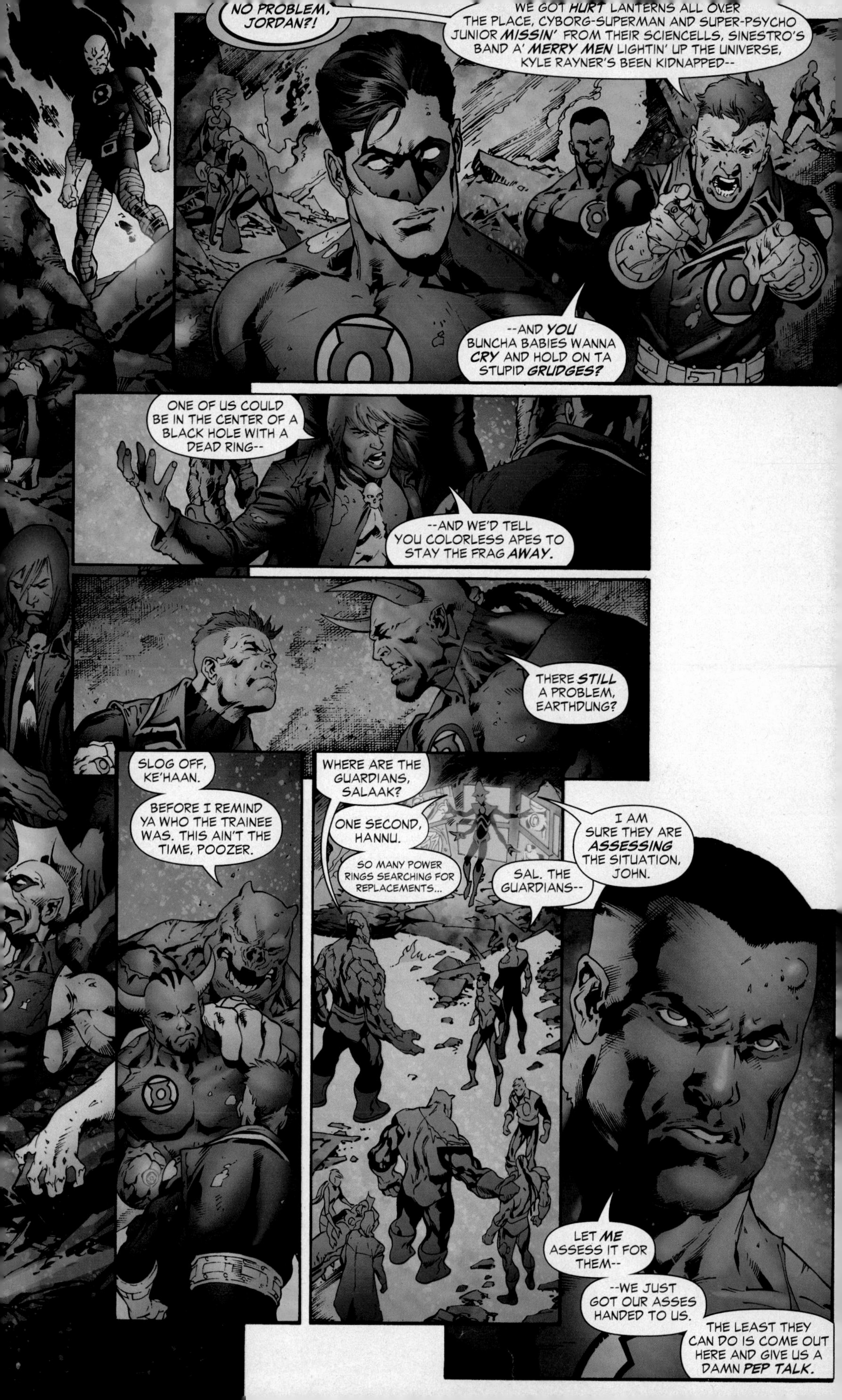
NO PROBLEM, JORDAN?!
WE GOT HURT LANTERNS ALL OVER THE PLACE, CYBORG-SUPERMAN AND SUPER-PSYCHO JUNIOR MISSIN' FROM THEIR SCIENCELLS, SINESTRO'S BAND A' MERRY MEN LIGHTIN' UP THE UNIVERSE, KYLE RAYNER'S BEEN KIDNAPPED--
--AND YOU BUNCHA BABIES WANNA CRY AND HOLD ON TA STUPID GRUDGES?
ONE OF US COULD BE IN THE CENTER OF A BLACK HOLE WITH A DEAD RING--
--AND WE'D TELL YOU COLORLESS APES TO STAY THE FRAG AWAY.
THERE STILL A PROBLEM, EARTHDUNG?
SLOG OFF, KE'HAAN.
BEFORE I REMIND YA WHO THE TRAINEE WAS. THIS AIN'T THE TIME, POOZER.
WHERE ARE THE GUARDIANS, SALAAK?
ONE SECOND, HANNU.
SO MANY POWER RINGS SEARCHING FOR REPLACEMENTS...
I AM SURE THEY ARE ASSESSING THE SITUATION, JOHN.
SAL. THE GUARDIANS--
LET ME ASSESS IT FOR THEM--
--WE JUST GOT OUR ASSES HANDED TO US.
THE LEAST THEY CAN DO IS COME OUT HERE AND GIVE US A DAMN PEP TALK.

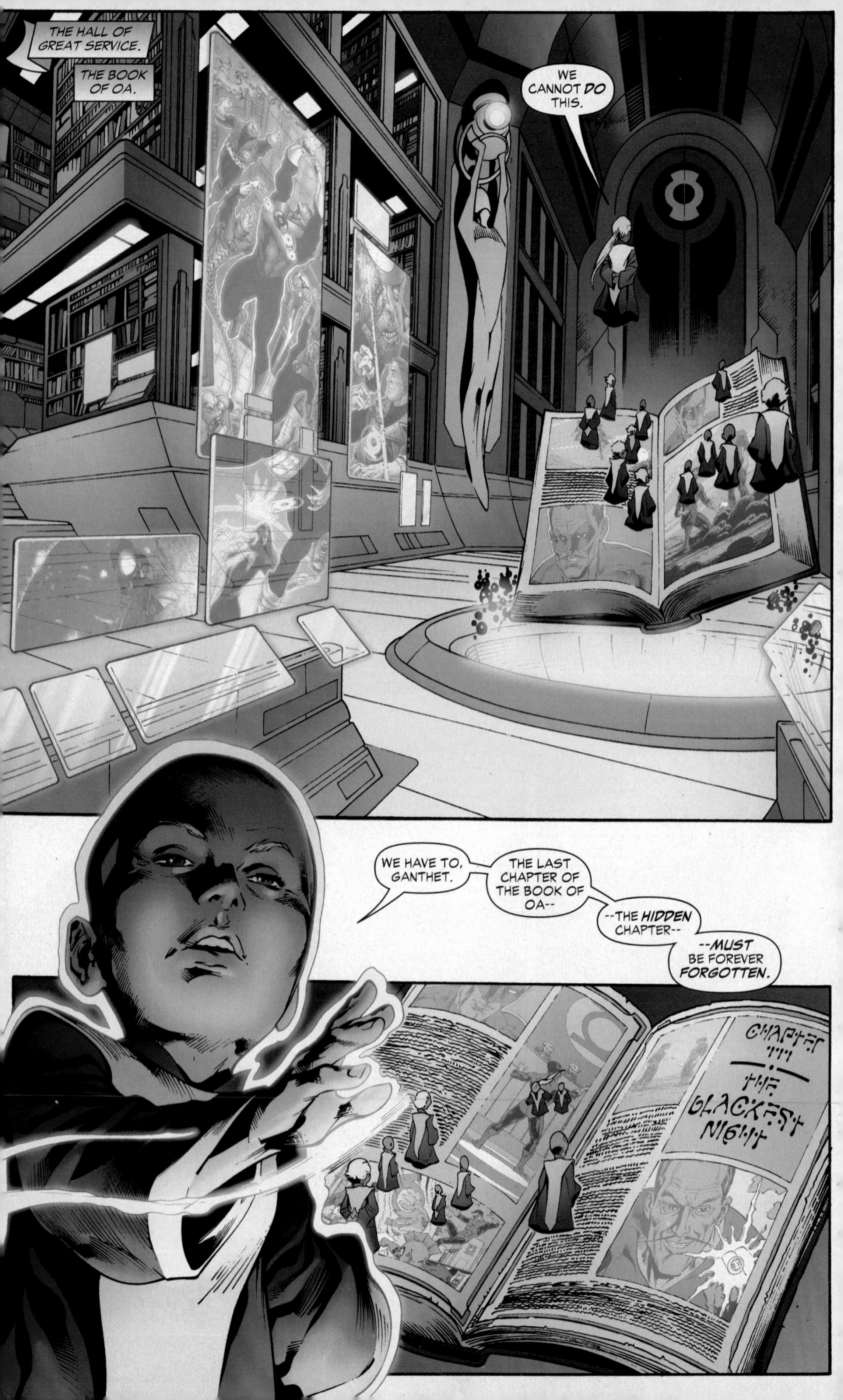
THE HALL OF GREAT SERVICE.
THE BOOK OF OA.
WE CANNOT DO THIS.
WE HAVE TO, GANTHET.
THE LAST CHAPTER OF THE BOOK OF OA--
--THE HIDDEN CHAPTER--
--MUST BE FOREVER FORGOTTEN.
CHAPTER ??? THE BLACKEST NIGHT

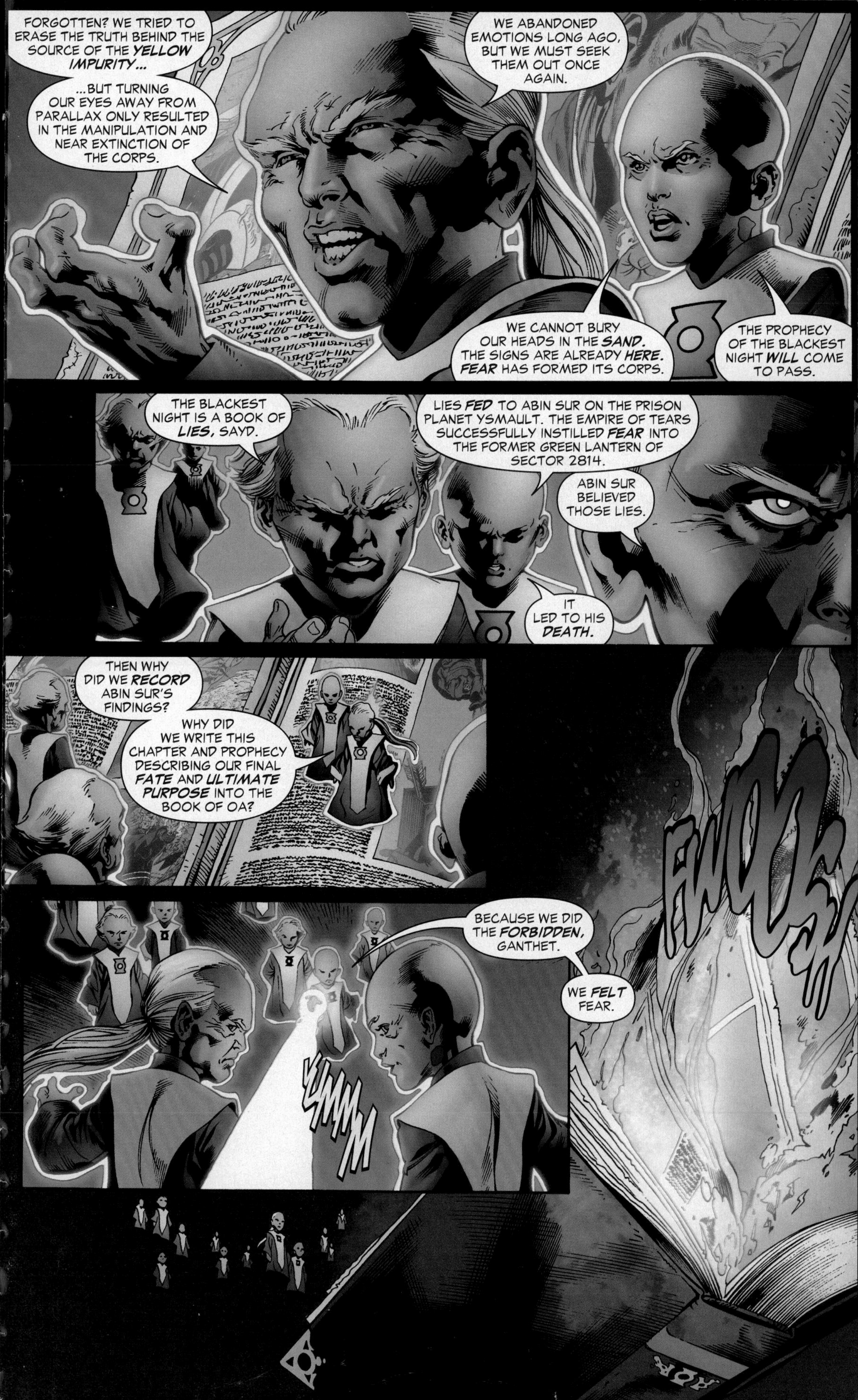

FORGOTTEN? WE TRIED TO ERASE THE TRUTH BEHIND THE SOURCE OF THE *YELLOW IMPURITY...*
...BUT TURNING OUR EYES AWAY FROM PARALLAX ONLY RESULTED IN THE MANIPULATION AND NEAR EXTINCTION OF THE CORPS.
WE ABANDONED EMOTIONS LONG AGO, BUT WE MUST SEEK THEM OUT ONCE AGAIN.
WE CANNOT BURY OUR HEADS IN THE *SAND*. THE SIGNS ARE ALREADY *HERE*. *FEAR* HAS FORMED ITS CORPS.
THE PROPHECY OF THE BLACKEST NIGHT *WILL* COME TO PASS.
THE BLACKEST NIGHT IS A BOOK OF *LIES*, SAYD.
LIES *FED* TO ABIN SUR ON THE PRISON PLANET YSMAULT. THE EMPIRE OF TEARS SUCCESSFULLY INSTILLED *FEAR* INTO THE FORMER GREEN LANTERN OF SECTOR 2814.
ABIN SUR BELIEVED THOSE LIES.
IT LED TO HIS *DEATH*.
THEN WHY DID WE *RECORD* ABIN SUR'S FINDINGS?
WHY DID WE WRITE THIS CHAPTER AND PROPHECY DESCRIBING OUR FINAL *FATE* AND *ULTIMATE PURPOSE* INTO THE BOOK OF OA?
BECAUSE WE DID THE *FORBIDDEN*, GANTHET.
WE *FELT* FEAR.

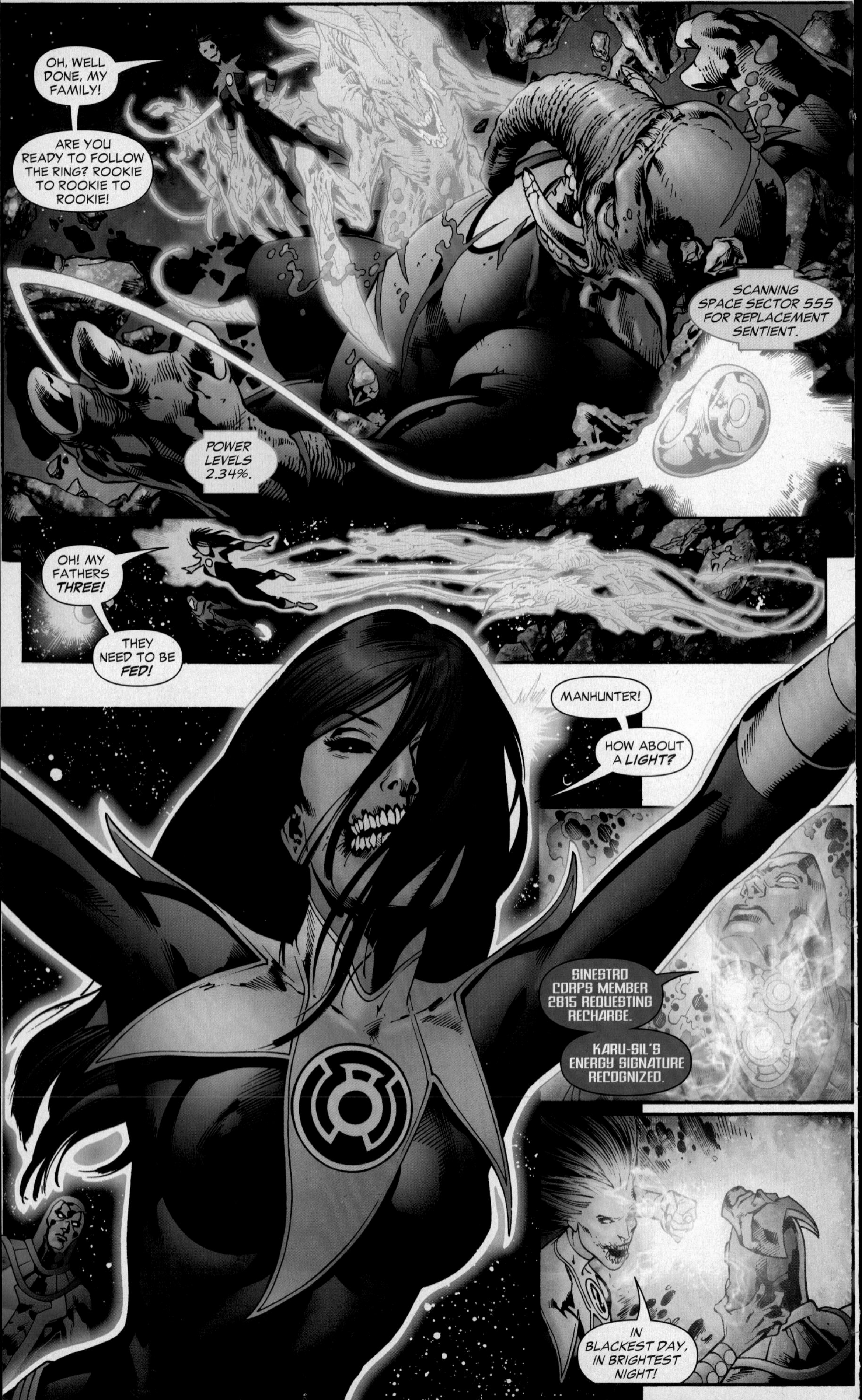

OH, WELL DONE, MY FAMILY!
ARE YOU READY TO FOLLOW THE RING? ROOKIE TO ROOKIE TO ROOKIE!
SCANNING SPACE SECTOR 555 FOR REPLACEMENT SENTIENT.
POWER LEVELS 2.34%.
OH! MY FATHERS THREE!
THEY NEED TO BE FED!
MANHUNTER!
HOW ABOUT A LIGHT?
SINESTRO CORPS MEMBER 2815 REQUESTING RECHARGE.
KARU-SIL'S ENERGY SIGNATURE RECOGNIZED.
IN BLACKEST DAY, IN BRIGHTEST NIGHT!

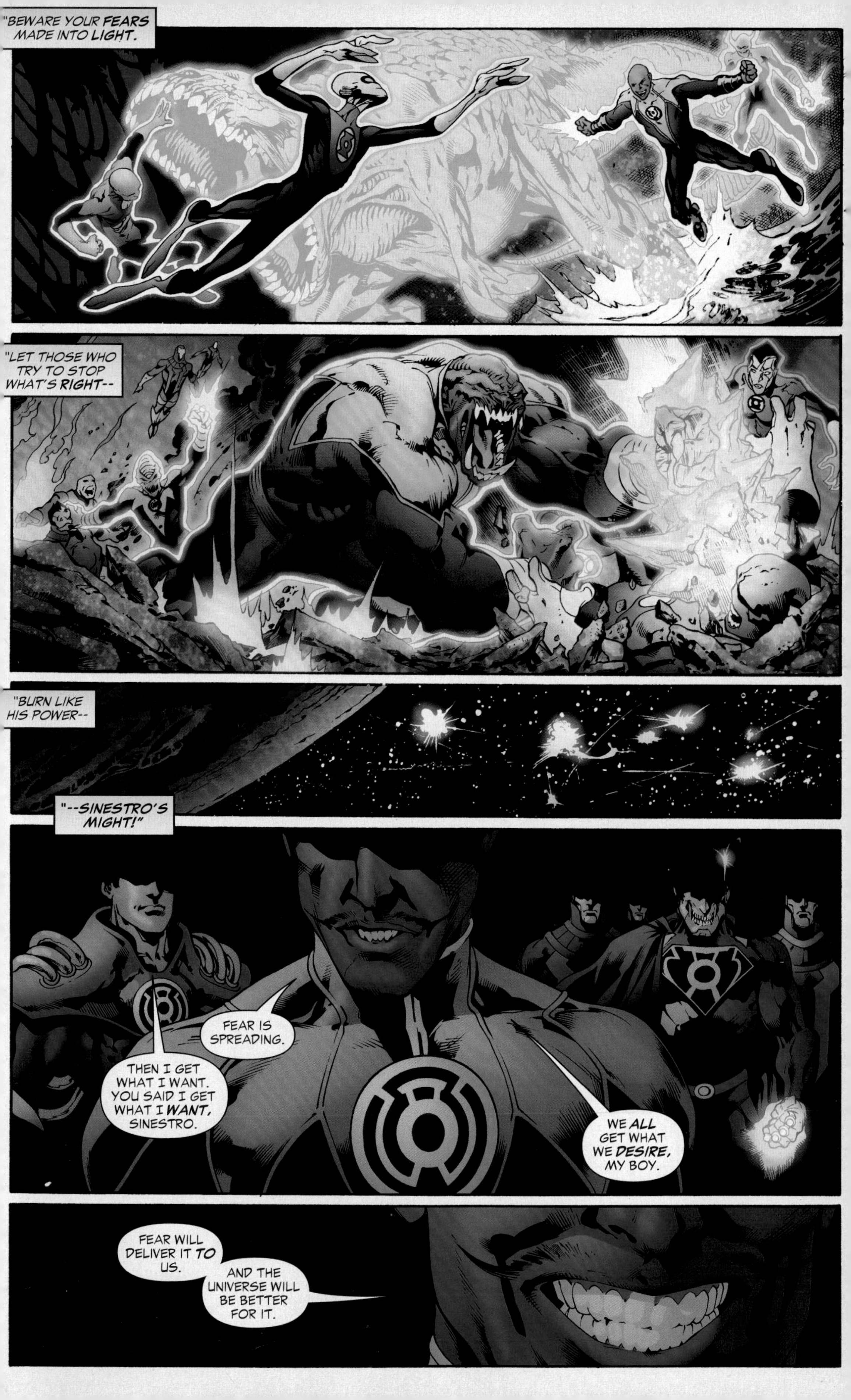
"BEWARE YOUR FEARS MADE INTO LIGHT.
"LET THOSE WHO TRY TO STOP WHAT'S RIGHT--
"BURN LIKE HIS POWER--
"--SINESTRO'S MIGHT!"
FEAR IS SPREADING.
THEN I GET WHAT I WANT. YOU SAID I GET WHAT I WANT, SINESTRO.
WE ALL GET WHAT WE DESIRE, MY BOY.
FEAR WILL DELIVER IT TO US.
AND THE UNIVERSE WILL BE BETTER FOR IT.

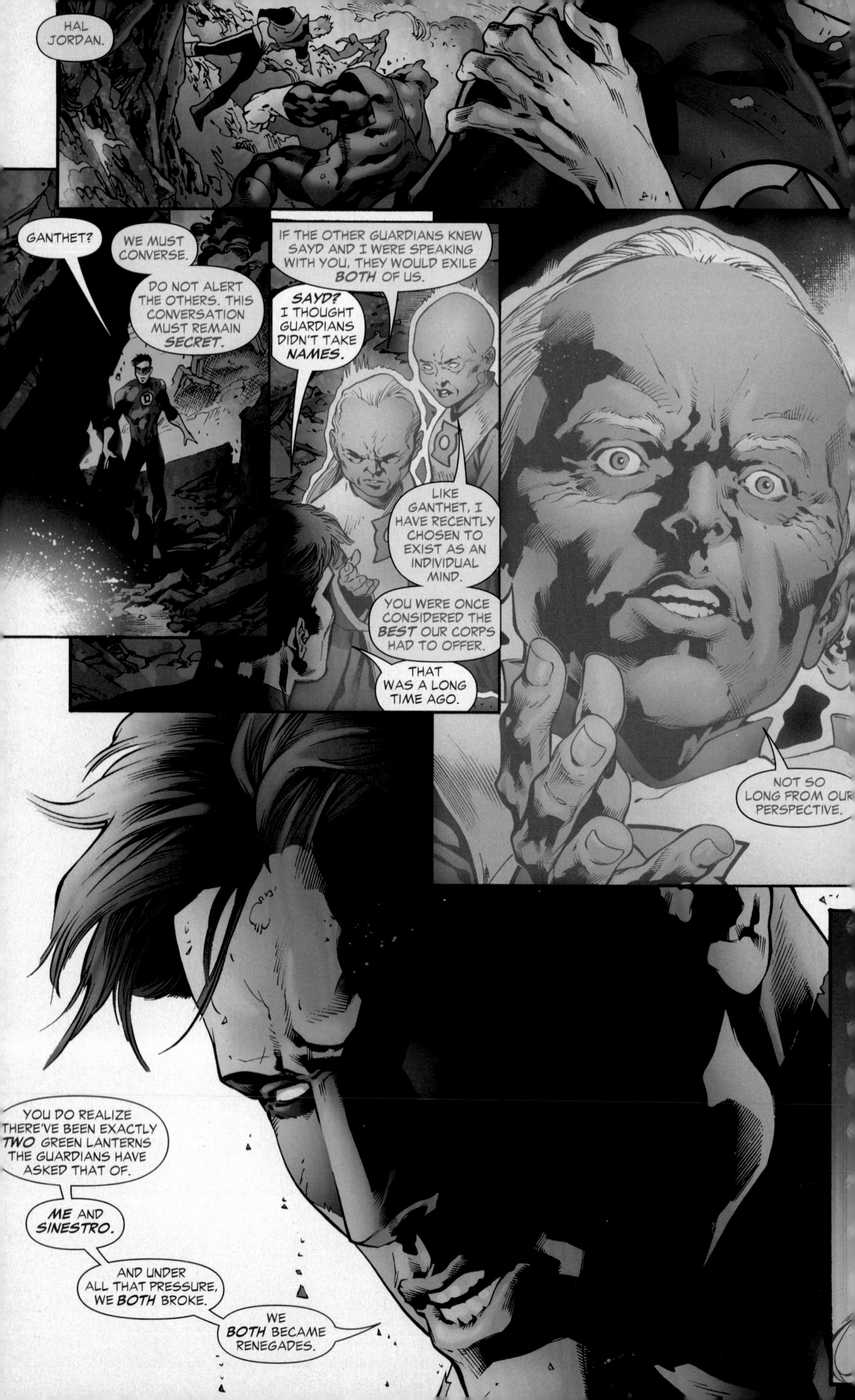
HAL JORDAN.
GANTHET?
WE MUST CONVERSE.
DO NOT ALERT THE OTHERS. THIS CONVERSATION MUST REMAIN SECRET.
IF THE OTHER GUARDIANS KNEW SAYD AND I WERE SPEAKING WITH YOU, THEY WOULD EXILE BOTH OF US.
SAYD? I THOUGHT GUARDIANS DIDN'T TAKE NAMES.
LIKE GANTHET, I HAVE RECENTLY CHOSEN TO EXIST AS AN INDIVIDUAL MIND.
YOU WERE ONCE CONSIDERED THE BEST OUR CORPS HAD TO OFFER.
THAT WAS A LONG TIME AGO.
NOT SO LONG FROM OUR PERSPECTIVE.
YOU DO REALIZE THERE'VE BEEN EXACTLY TWO GREEN LANTERNS THE GUARDIANS HAVE ASKED THAT OF.
ME AND SINESTRO.
AND UNDER ALL THAT PRESSURE, WE BOTH BROKE.
WE BOTH BECAME RENEGADES.

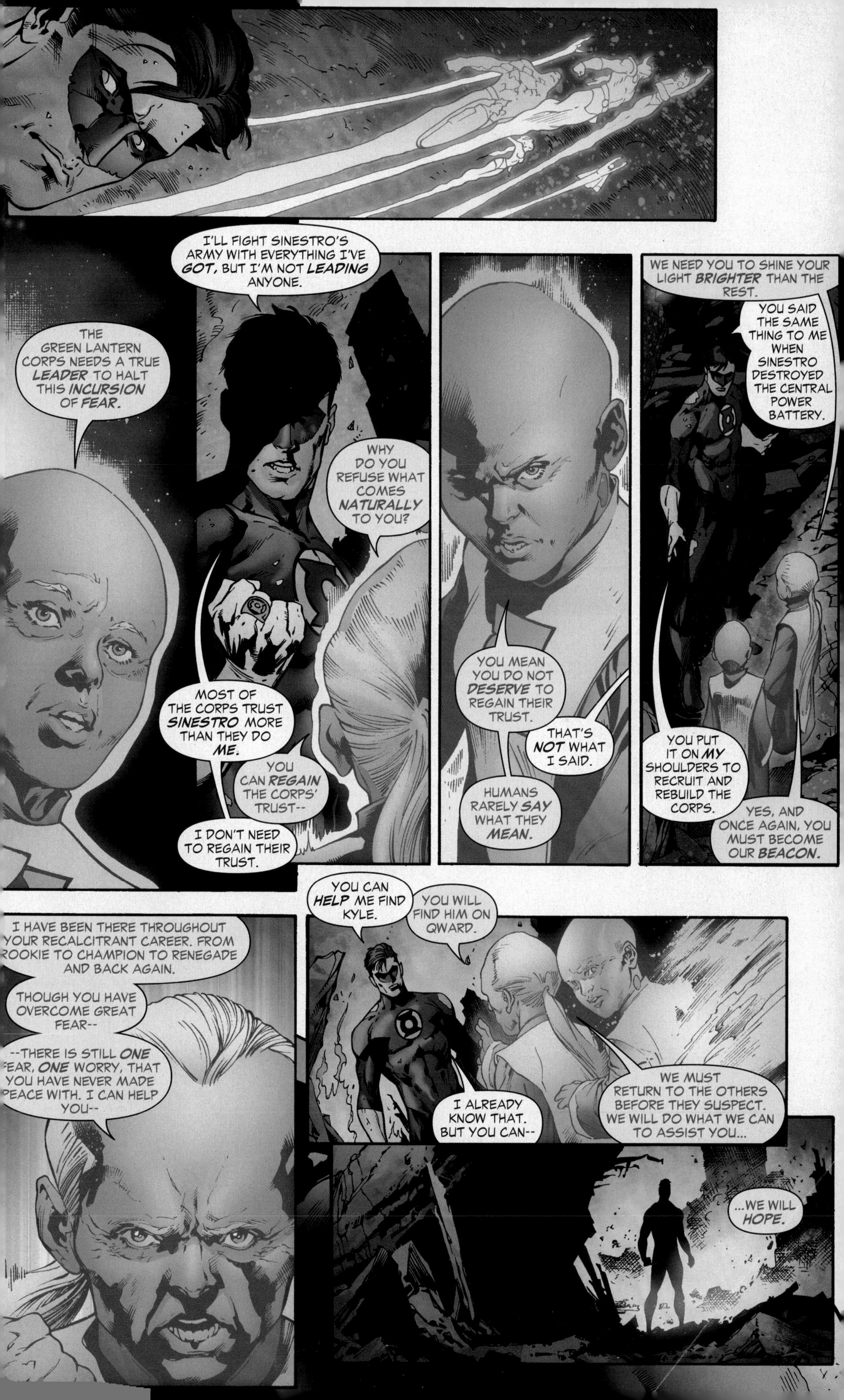

THE GREEN LANTERN CORPS NEEDS A TRUE LEADER TO HALT THIS INCURSION OF FEAR.
I'LL FIGHT SINESTRO'S ARMY WITH EVERYTHING I'VE GOT, BUT I'M NOT LEADING ANYONE.
WHY DO YOU REFUSE WHAT COMES NATURALLY TO YOU?
MOST OF THE CORPS TRUST SINESTRO MORE THAN THEY DO ME.
YOU CAN REGAIN THE CORPS' TRUST--
I DON'T NEED TO REGAIN THEIR TRUST.
YOU MEAN YOU DO NOT DESERVE TO REGAIN THEIR TRUST.
THAT'S NOT WHAT I SAID.
HUMANS RARELY SAY WHAT THEY MEAN.
WE NEED YOU TO SHINE YOUR LIGHT BRIGHTER THAN THE REST.
YOU SAID THE SAME THING TO ME WHEN SINESTRO DESTROYED THE CENTRAL POWER BATTERY.
YOU PUT IT ON MY SHOULDERS TO RECRUIT AND REBUILD THE CORPS.
YES, AND ONCE AGAIN, YOU MUST BECOME OUR BEACON.
I HAVE BEEN THERE THROUGHOUT YOUR RECALCITRANT CAREER. FROM ROOKIE TO CHAMPION TO RENEGADE AND BACK AGAIN.
THOUGH YOU HAVE OVERCOME GREAT FEAR--
--THERE IS STILL ONE FEAR, ONE WORRY, THAT YOU HAVE NEVER MADE PEACE WITH. I CAN HELP YOU--
YOU CAN HELP ME FIND KYLE.
YOU WILL FIND HIM ON QWARD.
I ALREADY KNOW THAT. BUT YOU CAN--
WE MUST RETURN TO THE OTHERS BEFORE THEY SUSPECT. WE WILL DO WHAT WE CAN TO ASSIST YOU...
...WE WILL HOPE.

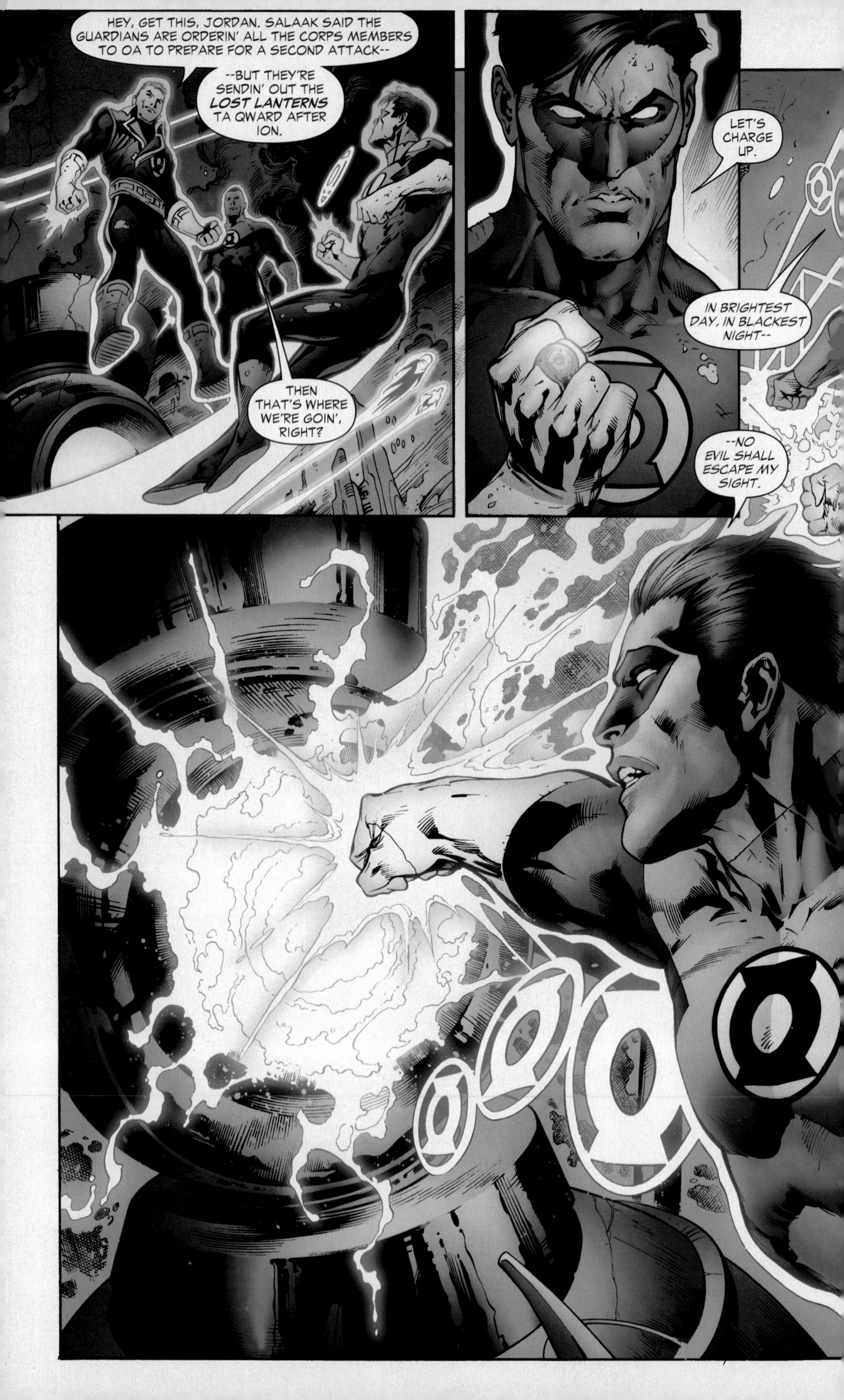
HEY, GET THIS, JORDAN. SALAAK SAID THE GUARDIANS ARE ORDERIN' ALL THE CORPS MEMBERS TO OA TO PREPARE FOR A SECOND ATTACK--
--BUT THEY'RE SENDIN' OUT THE LOST LANTERNS TA QWARD AFTER ION.
THEN THAT'S WHERE WE'RE GOIN', RIGHT?
LET'S CHARGE UP.
IN BRIGHTEST DAY, IN BLACKEST NIGHT--
--NO EVIL SHALL ESCAPE MY SIGHT.

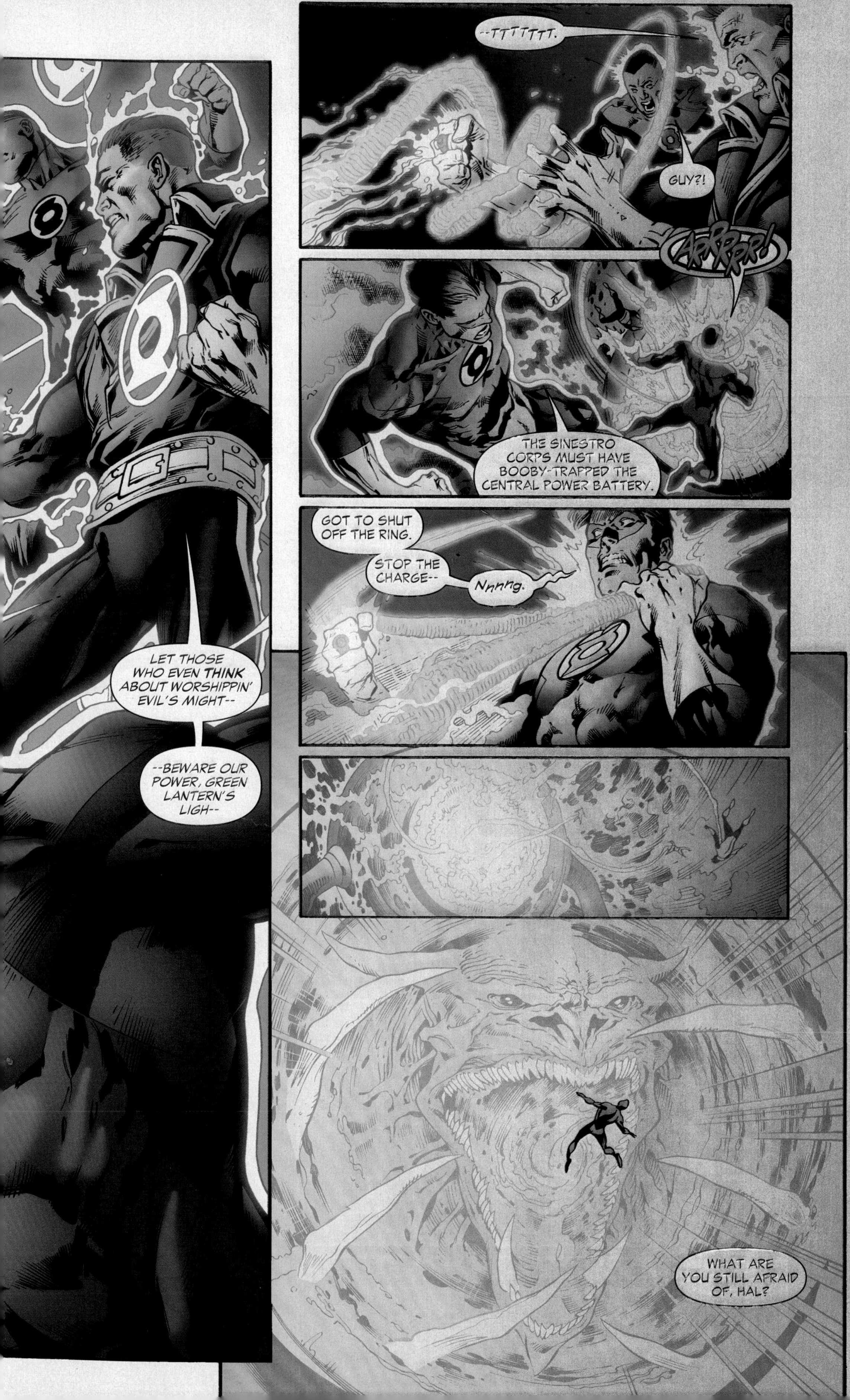
LET THOSE WHO EVEN THINK ABOUT WORSHIPPIN' EVIL'S MIGHT--
--BEWARE OUR POWER, GREEN LANTERN'S LIGH--
--TTTTTTT.
GUY?!
ARRRRRP!
THE SINESTRO CORPS MUST HAVE BOOBY-TRAPPED THE CENTRAL POWER BATTERY.
GOT TO SHUT OFF THE RING.
STOP THE CHARGE--
Nnnng.
WHAT ARE YOU STILL AFRAID OF, HAL?

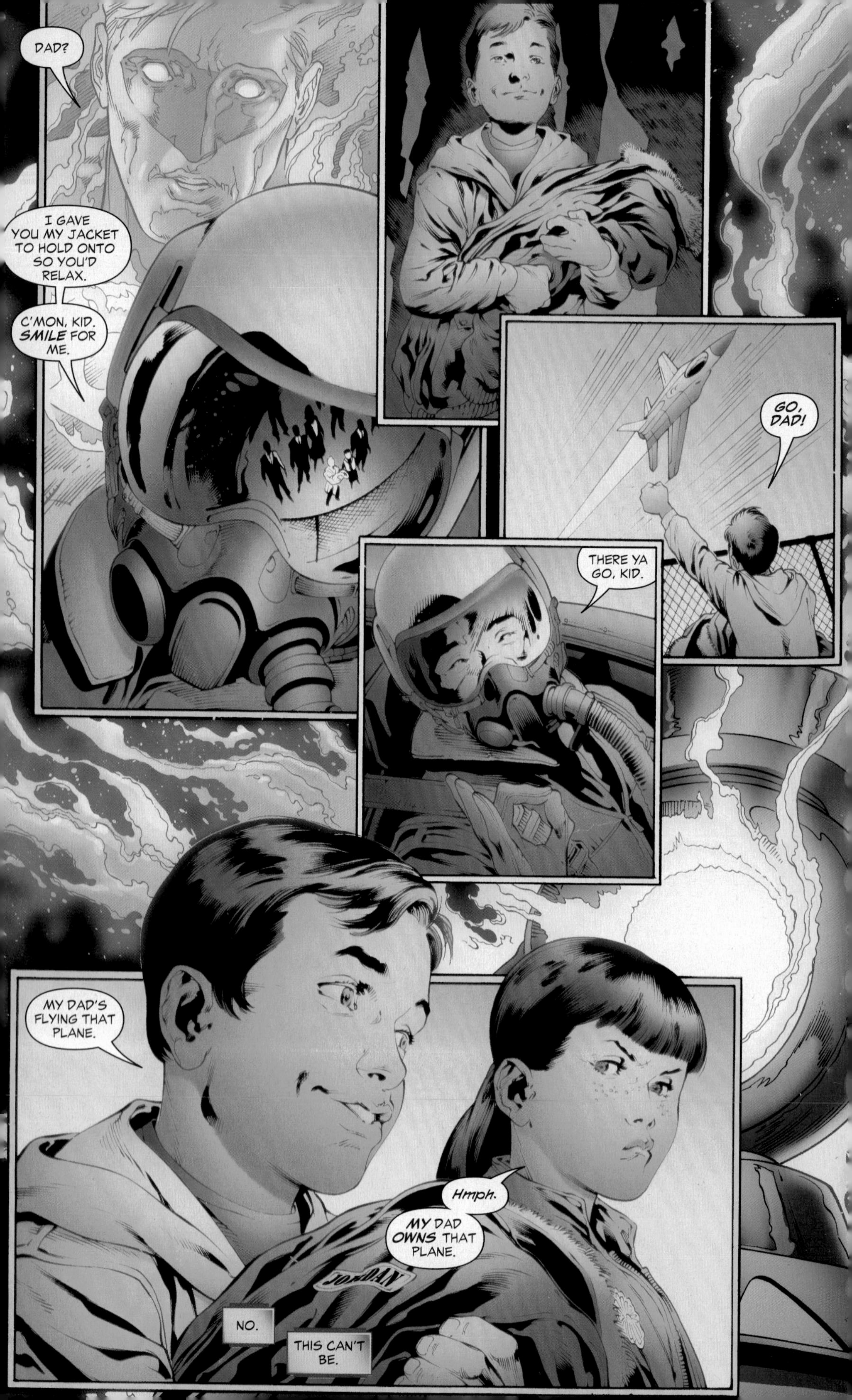
DAD?
I GAVE YOU MY JACKET TO HOLD ONTO SO YOU'D RELAX.
C'MON, KID. SMILE FOR ME.
GO, DAD!
THERE YA GO, KID.
MY DAD'S FLYING THAT PLANE.
Hmph.
MY DAD OWNS THAT PLANE.
JORDAN
NO.
THIS CAN'T BE.

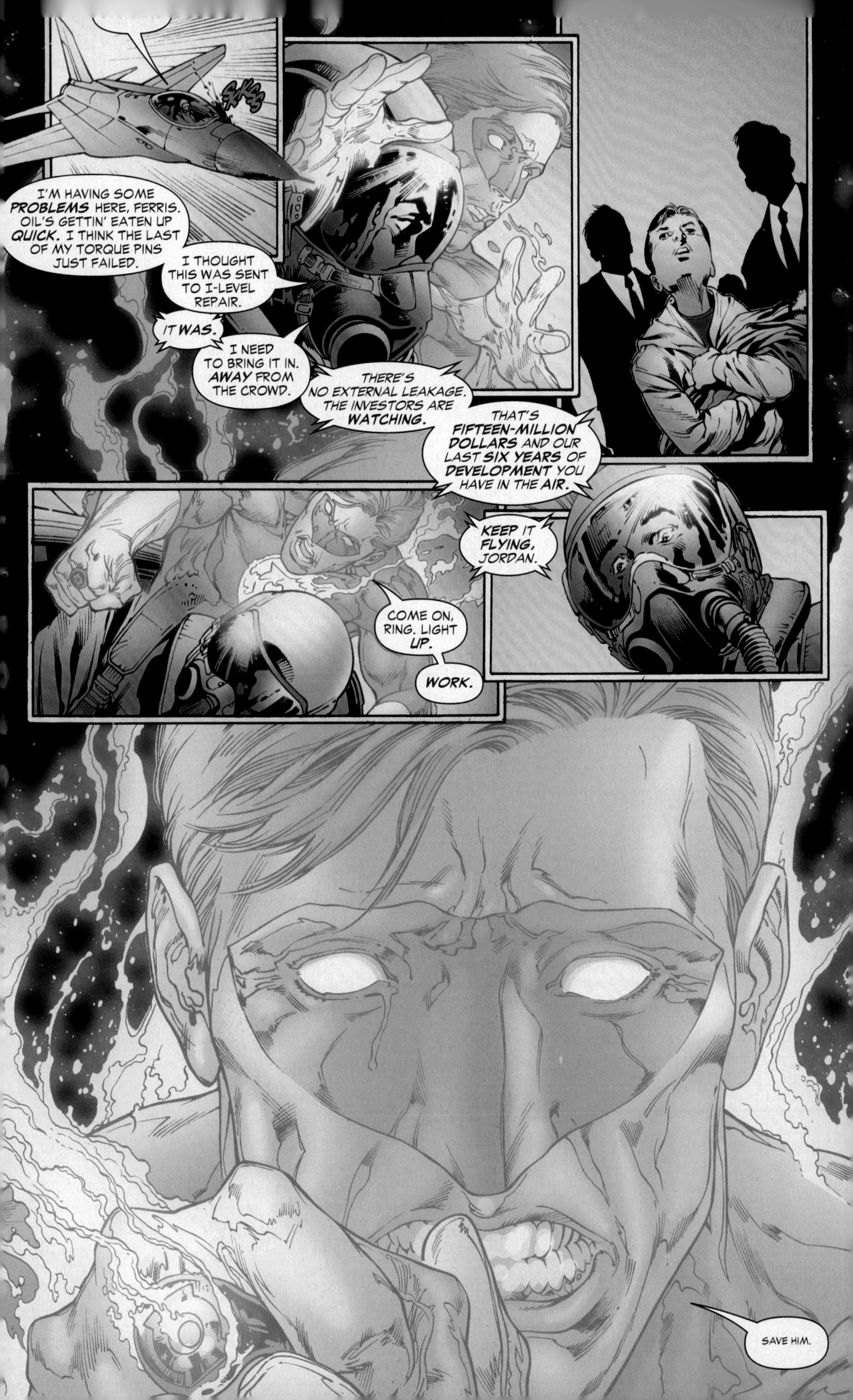

SKISS
I'M HAVING SOME PROBLEMS HERE, FERRIS. OIL'S GETTIN' EATEN UP QUICK. I THINK THE LAST OF MY TORQUE PINS JUST FAILED.
I THOUGHT THIS WAS SENT TO I-LEVEL REPAIR.
IT WAS.
I NEED TO BRING IT IN. AWAY FROM THE CROWD.
THERE'S NO EXTERNAL LEAKAGE. THE INVESTORS ARE WATCHING.
THAT'S FIFTEEN-MILLION DOLLARS AND OUR LAST SIX YEARS OF DEVELOPMENT YOU HAVE IN THE AIR.
KEEP IT FLYING, JORDAN.
COME ON, RING. LIGHT UP.
WORK.
SAVE HIM.

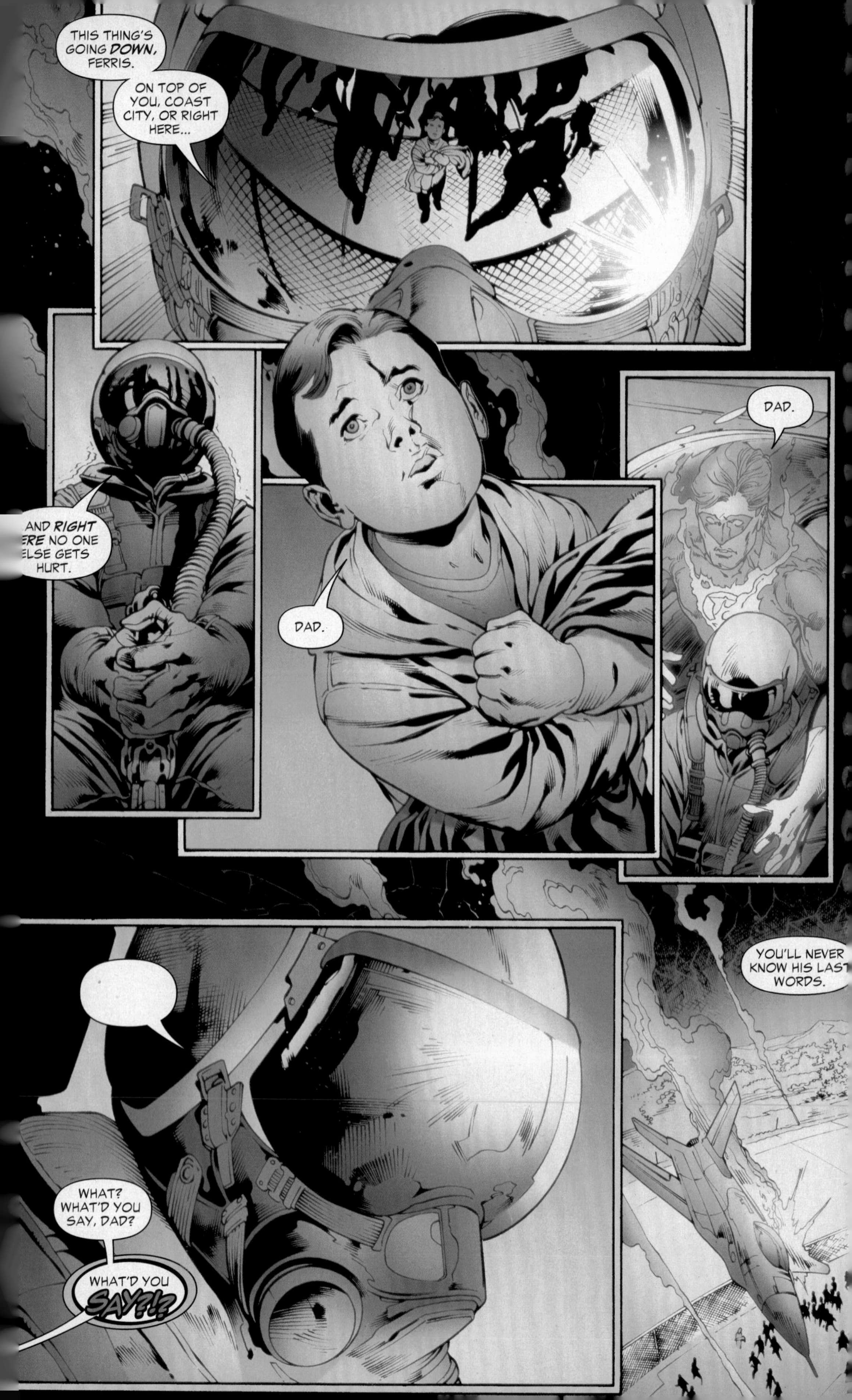
THIS THING'S GOING **DOWN,** FERRIS.
ON TOP OF YOU, COAST CITY, OR RIGHT HERE...
AND ***RIGHT*** ***ERE*** NO ONE ELSE GETS HURT.
DAD.
DAD.
YOU'LL NEVER KNOW HIS LAST WORDS.
WHAT? WHAT'D YOU SAY, DAD?
WHAT'D YOU ***SAY?!?***

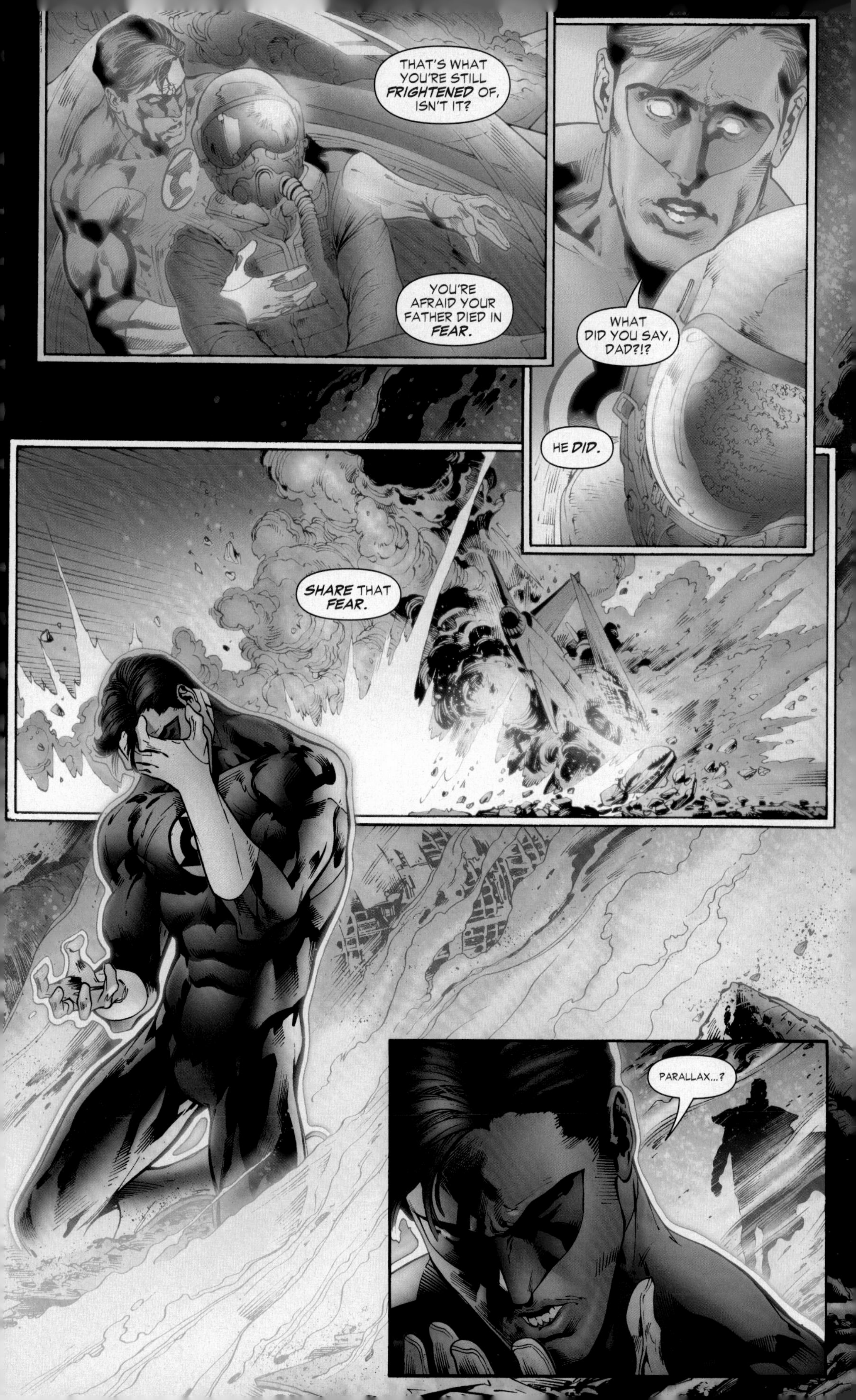

THAT'S WHAT YOU'RE STILL FRIGHTENED OF, ISN'T IT?
YOU'RE AFRAID YOUR FATHER DIED IN FEAR.
WHAT DID YOU SAY, DAD?!?
HE DID.
SHARE THAT FEAR.
PARALLAX...?

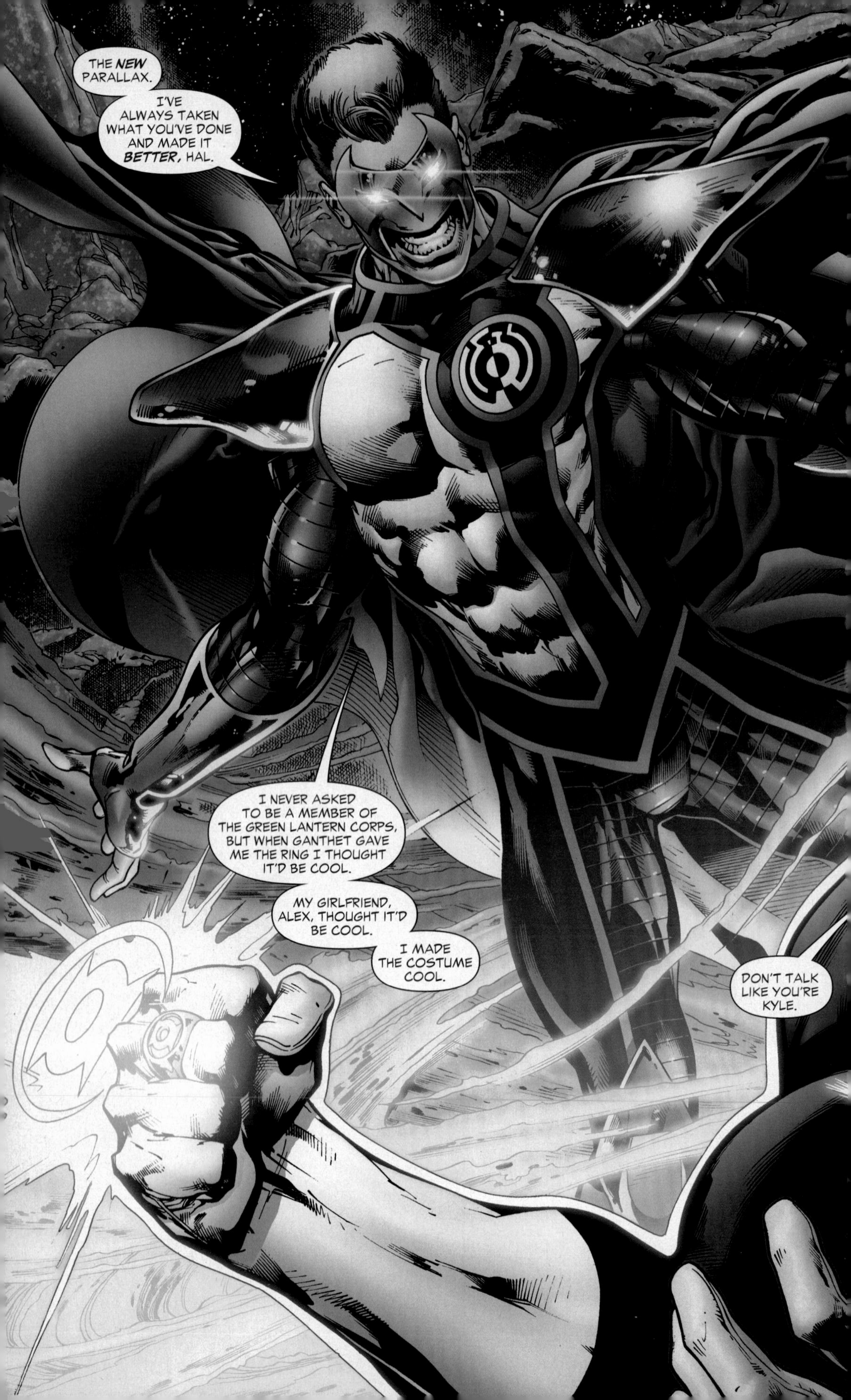
THE NEW PARALLAX.
I'VE ALWAYS TAKEN WHAT YOU'VE DONE AND MADE IT BETTER, HAL.
I NEVER ASKED TO BE A MEMBER OF THE GREEN LANTERN CORPS, BUT WHEN GANTHET GAVE ME THE RING I THOUGHT IT'D BE COOL.
MY GIRLFRIEND, ALEX, THOUGHT IT'D BE COOL.
I MADE THE COSTUME COOL.
DON'T TALK LIKE YOU'RE KYLE.

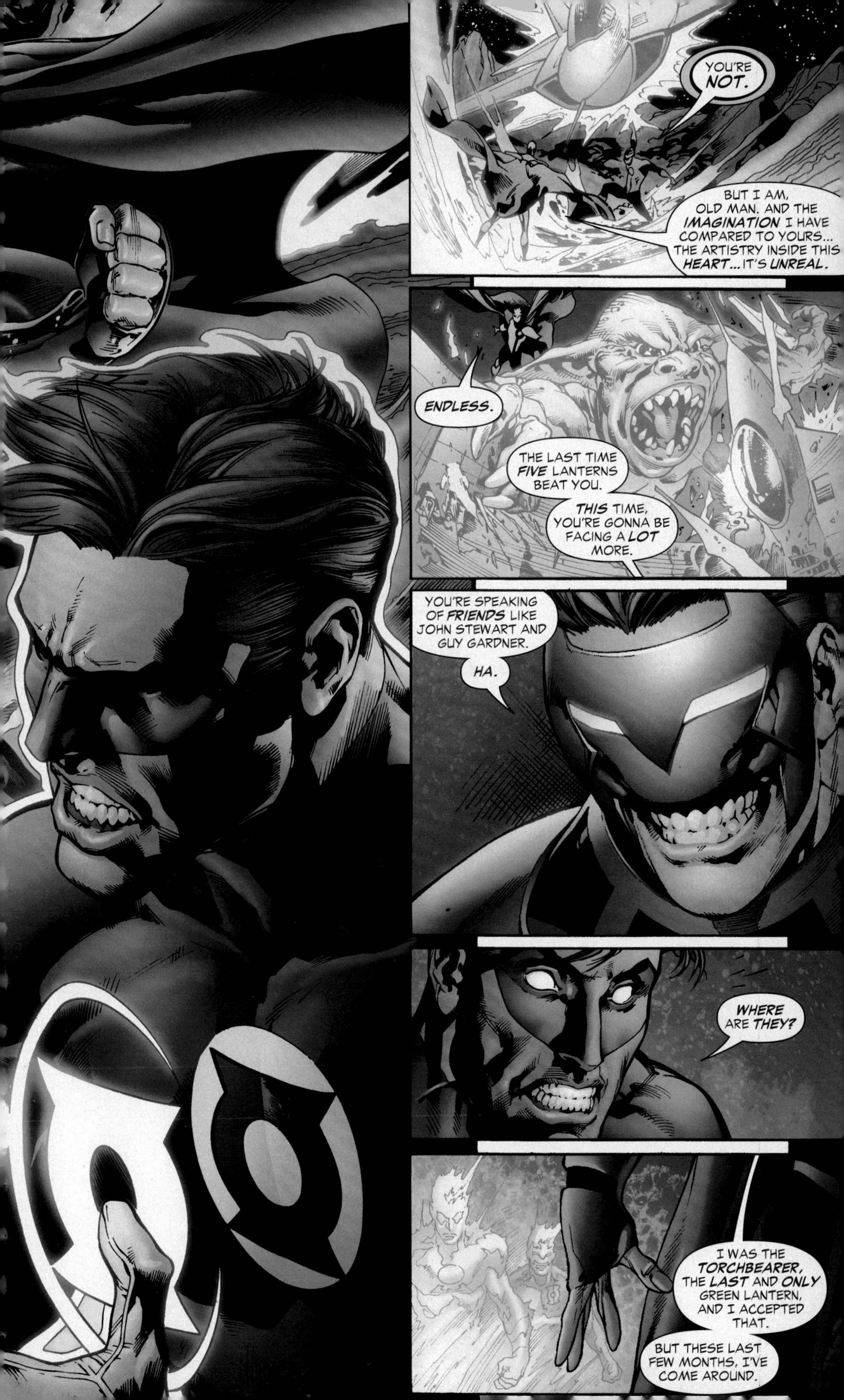
YOU'RE NOT.
BUT I AM, OLD MAN. AND THE IMAGINATION I HAVE COMPARED TO YOURS... THE ARTISTRY INSIDE THIS HEART... IT'S UNREAL.
ENDLESS.
THE LAST TIME FIVE LANTERNS BEAT YOU.
THIS TIME, YOU'RE GONNA BE FACING A LOT MORE.
YOU'RE SPEAKING OF FRIENDS LIKE JOHN STEWART AND GUY GARDNER.
HA.
WHERE ARE THEY?
I WAS THE TORCHBEARER, THE LAST AND ONLY GREEN LANTERN, AND I ACCEPTED THAT.
BUT THESE LAST FEW MONTHS, I'VE COME AROUND.

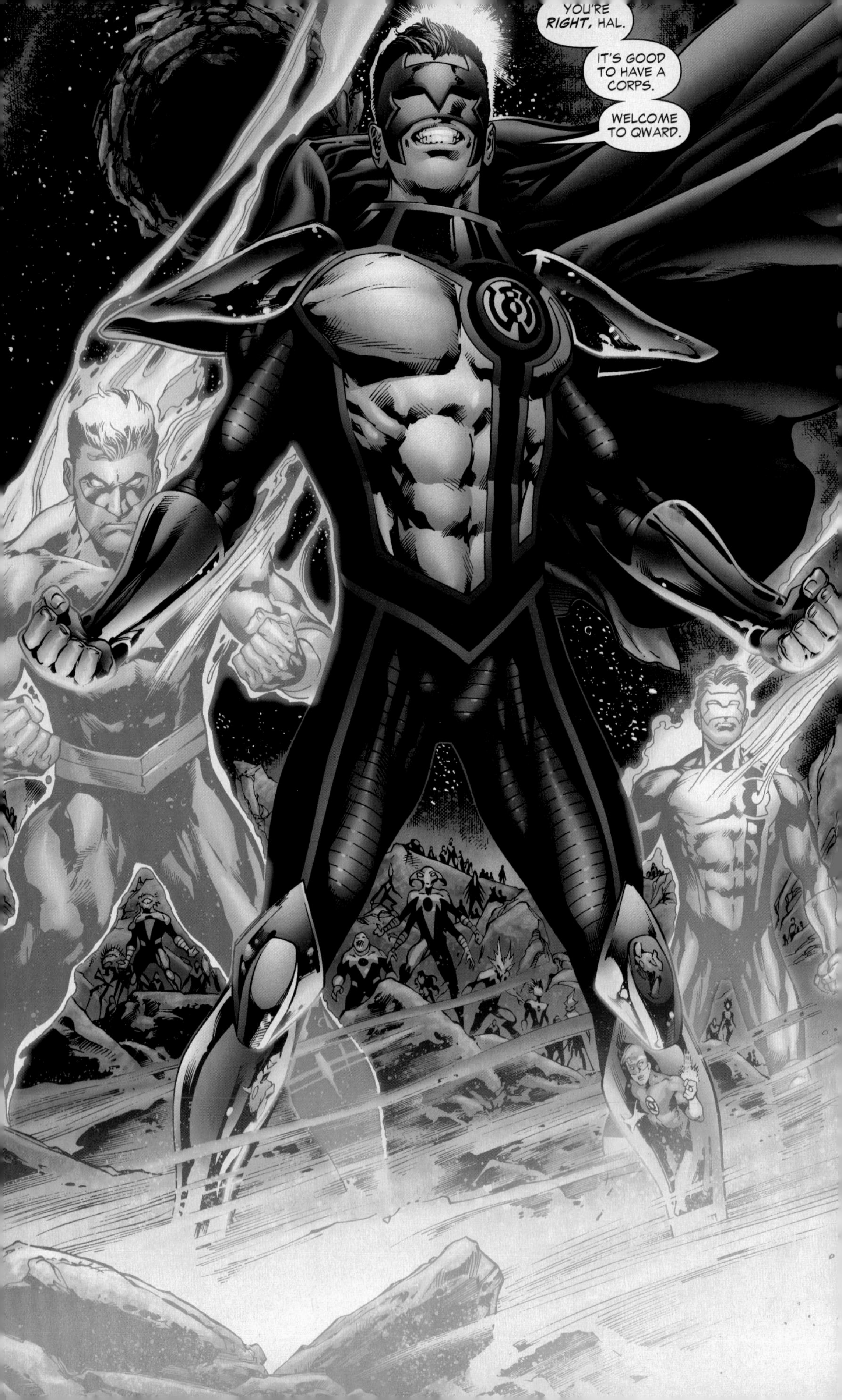
YOU'RE RIGHT, HAL.
IT'S GOOD TO HAVE A CORPS.
WELCOME TO QWARD.

GREEN LANTERN CORPS 14
Patrick Gleason
Prentis Rollins
Moose Baumann

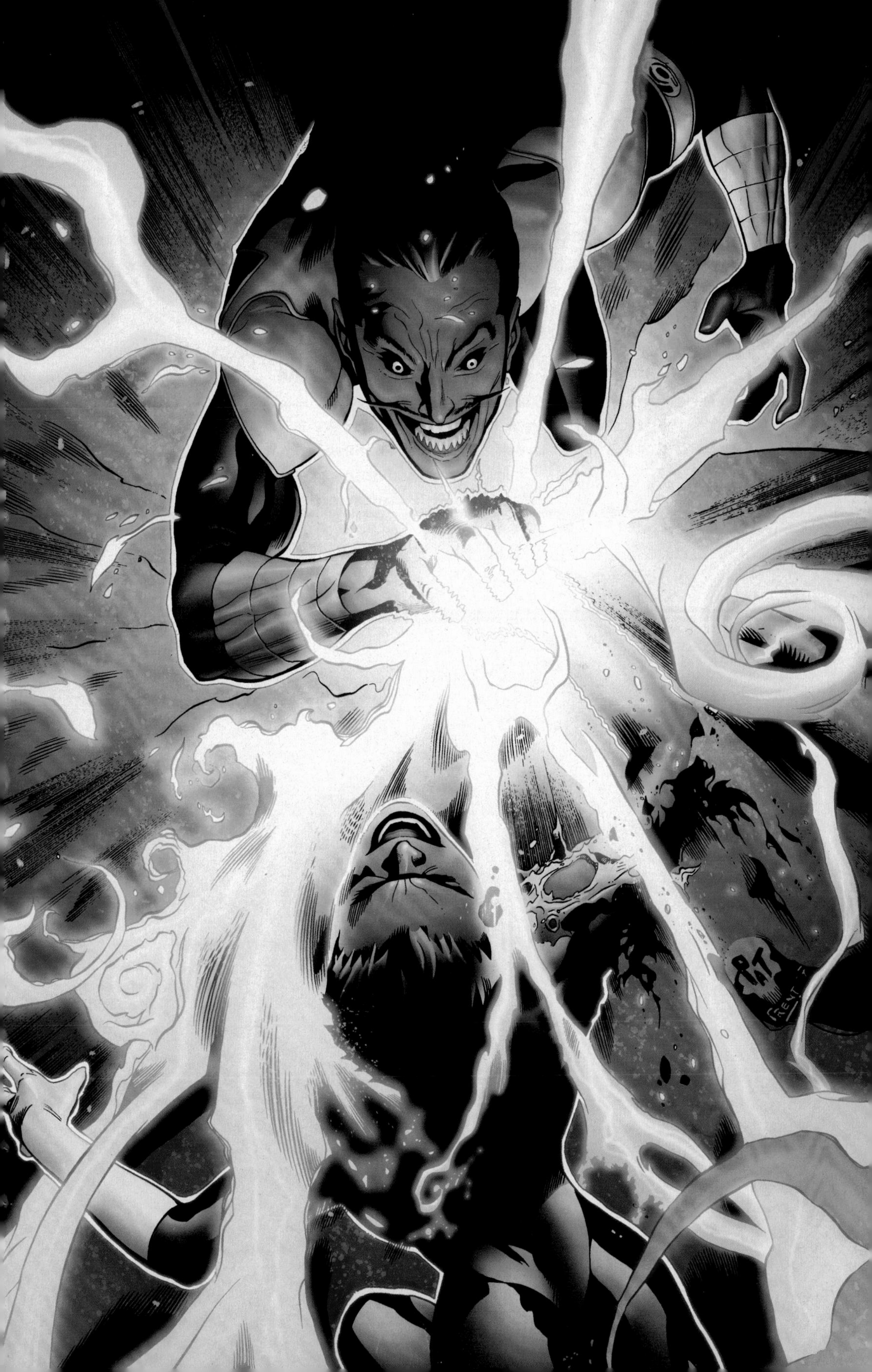

THE SINESTRO CORPS WAR
Chapter Two
THE GATHERING STORM

Penciller: **Patrick Gleason** (pages 81-91, 94-97, 100-102)
Penciller: **Angel Unzueta** (pages 92-93, 98-99)
Inker: **Prentis Rollins**
Colorist: **Guy Major**
Letterer: **Phil Balsman**

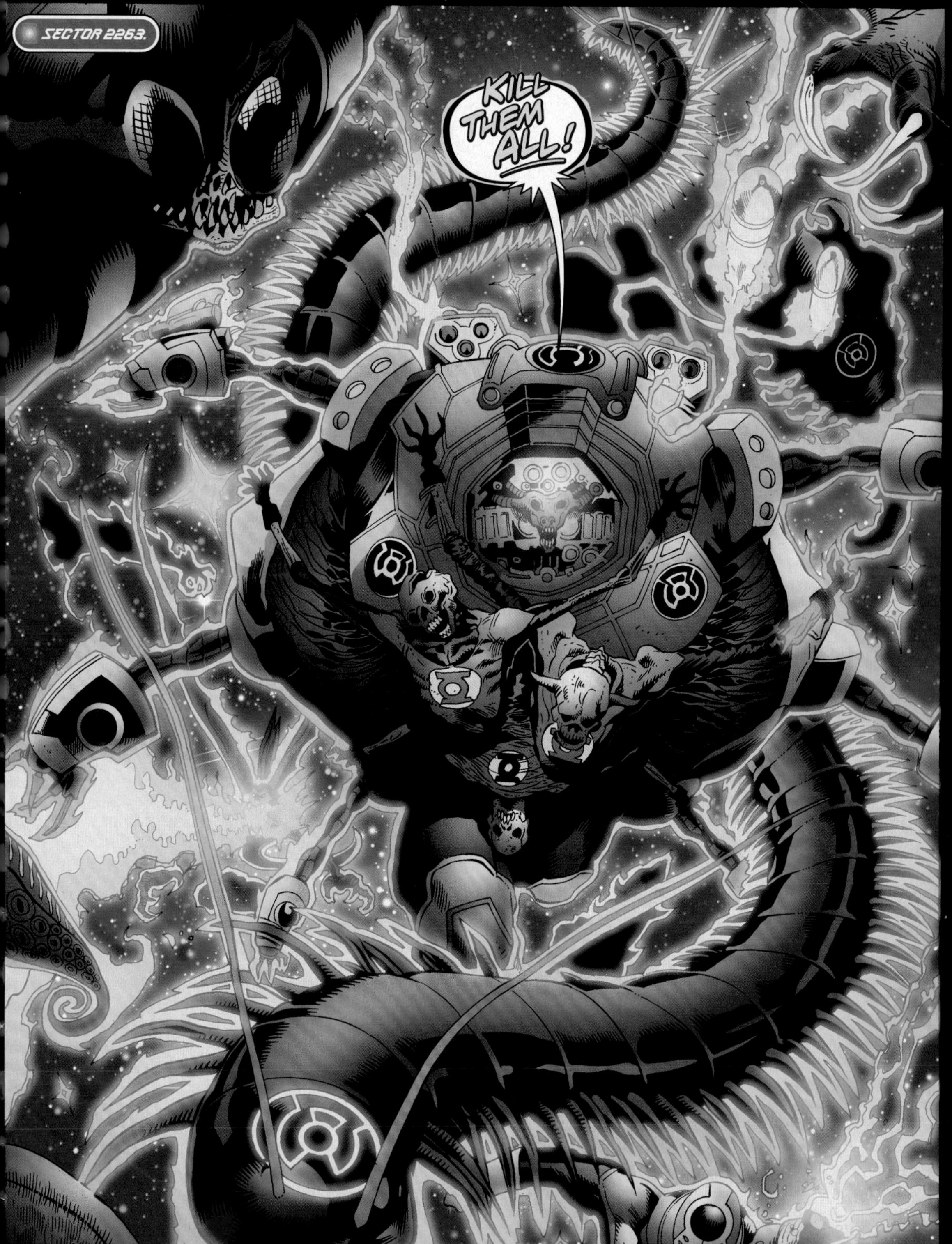
SECTOR 2263.
KILL THEM ALL!

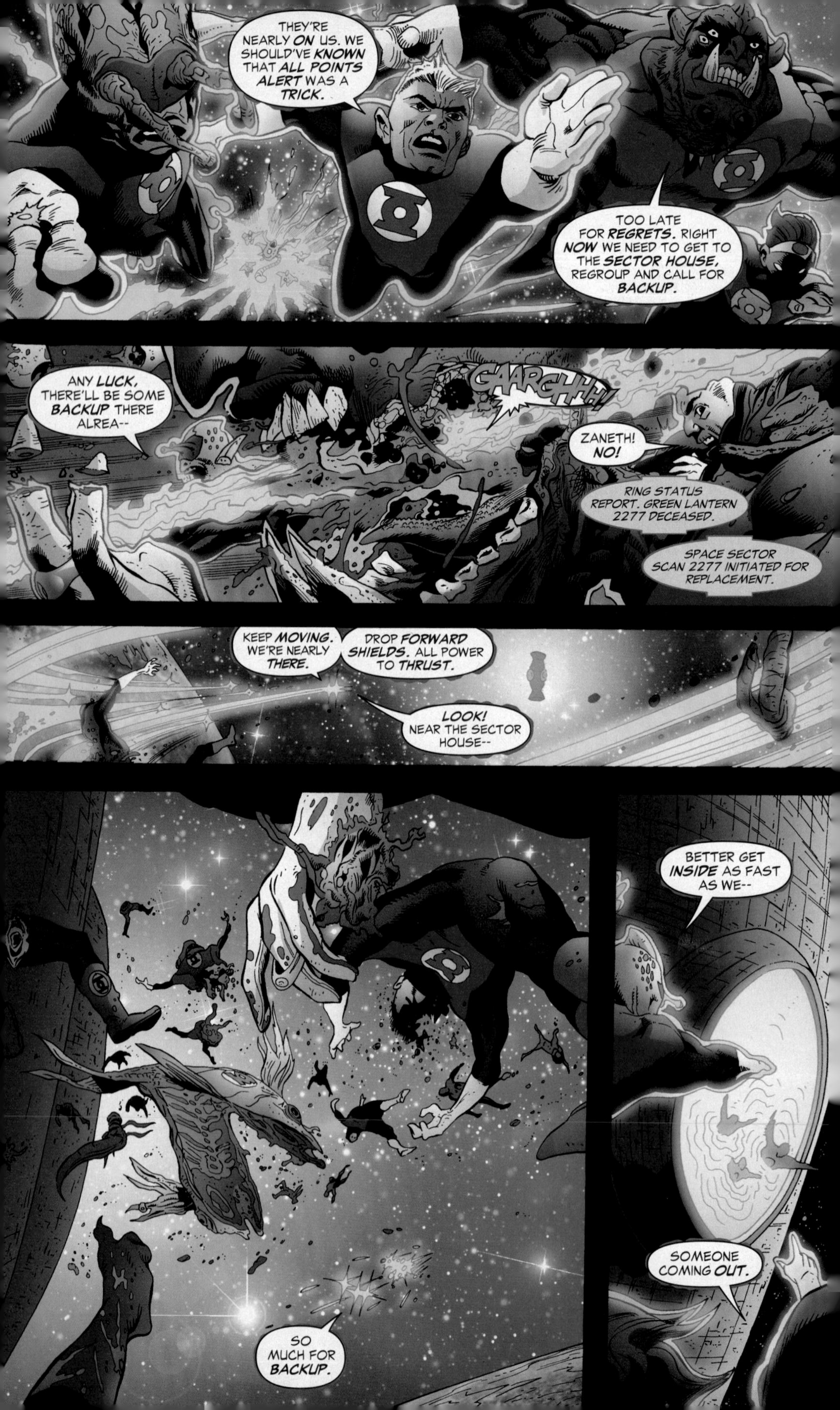

THEY'RE NEARLY ON US. WE SHOULD'VE KNOWN THAT ALL POINTS ALERT WAS A TRICK.
TOO LATE FOR REGRETS. RIGHT NOW WE NEED TO GET TO THE SECTOR HOUSE, REGROUP AND CALL FOR BACKUP.
ANY LUCK, THERE'LL BE SOME BACKUP THERE ALREA--
GAARGHHH!
ZANETH! NO!
RING STATUS REPORT. GREEN LANTERN 2277 DECEASED.
SPACE SECTOR SCAN 2277 INITIATED FOR REPLACEMENT.
KEEP MOVING. WE'RE NEARLY THERE.
DROP FORWARD SHIELDS. ALL POWER TO THRUST.
LOOK! NEAR THE SECTOR HOUSE--
SO MUCH FOR BACKUP.
BETTER GET INSIDE AS FAST AS WE--
SOMEONE COMING OUT.

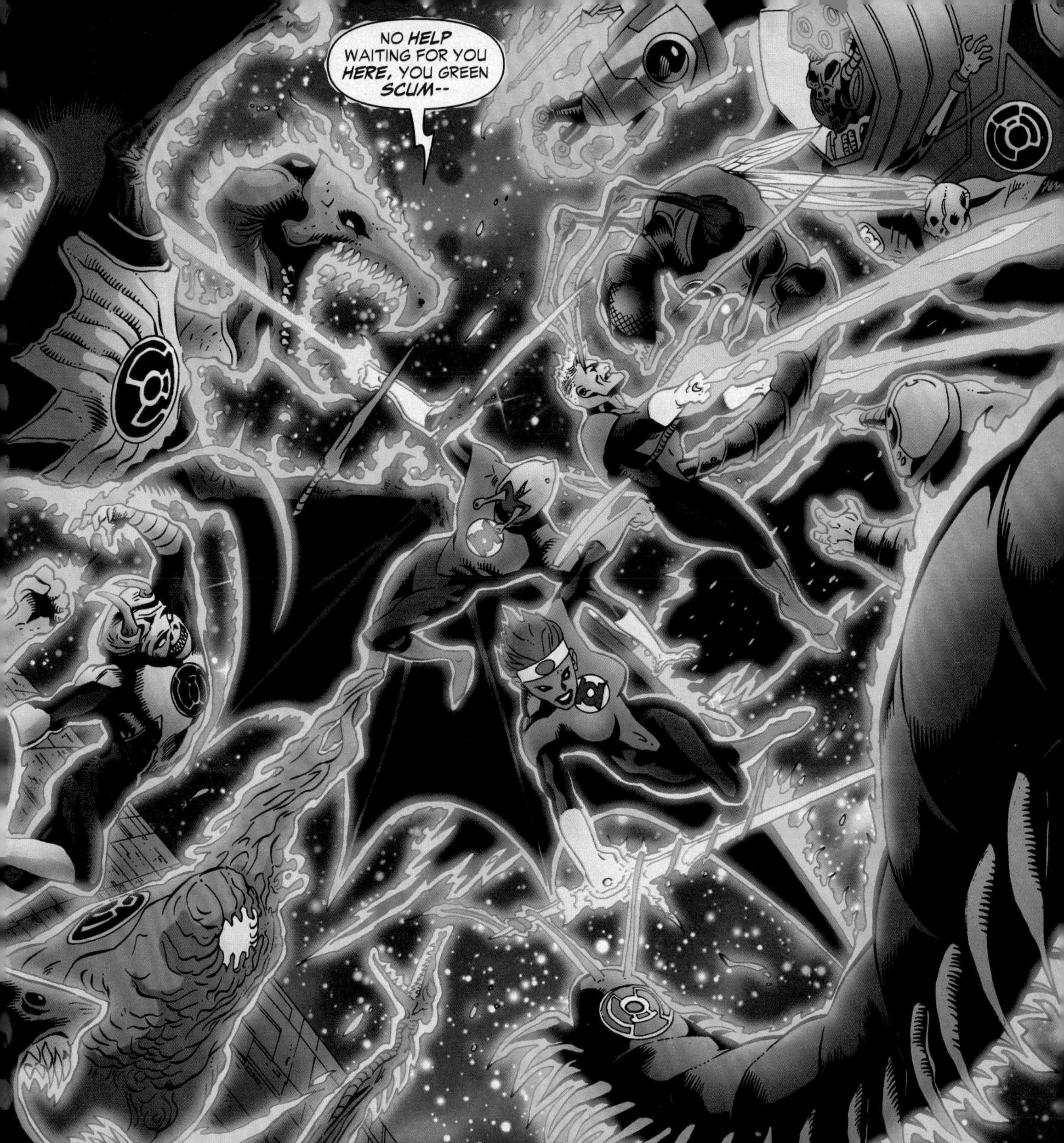
NO HELP WAITING FOR YOU HERE, YOU GREEN SCUM--
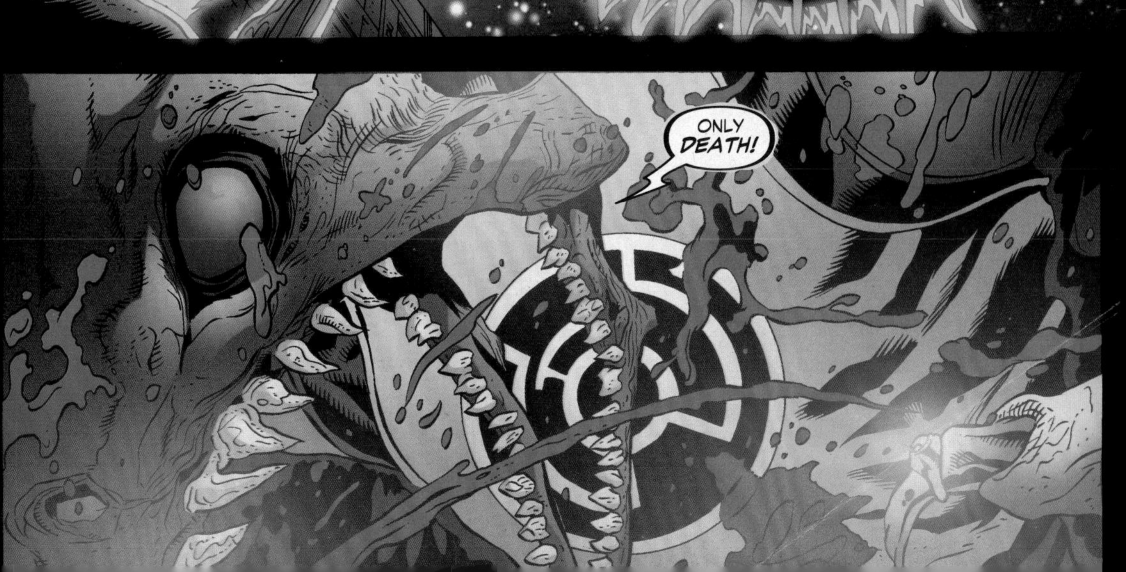
ONLY DEATH!

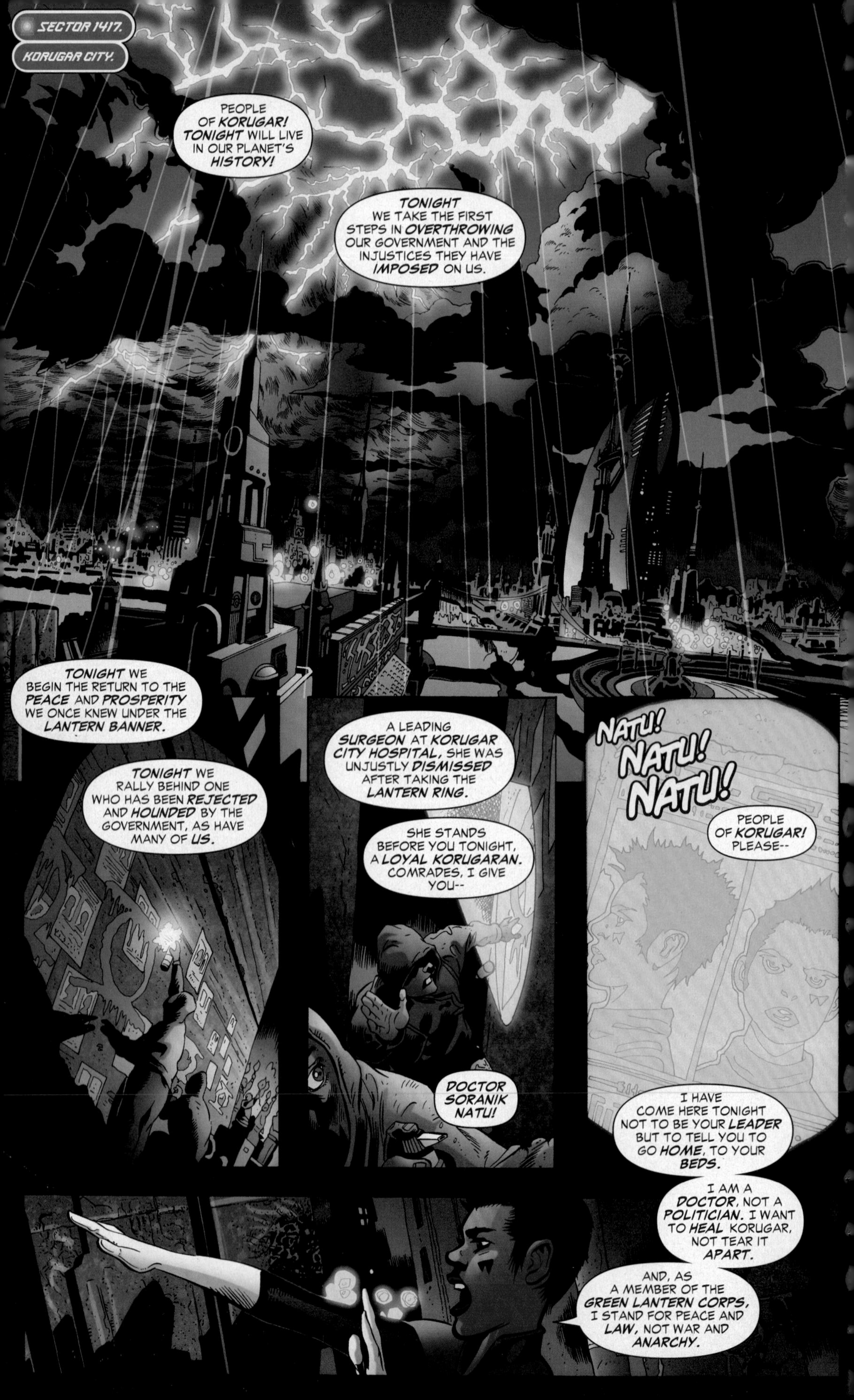
SECTOR 1417.
KORUGAR CITY.
PEOPLE OF KORUGAR! TONIGHT WILL LIVE IN OUR PLANET'S HISTORY!
TONIGHT WE TAKE THE FIRST STEPS IN OVERTHROWING OUR GOVERNMENT AND THE INJUSTICES THEY HAVE IMPOSED ON US.
TONIGHT WE BEGIN THE RETURN TO THE PEACE AND PROSPERITY WE ONCE KNEW UNDER THE LANTERN BANNER.
TONIGHT WE RALLY BEHIND ONE WHO HAS BEEN REJECTED AND HOUNDED BY THE GOVERNMENT, AS HAVE MANY OF US.
A LEADING SURGEON AT KORUGAR CITY HOSPITAL, SHE WAS UNJUSTLY DISMISSED AFTER TAKING THE LANTERN RING.
SHE STANDS BEFORE YOU TONIGHT, A LOYAL KORUGARAN. COMRADES, I GIVE YOU--
DOCTOR SORANIK NATU!
NATU! NATU! NATU!
PEOPLE OF KORUGAR! PLEASE--
I HAVE COME HERE TONIGHT NOT TO BE YOUR LEADER BUT TO TELL YOU TO GO HOME, TO YOUR BEDS.
I AM A DOCTOR, NOT A POLITICIAN. I WANT TO HEAL KORUGAR, NOT TEAR IT APART.
AND, AS A MEMBER OF THE GREEN LANTERN CORPS, I STAND FOR PEACE AND LAW, NOT WAR AND ANARCHY.

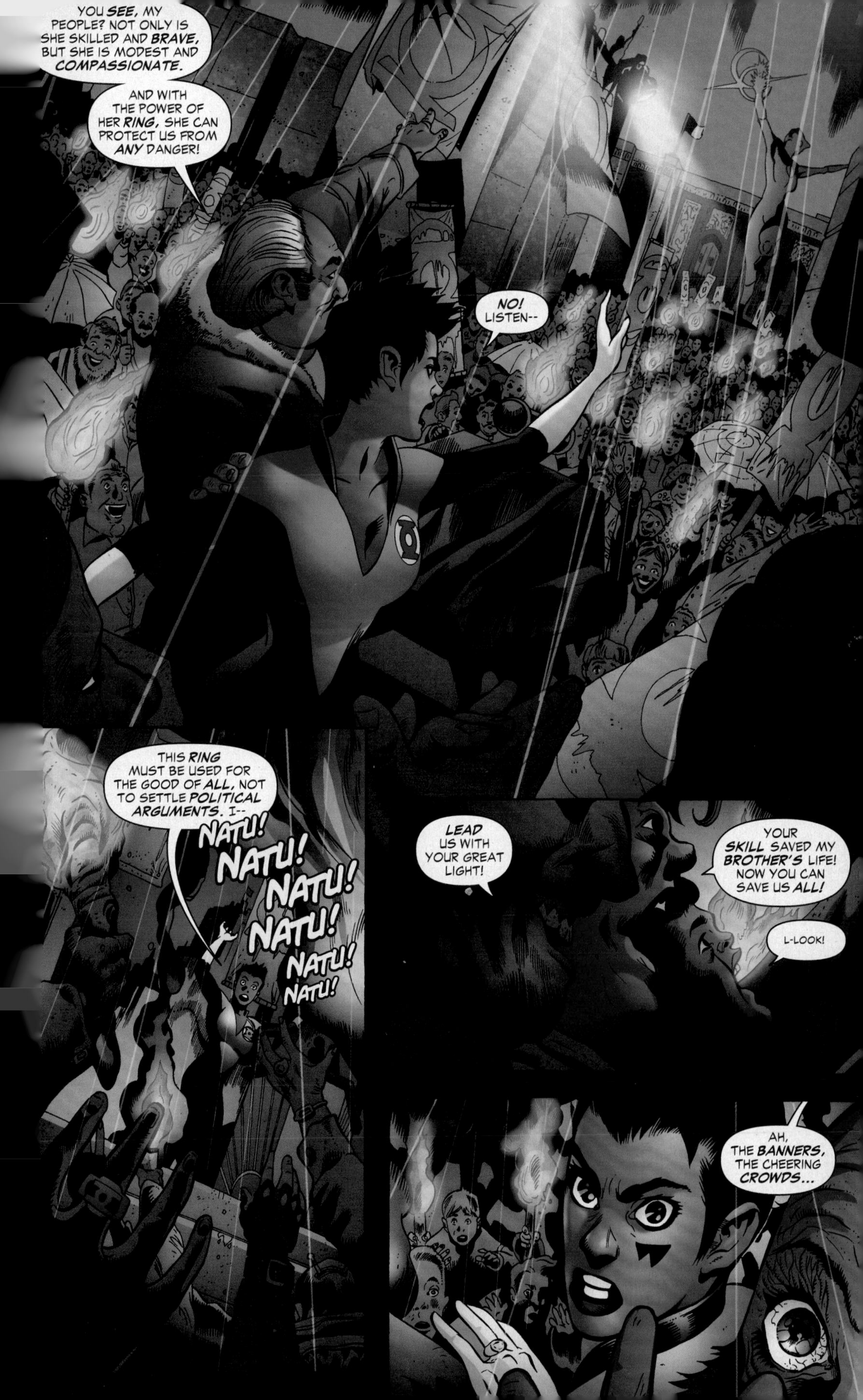
YOU SEE, MY PEOPLE? NOT ONLY IS SHE SKILLED AND BRAVE, BUT SHE IS MODEST AND COMPASSIONATE.
AND WITH THE POWER OF HER RING, SHE CAN PROTECT US FROM ANY DANGER!
NO! LISTEN--
THIS RING MUST BE USED FOR THE GOOD OF ALL, NOT TO SETTLE POLITICAL ARGUMENTS. I--
NATU! NATU! NATU! NATU! NATU! NATU!
LEAD US WITH YOUR GREAT LIGHT!
YOUR SKILL SAVED MY BROTHER'S LIFE! NOW YOU CAN SAVE US ALL!
L-LOOK!
AH, THE BANNERS, THE CHEERING CROWDS...

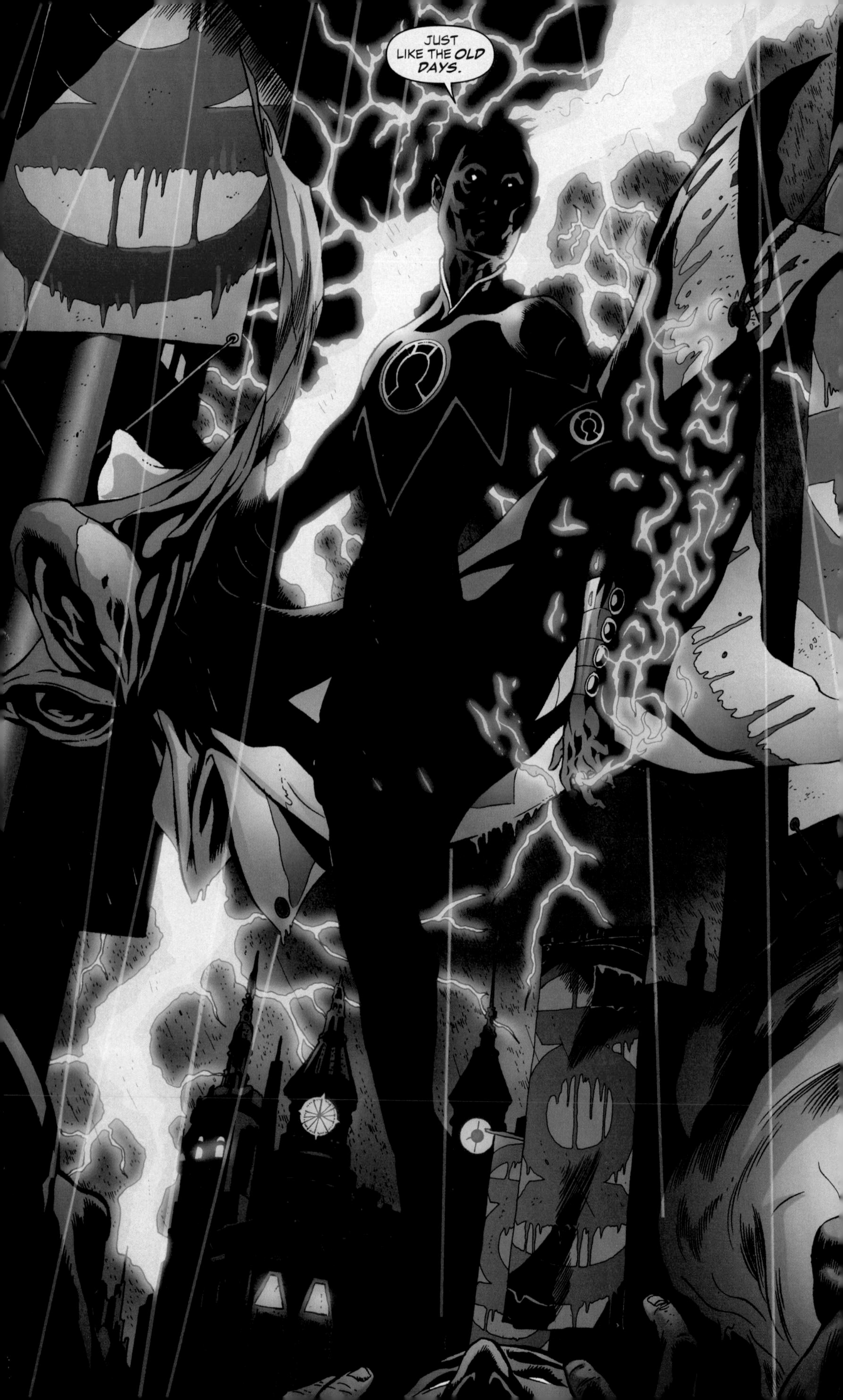
JUST LIKE THE OLD DAYS.

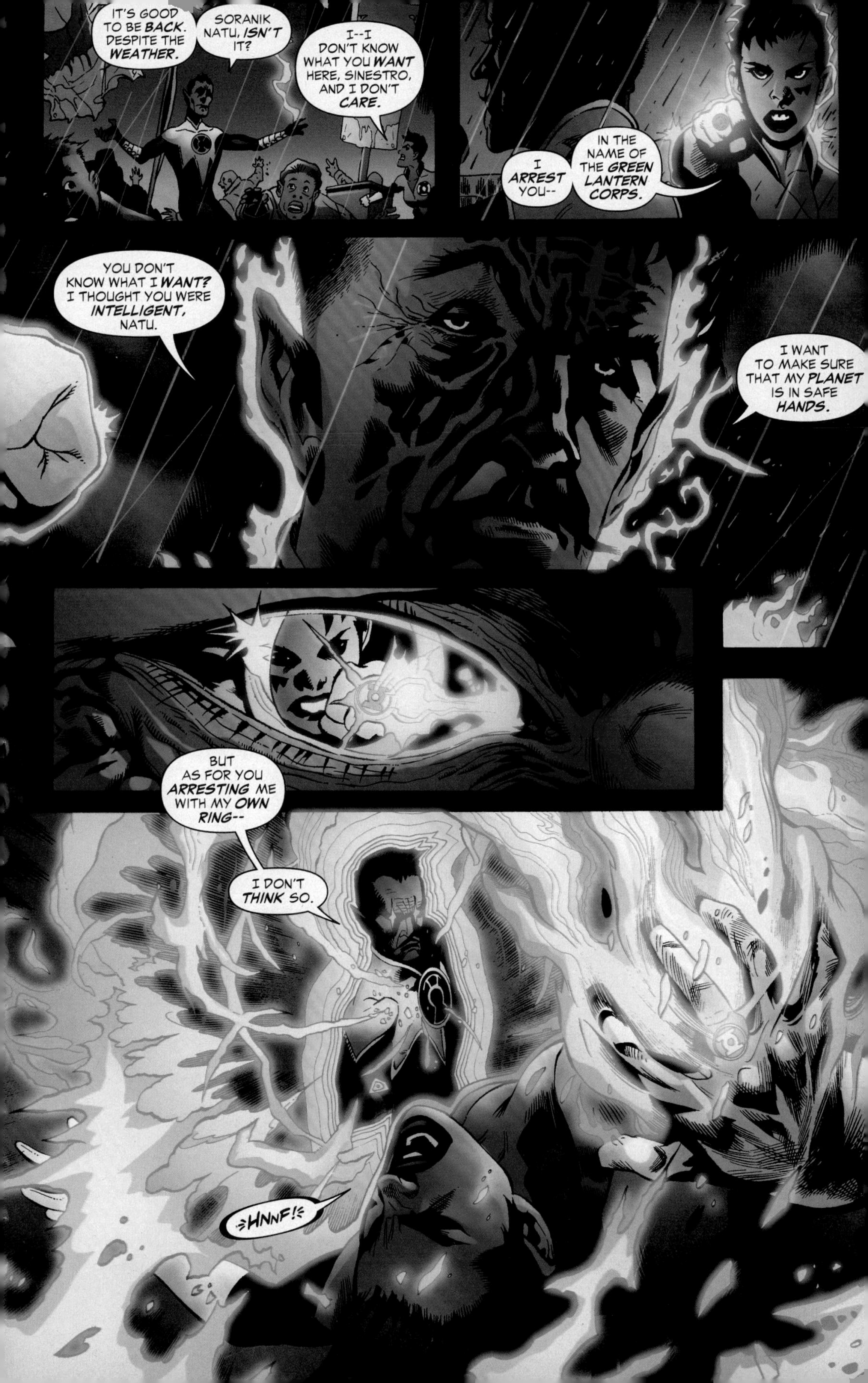
IT'S GOOD TO BE BACK. DESPITE THE WEATHER.
SORANIK NATU, ISN'T IT?
I--I DON'T KNOW WHAT YOU WANT HERE, SINESTRO, AND I DON'T CARE.
I ARREST YOU--
IN THE NAME OF THE GREEN LANTERN CORPS.
YOU DON'T KNOW WHAT I WANT? I THOUGHT YOU WERE INTELLIGENT, NATU.
I WANT TO MAKE SURE THAT MY PLANET IS IN SAFE HANDS.
BUT AS FOR YOU ARRESTING ME WITH MY OWN RING--
I DON'T THINK SO.
HNNF!

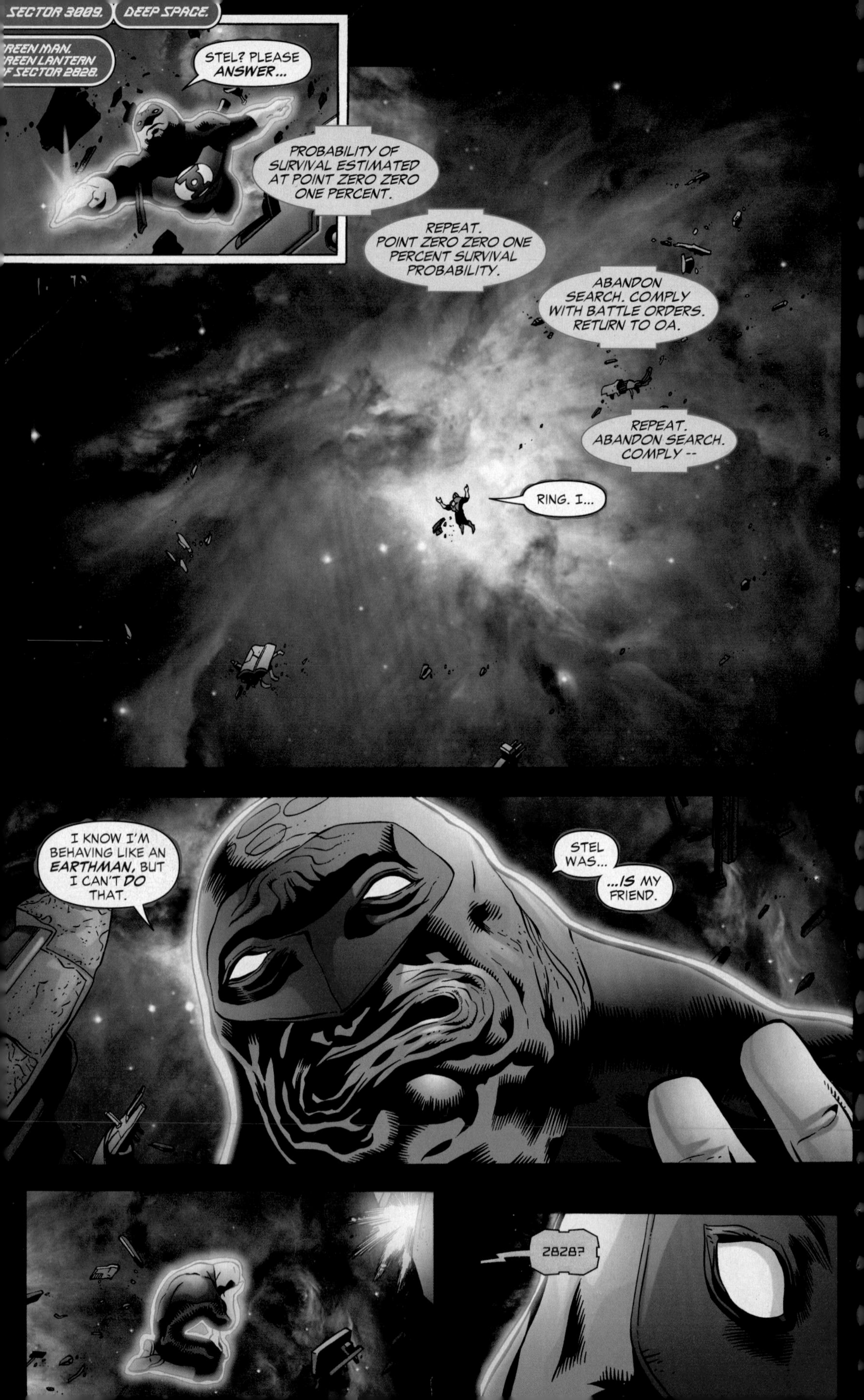
SECTOR 3009.
DEEP SPACE.
REEN MAN. REEN LANTERN F SECTOR 2828.
STEL? PLEASE ANSWER...
PROBABILITY OF SURVIVAL ESTIMATED AT POINT ZERO ZERO ONE PERCENT.
REPEAT. POINT ZERO ZERO ONE PERCENT SURVIVAL PROBABILITY.
ABANDON SEARCH. COMPLY WITH BATTLE ORDERS. RETURN TO OA.
REPEAT. ABANDON SEARCH. COMPLY --
RING. I...
I KNOW I'M BEHAVING LIKE AN EARTHMAN, BUT I CAN'T DO THAT.
STEL WAS...
...IS MY FRIEND.
2828?

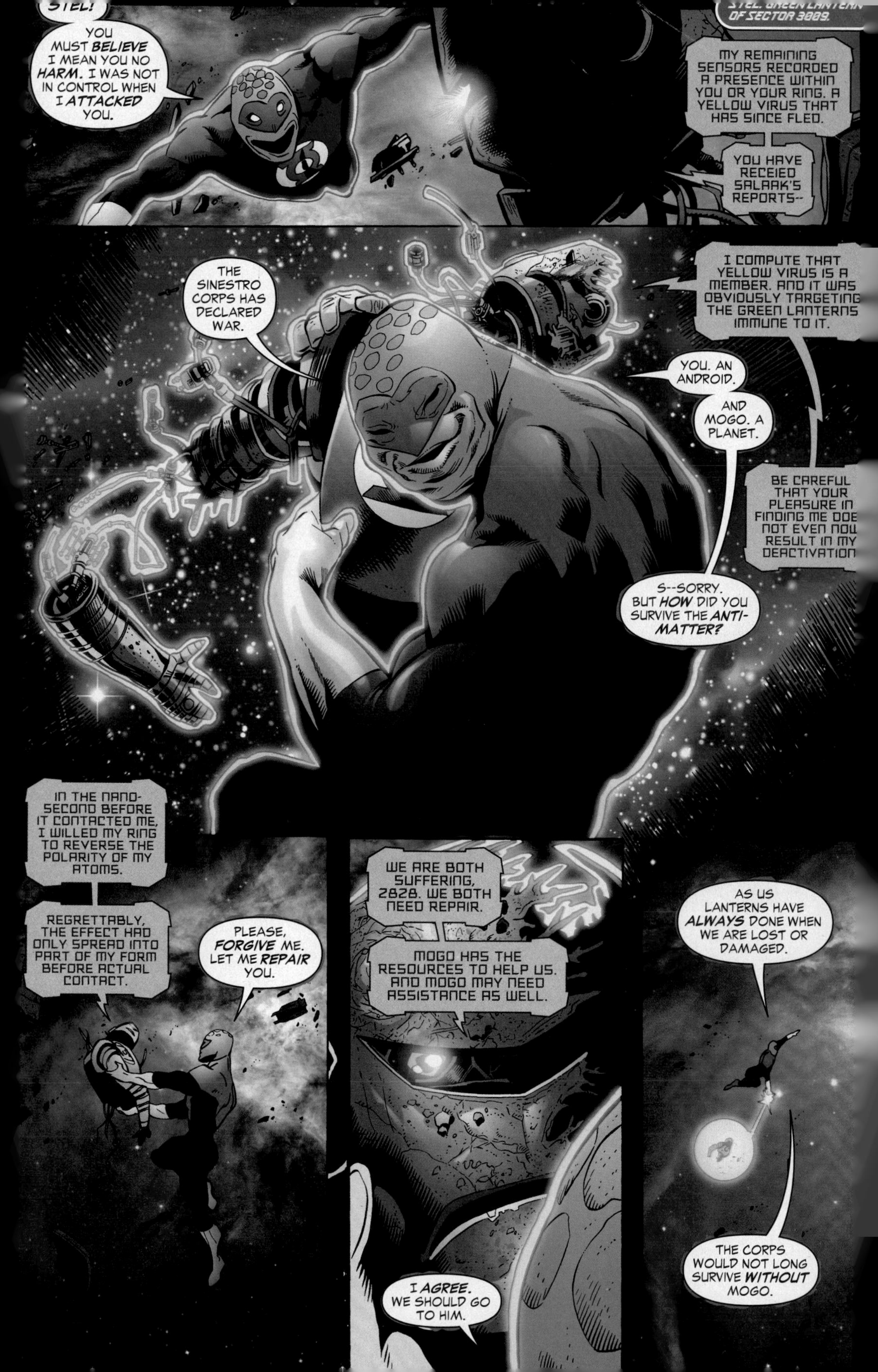
STEL!
YOU MUST BELIEVE I MEAN YOU NO HARM. I WAS NOT IN CONTROL WHEN I ATTACKED YOU.
STEL. GREEN LANTERN OF SECTOR 3009.
MY REMAINING SENSORS RECORDED A PRESENCE WITHIN YOU OR YOUR RING. A YELLOW VIRUS THAT HAS SINCE FLED.
YOU HAVE RECEIED SALAAK'S REPORTS--
THE SINESTRO CORPS HAS DECLARED WAR.
I COMPUTE THAT YELLOW VIRUS IS A MEMBER. AND IT WAS OBVIOUSLY TARGETING THE GREEN LANTERNS IMMUNE TO IT.
YOU. AN ANDROID.
AND MOGO. A PLANET.
BE CAREFUL THAT YOUR PLEASURE IN FINDING ME DOES NOT EVEN NOW RESULT IN MY DEACTIVATION
S--SORRY. BUT HOW DID YOU SURVIVE THE ANTI-MATTER?
IN THE NANO-SECOND BEFORE IT CONTACTED ME, I WILLED MY RING TO REVERSE THE POLARITY OF MY ATOMS.
REGRETTABLY, THE EFFECT HAD ONLY SPREAD INTO PART OF MY FORM BEFORE ACTUAL CONTACT.
PLEASE, FORGIVE ME. LET ME REPAIR YOU.
WE ARE BOTH SUFFERING, 2828. WE BOTH NEED REPAIR.
MOGO HAS THE RESOURCES TO HELP US. AND MOGO MAY NEED ASSISTANCE AS WELL.
I AGREE. WE SHOULD GO TO HIM.
AS US LANTERNS HAVE ALWAYS DONE WHEN WE ARE LOST OR DAMAGED.
THE CORPS WOULD NOT LONG SURVIVE WITHOUT MOGO.

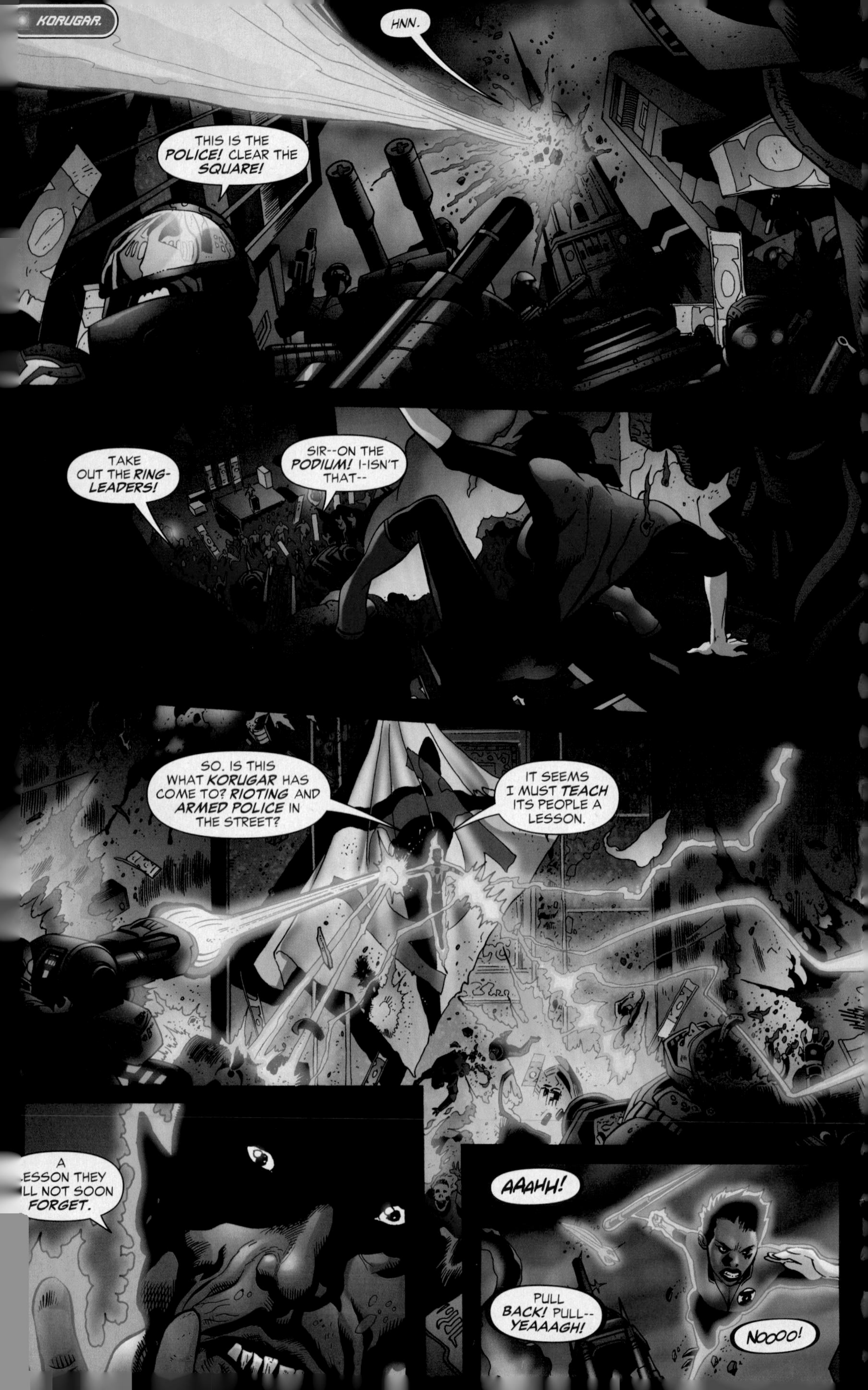
KORUGAR.
HNN.
THIS IS THE POLICE! CLEAR THE SQUARE!
TAKE OUT THE RING-LEADERS!
SIR--ON THE PODIUM! I-ISN'T THAT--
SO. IS THIS WHAT KORUGAR HAS COME TO? RIOTING AND ARMED POLICE IN THE STREET?
IT SEEMS I MUST TEACH ITS PEOPLE A LESSON.
A LESSON THEY LL NOT SOON FORGET.
AAAHH!
PULL BACK! PULL-- YEAAAGH!
NOOOO!

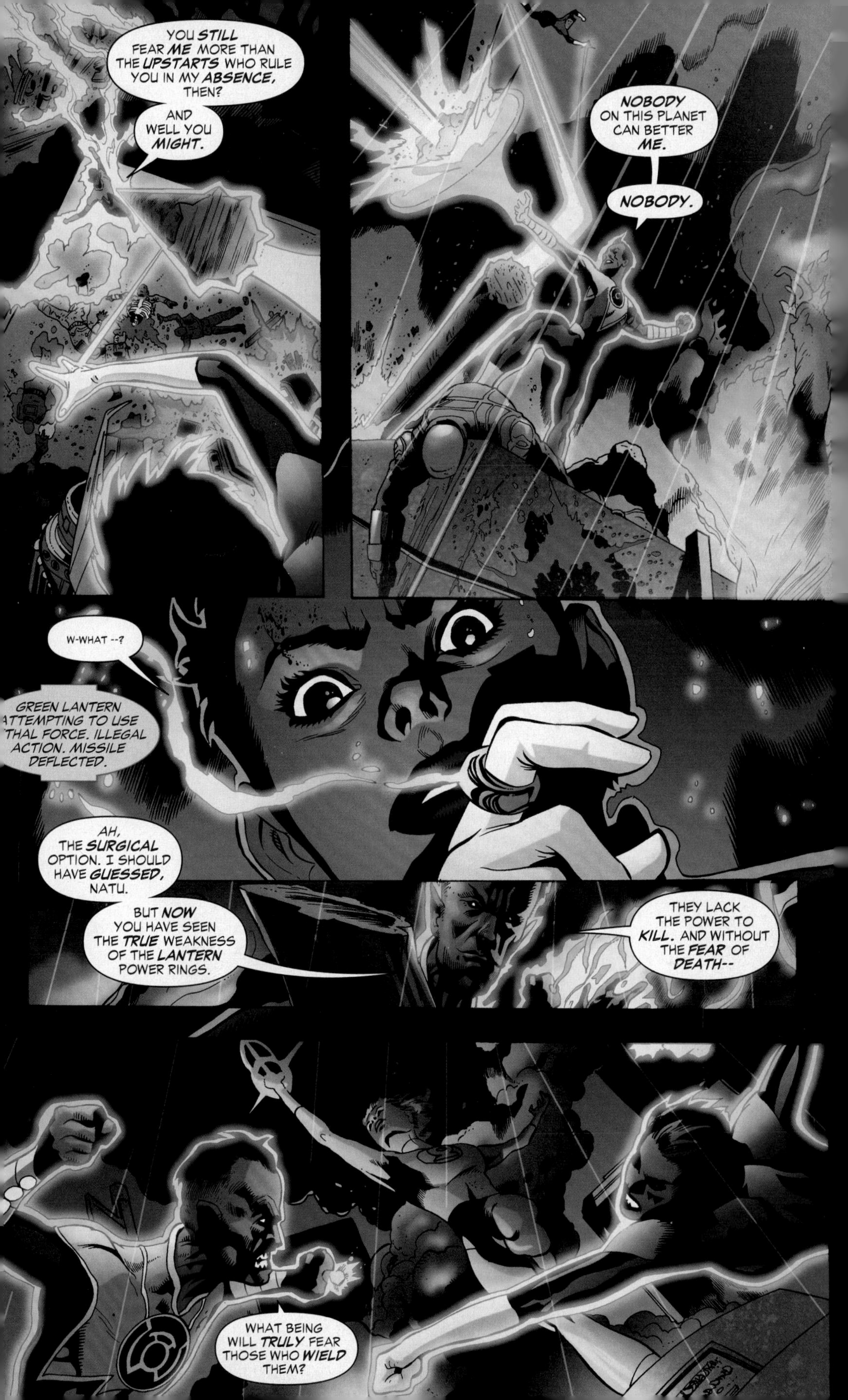

YOU STILL FEAR ME MORE THAN THE UPSTARTS WHO RULE YOU IN MY ABSENCE, THEN?
AND WELL YOU MIGHT.
NOBODY ON THIS PLANET CAN BETTER ME.
NOBODY.
W-WHAT --?
GREEN LANTERN ATTEMPTING TO USE THAL FORCE. ILLEGAL ACTION. MISSILE DEFLECTED.
AH, THE SURGICAL OPTION. I SHOULD HAVE GUESSED, NATU.
BUT NOW YOU HAVE SEEN THE TRUE WEAKNESS OF THE LANTERN POWER RINGS.
THEY LACK THE POWER TO KILL. AND WITHOUT THE FEAR OF DEATH--
WHAT BEING WILL TRULY FEAR THOSE WHO WIELD THEM?

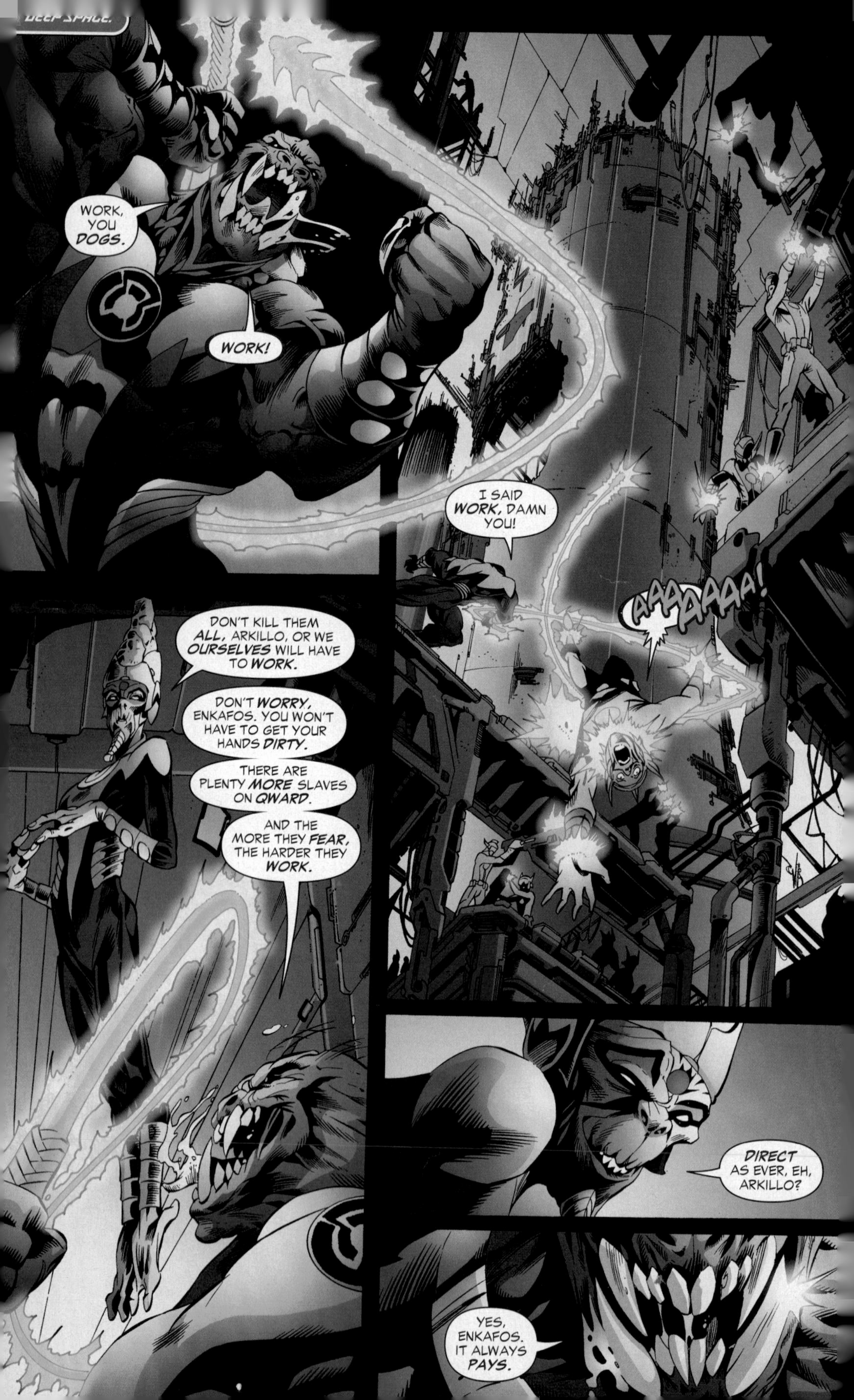
WORK, YOU DOGS.
WORK!
I SAID WORK, DAMN YOU!
AAAAAAA!
DON'T KILL THEM ALL, ARKILLO, OR WE OURSELVES WILL HAVE TO WORK.
DON'T WORRY, ENKAFOS. YOU WON'T HAVE TO GET YOUR HANDS DIRTY.
THERE ARE PLENTY MORE SLAVES ON QWARD.
AND THE MORE THEY FEAR, THE HARDER THEY WORK.
DIRECT AS EVER, EH, ARKILLO?
YES, ENKAFOS. IT ALWAYS PAYS.

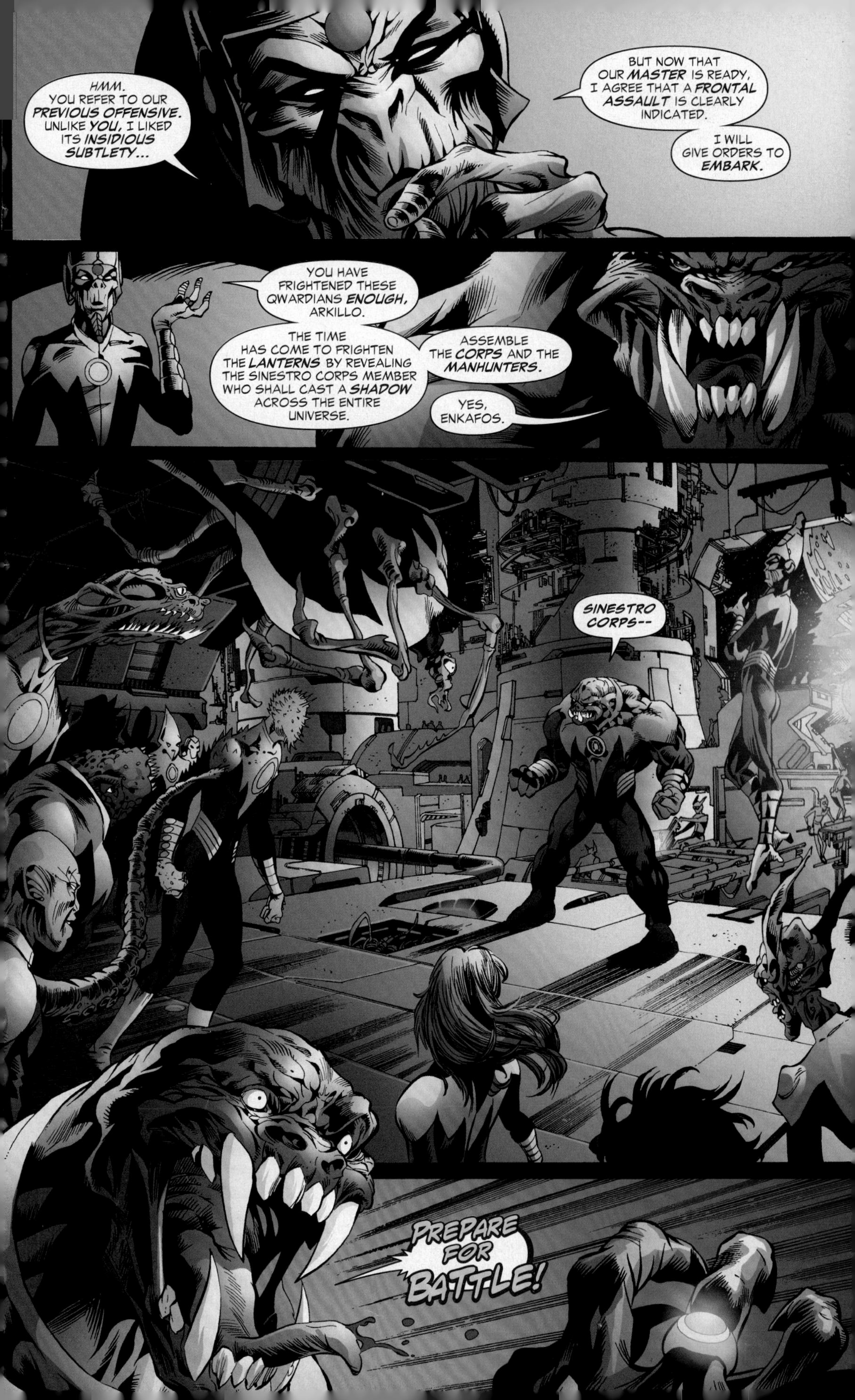
HMM. YOU REFER TO OUR PREVIOUS OFFENSIVE. UNLIKE YOU, I LIKED ITS INSIDIOUS SUBTLETY...
BUT NOW THAT OUR MASTER IS READY, I AGREE THAT A FRONTAL ASSAULT IS CLEARLY INDICATED.
I WILL GIVE ORDERS TO EMBARK.
YOU HAVE FRIGHTENED THESE QWARDIANS ENOUGH, ARKILLO.
THE TIME HAS COME TO FRIGHTEN THE LANTERNS BY REVEALING THE SINESTRO CORPS MEMBER WHO SHALL CAST A SHADOW ACROSS THE ENTIRE UNIVERSE.
ASSEMBLE THE CORPS AND THE MANHUNTERS.
YES, ENKAFOS.
SINESTRO CORPS--
PREPARE FOR BATTLE!

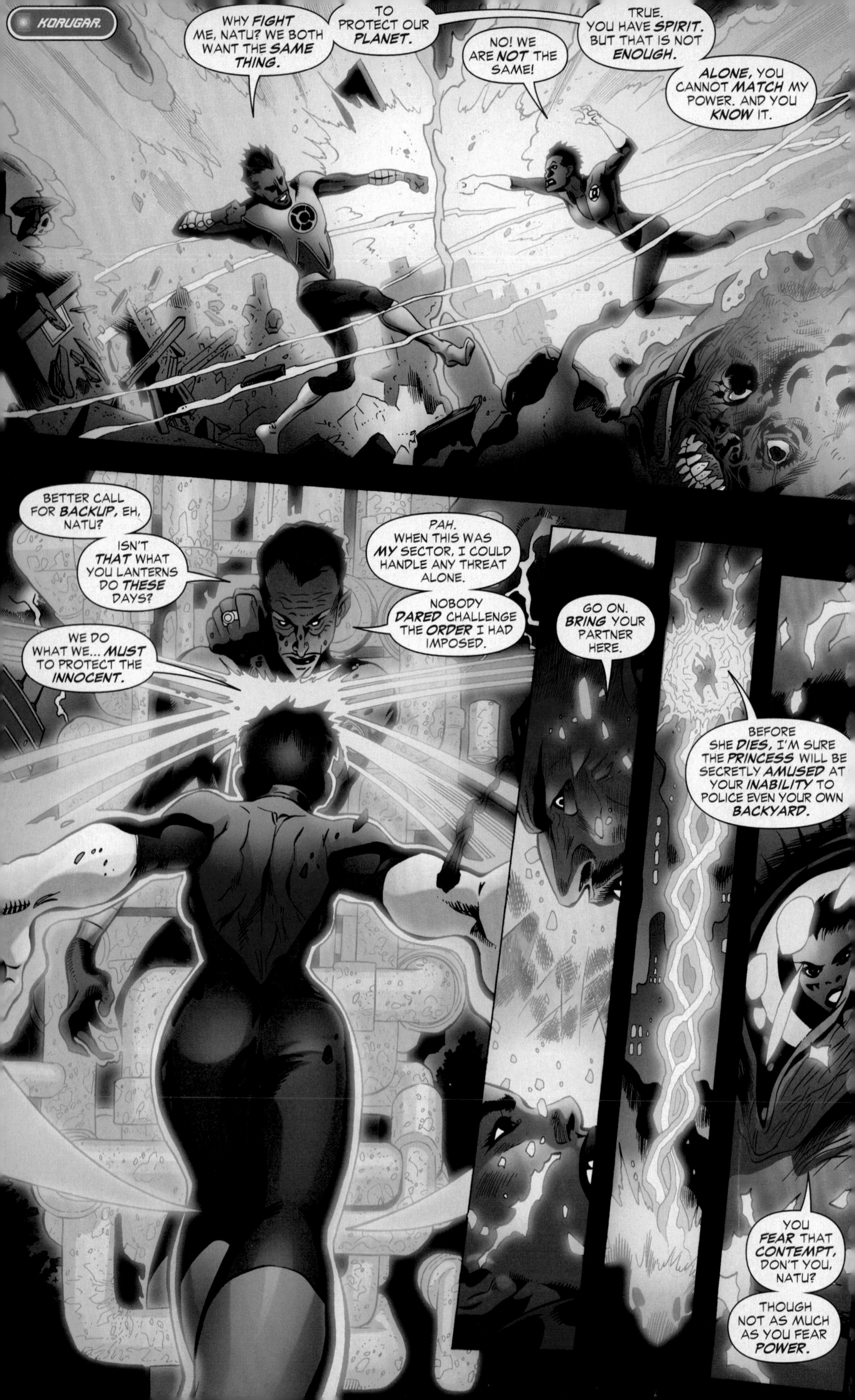
KORUGAR.
WHY FIGHT ME, NATU? WE BOTH WANT THE SAME THING.
TO PROTECT OUR PLANET.
NO! WE ARE NOT THE SAME!
TRUE. YOU HAVE SPIRIT. BUT THAT IS NOT ENOUGH.
ALONE, YOU CANNOT MATCH MY POWER. AND YOU KNOW IT.
BETTER CALL FOR BACKUP, EH, NATU?
ISN'T THAT WHAT YOU LANTERNS DO THESE DAYS?
WE DO WHAT WE... MUST TO PROTECT THE INNOCENT.
PAH. WHEN THIS WAS MY SECTOR, I COULD HANDLE ANY THREAT ALONE.
NOBODY DARED CHALLENGE THE ORDER I HAD IMPOSED.
GO ON. BRING YOUR PARTNER HERE.
BEFORE SHE DIES, I'M SURE THE PRINCESS WILL BE SECRETLY AMUSED AT YOUR INABILITY TO POLICE EVEN YOUR OWN BACKYARD.
YOU FEAR THAT CONTEMPT, DON'T YOU, NATU?
THOUGH NOT AS MUCH AS YOU FEAR POWER.

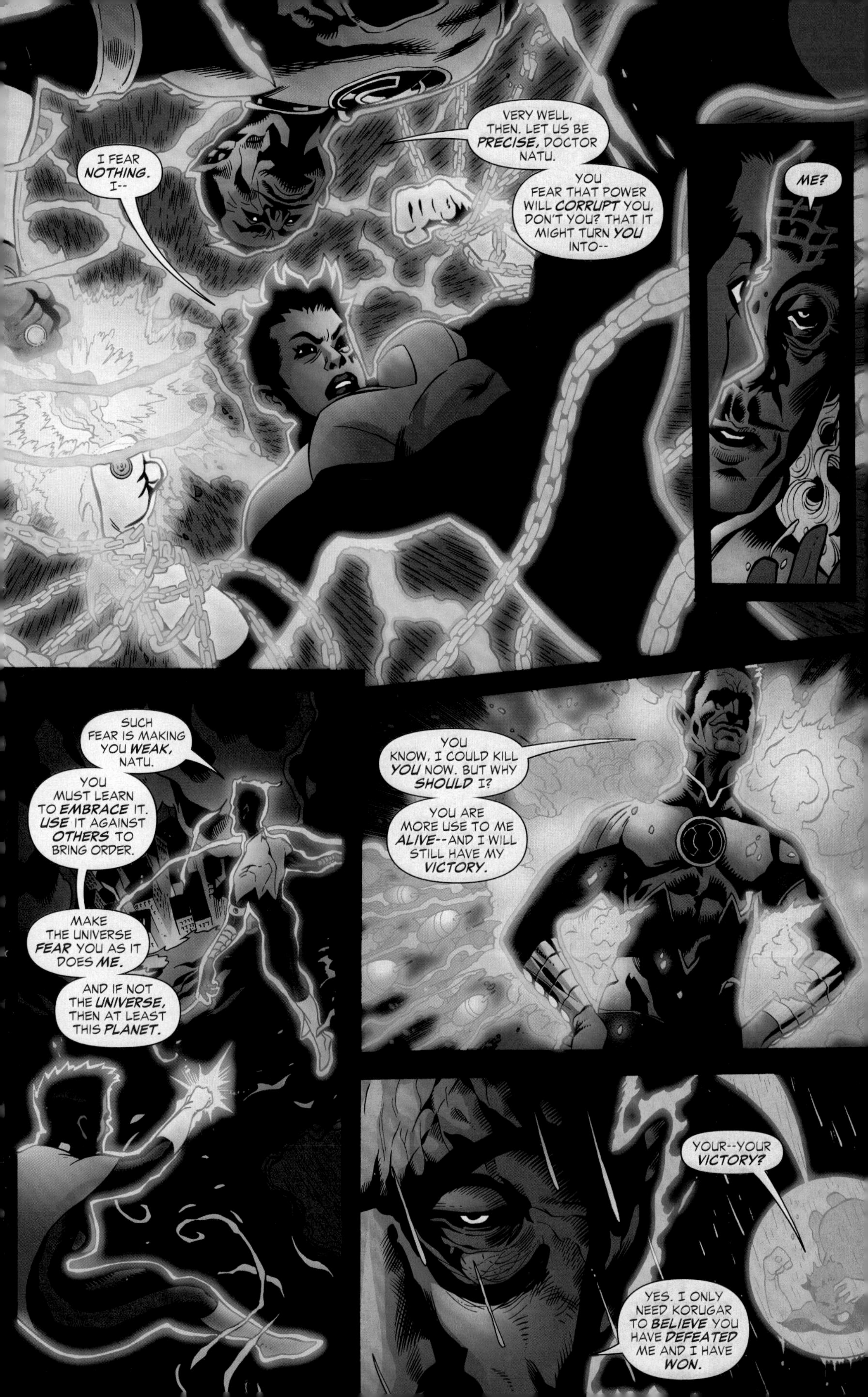
I FEAR NOTHING. I--
VERY WELL, THEN. LET US BE PRECISE, DOCTOR NATU.
YOU FEAR THAT POWER WILL CORRUPT YOU, DON'T YOU? THAT IT MIGHT TURN YOU INTO--
ME?
SUCH FEAR IS MAKING YOU WEAK, NATU.
YOU MUST LEARN TO EMBRACE IT. USE IT AGAINST OTHERS TO BRING ORDER.
MAKE THE UNIVERSE FEAR YOU AS IT DOES ME.
AND IF NOT THE UNIVERSE, THEN AT LEAST THIS PLANET.
YOU KNOW, I COULD KILL YOU NOW. BUT WHY SHOULD I?
YOU ARE MORE USE TO ME ALIVE--AND I WILL STILL HAVE MY VICTORY.
YOUR--YOUR VICTORY?
YES. I ONLY NEED KORUGAR TO BELIEVE YOU HAVE DEFEATED ME AND I HAVE WON.

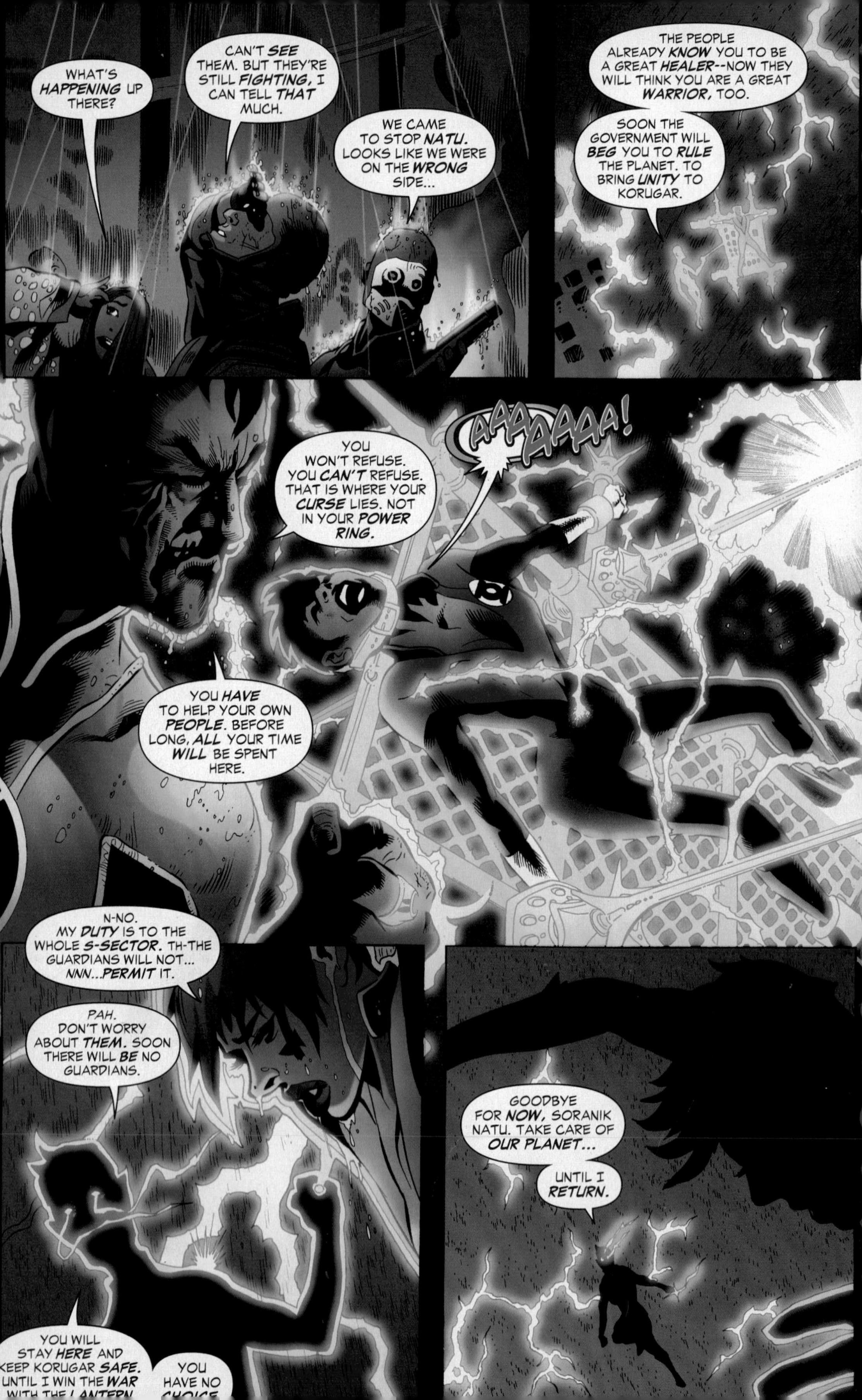
WHAT'S HAPPENING UP THERE?
CAN'T SEE THEM. BUT THEY'RE STILL FIGHTING, I CAN TELL THAT MUCH.
WE CAME TO STOP NATU. LOOKS LIKE WE WERE ON THE WRONG SIDE...
THE PEOPLE ALREADY KNOW YOU TO BE A GREAT HEALER--NOW THEY WILL THINK YOU ARE A GREAT WARRIOR, TOO.
SOON THE GOVERNMENT WILL BEG YOU TO RULE THE PLANET. TO BRING UNITY TO KORUGAR.
AAAAAAA!
YOU WON'T REFUSE. YOU CAN'T REFUSE. THAT IS WHERE YOUR CURSE LIES. NOT IN YOUR POWER RING.
YOU HAVE TO HELP YOUR OWN PEOPLE. BEFORE LONG, ALL YOUR TIME WILL BE SPENT HERE.
N-NO. MY DUTY IS TO THE WHOLE S-SECTOR. TH-THE GUARDIANS WILL NOT... NNN...PERMIT IT.
PAH. DON'T WORRY ABOUT THEM. SOON THERE WILL BE NO GUARDIANS.
YOU WILL STAY HERE AND KEEP KORUGAR SAFE. UNTIL I WIN THE WAR
YOU HAVE NO
GOODBYE FOR NOW, SORANIK NATU. TAKE CARE OF OUR PLANET...
UNTIL I RETURN.

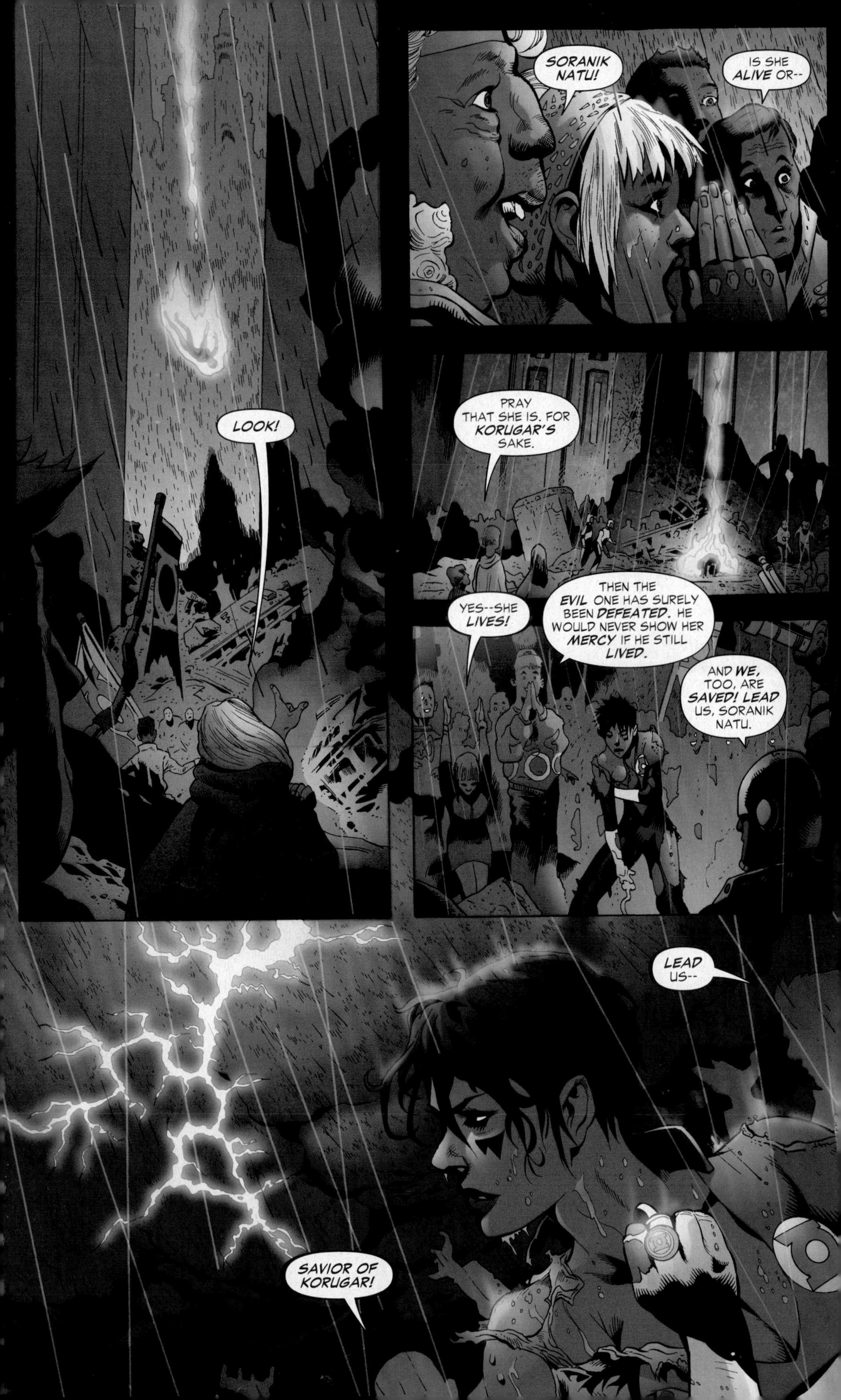
LOOK!
SORANIK NATU!
IS SHE ALIVE OR--
PRAY THAT SHE IS. FOR KORUGAR'S SAKE.
YES--SHE LIVES!
THEN THE EVIL ONE HAS SURELY BEEN DEFEATED. HE WOULD NEVER SHOW HER MERCY IF HE STILL LIVED.
AND WE, TOO, ARE SAVED! LEAD US, SORANIK NATU.
LEAD US--
SAVIOR OF KORUGAR!

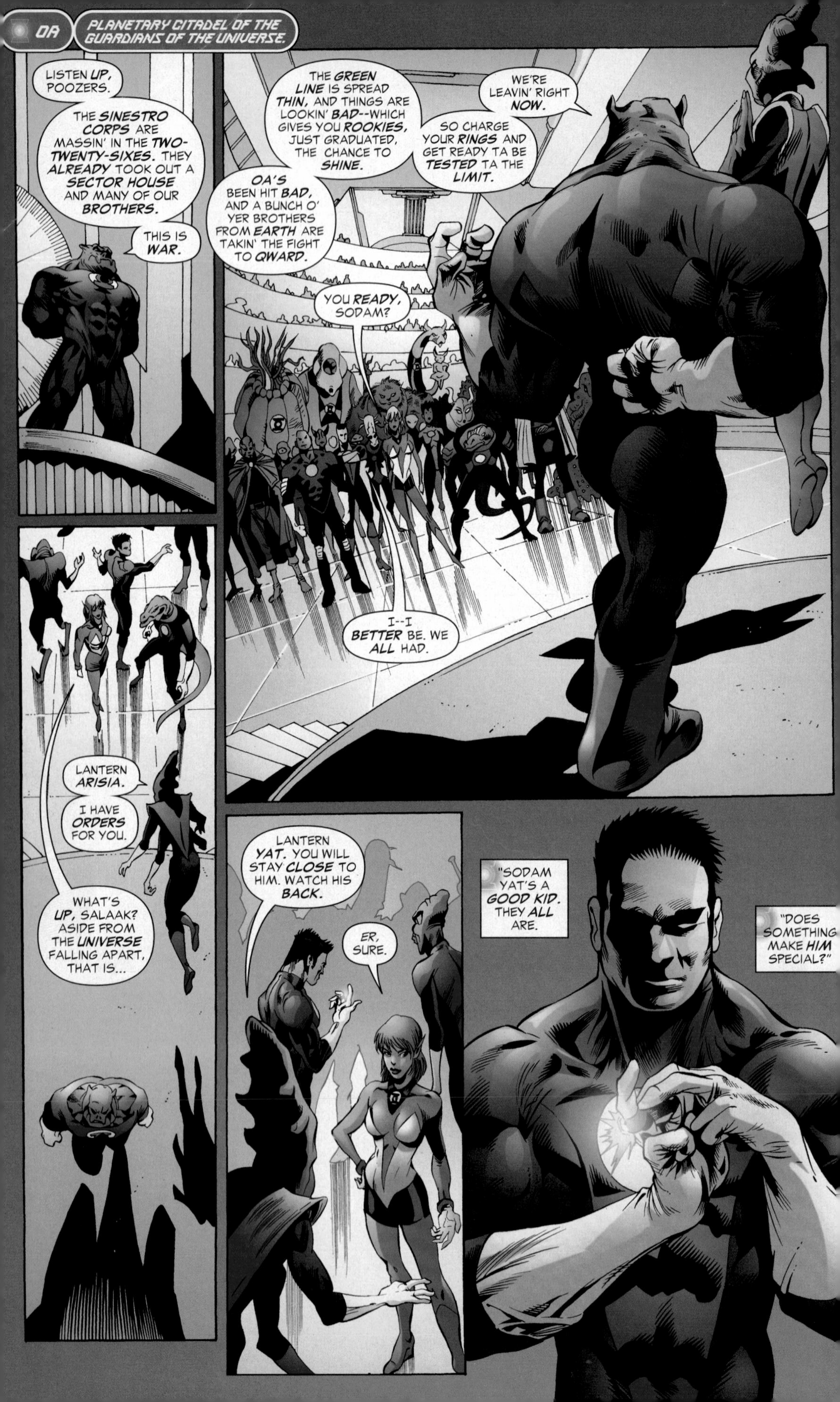
OA
PLANETARY CITADEL OF THE GUARDIANS OF THE UNIVERSE.
LISTEN UP, POOZERS.
THE SINESTRO CORPS ARE MASSIN' IN THE TWO-TWENTY-SIXES. THEY ALREADY TOOK OUT A SECTOR HOUSE AND MANY OF OUR BROTHERS.
THIS IS WAR.
THE GREEN LINE IS SPREAD THIN, AND THINGS ARE LOOKIN' BAD--WHICH GIVES YOU ROOKIES, JUST GRADUATED, THE CHANCE TO SHINE.
OA'S BEEN HIT BAD, AND A BUNCH O' YER BROTHERS FROM EARTH ARE TAKIN' THE FIGHT TO QWARD.
WE'RE LEAVIN' RIGHT NOW.
SO CHARGE YOUR RINGS AND GET READY TA BE TESTED TA THE LIMIT.
YOU READY, SODAM?
I--I BETTER BE. WE ALL HAD.
LANTERN ARISIA.
I HAVE ORDERS FOR YOU.
WHAT'S UP, SALAAK? ASIDE FROM THE UNIVERSE FALLING APART, THAT IS...
LANTERN YAT. YOU WILL STAY CLOSE TO HIM. WATCH HIS BACK.
ER, SURE.
"SODAM YAT'S A GOOD KID. THEY ALL ARE.
"DOES SOMETHING MAKE HIM SPECIAL?"

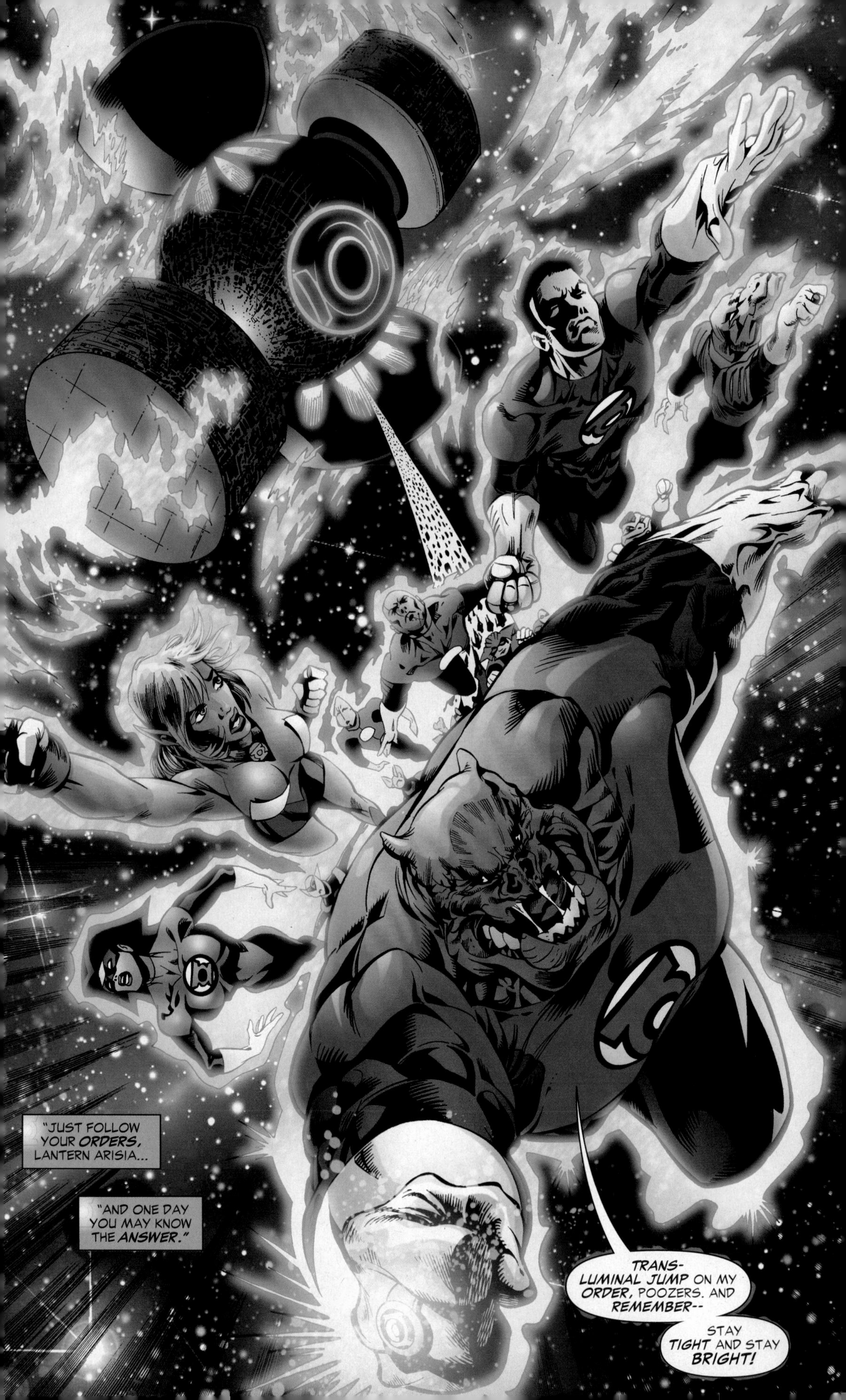
"JUST FOLLOW YOUR ORDERS, LANTERN ARISIA...
"AND ONE DAY YOU MAY KNOW THE ANSWER."
TRANS-LUMINAL JUMP ON MY ORDER, POOZERS. AND REMEMBER--
STAY TIGHT AND STAY BRIGHT!

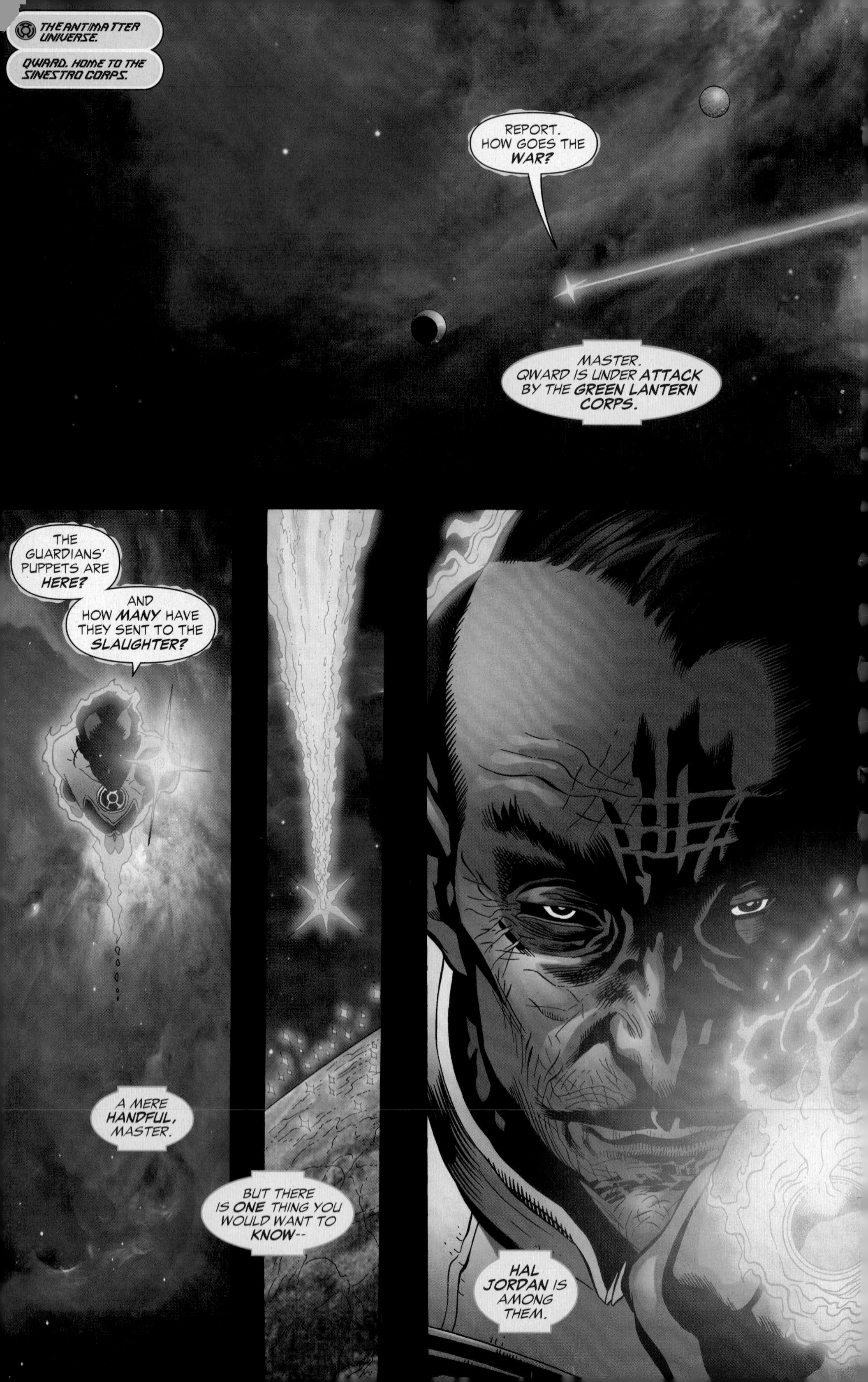
THE ANTIMATTER UNIVERSE.
QWARD. HOME TO THE SINESTRO CORPS.
REPORT. HOW GOES THE WAR?
MASTER. QWARD IS UNDER ATTACK BY THE GREEN LANTERN CORPS.
THE GUARDIANS' PUPPETS ARE HERE?
AND HOW MANY HAVE THEY SENT TO THE SLAUGHTER?
A MERE HANDFUL, MASTER.
BUT THERE IS ONE THING YOU WOULD WANT TO KNOW--
HAL JORDAN IS AMONG THEM.

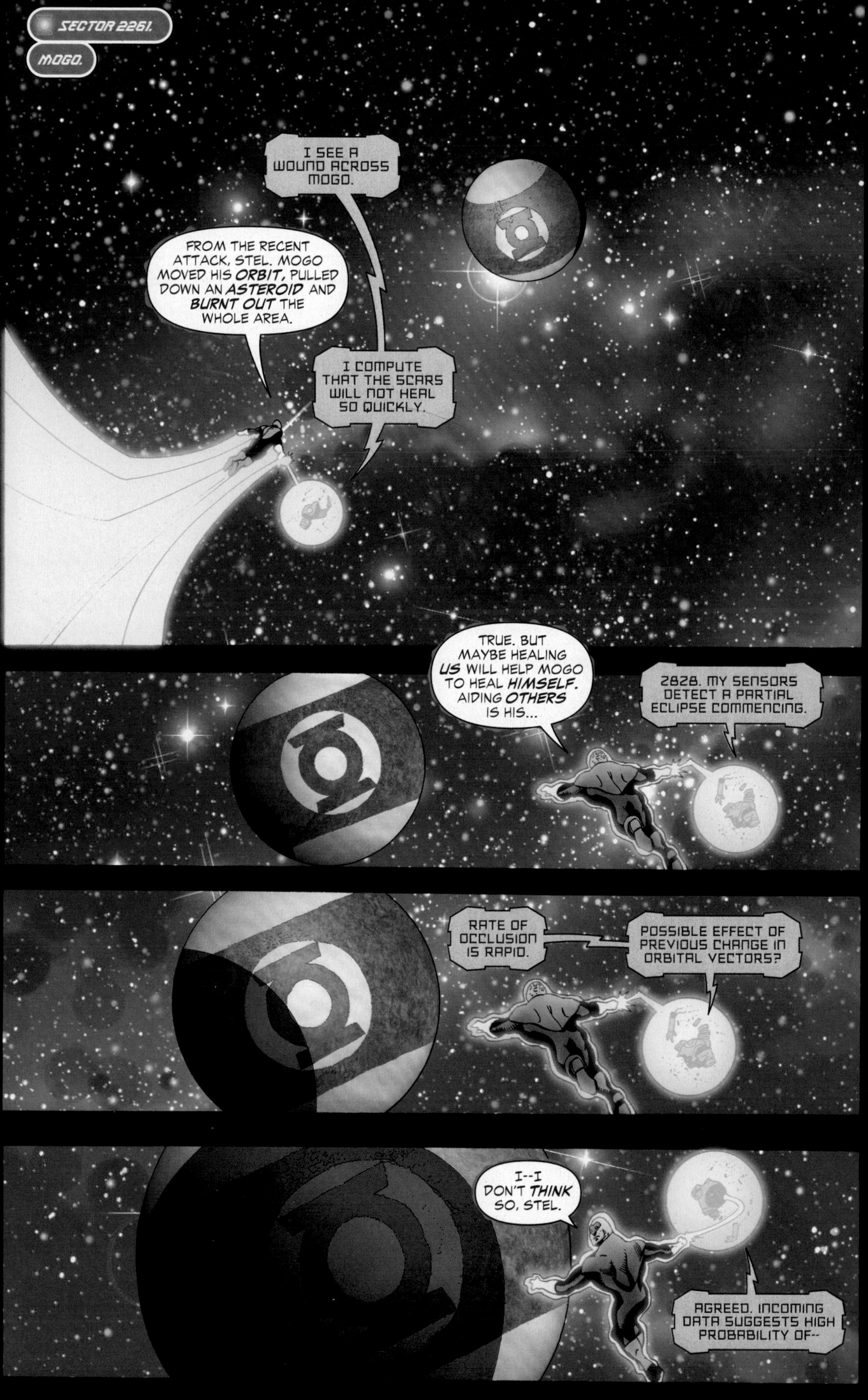
SECTOR 2261.
MOGO.
I SEE A WOUND ACROSS MOGO.
FROM THE RECENT ATTACK, STEL. MOGO MOVED HIS ORBIT, PULLED DOWN AN ASTEROID AND BURNT OUT THE WHOLE AREA.
I COMPUTE THAT THE SCARS WILL NOT HEAL SO QUICKLY.
TRUE. BUT MAYBE HEALING US WILL HELP MOGO TO HEAL HIMSELF. AIDING OTHERS IS HIS...
2828. MY SENSORS DETECT A PARTIAL ECLIPSE COMMENCING.
RATE OF OCCLUSION IS RAPID.
POSSIBLE EFFECT OF PREVIOUS CHANGE IN ORBITAL VECTORS?
I--I DON'T THINK SO, STEL.
AGREED. INCOMING DATA SUGGESTS HIGH PROBABILITY OF--

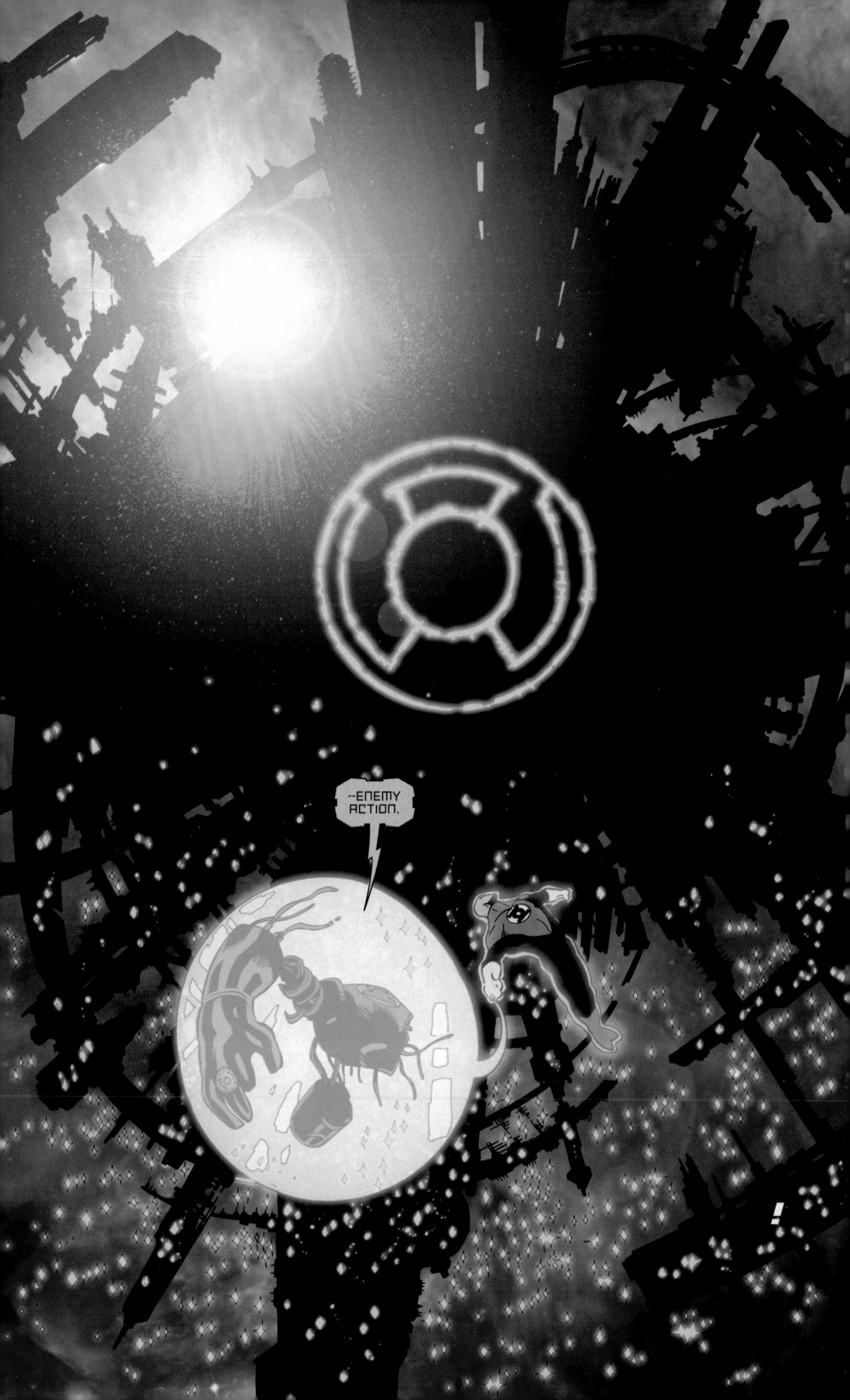
--ENEMY ACTION.
!

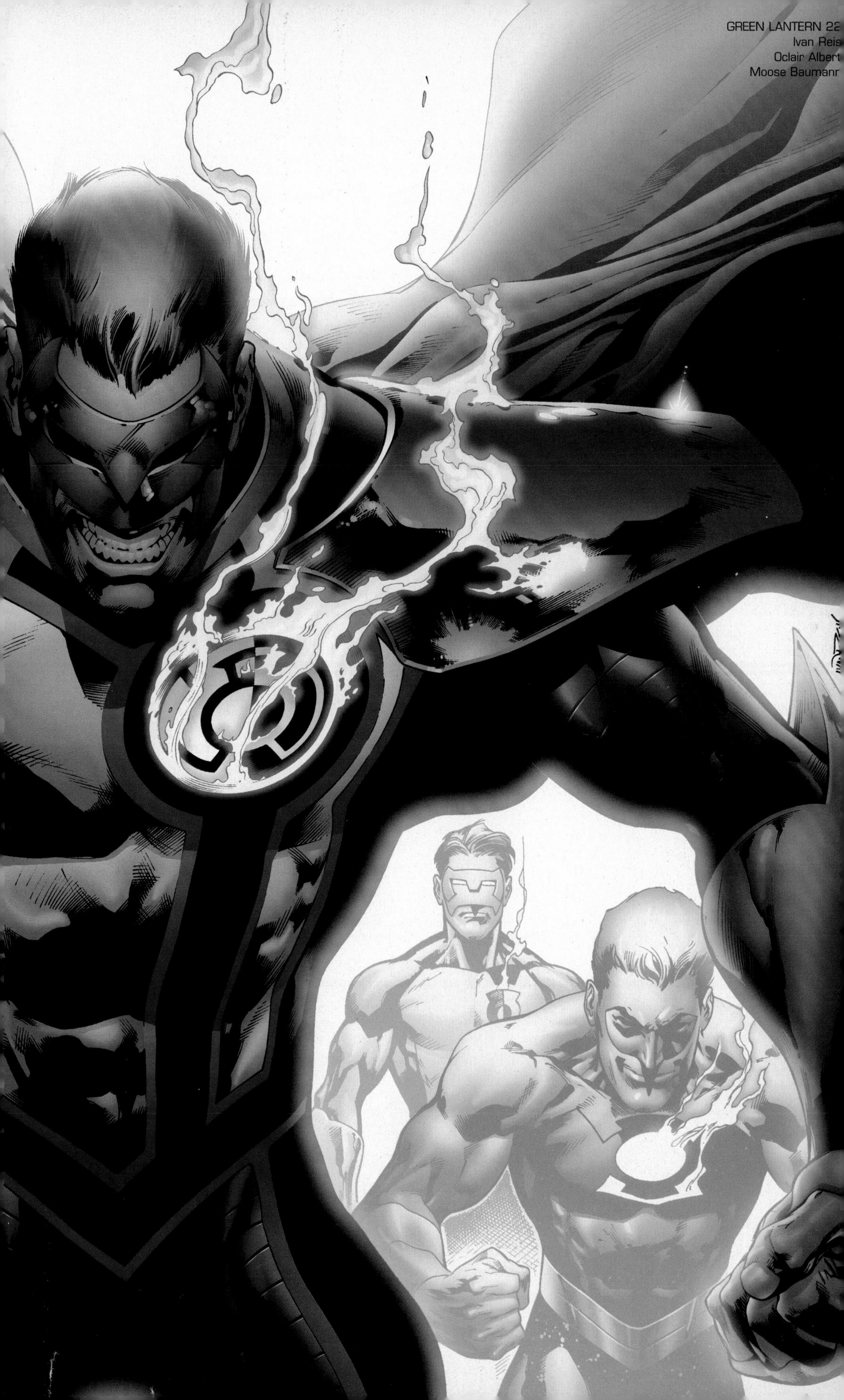

GREEN LANTERN 22
Ivan Reis
Oclair Albert
Moose Baumann

THE SINESTRO CORPS WAR
Chapter Three
RUNNING SCARED

Writer: **Geoff Johns**
Penciller: **Ivan Reis**
Inker: **Oclair Albert**
Colorist: **Moose Baumann**
Letterer: **Rob Leigh**

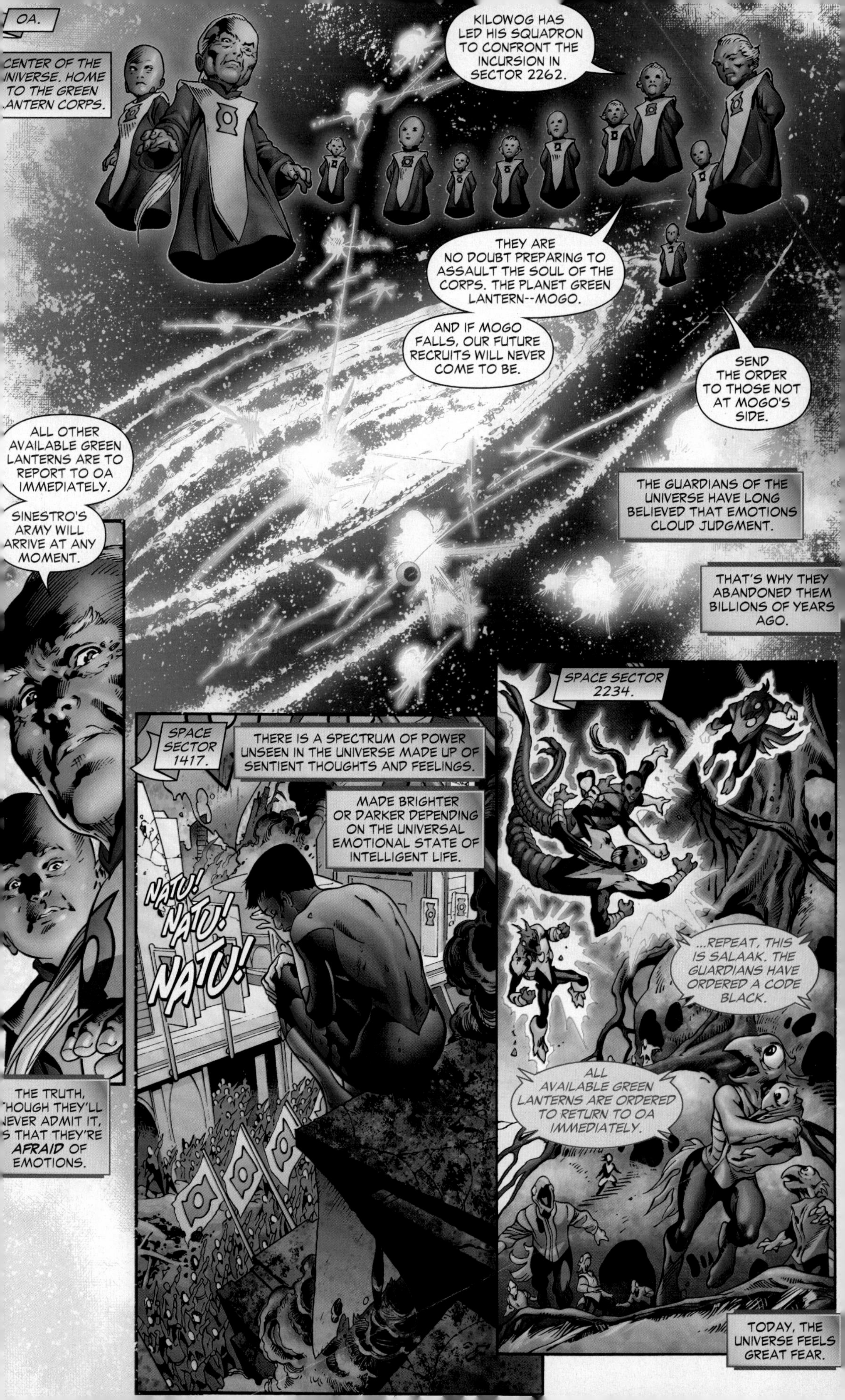
OA.
CENTER OF THE UNIVERSE. HOME TO THE GREEN LANTERN CORPS.
KILOWOG HAS LED HIS SQUADRON TO CONFRONT THE INCURSION IN SECTOR 2262.
THEY ARE NO DOUBT PREPARING TO ASSAULT THE SOUL OF THE CORPS. THE PLANET GREEN LANTERN--MOGO.
AND IF MOGO FALLS, OUR FUTURE RECRUITS WILL NEVER COME TO BE.
SEND THE ORDER TO THOSE NOT AT MOGO'S SIDE.
ALL OTHER AVAILABLE GREEN LANTERNS ARE TO REPORT TO OA IMMEDIATELY.
SINESTRO'S ARMY WILL ARRIVE AT ANY MOMENT.
THE GUARDIANS OF THE UNIVERSE HAVE LONG BELIEVED THAT EMOTIONS CLOUD JUDGMENT.
THAT'S WHY THEY ABANDONED THEM BILLIONS OF YEARS AGO.
THE TRUTH, THOUGH THEY'LL NEVER ADMIT IT, IS THAT THEY'RE *AFRAID* OF EMOTIONS.
SPACE SECTOR 1417.
THERE IS A SPECTRUM OF POWER UNSEEN IN THE UNIVERSE MADE UP OF SENTIENT THOUGHTS AND FEELINGS.
MADE BRIGHTER OR DARKER DEPENDING ON THE UNIVERSAL EMOTIONAL STATE OF INTELLIGENT LIFE.
NATU! NATU! NATU!
SPACE SECTOR 2234.
...REPEAT, THIS IS SALAAK. THE GUARDIANS HAVE ORDERED A CODE BLACK.
ALL AVAILABLE GREEN LANTERNS ARE ORDERED TO RETURN TO OA IMMEDIATELY.
TODAY, THE UNIVERSE FEELS GREAT FEAR.

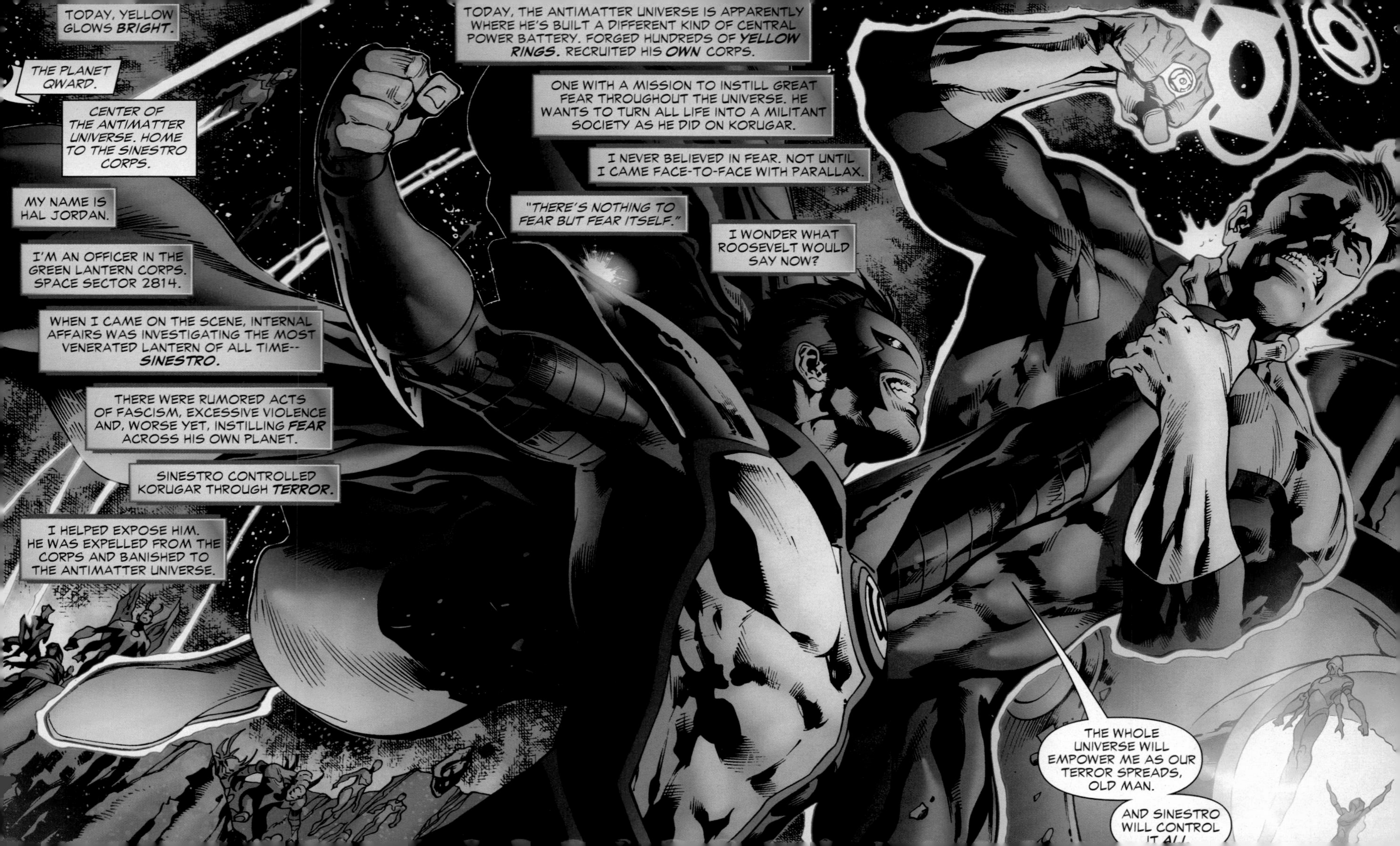
TODAY, YELLOW GLOWS **BRIGHT**.
THE PLANET QWARD.
CENTER OF THE ANTIMATTER UNIVERSE. HOME TO THE SINESTRO CORPS.
MY NAME IS HAL JORDAN.
I'M AN OFFICER IN THE GREEN LANTERN CORPS. SPACE SECTOR 2814.
WHEN I CAME ON THE SCENE, INTERNAL AFFAIRS WAS INVESTIGATING THE MOST VENERATED LANTERN OF ALL TIME-- **SINESTRO**.
THERE WERE RUMORED ACTS OF FASCISM, EXCESSIVE VIOLENCE AND, WORSE YET, INSTILLING **FEAR** ACROSS HIS OWN PLANET.
SINESTRO CONTROLLED KORUGAR THROUGH **TERROR**.
I HELPED EXPOSE HIM. HE WAS EXPELLED FROM THE CORPS AND BANISHED TO THE ANTIMATTER UNIVERSE.
TODAY, THE ANTIMATTER UNIVERSE IS APPARENTLY WHERE HE'S BUILT A DIFFERENT KIND OF CENTRAL POWER BATTERY. FORGED HUNDREDS OF ***YELLOW RINGS***. RECRUITED HIS ***OWN*** CORPS.
ONE WITH A MISSION TO INSTILL GREAT FEAR THROUGHOUT THE UNIVERSE. HE WANTS TO TURN ALL LIFE INTO A MILITANT SOCIETY AS HE DID ON KORUGAR.
I NEVER BELIEVED IN FEAR. NOT UNTIL I CAME FACE-TO-FACE WITH PARALLAX.
"THERE'S NOTHING TO FEAR BUT FEAR ITSELF."
I WONDER WHAT ROOSEVELT WOULD SAY NOW?
THE WHOLE UNIVERSE WILL EMPOWER ME AS OUR TERROR SPREADS, OLD MAN.
AND SINESTRO WILL CONTROL IT ***ALL***.

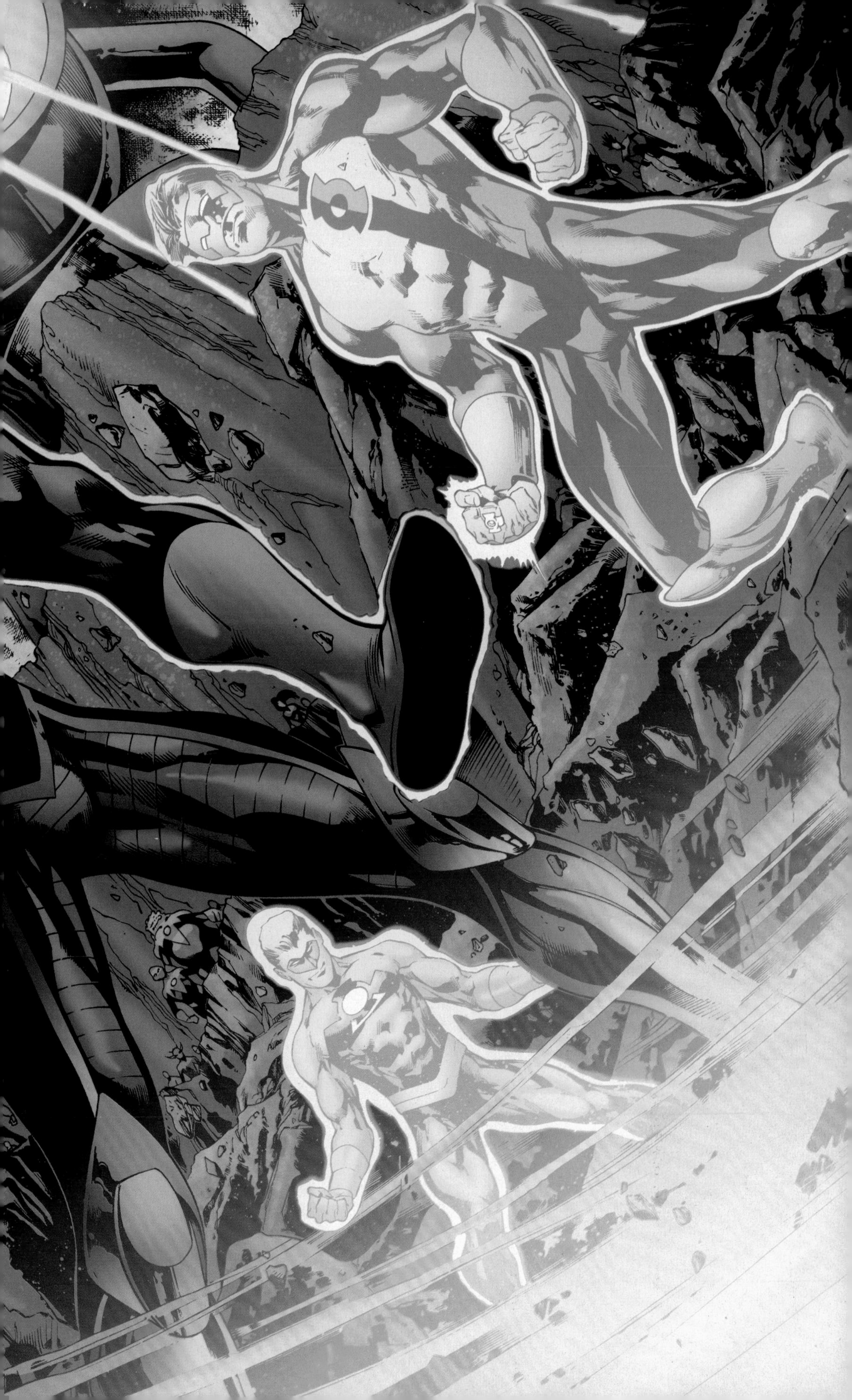

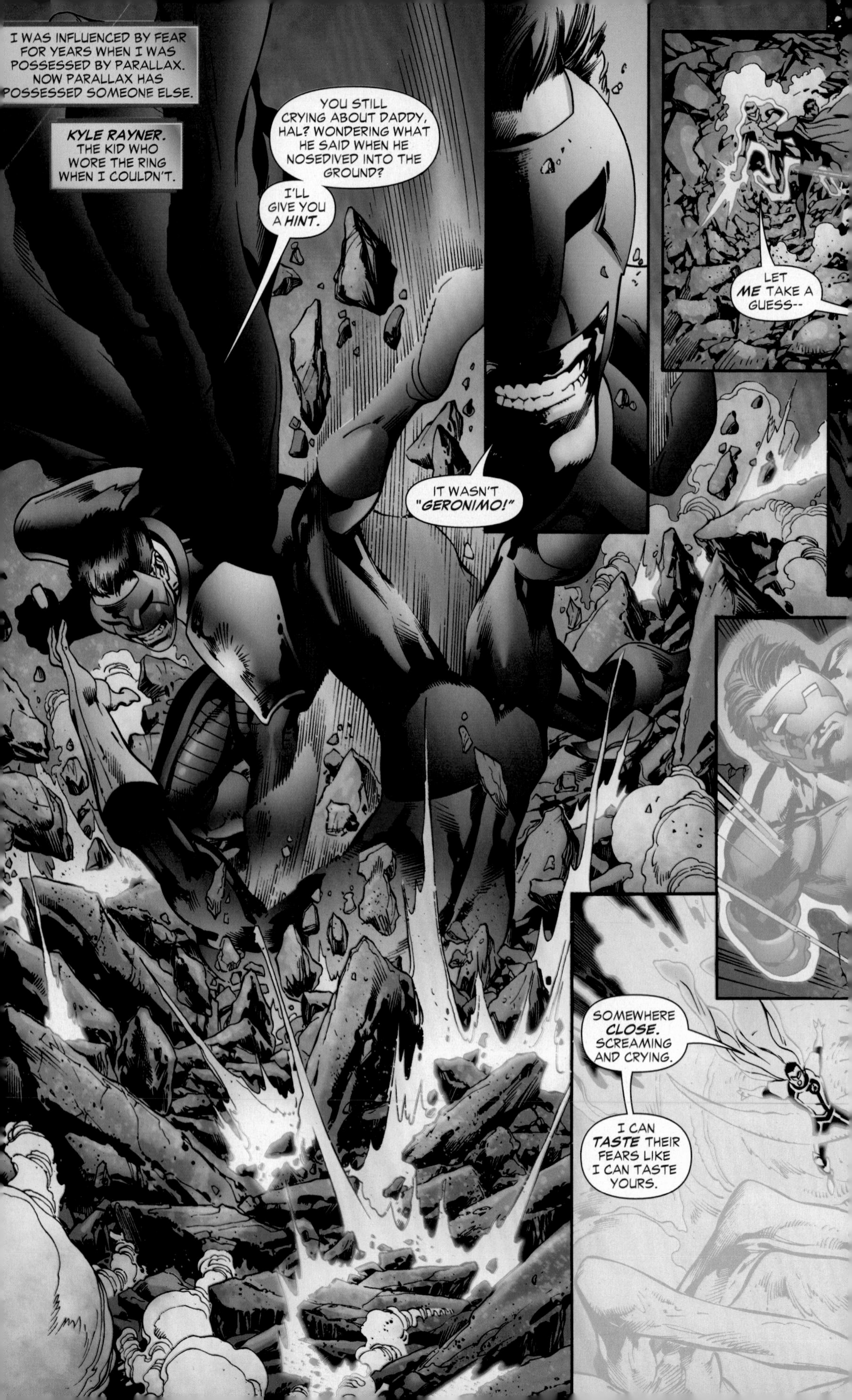
I WAS INFLUENCED BY FEAR FOR YEARS WHEN I WAS POSSESSED BY PARALLAX. NOW PARALLAX HAS POSSESSED SOMEONE ELSE.
KYLE RAYNER. THE KID WHO WORE THE RING WHEN I COULDN'T.
YOU STILL CRYING ABOUT DADDY, HAL? WONDERING WHAT HE SAID WHEN HE NOSEDIVED INTO THE GROUND?
I'LL GIVE YOU A HINT.
LET ME TAKE A GUESS--
IT WASN'T "GERONIMO!"
SOMEWHERE CLOSE. SCREAMING AND CRYING.
I CAN TASTE THEIR FEARS LIKE I CAN TASTE YOURS.

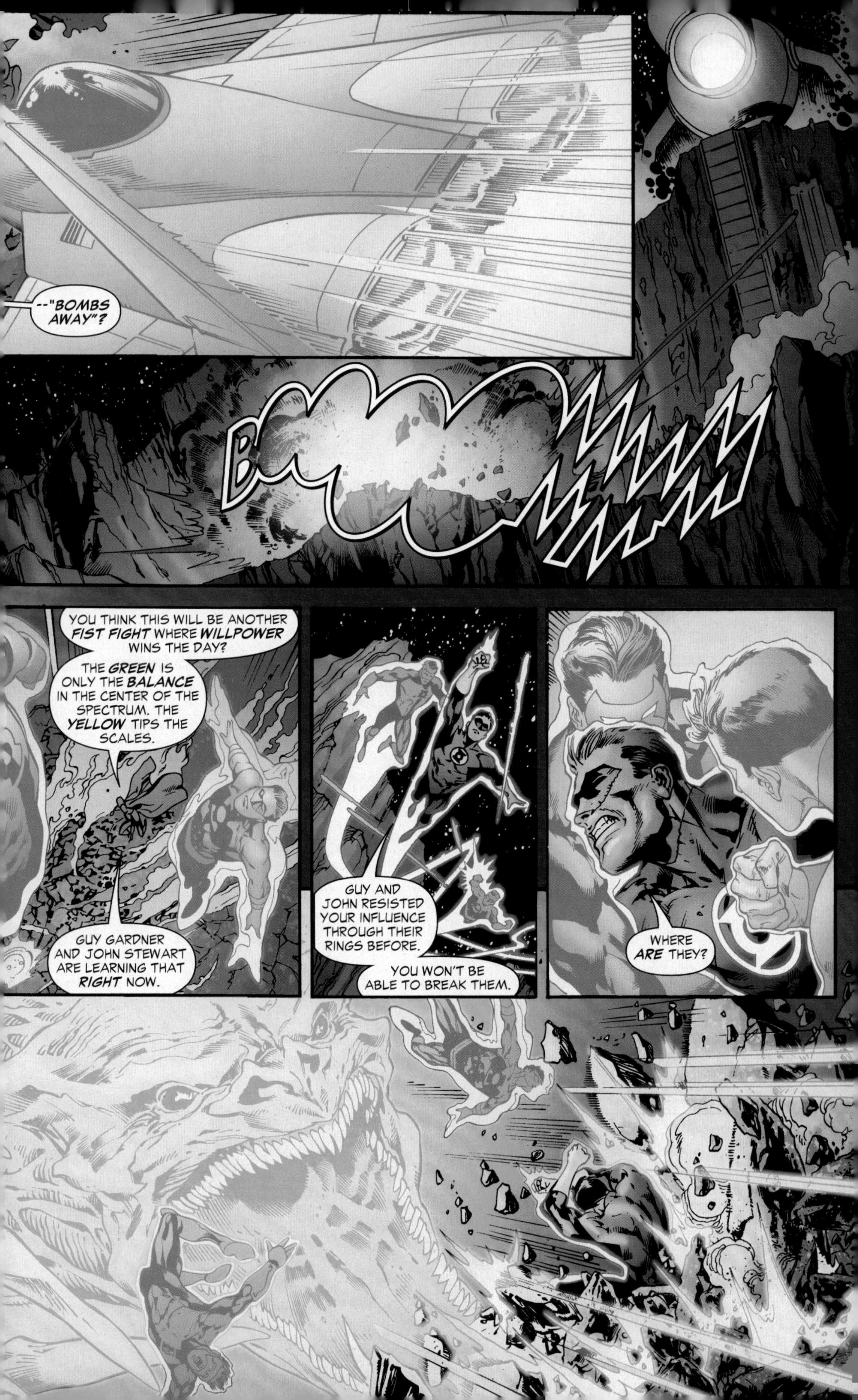
--"BOMBS AWAY"?
BOOOOM
YOU THINK THIS WILL BE ANOTHER FIST FIGHT WHERE WILLPOWER WINS THE DAY?
THE GREEN IS ONLY THE BALANCE IN THE CENTER OF THE SPECTRUM. THE YELLOW TIPS THE SCALES.
GUY GARDNER AND JOHN STEWART ARE LEARNING THAT RIGHT NOW.
GUY AND JOHN RESISTED YOUR INFLUENCE THROUGH THEIR RINGS BEFORE.
YOU WON'T BE ABLE TO BREAK THEM.
WHERE ARE THEY?

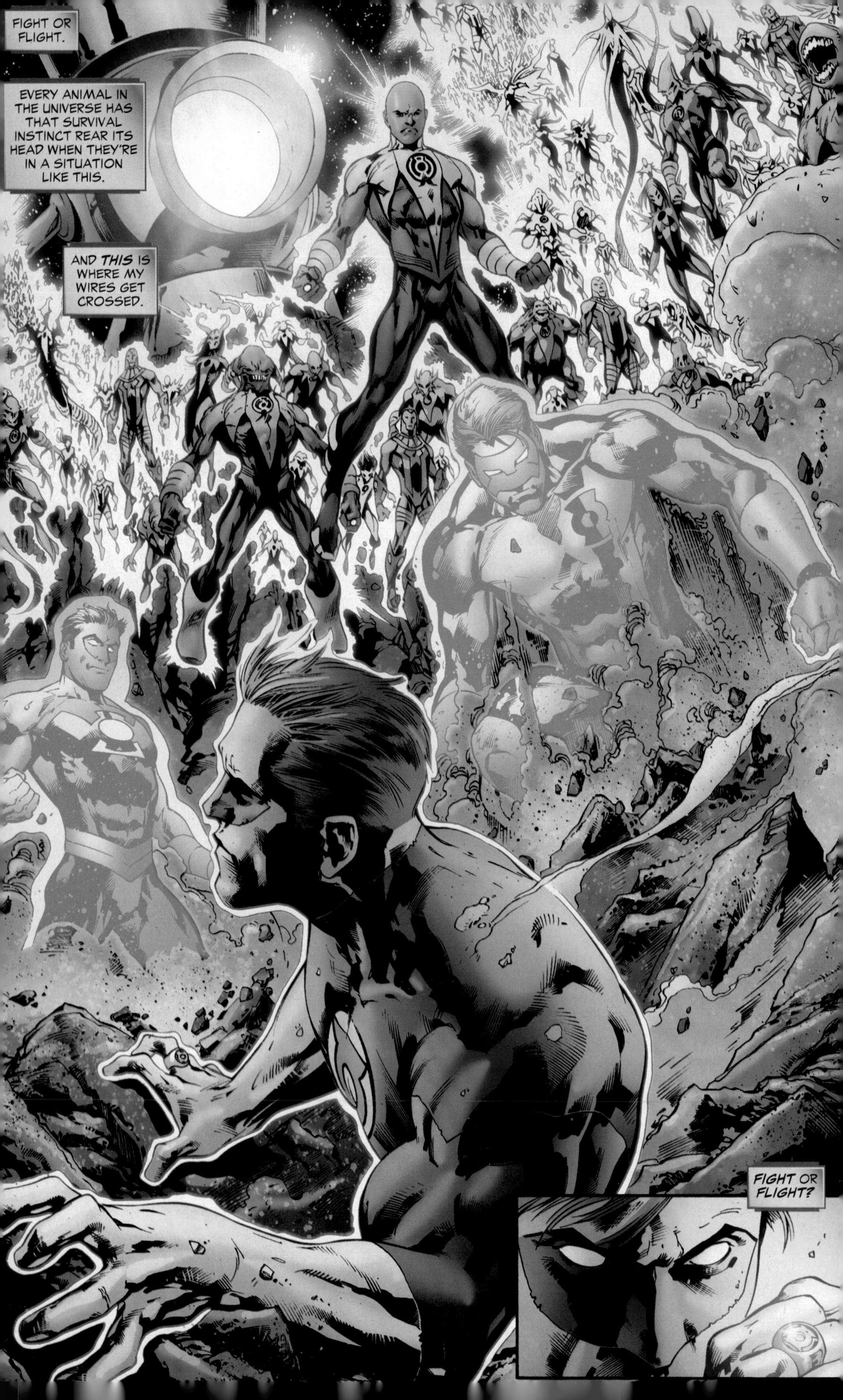
FIGHT OR FLIGHT.
EVERY ANIMAL IN THE UNIVERSE HAS THAT SURVIVAL INSTINCT REAR ITS HEAD WHEN THEY'RE IN A SITUATION LIKE THIS.
AND *THIS* IS WHERE MY WIRES GET CROSSED.
FIGHT OR FLIGHT?

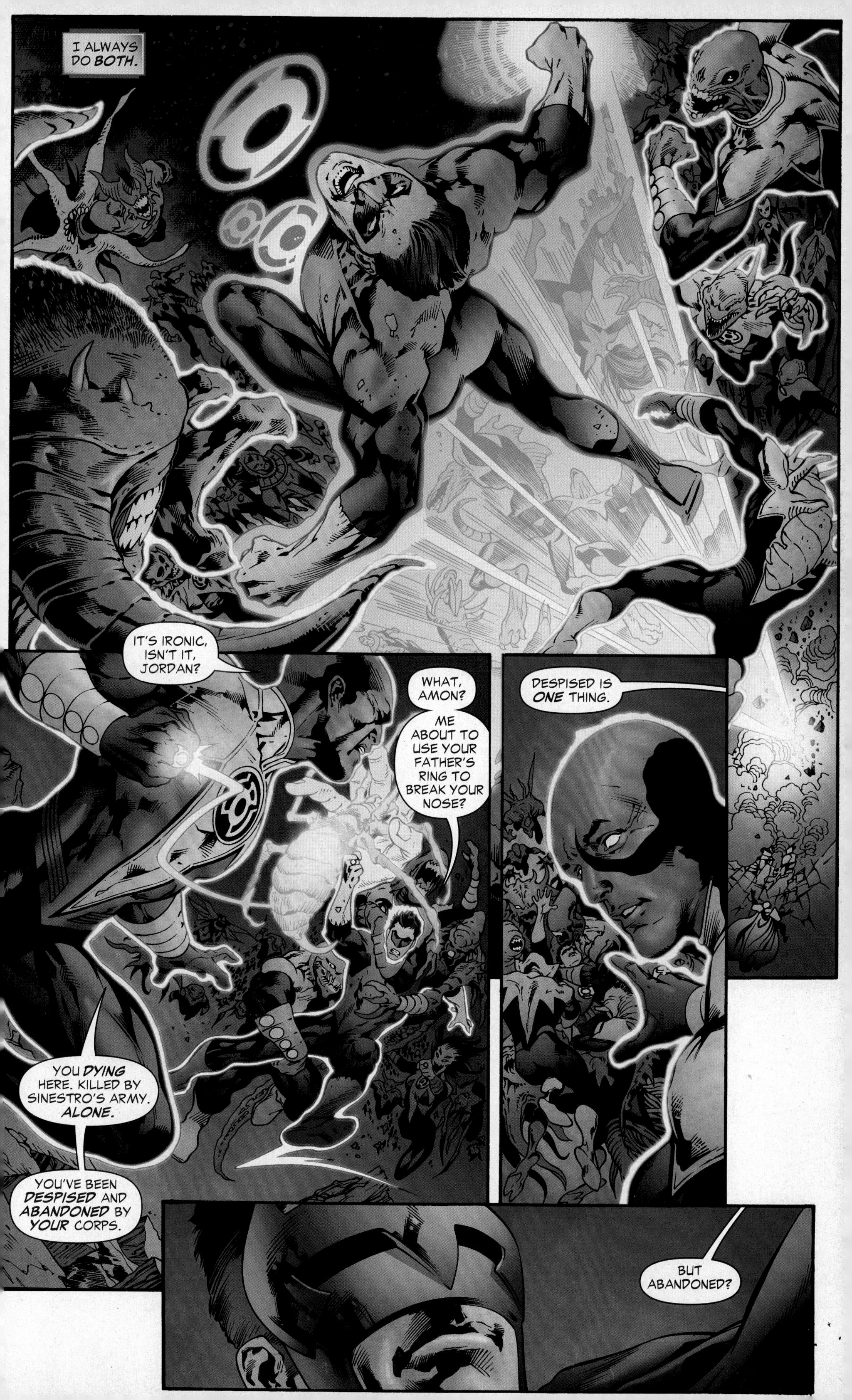
I ALWAYS DO BOTH.
IT'S IRONIC, ISN'T IT, JORDAN?
WHAT, AMON?
ME ABOUT TO USE YOUR FATHER'S RING TO BREAK YOUR NOSE?
YOU DYING HERE. KILLED BY SINESTRO'S ARMY. ALONE.
YOU'VE BEEN DESPISED AND ABANDONED BY YOUR CORPS.
DESPISED IS ONE THING.
BUT ABANDONED?

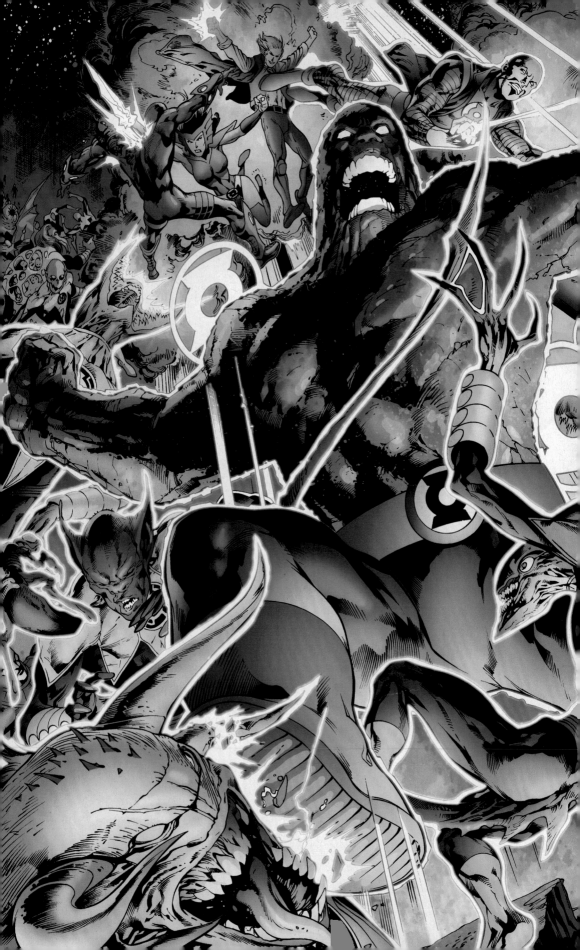

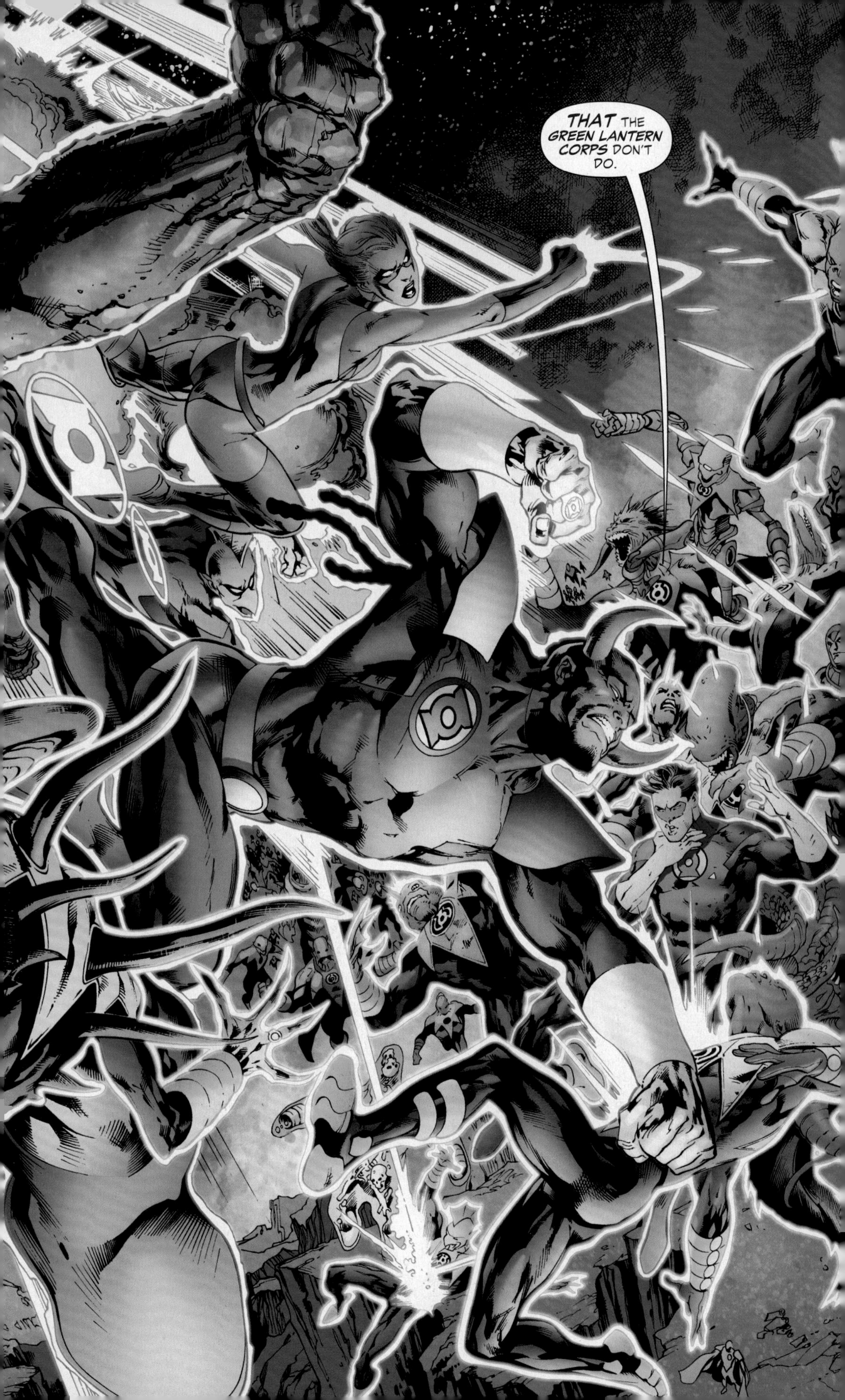
THAT THE GREEN LANTERN CORPS DON'T DO.

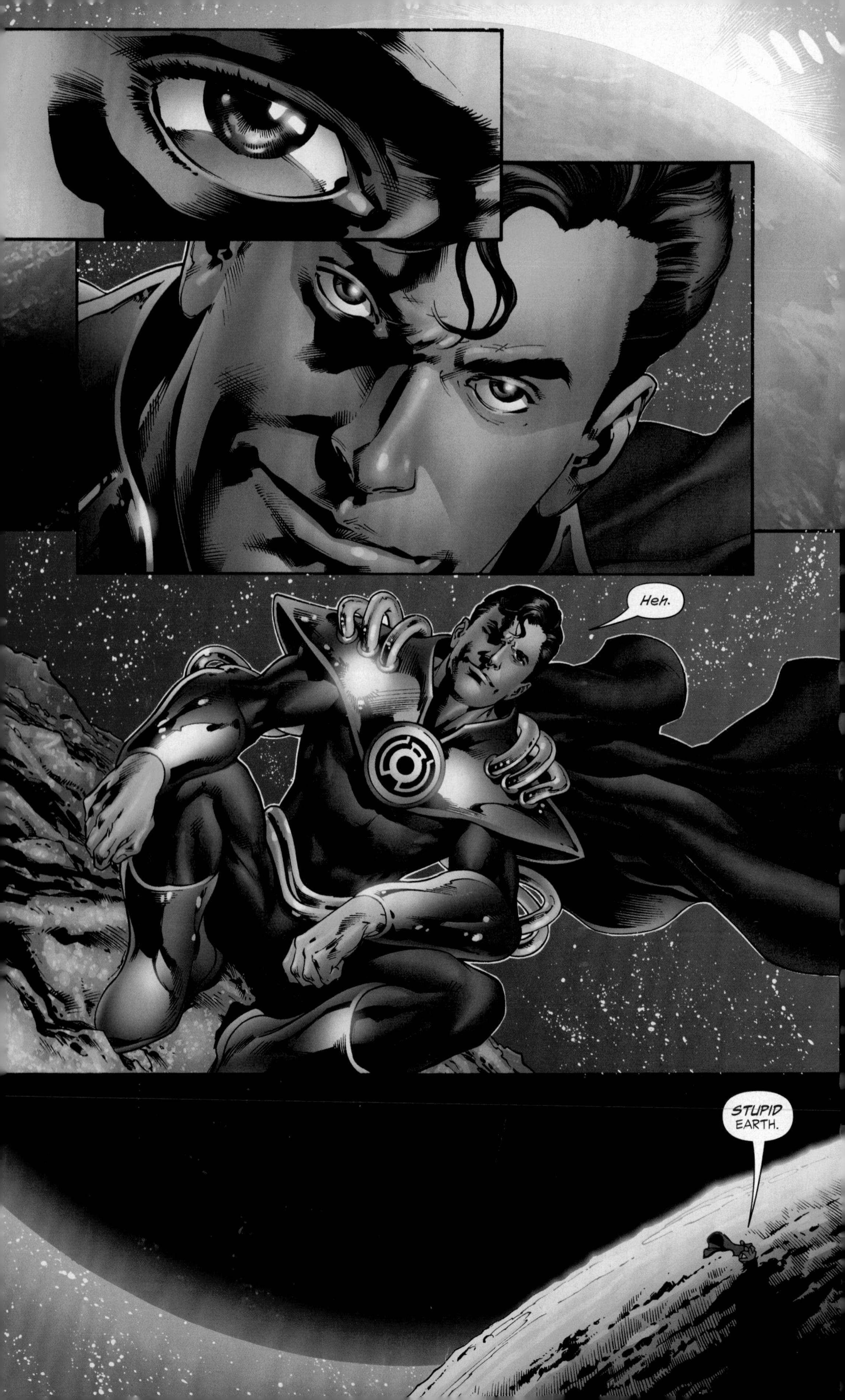
Heh.
STUPID EARTH.

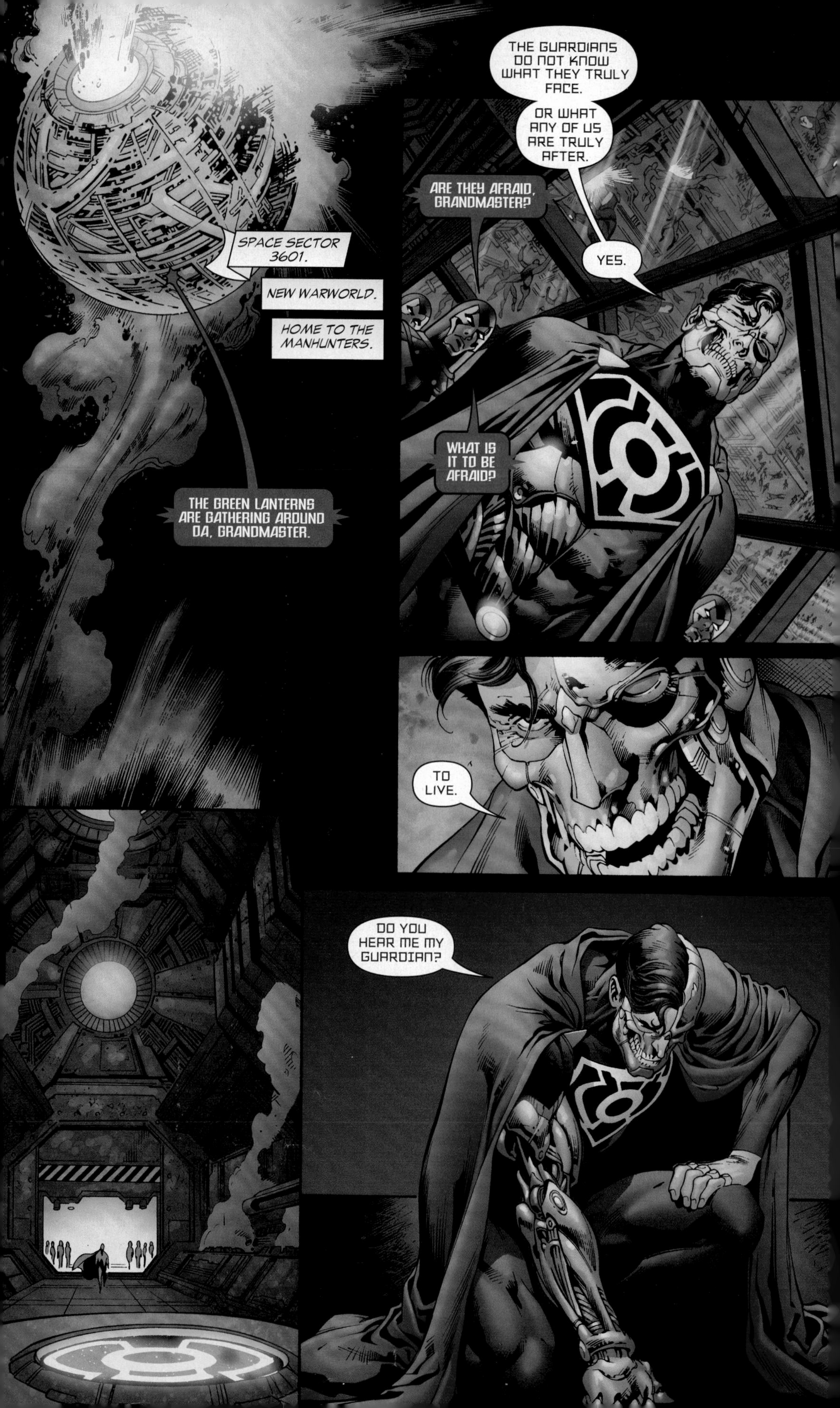

SPACE SECTOR 3601.
NEW WARWORLD.
HOME TO THE MANHUNTERS.
THE GREEN LANTERNS ARE GATHERING AROUND OA, GRANDMASTER.
THE GUARDIANS DO NOT KNOW WHAT THEY TRULY FACE.
OR WHAT ANY OF US ARE TRULY AFTER.
ARE THEY AFRAID, GRANDMASTER?
YES.
WHAT IS IT TO BE AFRAID?
TO LIVE.
DO YOU HEAR ME MY GUARDIAN?

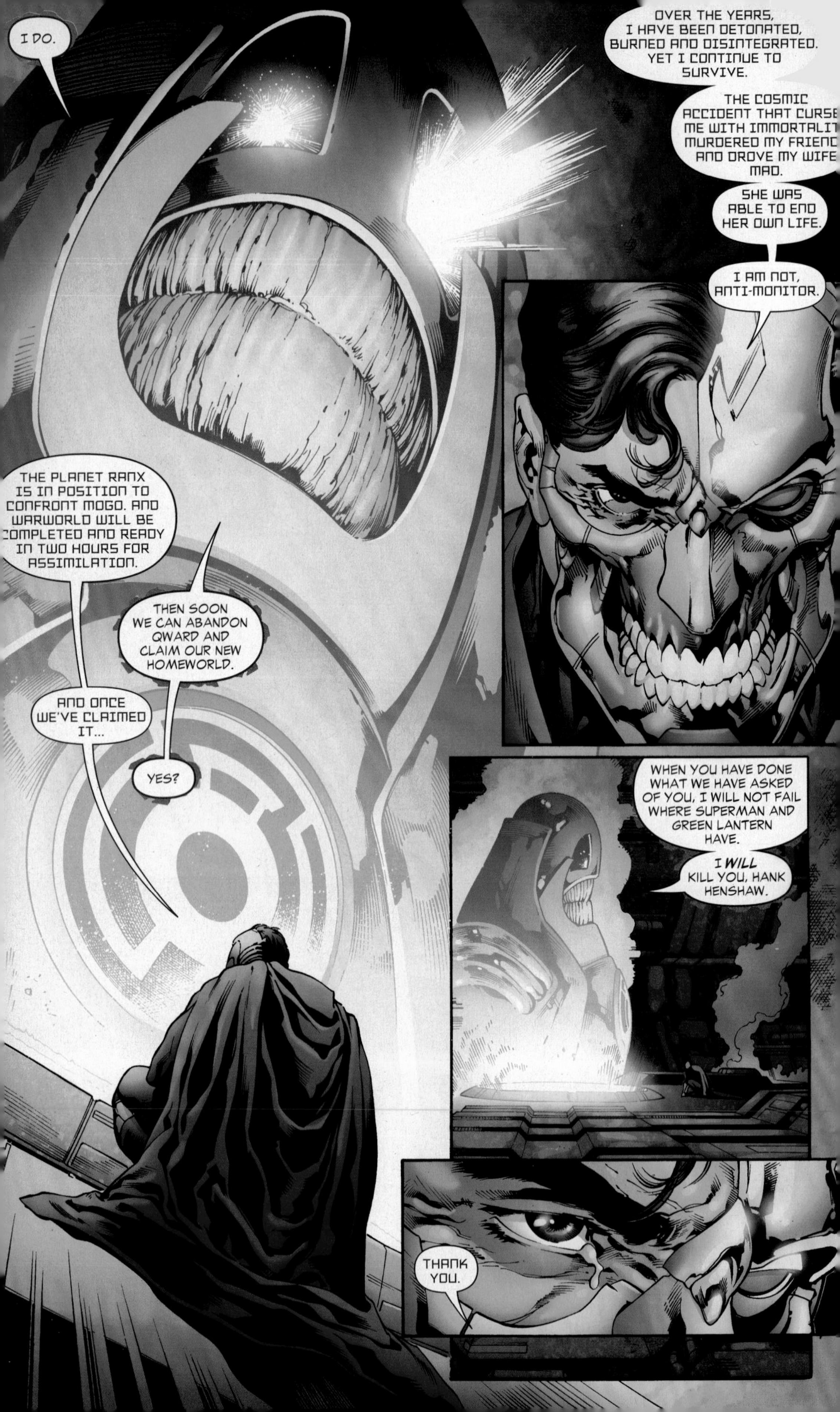
I DO.
OVER THE YEARS, I HAVE BEEN DETONATED, BURNED AND DISINTEGRATED. YET I CONTINUE TO SURVIVE.
THE COSMIC ACCIDENT THAT CURSE ME WITH IMMORTALIT MURDERED MY FRIEND AND DROVE MY WIFE MAD.
SHE WAS ABLE TO END HER OWN LIFE.
I AM NOT, ANTI-MONITOR.
THE PLANET RANX IS IN POSITION TO CONFRONT MOGO. AND WARWORLD WILL BE COMPLETED AND READY IN TWO HOURS FOR ASSIMILATION.
THEN SOON WE CAN ABANDON QWARD AND CLAIM OUR NEW HOMEWORLD.
AND ONCE WE'VE CLAIMED IT...
YES?
WHEN YOU HAVE DONE WHAT WE HAVE ASKED OF YOU, I WILL NOT FAIL WHERE SUPERMAN AND GREEN LANTERN HAVE.
I WILL KILL YOU, HANK HENSHAW.
THANK YOU.

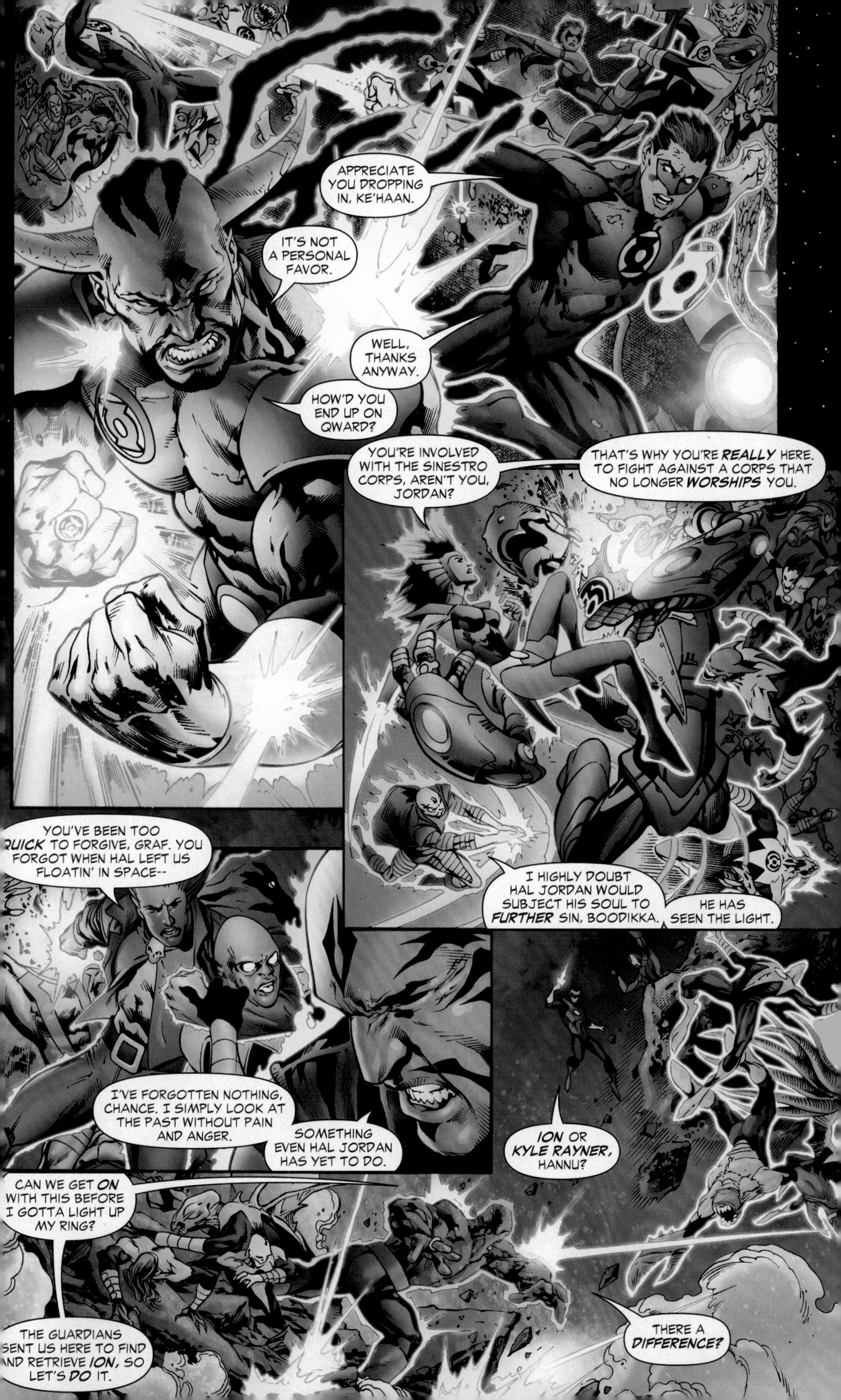
APPRECIATE YOU DROPPING IN, KE'HAAN.
IT'S NOT A PERSONAL FAVOR.
WELL, THANKS ANYWAY.
HOW'D YOU END UP ON QWARD?
YOU'RE INVOLVED WITH THE SINESTRO CORPS, AREN'T YOU, JORDAN?
THAT'S WHY YOU'RE REALLY HERE. TO FIGHT AGAINST A CORPS THAT NO LONGER WORSHIPS YOU.
I HIGHLY DOUBT HAL JORDAN WOULD SUBJECT HIS SOUL TO FURTHER SIN, BOODIKKA.
HE HAS SEEN THE LIGHT.
YOU'VE BEEN TOO QUICK TO FORGIVE, GRAF. YOU FORGOT WHEN HAL LEFT US FLOATIN' IN SPACE--
I'VE FORGOTTEN NOTHING, CHANCE. I SIMPLY LOOK AT THE PAST WITHOUT PAIN AND ANGER.
SOMETHING EVEN HAL JORDAN HAS YET TO DO.
ION OR KYLE RAYNER, HANNU?
CAN WE GET ON WITH THIS BEFORE I GOTTA LIGHT UP MY RING?
THE GUARDIANS SENT US HERE TO FIND AND RETRIEVE ION, SO LET'S DO IT.
THERE A DIFFERENCE?

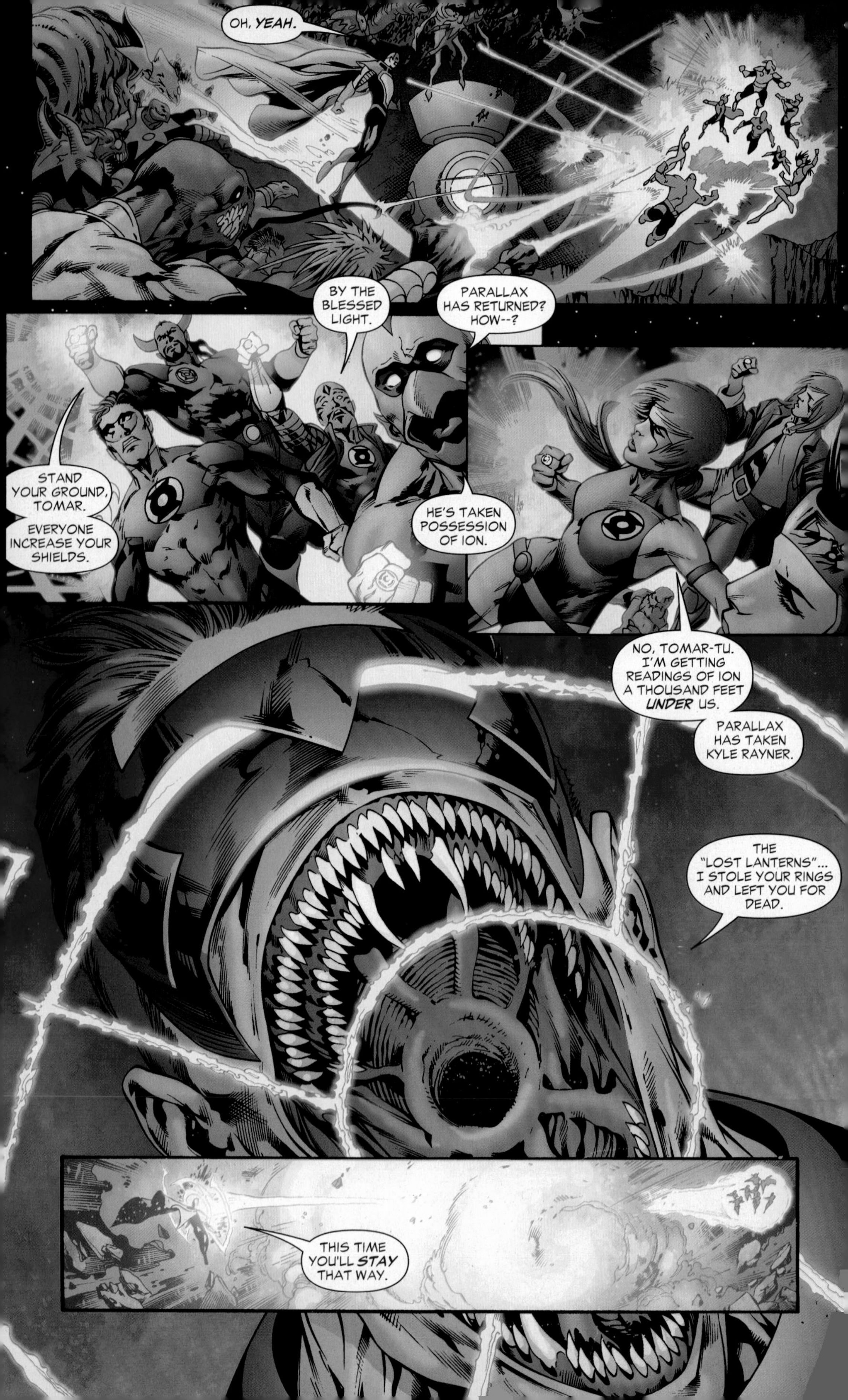

OH, YEAH.
BY THE BLESSED LIGHT.
PARALLAX HAS RETURNED? HOW--?
STAND YOUR GROUND, TOMAR.
EVERYONE INCREASE YOUR SHIELDS.
HE'S TAKEN POSSESSION OF ION.
NO, TOMAR-TU. I'M GETTING READINGS OF ION A THOUSAND FEET UNDER US.
PARALLAX HAS TAKEN KYLE RAYNER.
THE "LOST LANTERNS"... I STOLE YOUR RINGS AND LEFT YOU FOR DEAD.
THIS TIME YOU'LL STAY THAT WAY.

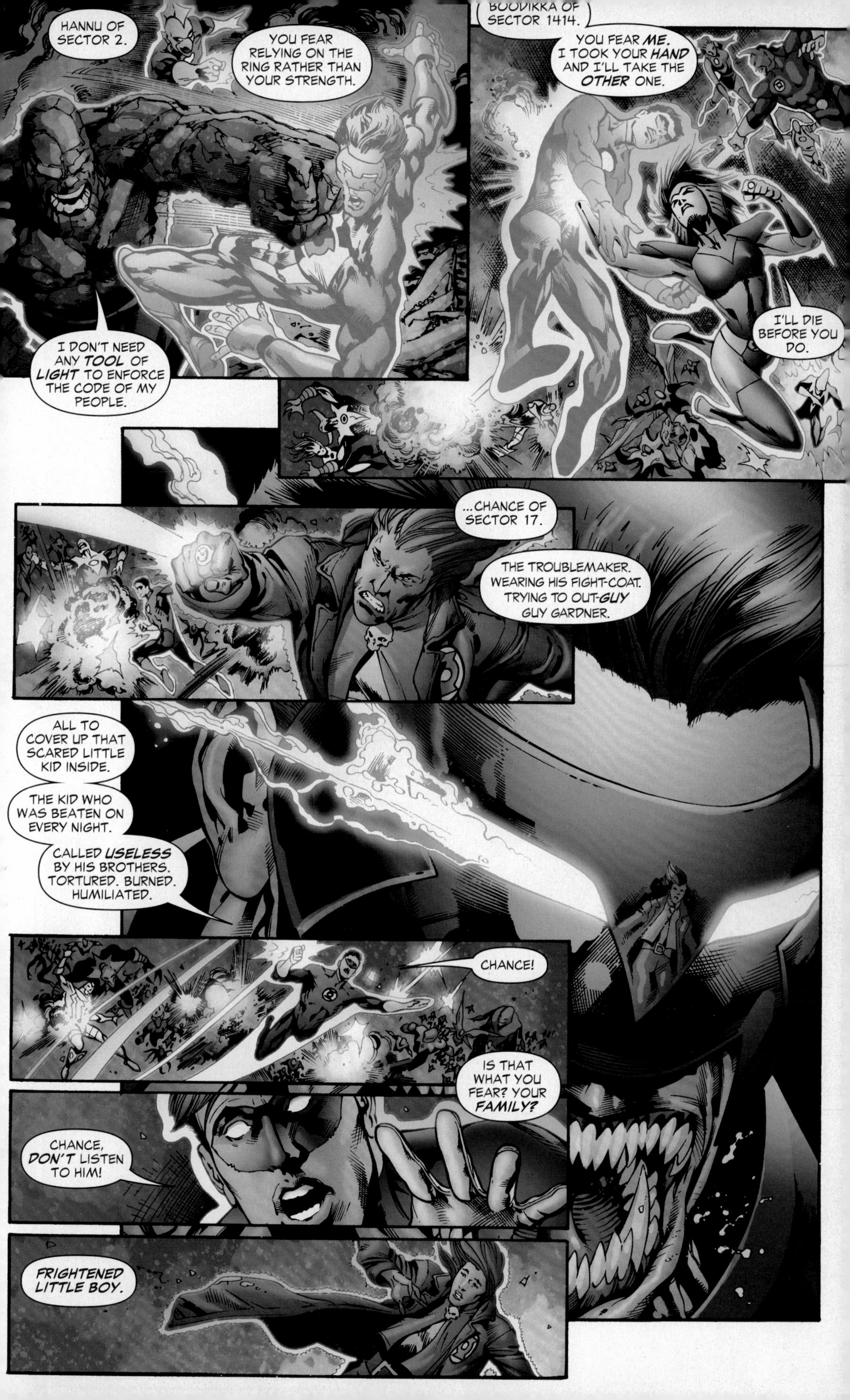
HANNU OF SECTOR 2.
YOU FEAR RELYING ON THE RING RATHER THAN YOUR STRENGTH.
I DON'T NEED ANY TOOL OF LIGHT TO ENFORCE THE CODE OF MY PEOPLE.
BOODIKKA OF SECTOR 1414.
YOU FEAR ME. I TOOK YOUR HAND AND I'LL TAKE THE OTHER ONE.
I'LL DIE BEFORE YOU DO.
...CHANCE OF SECTOR 17.
THE TROUBLEMAKER. WEARING HIS FIGHT-COAT. TRYING TO OUT-GUY GUY GARDNER.
ALL TO COVER UP THAT SCARED LITTLE KID INSIDE.
THE KID WHO WAS BEATEN ON EVERY NIGHT.
CALLED USELESS BY HIS BROTHERS. TORTURED. BURNED. HUMILIATED.
CHANCE!
IS THAT WHAT YOU FEAR? YOUR FAMILY?
CHANCE, DON'T LISTEN TO HIM!
FRIGHTENED LITTLE BOY.

VZZP

VZZP

VZZP

VZZP

VZZP

AARRGHH!

RING STATUS REPORT. GREEN LANTERN 17 DECEASED.

SPACE SECTOR SCAN 17 INITIATED FOR REPLACEMENT--

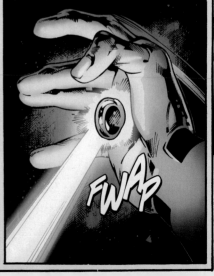

FWAP

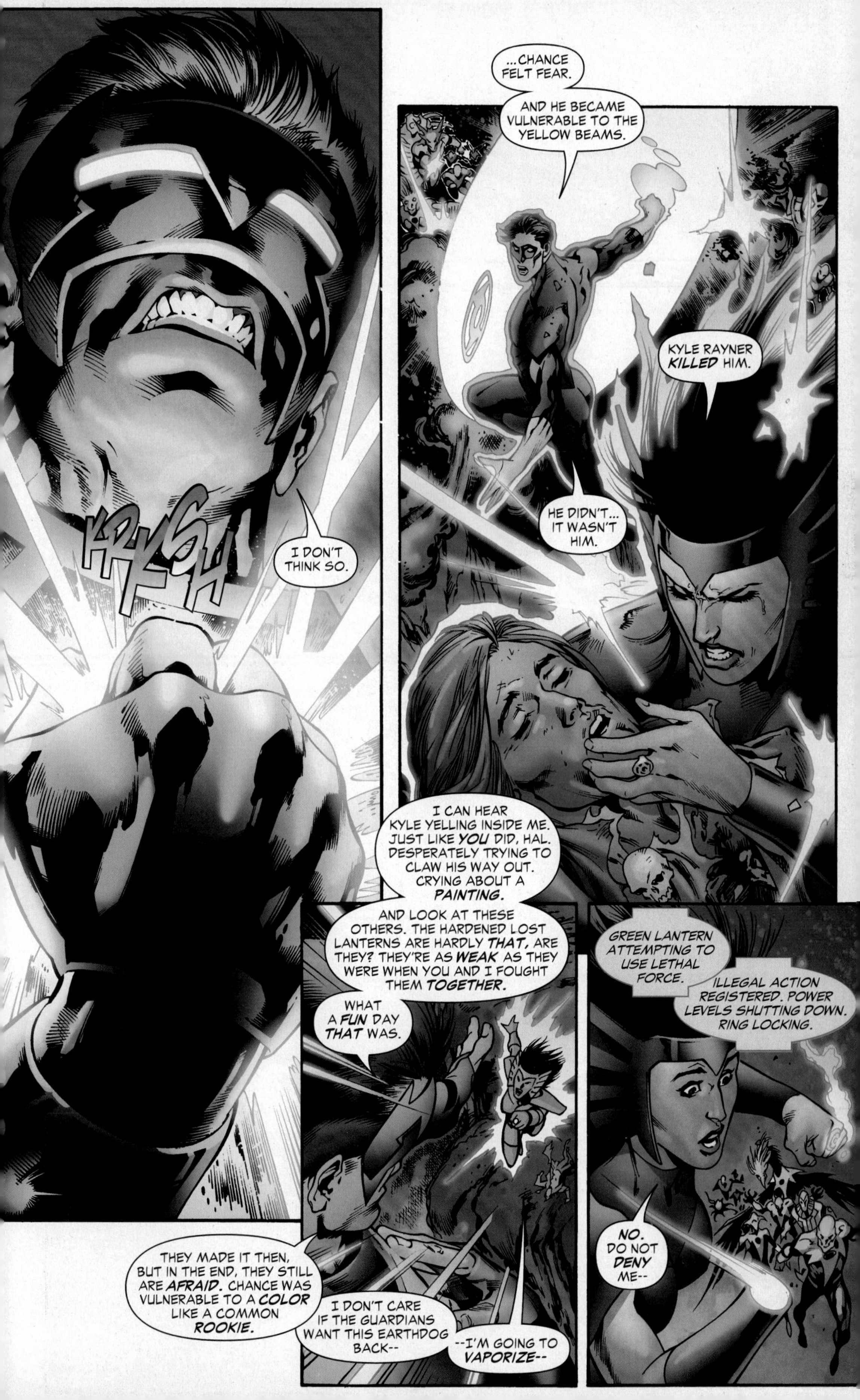
KRKSH
I DON'T THINK SO.
...CHANCE FELT FEAR.
AND HE BECAME VULNERABLE TO THE YELLOW BEAMS.
KYLE RAYNER KILLED HIM.
HE DIDN'T... IT WASN'T HIM.
I CAN HEAR KYLE YELLING INSIDE ME. JUST LIKE YOU DID, HAL. DESPERATELY TRYING TO CLAW HIS WAY OUT. CRYING ABOUT A PAINTING.
AND LOOK AT THESE OTHERS. THE HARDENED LOST LANTERNS ARE HARDLY THAT, ARE THEY? THEY'RE AS WEAK AS THEY WERE WHEN YOU AND I FOUGHT THEM TOGETHER.
WHAT A FUN DAY THAT WAS.
THEY MADE IT THEN, BUT IN THE END, THEY STILL ARE AFRAID. CHANCE WAS VULNERABLE TO A COLOR LIKE A COMMON ROOKIE.
I DON'T CARE IF THE GUARDIANS WANT THIS EARTHDOG BACK--
--I'M GOING TO VAPORIZE--
GREEN LANTERN ATTEMPTING TO USE LETHAL FORCE.
ILLEGAL ACTION REGISTERED. POWER LEVELS SHUTTING DOWN. RING LOCKING.
NO. DO NOT DENY ME--

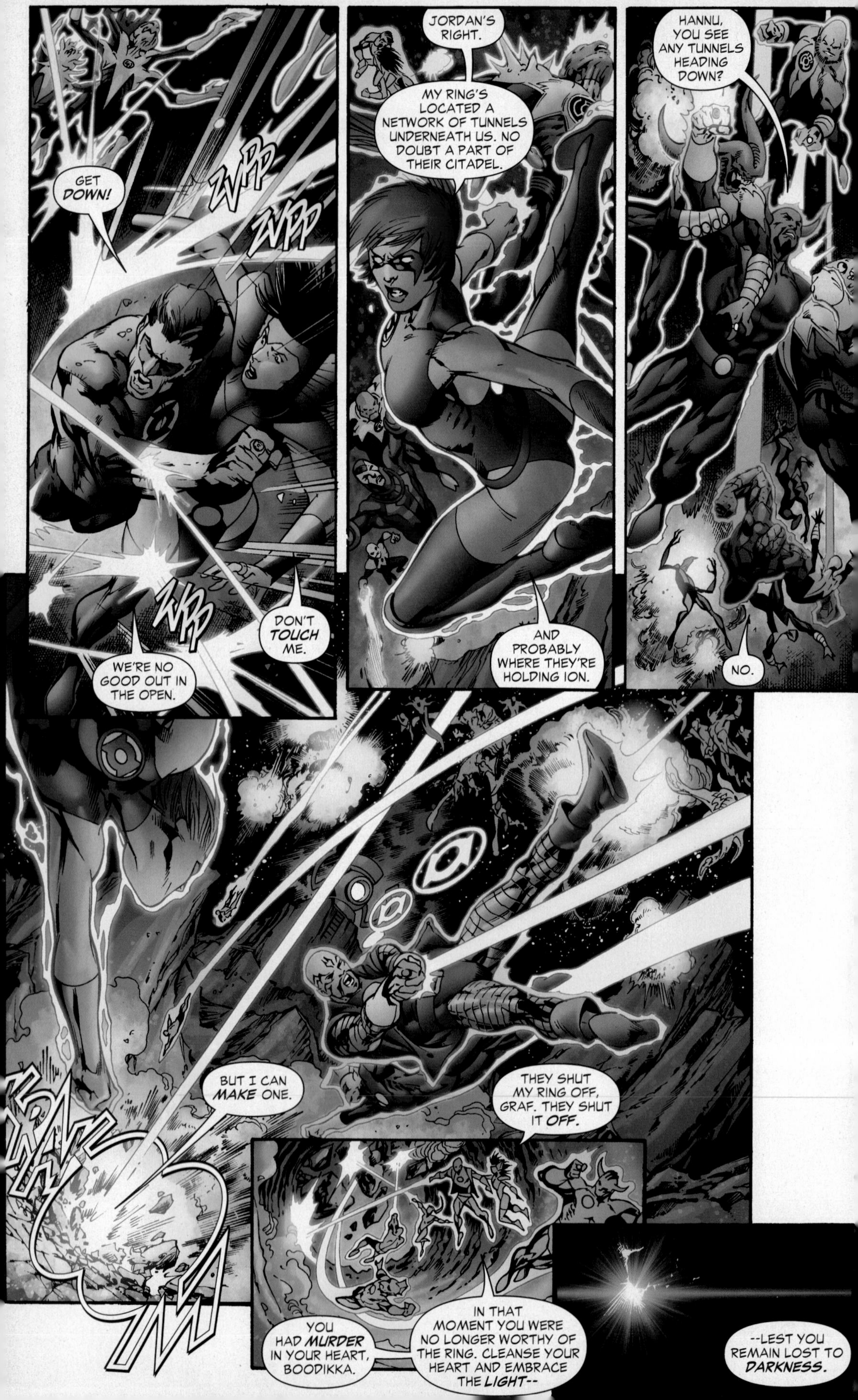
GET DOWN!
ZVPP
ZVPP
ZKPP
WE'RE NO GOOD OUT IN THE OPEN.
DON'T TOUCH ME.
JORDAN'S RIGHT.
MY RING'S LOCATED A NETWORK OF TUNNELS UNDERNEATH US. NO DOUBT A PART OF THEIR CITADEL.
AND PROBABLY WHERE THEY'RE HOLDING ION.
HANNU, YOU SEE ANY TUNNELS HEADING DOWN?
NO.
BUT I CAN MAKE ONE.
THEY SHUT MY RING OFF, GRAF. THEY SHUT IT OFF.
YOU HAD MURDER IN YOUR HEART, BOODIKKA.
IN THAT MOMENT YOU WERE NO LONGER WORTHY OF THE RING. CLEANSE YOUR HEART AND EMBRACE THE LIGHT--
--LEST YOU REMAIN LOST TO DARKNESS.

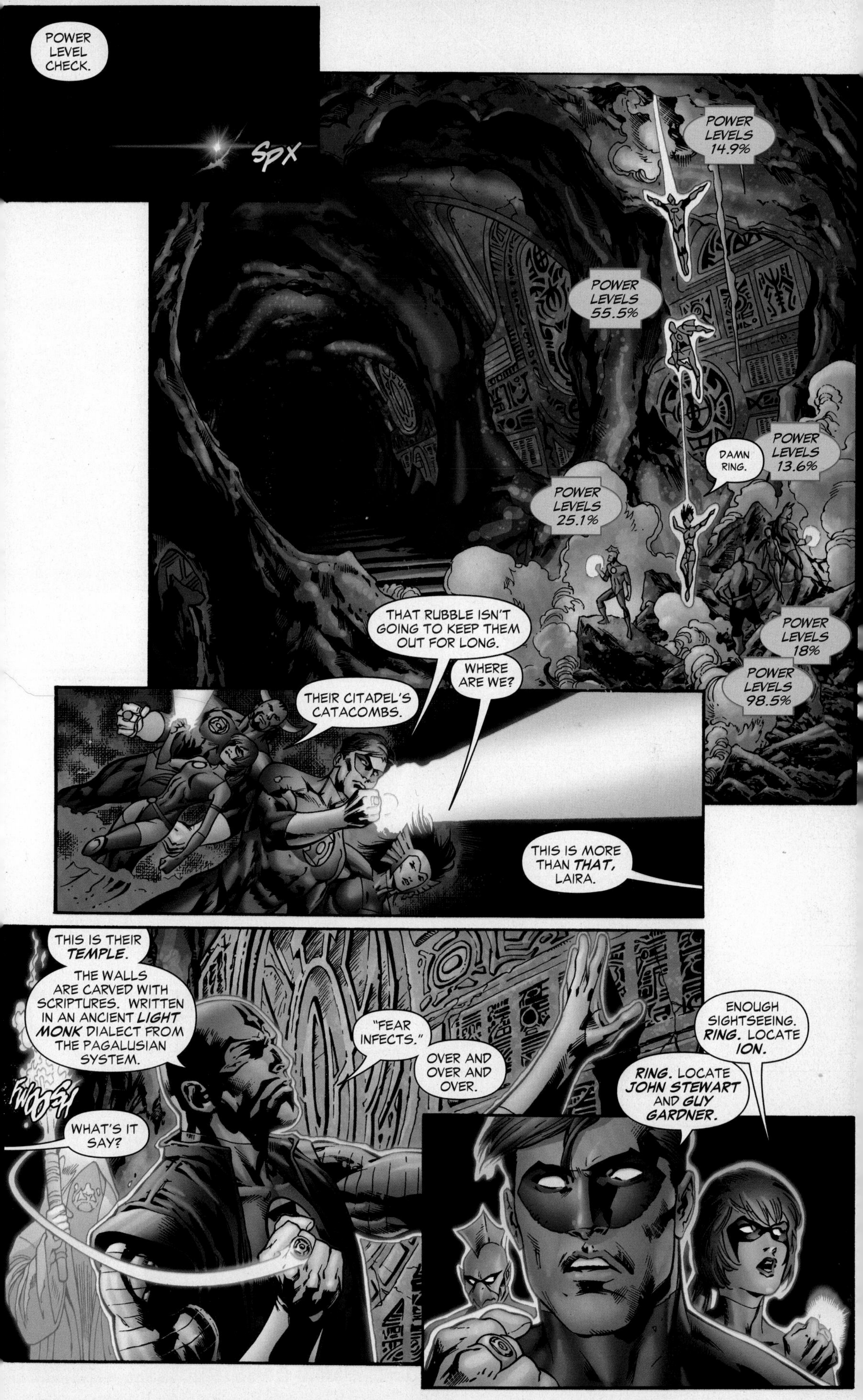
POWER LEVEL CHECK.
SPX
POWER LEVELS 14.9%
POWER LEVELS 55.5%
DAMN RING.
POWER LEVELS 13.6%
POWER LEVELS 25.1%
THAT RUBBLE ISN'T GOING TO KEEP THEM OUT FOR LONG.
POWER LEVELS 18%
POWER LEVELS 98.5%
WHERE ARE WE?
THEIR CITADEL'S CATACOMBS.
THIS IS MORE THAN THAT, LAIRA.
THIS IS THEIR TEMPLE.
THE WALLS ARE CARVED WITH SCRIPTURES. WRITTEN IN AN ANCIENT LIGHT MONK DIALECT FROM THE PAGALUSIAN SYSTEM.
FWOOSH
WHAT'S IT SAY?
"FEAR INFECTS."
OVER AND OVER AND OVER.
ENOUGH SIGHTSEEING. RING. LOCATE ION.
RING. LOCATE JOHN STEWART AND GUY GARDNER.

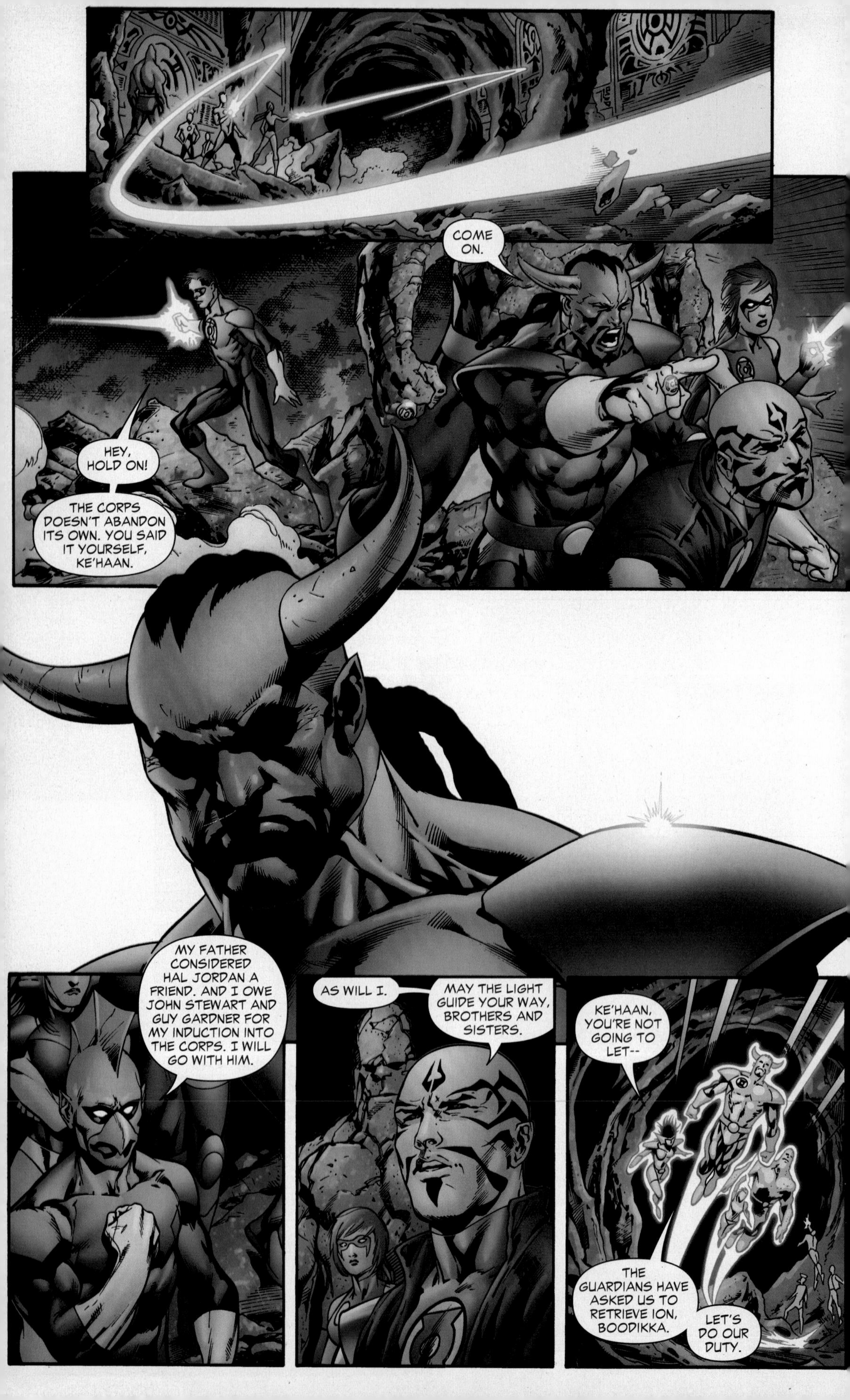
COME ON.
HEY, HOLD ON!
THE CORPS DOESN'T ABANDON ITS OWN. YOU SAID IT YOURSELF, KE'HAAN.
MY FATHER CONSIDERED HAL JORDAN A FRIEND. AND I OWE JOHN STEWART AND GUY GARDNER FOR MY INDUCTION INTO THE CORPS. I WILL GO WITH HIM.
AS WILL I.
MAY THE LIGHT GUIDE YOUR WAY, BROTHERS AND SISTERS.
KE'HAAN, YOU'RE NOT GOING TO LET--
THE GUARDIANS HAVE ASKED US TO RETRIEVE ION, BOODIKKA.
LET'S DO OUR DUTY.

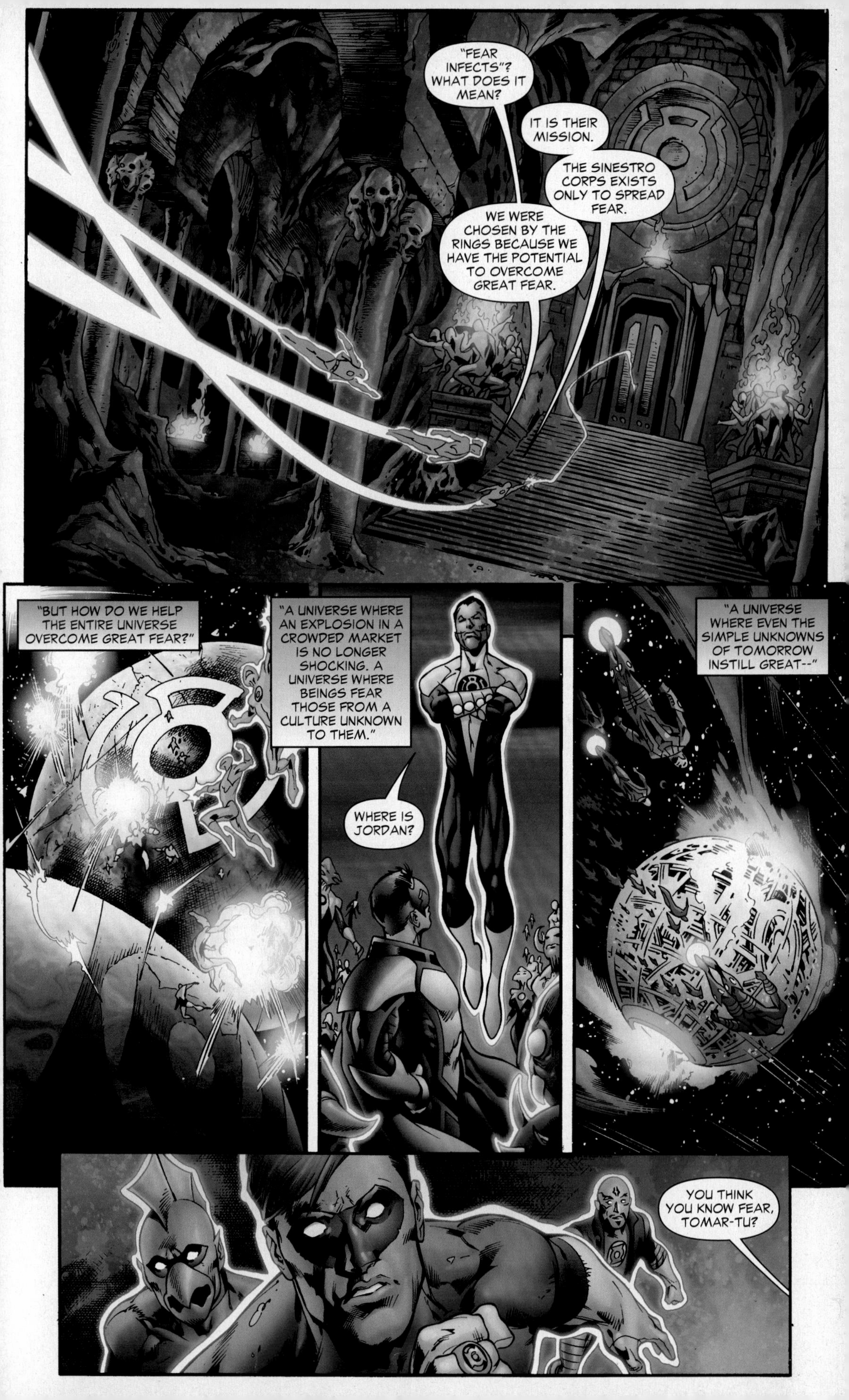
"FEAR INFECTS"? WHAT DOES IT MEAN?
IT IS THEIR MISSION.
THE SINESTRO CORPS EXISTS ONLY TO SPREAD FEAR.
WE WERE CHOSEN BY THE RINGS BECAUSE WE HAVE THE POTENTIAL TO OVERCOME GREAT FEAR.
"BUT HOW DO WE HELP THE ENTIRE UNIVERSE OVERCOME GREAT FEAR?"
"A UNIVERSE WHERE AN EXPLOSION IN A CROWDED MARKET IS NO LONGER SHOCKING. A UNIVERSE WHERE BEINGS FEAR THOSE FROM A CULTURE UNKNOWN TO THEM."
WHERE IS JORDAN?
"A UNIVERSE WHERE EVEN THE SIMPLE UNKNOWNS OF TOMORROW INSTILL GREAT--"
YOU THINK YOU KNOW FEAR, TOMAR-TU?

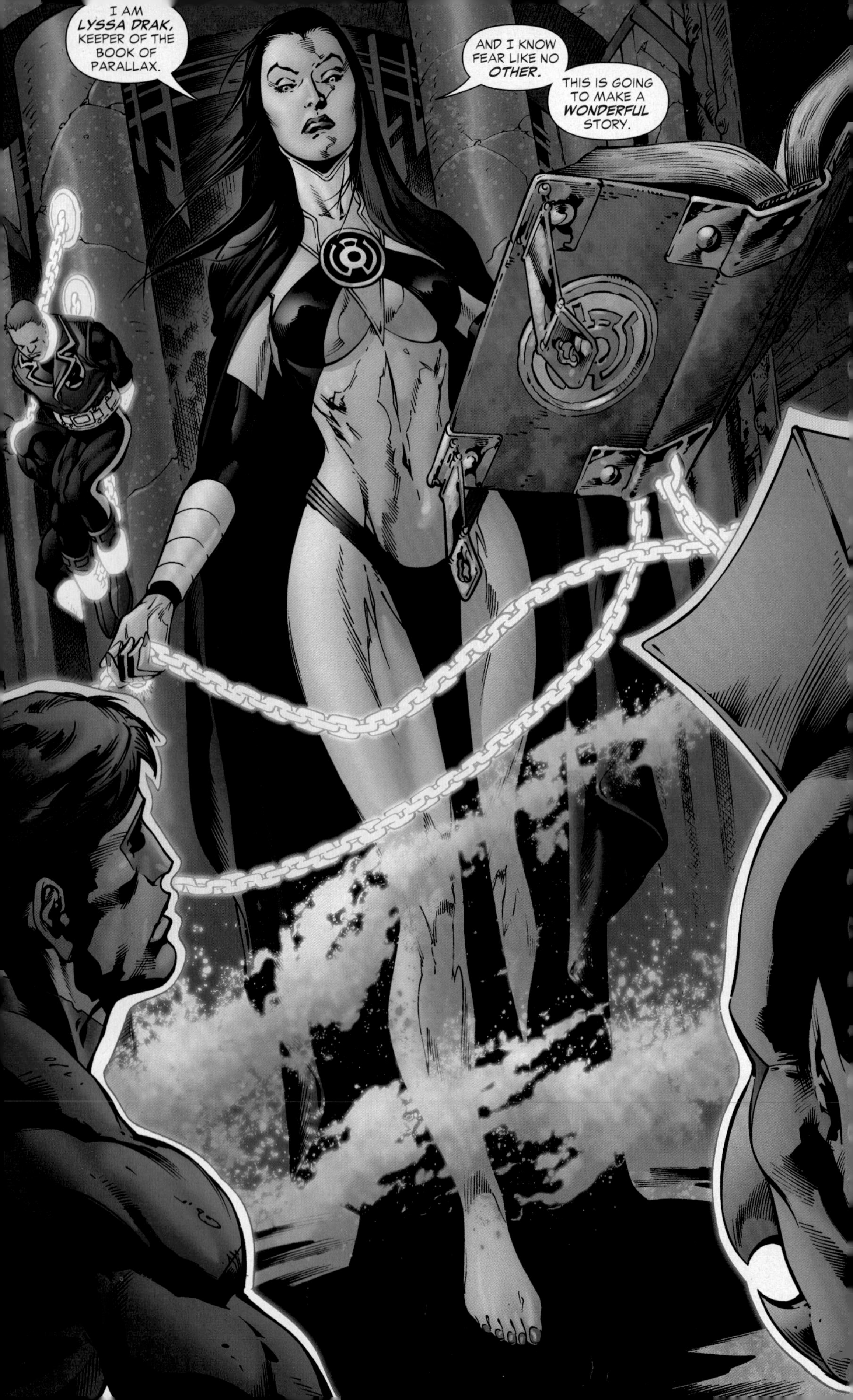
I AM **LYSSA DRAK,** KEEPER OF THE BOOK OF PARALLAX.
AND I KNOW FEAR LIKE NO **OTHER.**
THIS IS GOING TO MAKE A **WONDERFUL** STORY.

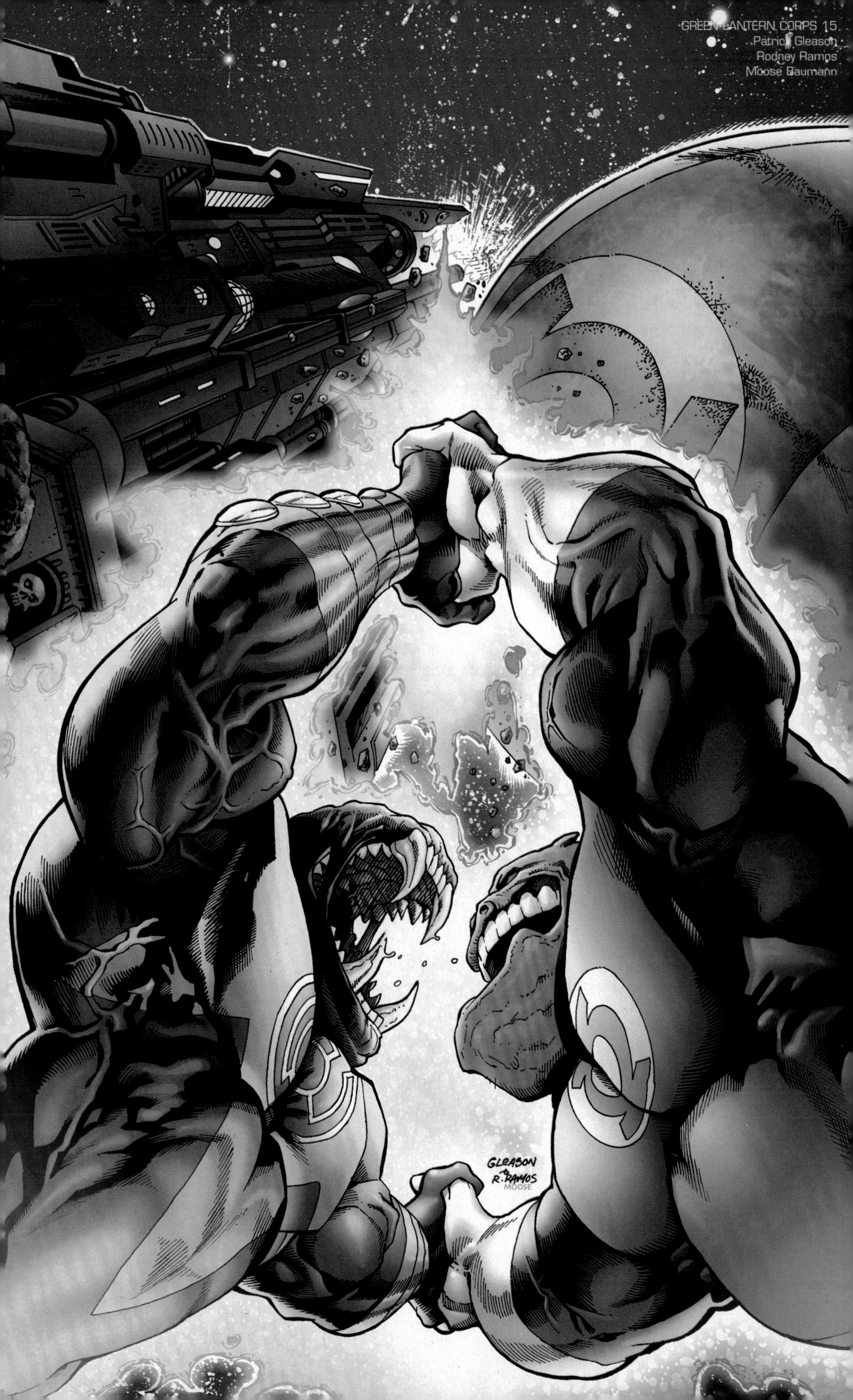
GREEN LANTERN CORPS 15
Patrick Gleason
Rodney Ramos
Moose Baumann
GLEASON
R. RAMOS
MOOSE

THE SINESTRO CORPS WAR
Chapter Four
THE BATTLE OF MOGO

Penciller: **Patrick Gleason** (pages 129-135, 142-147)
Penciller: **Angel Unzueta** (pages 136-141, 148-150)
Inker: **Prentis Rollins** (pages 129-136, 140-150)
Inker: **Drew Geraci** (pages 137-139)
Colorist: **Guy Major**
Letterer: **Phil Balsman**

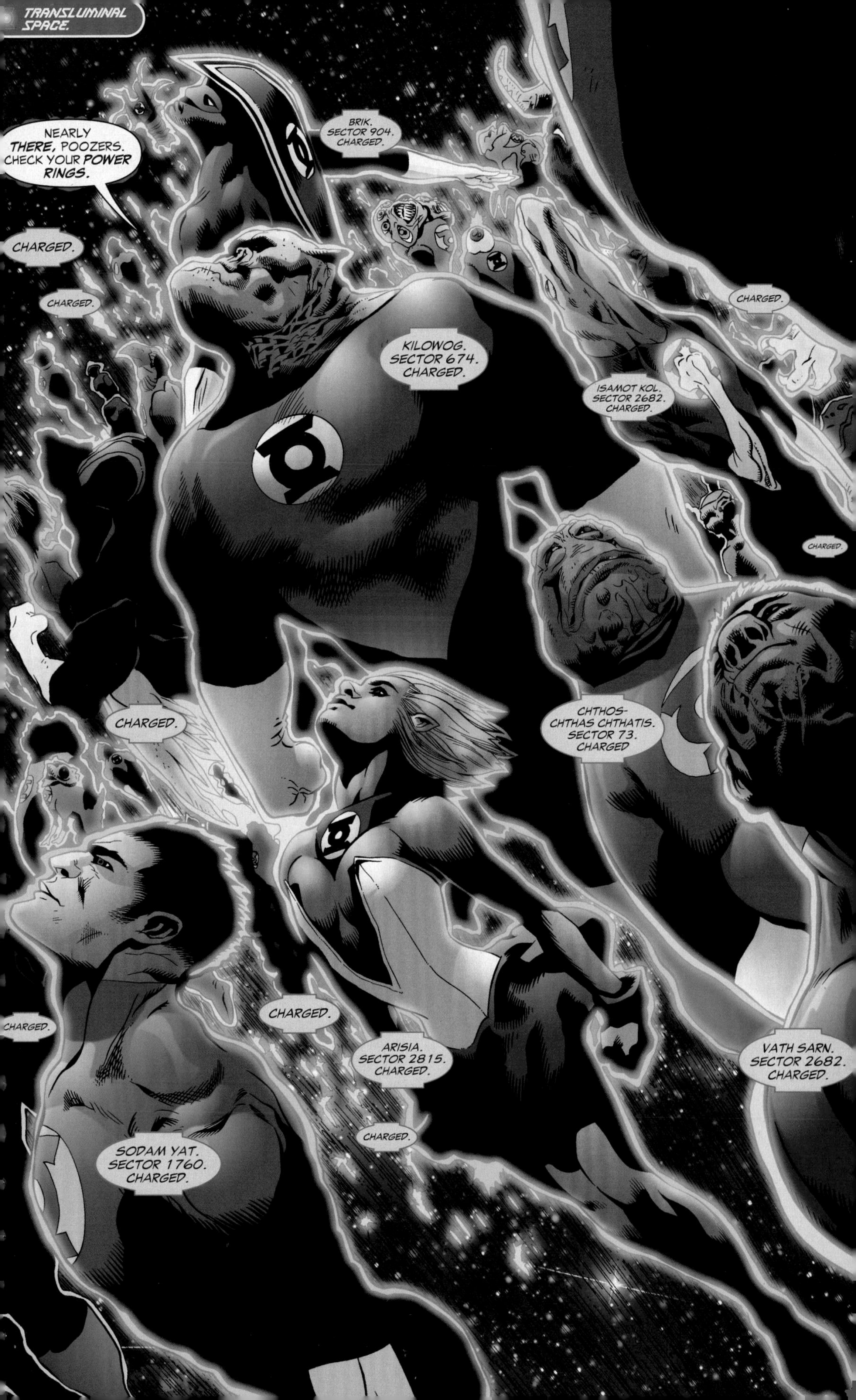
TRANSLUMINAL SPACE.
NEARLY THERE, POOZERS. CHECK YOUR POWER RINGS.
BRIK. SECTOR 904. CHARGED.
CHARGED.
CHARGED.
KILOWOG. SECTOR 674. CHARGED.
CHARGED.
ISAMOT KOL. SECTOR 2682. CHARGED.
CHARGED.
CHARGED.
CHTHOS-CHTHAS CHTHATIS. SECTOR 73. CHARGED
CHARGED.
CHARGED.
ARISIA. SECTOR 2815. CHARGED.
VATH SARN. SECTOR 2682. CHARGED.
CHARGED.
SODAM YAT. SECTOR 1760. CHARGED.

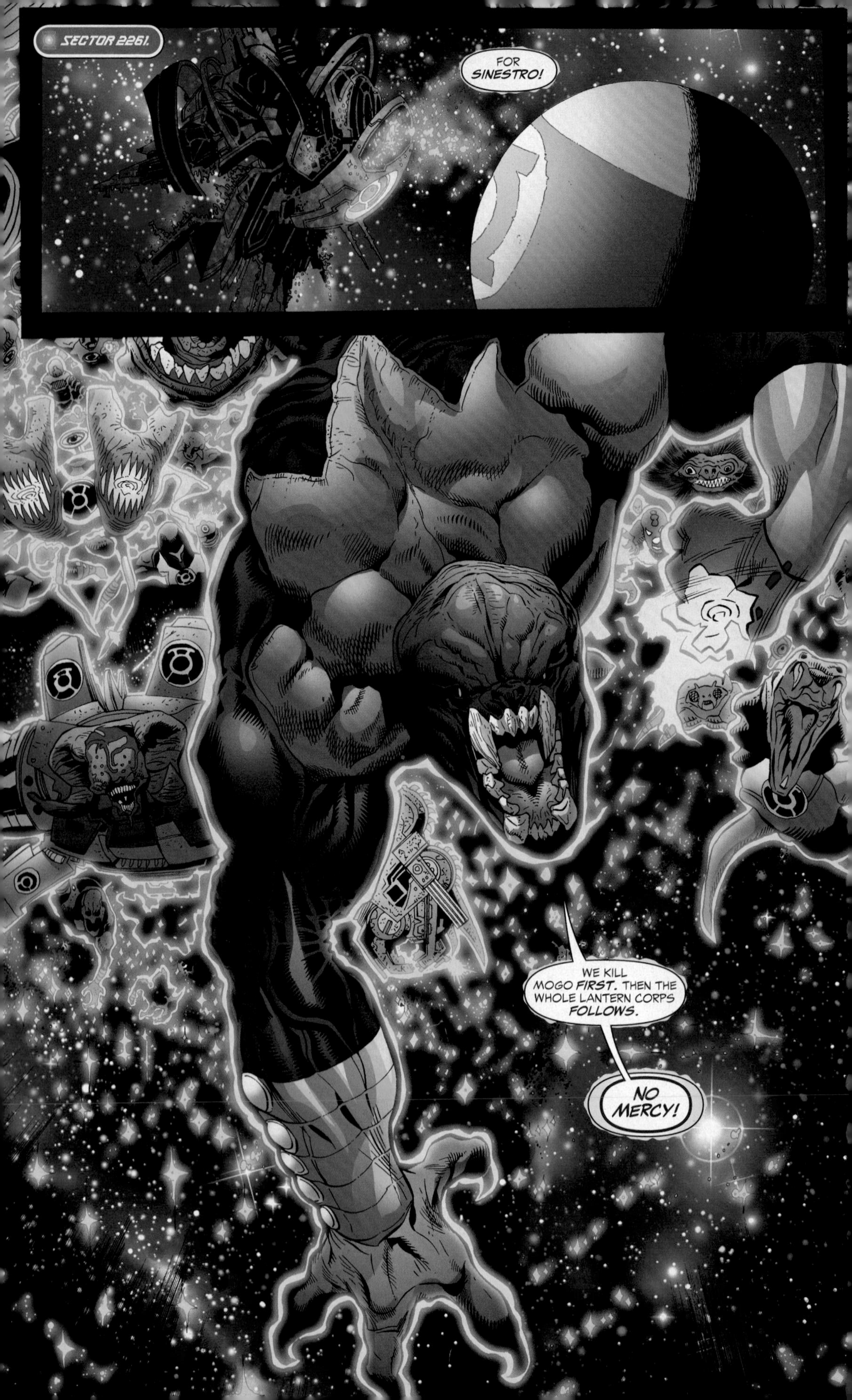
SECTOR 2261.
FOR SINESTRO!
WE KILL MOGO FIRST. THEN THE WHOLE LANTERN CORPS FOLLOWS.
NO MERCY!

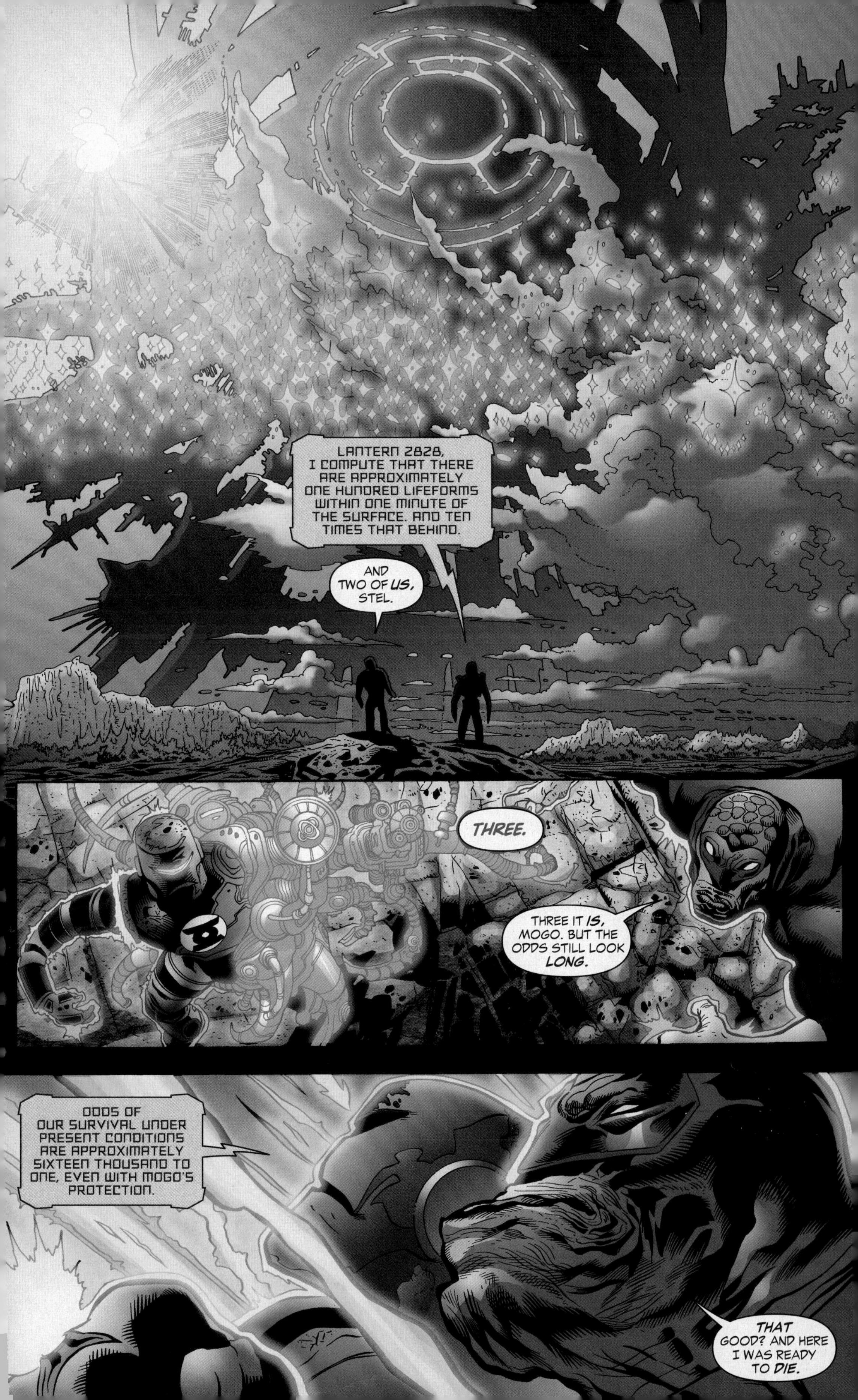
LANTERN 2828, I COMPUTE THAT THERE ARE APPROXIMATELY ONE HUNDRED LIFEFORMS WITHIN ONE MINUTE OF THE SURFACE. AND TEN TIMES THAT BEHIND.
AND TWO OF US, STEL.
THREE.
THREE IT IS, MOGO. BUT THE ODDS STILL LOOK LONG.
ODDS OF OUR SURVIVAL UNDER PRESENT CONDITIONS ARE APPROXIMATELY SIXTEEN THOUSAND TO ONE, EVEN WITH MOGO'S PROTECTION.
THAT GOOD? AND HERE I WAS READY TO DIE.

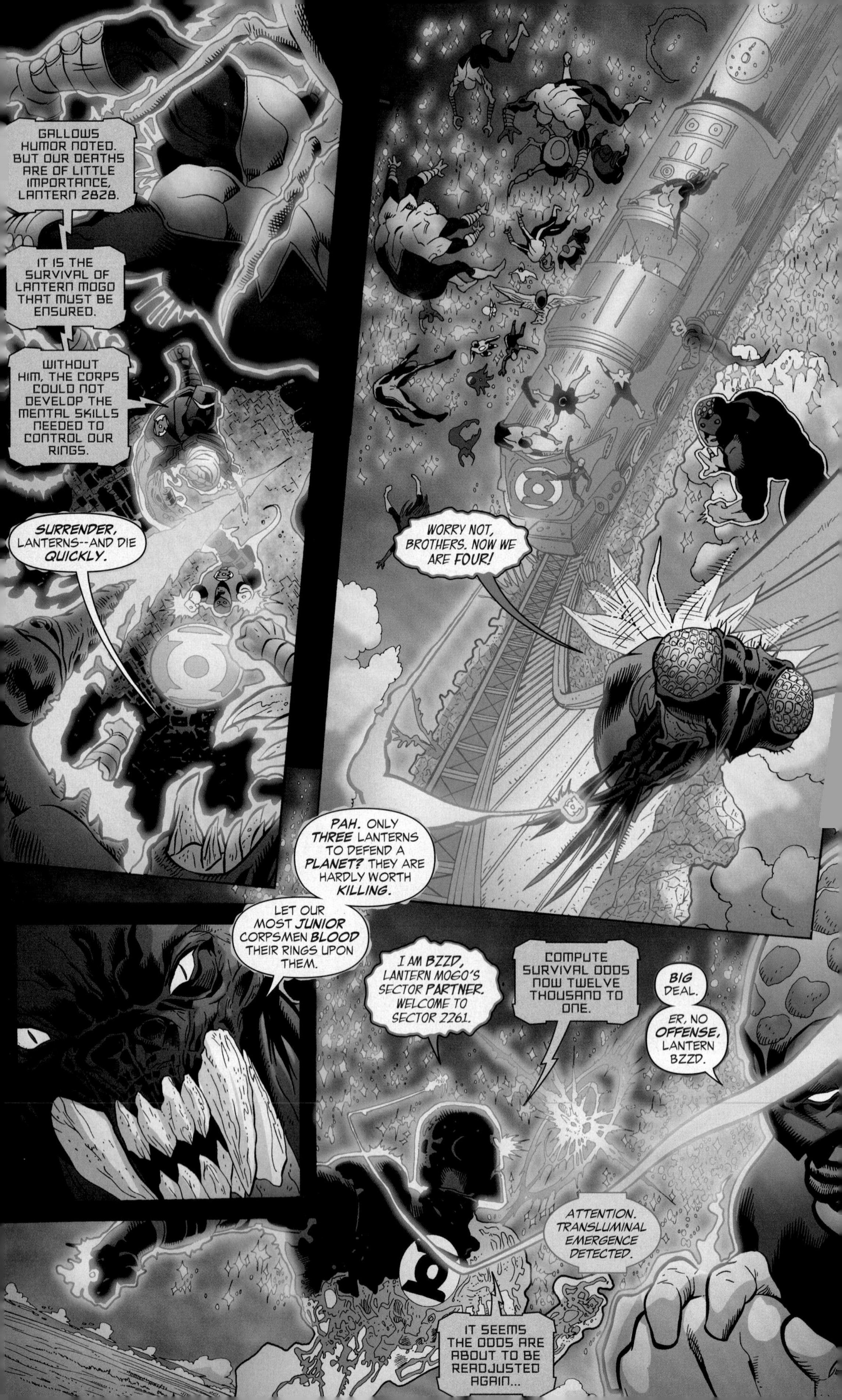
GALLOWS HUMOR NOTED. BUT OUR DEATHS ARE OF LITTLE IMPORTANCE, LANTERN 2828.
IT IS THE SURVIVAL OF LANTERN MOGO THAT MUST BE ENSURED.
WITHOUT HIM, THE CORPS COULD NOT DEVELOP THE MENTAL SKILLS NEEDED TO CONTROL OUR RINGS.
SURRENDER, LANTERNS--AND DIE QUICKLY.
WORRY NOT, BROTHERS. NOW WE ARE FOUR!
PAH. ONLY THREE LANTERNS TO DEFEND A PLANET? THEY ARE HARDLY WORTH KILLING.
LET OUR MOST JUNIOR CORPSMEN BLOOD THEIR RINGS UPON THEM.
I AM BZZD, LANTERN MOGO'S SECTOR PARTNER. WELCOME TO SECTOR 2261.
COMPUTE SURVIVAL ODDS NOW TWELVE THOUSAND TO ONE.
BIG DEAL.
ER, NO OFFENSE, LANTERN BZZD.
ATTENTION. TRANSLUMINAL EMERGENCE DETECTED.
IT SEEMS THE ODDS ARE ABOUT TO BE READJUSTED AGAIN...

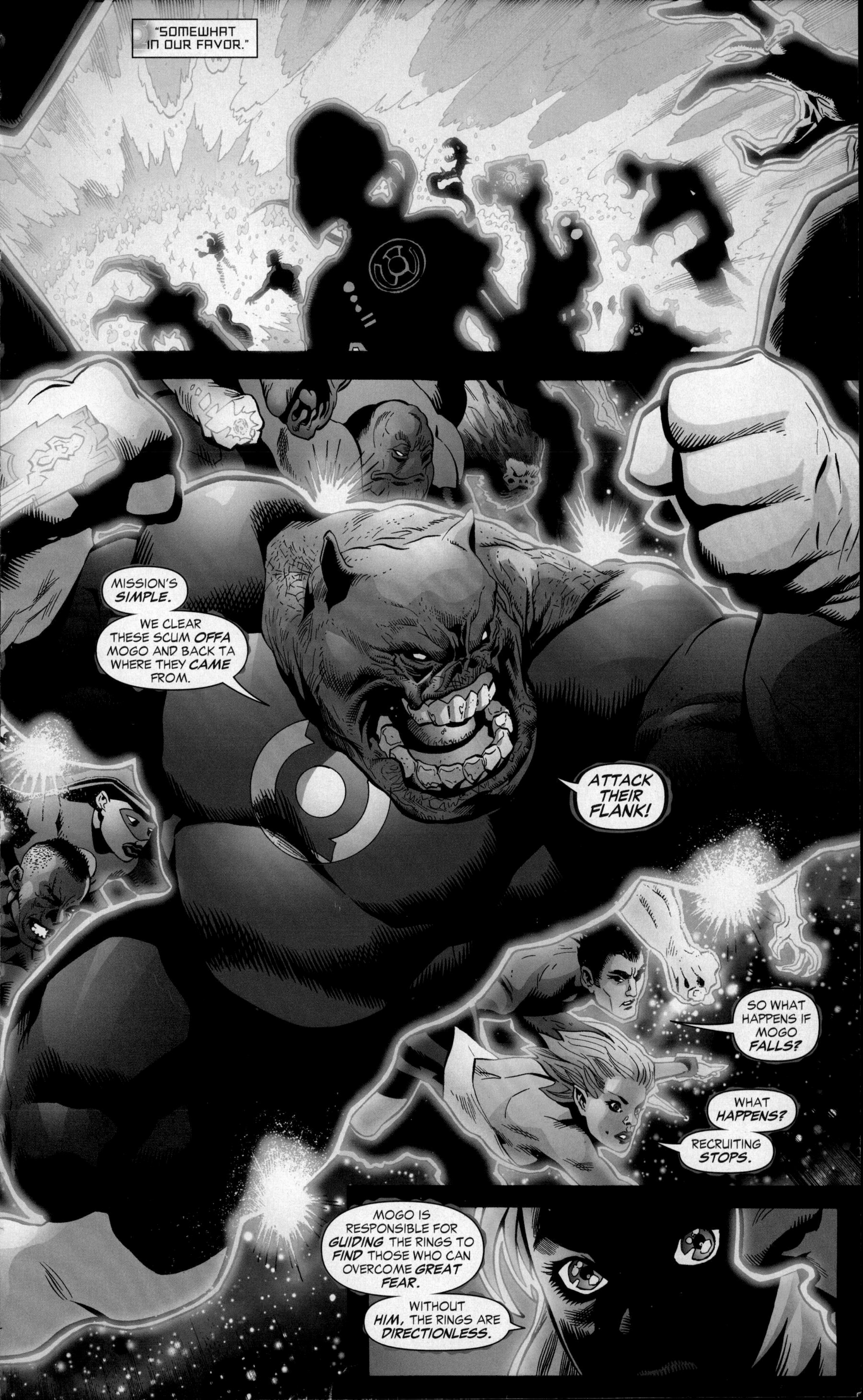
"SOMEWHAT IN OUR FAVOR."
MISSION'S SIMPLE.
WE CLEAR THESE SCUM OFFA MOGO AND BACK TA WHERE THEY CAME FROM.
ATTACK THEIR FLANK!
SO WHAT HAPPENS IF MOGO FALLS?
WHAT HAPPENS?
RECRUITING STOPS.
MOGO IS RESPONSIBLE FOR GUIDING THE RINGS TO FIND THOSE WHO CAN OVERCOME GREAT FEAR.
WITHOUT HIM, THE RINGS ARE DIRECTIONLESS.

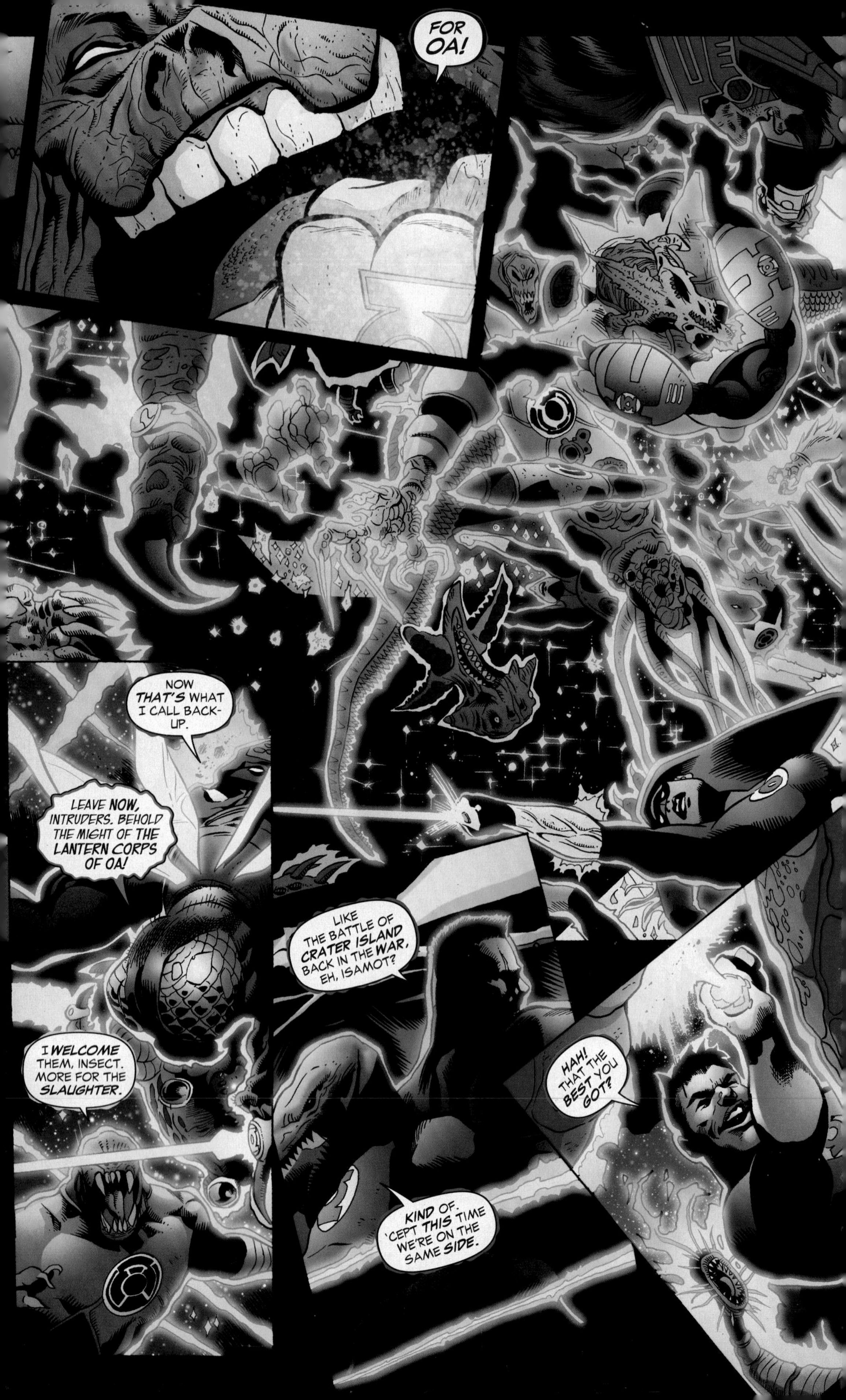
FOR OA!
NOW THAT'S WHAT I CALL BACK-UP.
LEAVE NOW, INTRUDERS. BEHOLD THE MIGHT OF THE LANTERN CORPS OF OA!
I WELCOME THEM, INSECT. MORE FOR THE SLAUGHTER.
LIKE THE BATTLE OF CRATER ISLAND BACK IN THE WAR, EH, ISAMOT?
KIND OF. 'CEPT THIS TIME WE'RE ON THE SAME SIDE.
HAH! THAT THE BEST YOU GOT?

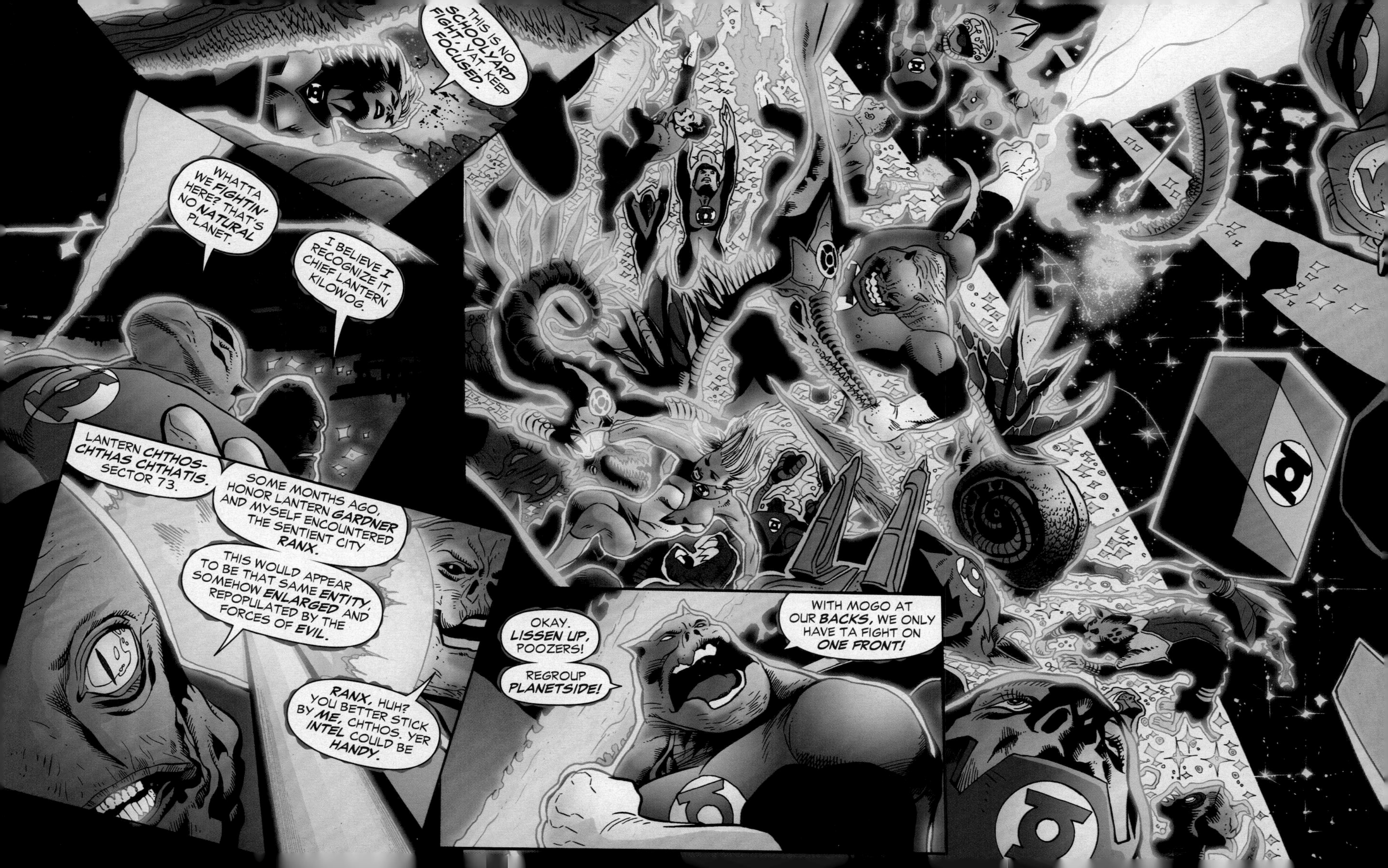
THIS IS NO SCHOOLYARD FIGHT, YAT. KEEP FOCUSED.
WHATTA WE FIGHTIN' HERE? THAT'S NO NATURAL PLANET.
I BELIEVE I RECOGNIZE IT, CHIEF LANTERN KILOWOG.
LANTERN CHTHOS-CHTHAS CHTHATIS. SECTOR 73.
SOME MONTHS AGO, HONOR LANTERN GARDNER AND MYSELF ENCOUNTERED THE SENTIENT CITY RANX.
THIS WOULD APPEAR TO BE THAT SAME ENTITY, SOMEHOW ENLARGED AND REPOPULATED BY THE FORCES OF EVIL.
RANX, HUH? YOU BETTER STICK BY ME, CHTHOS. YER INTEL COULD BE HANDY.
WITH MOGO AT OUR BACKS, WE ONLY HAVE TA FIGHT ON ONE FRONT!
OKAY. LISSEN UP, POOZERS!
REGROUP PLANETSIDE!

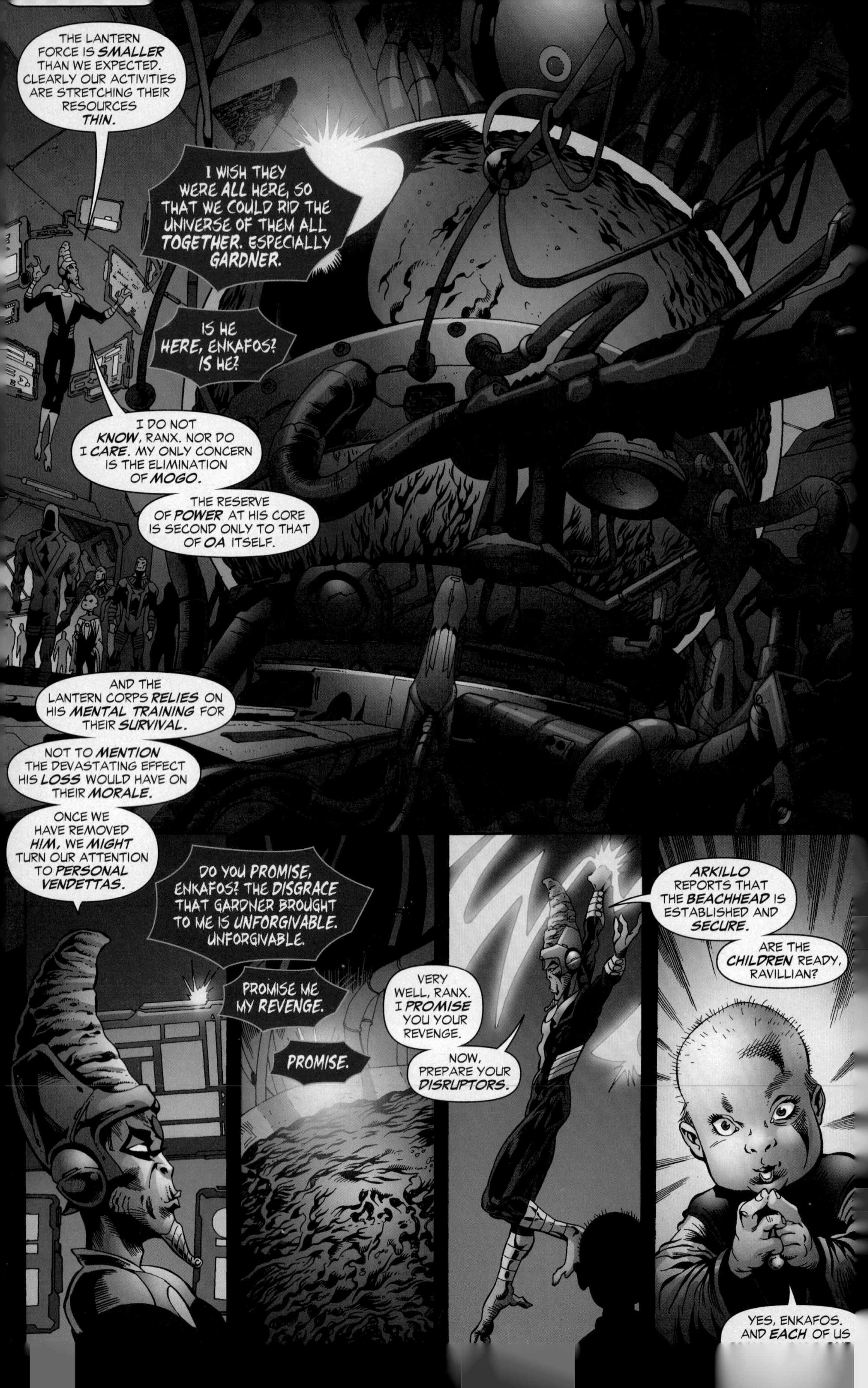

THE LANTERN FORCE IS SMALLER THAN WE EXPECTED. CLEARLY OUR ACTIVITIES ARE STRETCHING THEIR RESOURCES THIN.
I WISH THEY WERE ALL HERE, SO THAT WE COULD RID THE UNIVERSE OF THEM ALL TOGETHER. ESPECIALLY GARDNER.
IS HE HERE, ENKAFOS? IS HE?
I DO NOT KNOW, RANX. NOR DO I CARE. MY ONLY CONCERN IS THE ELIMINATION OF MOGO.
THE RESERVE OF POWER AT HIS CORE IS SECOND ONLY TO THAT OF OA ITSELF.
AND THE LANTERN CORPS RELIES ON HIS MENTAL TRAINING FOR THEIR SURVIVAL.
NOT TO MENTION THE DEVASTATING EFFECT HIS LOSS WOULD HAVE ON THEIR MORALE.
ONCE WE HAVE REMOVED HIM, WE MIGHT TURN OUR ATTENTION TO PERSONAL VENDETTAS.
DO YOU PROMISE, ENKAFOS? THE DISGRACE THAT GARDNER BROUGHT TO ME IS UNFORGIVABLE. UNFORGIVABLE.
PROMISE ME MY REVENGE.
PROMISE.
VERY WELL, RANX. I PROMISE YOU YOUR REVENGE.
NOW, PREPARE YOUR DISRUPTORS.
ARKILLO REPORTS THAT THE BEACHHEAD IS ESTABLISHED AND SECURE.
ARE THE CHILDREN READY, RAVILLIAN?
YES, ENKAFOS. AND EACH OF US

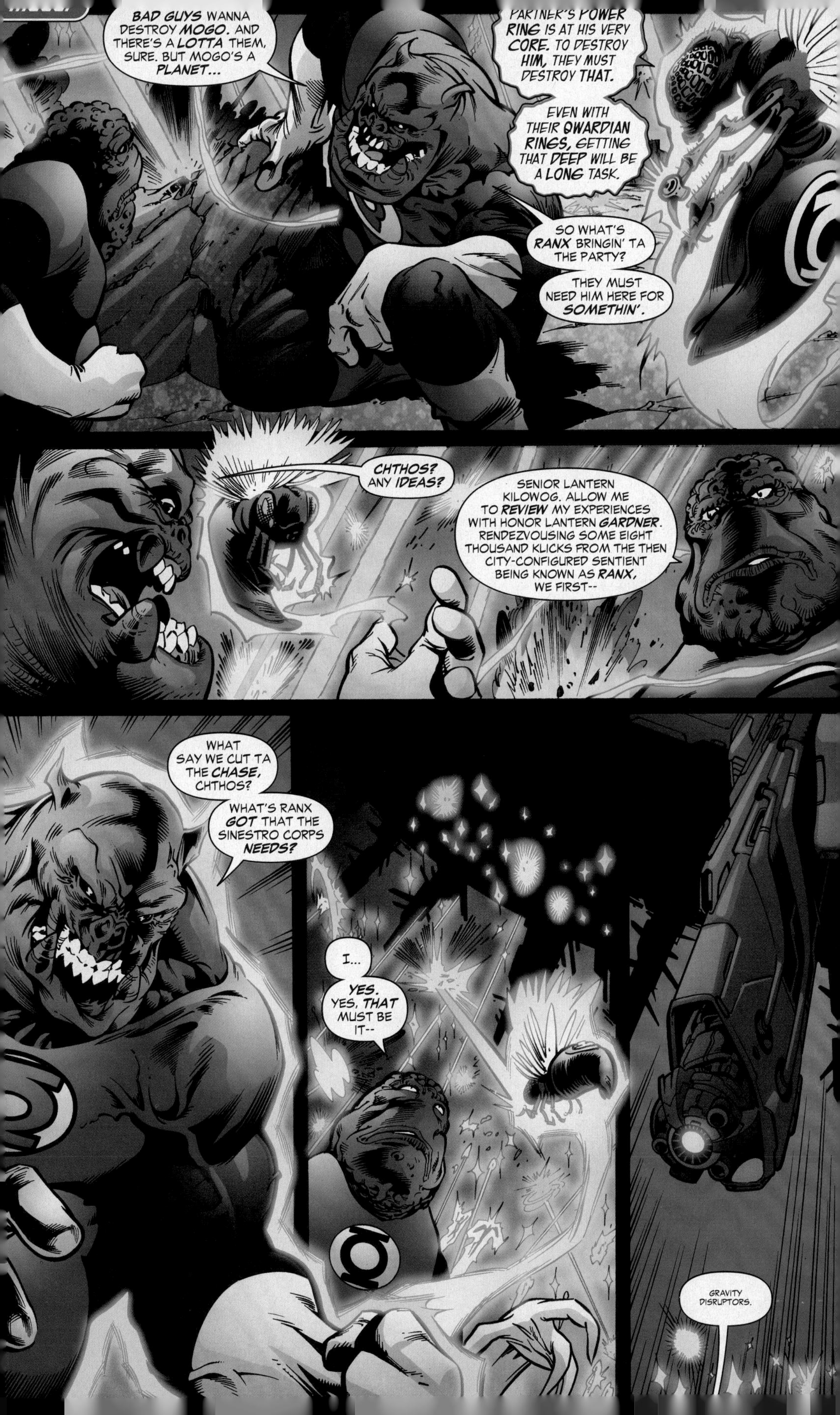
BAD GUYS WANNA DESTROY MOGO. AND THERE'S A LOTTA THEM, SURE. BUT MOGO'S A PLANET...
PARTNER'S POWER RING IS AT HIS VERY CORE. TO DESTROY HIM, THEY MUST DESTROY THAT.
EVEN WITH THEIR QWARDIAN RINGS, GETTING THAT DEEP WILL BE A LONG TASK.
SO WHAT'S RANX BRINGIN' TA THE PARTY?
THEY MUST NEED HIM HERE FOR SOMETHIN'.
CHTHOS? ANY IDEAS?
SENIOR LANTERN KILOWOG. ALLOW ME TO REVIEW MY EXPERIENCES WITH HONOR LANTERN GARDNER. RENDEZVOUSING SOME EIGHT THOUSAND KLICKS FROM THE THEN CITY-CONFIGURED SENTIENT BEING KNOWN AS RANX, WE FIRST--
WHAT SAY WE CUT TA THE CHASE, CHTHOS?
WHAT'S RANX GOT THAT THE SINESTRO CORPS NEEDS?
I...
YES. YES, THAT MUST BE IT--
GRAVITY DISRUPTORS.

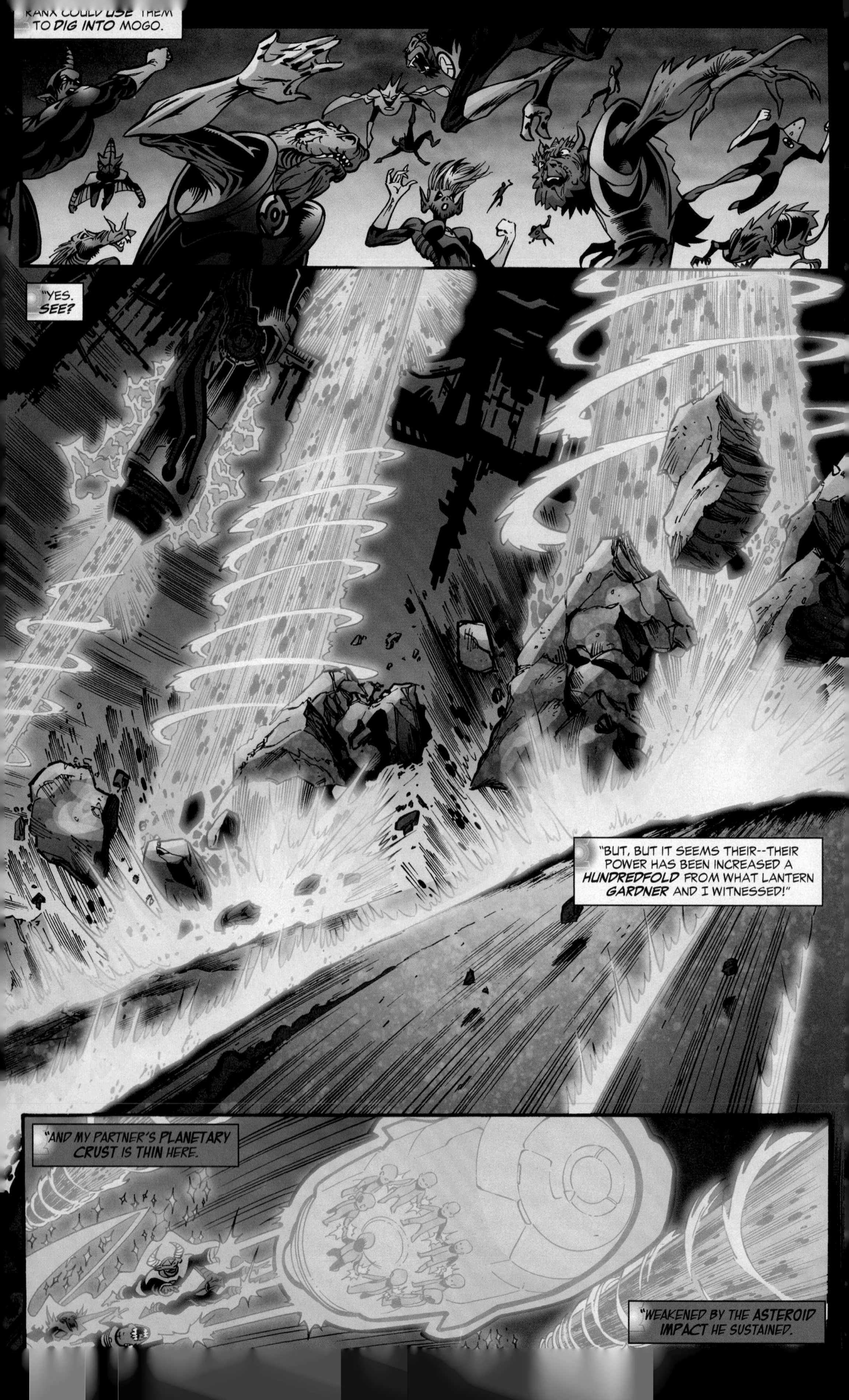
RANX COULD USE THEM TO DIG INTO MOGO.
"YES. SEE?
"BUT, BUT IT SEEMS THEIR--THEIR POWER HAS BEEN INCREASED A HUNDREDFOLD FROM WHAT LANTERN GARDNER AND I WITNESSED!"
"AND MY PARTNER'S PLANETARY CRUST IS THIN HERE.
"WEAKENED BY THE ASTEROID IMPACT HE SUSTAINED.

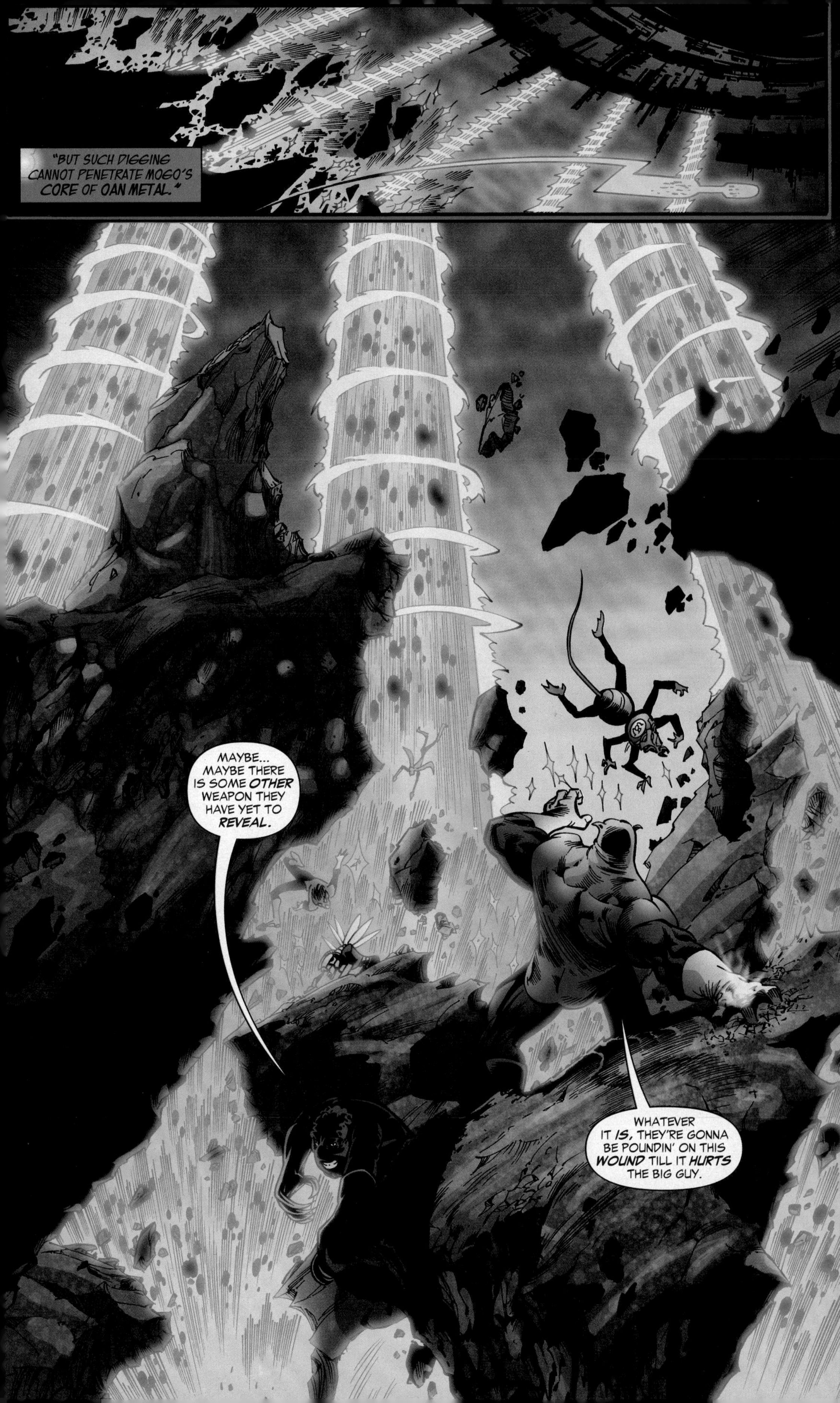
"BUT SUCH DIGGING CANNOT PENETRATE MOGO'S CORE OF OAN METAL."
MAYBE... MAYBE THERE IS SOME OTHER WEAPON THEY HAVE YET TO REVEAL.
WHATEVER IT IS, THEY'RE GONNA BE POUNDIN' ON THIS WOUND TILL IT HURTS THE BIG GUY.

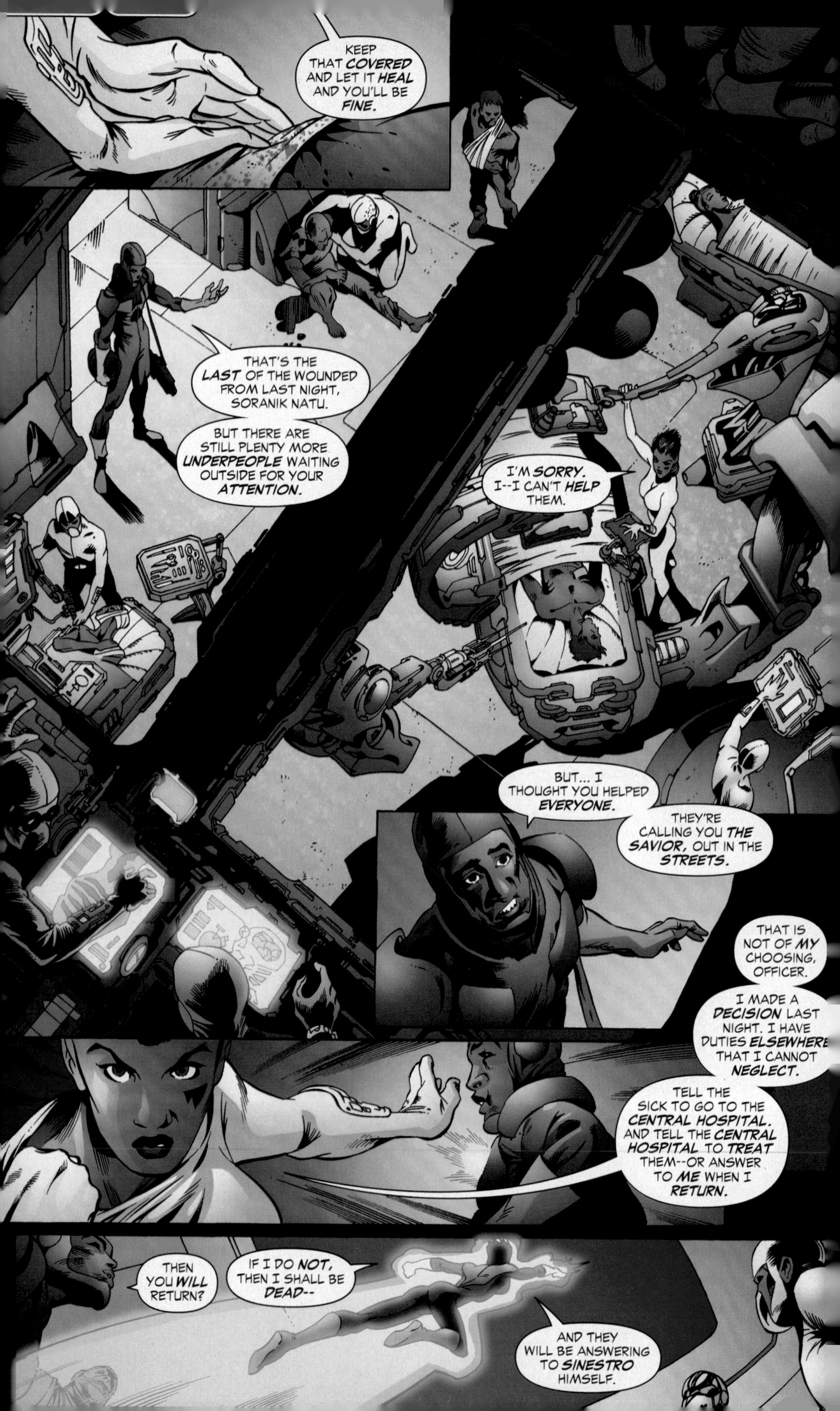
KEEP THAT COVERED AND LET IT HEAL AND YOU'LL BE FINE.
THAT'S THE LAST OF THE WOUNDED FROM LAST NIGHT, SORANIK NATU.
BUT THERE ARE STILL PLENTY MORE UNDERPEOPLE WAITING OUTSIDE FOR YOUR ATTENTION.
I'M SORRY. I--I CAN'T HELP THEM.
BUT... I THOUGHT YOU HELPED EVERYONE.
THEY'RE CALLING YOU THE SAVIOR, OUT IN THE STREETS.
THAT IS NOT OF MY CHOOSING, OFFICER.
I MADE A DECISION LAST NIGHT. I HAVE DUTIES ELSEWHERE THAT I CANNOT NEGLECT.
TELL THE SICK TO GO TO THE CENTRAL HOSPITAL. AND TELL THE CENTRAL HOSPITAL TO TREAT THEM--OR ANSWER TO ME WHEN I RETURN.
THEN YOU WILL RETURN?
IF I DO NOT, THEN I SHALL BE DEAD--
AND THEY WILL BE ANSWERING TO SINESTRO HIMSELF.

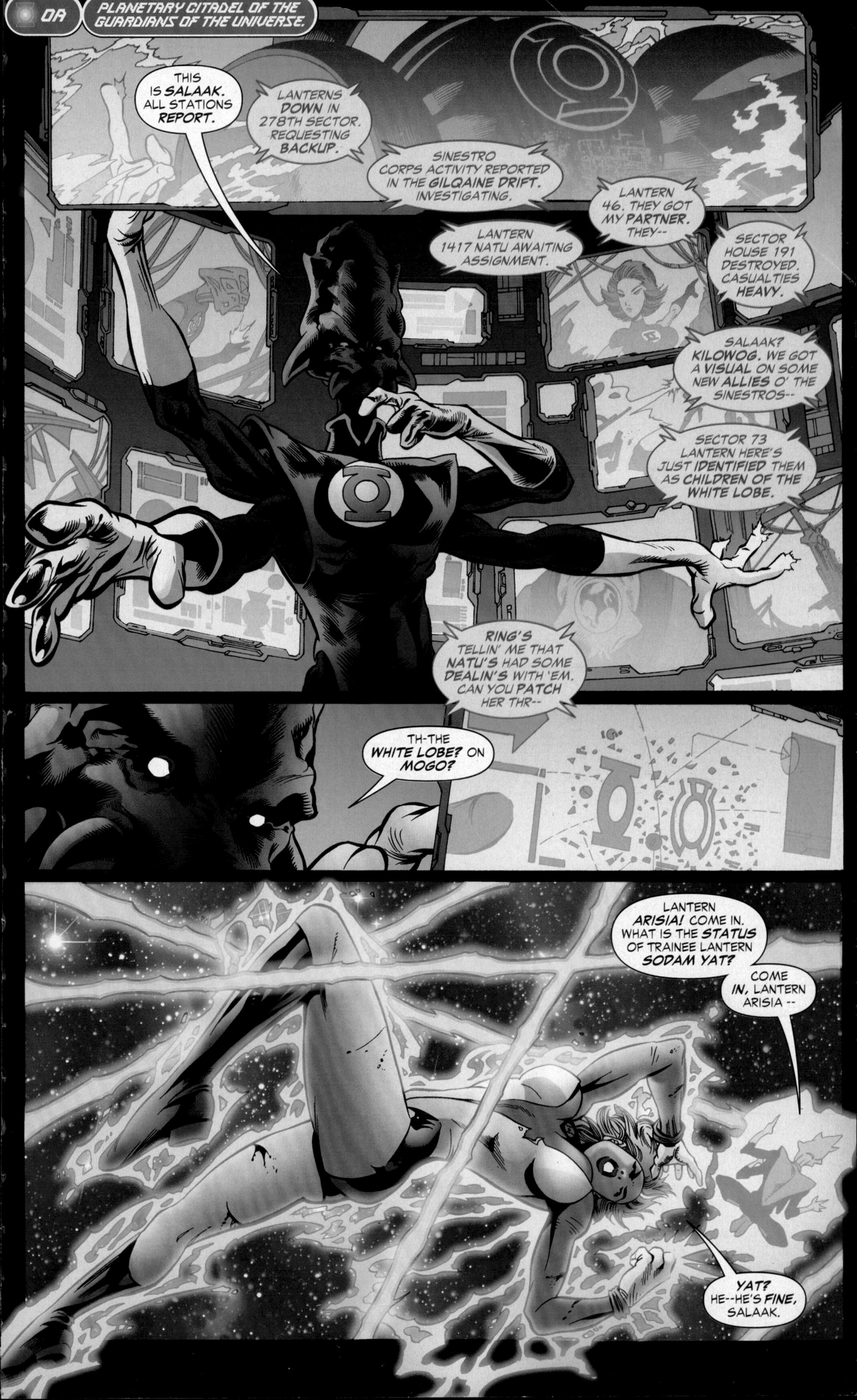
OA
PLANETARY CITADEL OF THE GUARDIANS OF THE UNIVERSE.
THIS IS SALAAK. ALL STATIONS REPORT.
LANTERNS DOWN IN 278TH SECTOR. REQUESTING BACKUP.
SINESTRO CORPS ACTIVITY REPORTED IN THE GILQAINE DRIFT. INVESTIGATING.
LANTERN 46. THEY GOT MY PARTNER. THEY--
LANTERN 1417 NATU AWAITING ASSIGNMENT.
SECTOR HOUSE 191 DESTROYED. CASUALTIES HEAVY.
SALAAK? KILOWOG. WE GOT A VISUAL ON SOME NEW ALLIES O' THE SINESTROS--
SECTOR 73 LANTERN HERE'S JUST IDENTIFIED THEM AS CHILDREN OF THE WHITE LOBE.
RING'S TELLIN' ME THAT NATU'S HAD SOME DEALIN'S WITH 'EM. CAN YOU PATCH HER THR--
TH-THE WHITE LOBE? ON MOGO?
LANTERN ARISIA! COME IN. WHAT IS THE STATUS OF TRAINEE LANTERN SODAM YAT?
COME IN, LANTERN ARISIA --
YAT? HE--HE'S FINE, SALAAK.

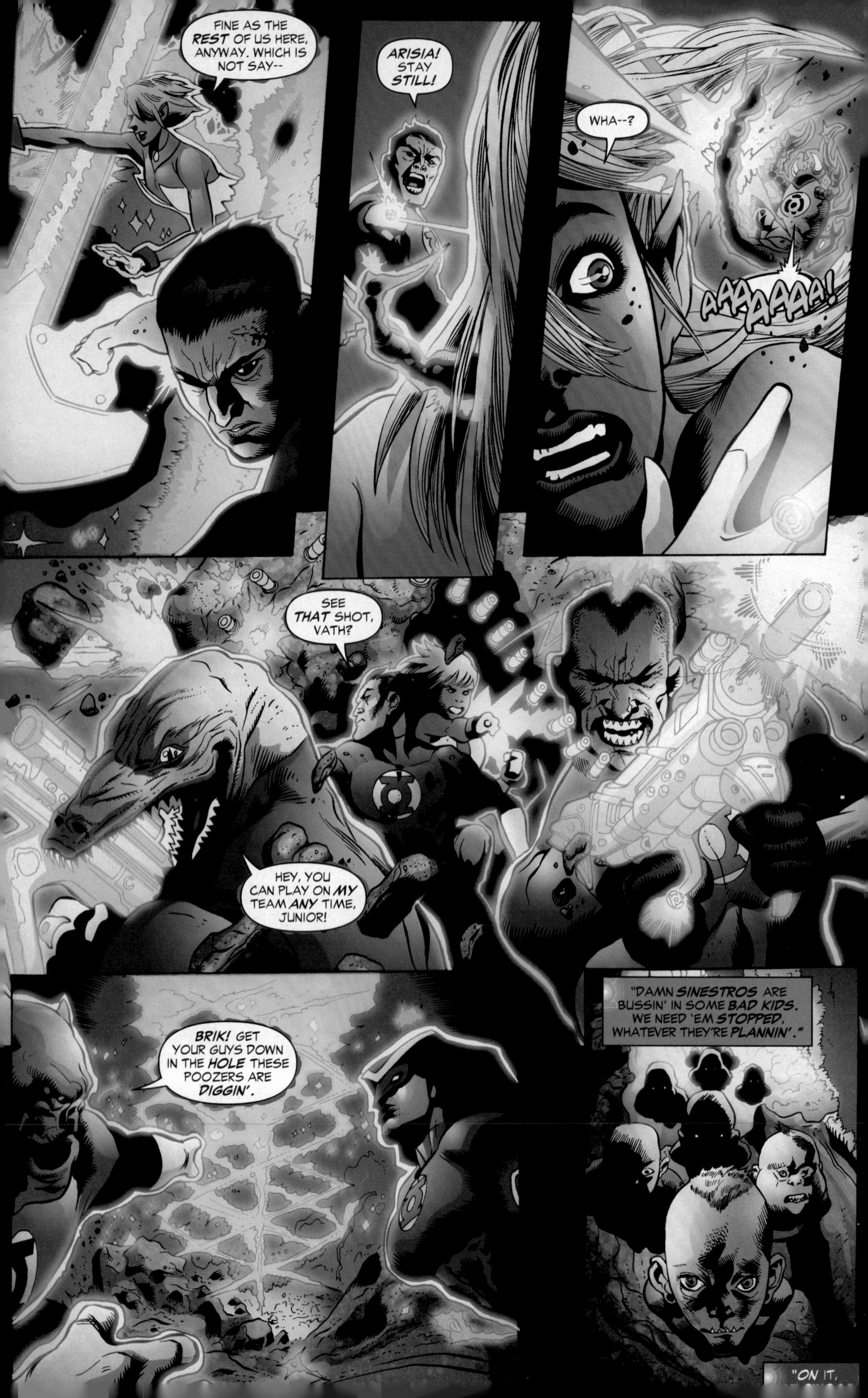
FINE AS THE REST OF US HERE, ANYWAY. WHICH IS NOT SAY--
ARISIA! STAY STILL!
WHA--?
AAAAAAAA!
SEE THAT SHOT, VATH?
HEY, YOU CAN PLAY ON MY TEAM ANY TIME, JUNIOR!
BRIK! GET YOUR GUYS DOWN IN THE HOLE THESE POOZERS ARE DIGGIN'.
"DAMN SINESTROS ARE BUSSIN' IN SOME BAD KIDS. WE NEED 'EM STOPPED, WHATEVER THEY'RE PLANNIN'."
"ON IT,

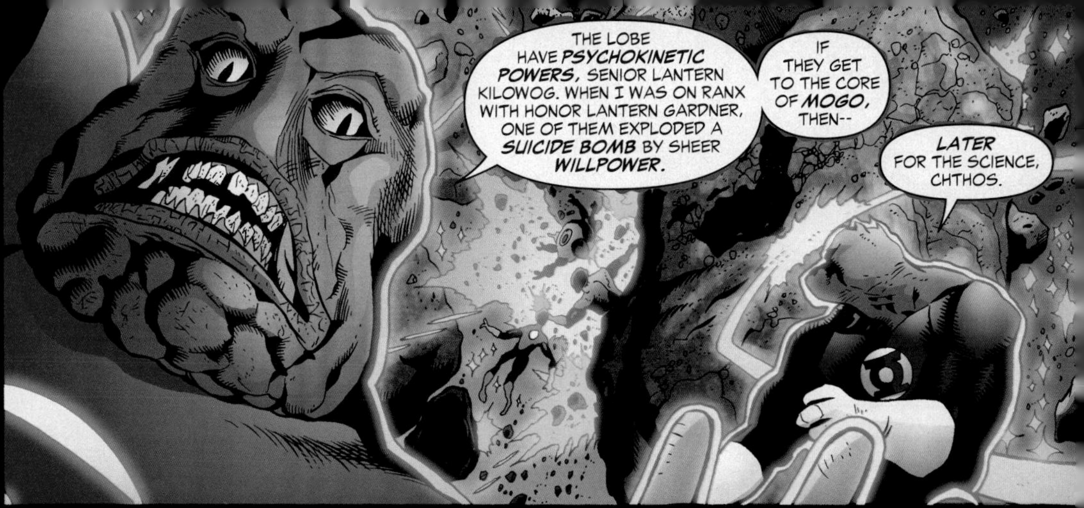
THE LOBE HAVE PSYCHOKINETIC POWERS, SENIOR LANTERN KILOWOG. WHEN I WAS ON RANX WITH HONOR LANTERN GARDNER, ONE OF THEM EXPLODED A SUICIDE BOMB BY SHEER WILLPOWER.
IF THEY GET TO THE CORE OF MOGO, THEN--
LATER FOR THE SCIENCE, CHTHOS.

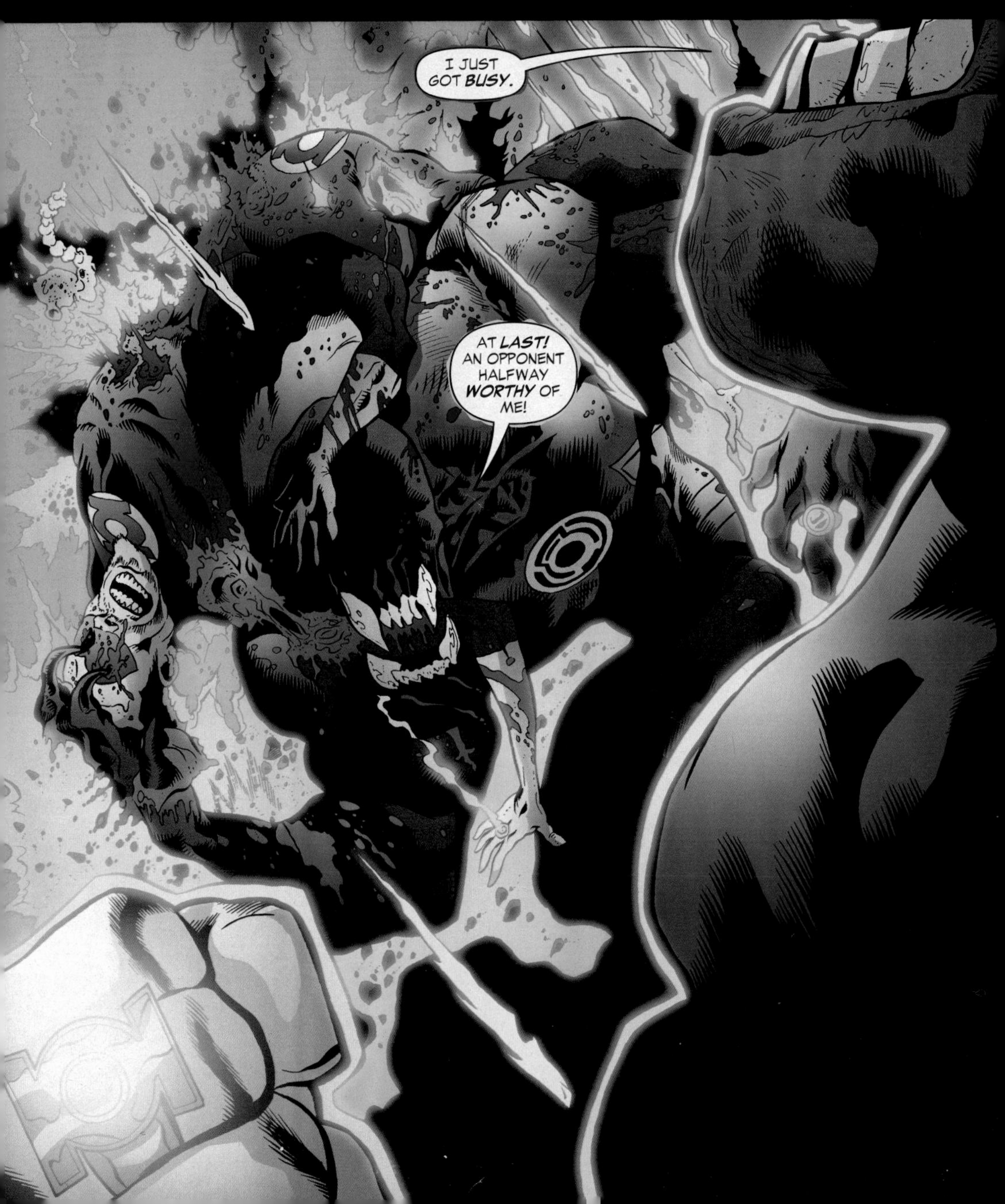
I JUST GOT BUSY.
AT LAST! AN OPPONENT HALFWAY WORTHY OF ME!

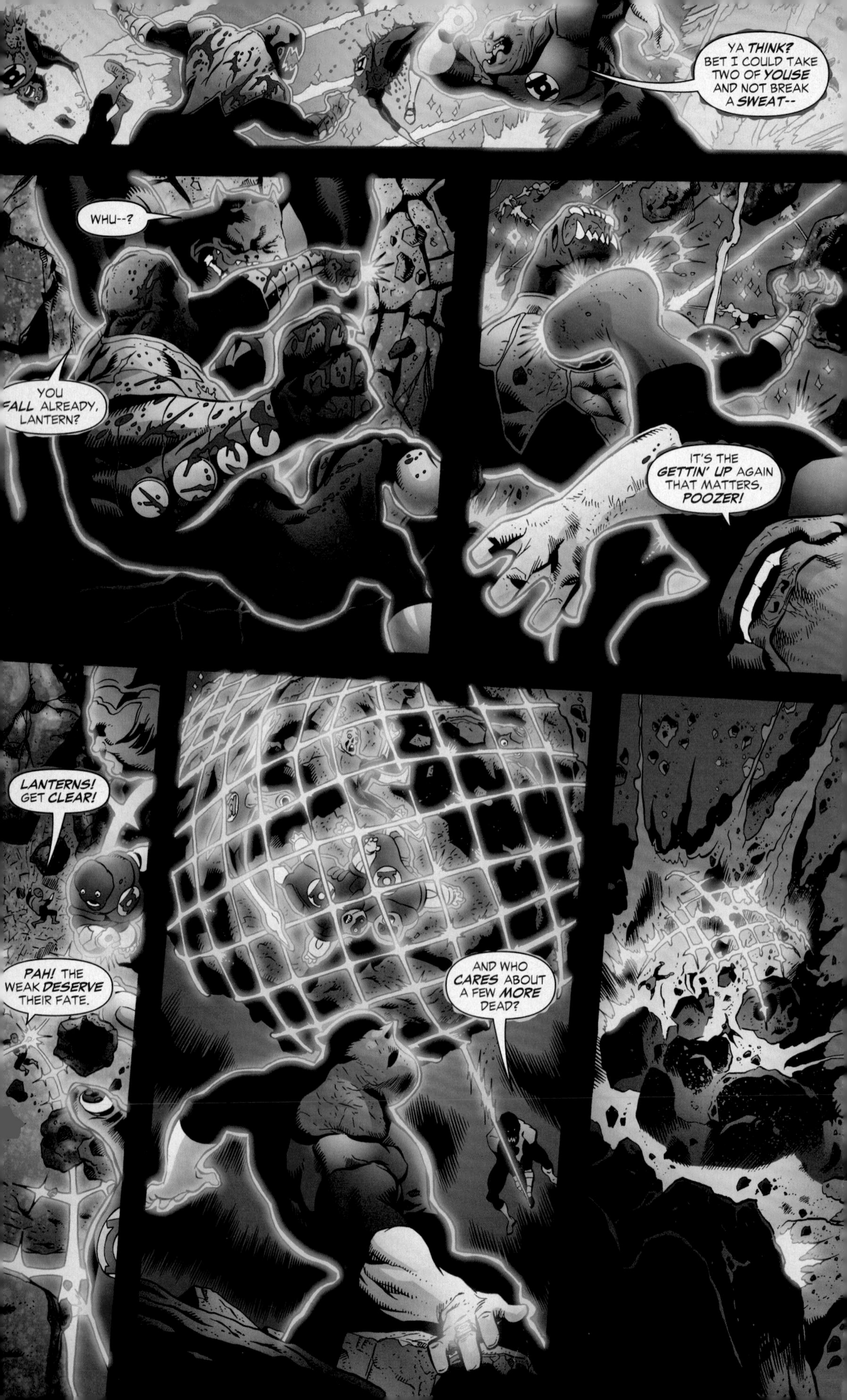
YA THINK? BET I COULD TAKE TWO OF YOUSE AND NOT BREAK A SWEAT--
WHU--?
YOU FALL ALREADY, LANTERN?
IT'S THE GETTIN' UP AGAIN THAT MATTERS, POOZER!
LANTERNS! GET CLEAR!
PAH! THE WEAK DESERVE THEIR FATE.
AND WHO CARES ABOUT A FEW MORE DEAD?

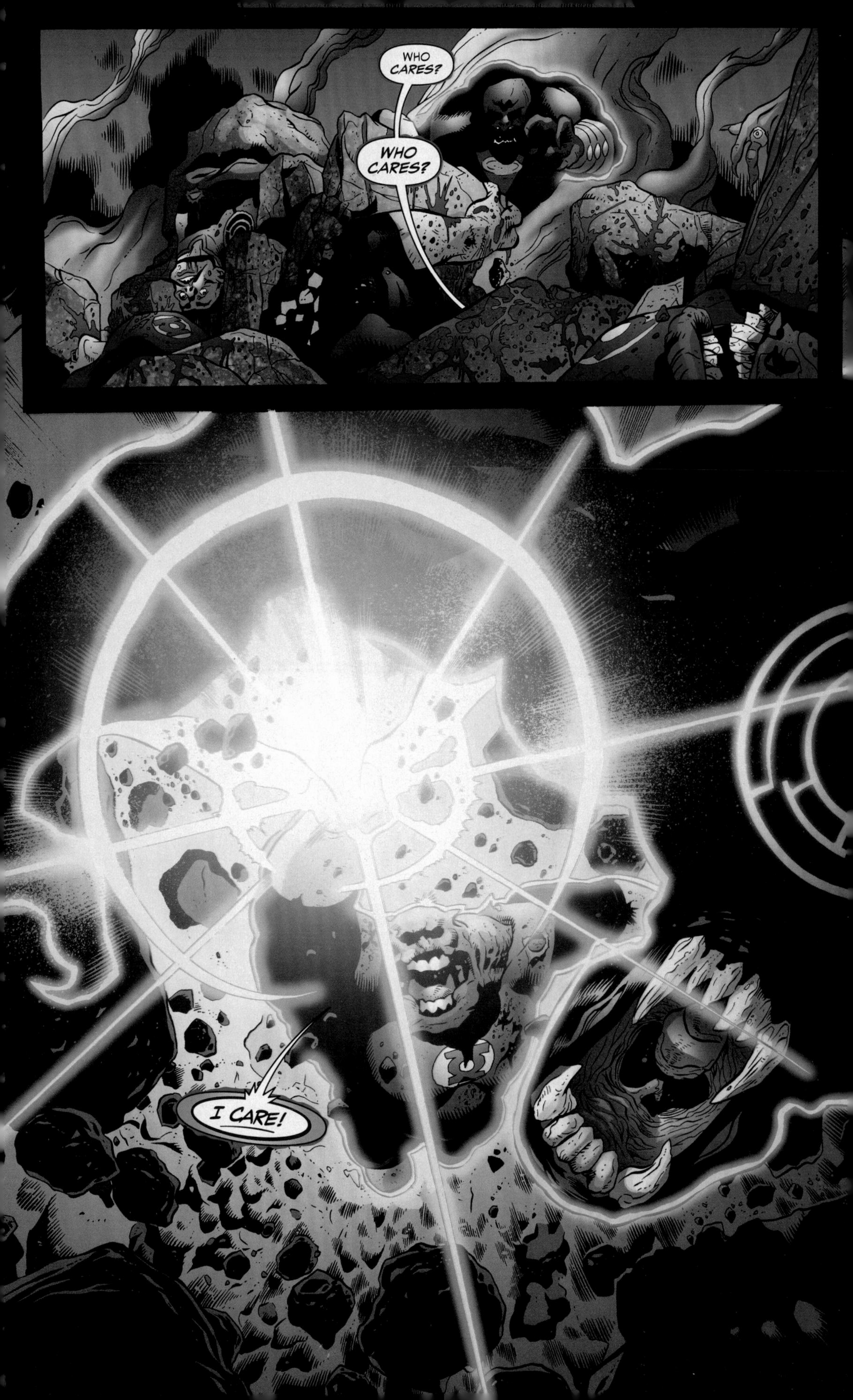
WHO CARES?
WHO CARES?
I CARE!

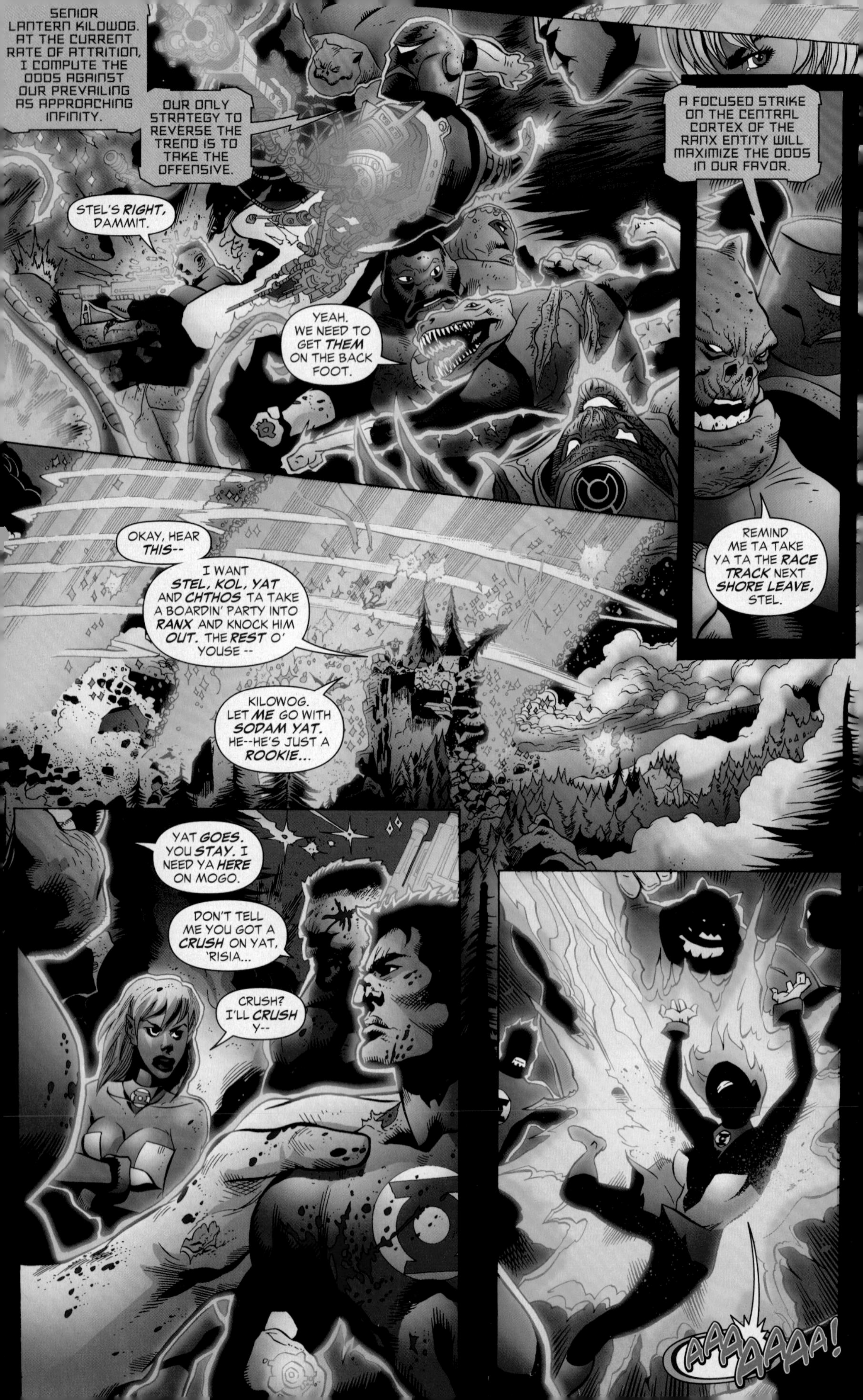

SENIOR LANTERN KILOWOG. AT THE CURRENT RATE OF ATTRITION, I COMPUTE THE ODDS AGAINST OUR PREVAILING AS APPROACHING INFINITY.
OUR ONLY STRATEGY TO REVERSE THE TREND IS TO TAKE THE OFFENSIVE.
STEL'S RIGHT, DAMMIT.
YEAH. WE NEED TO GET THEM ON THE BACK FOOT.
A FOCUSED STRIKE ON THE CENTRAL CORTEX OF THE RANX ENTITY WILL MAXIMIZE THE ODDS IN OUR FAVOR.
REMIND ME TA TAKE YA TA THE RACE TRACK NEXT SHORE LEAVE, STEL.
OKAY, HEAR THIS--
I WANT STEL, KOL, YAT AND CHTHOS TA TAKE A BOARDIN' PARTY INTO RANX AND KNOCK HIM OUT. THE REST O' YOUSE --
KILOWOG. LET ME GO WITH SODAM YAT. HE--HE'S JUST A ROOKIE...
YAT GOES. YOU STAY. I NEED YA HERE ON MOGO.
DON'T TELL ME YOU GOT A CRUSH ON YAT, 'RISIA...
CRUSH? I'LL CRUSH Y--
AAAAAAA!

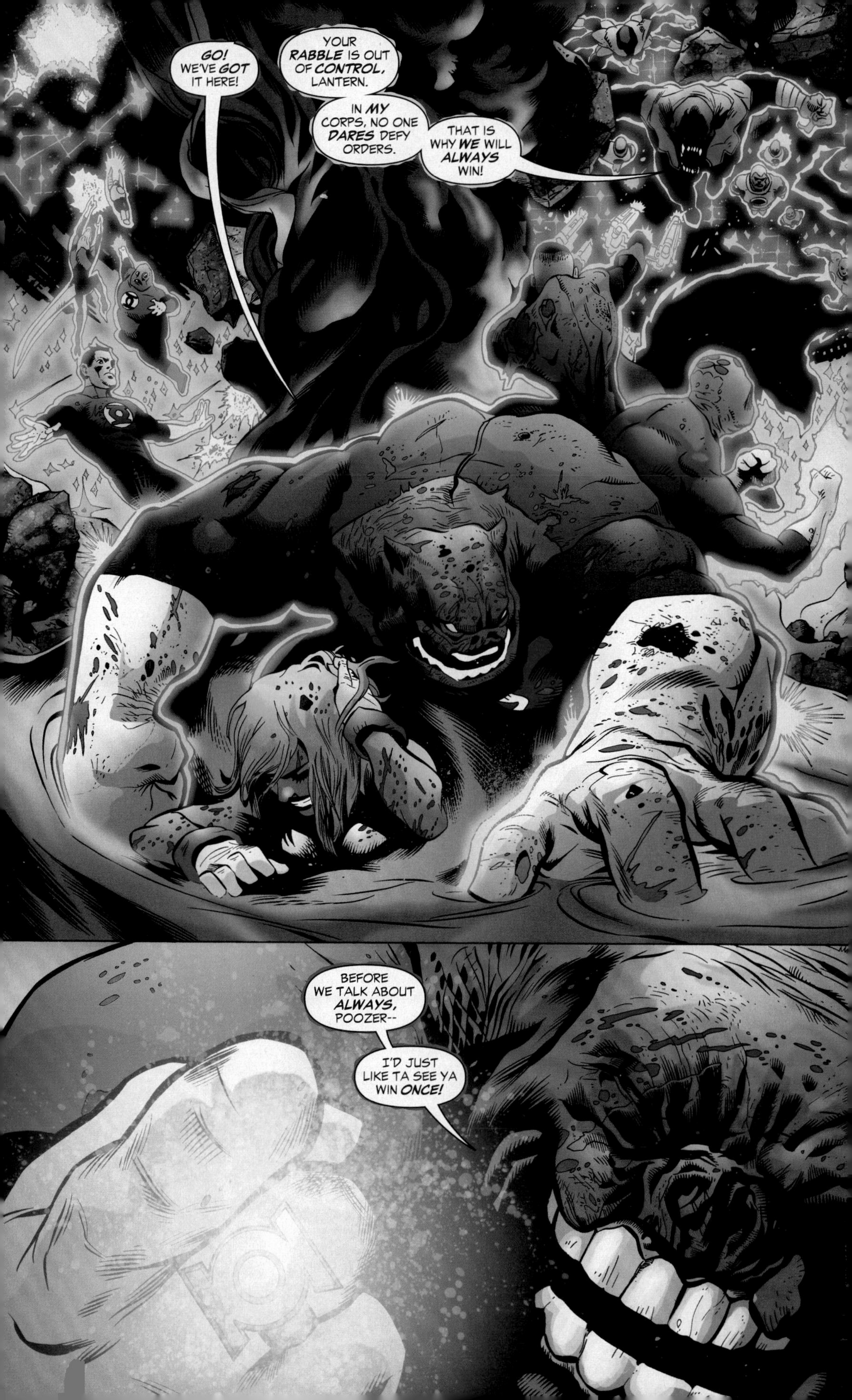
GO! WE'VE GOT IT HERE!
YOUR RABBLE IS OUT OF CONTROL, LANTERN.
IN MY CORPS, NO ONE DARES DEFY ORDERS.
THAT IS WHY WE WILL ALWAYS WIN!
BEFORE WE TALK ABOUT ALWAYS, POOZER--
I'D JUST LIKE TA SEE YA WIN ONCE!

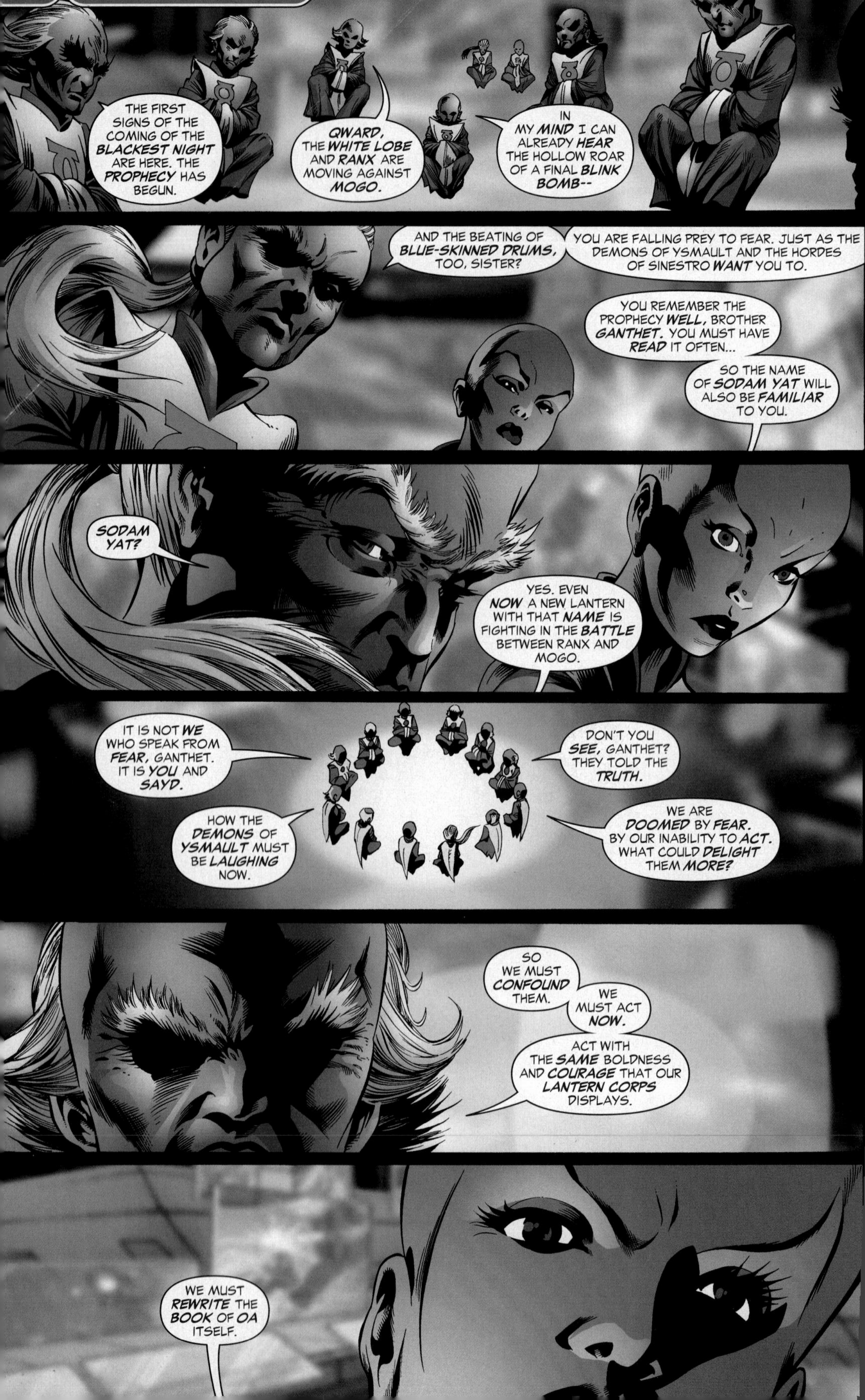
THE FIRST SIGNS OF THE COMING OF THE BLACKEST NIGHT ARE HERE. THE PROPHECY HAS BEGUN.
QWARD, THE WHITE LOBE AND RANX ARE MOVING AGAINST MOGO.
IN MY MIND I CAN ALREADY HEAR THE HOLLOW ROAR OF A FINAL BLINK BOMB--
AND THE BEATING OF BLUE-SKINNED DRUMS, TOO, SISTER?
YOU ARE FALLING PREY TO FEAR. JUST AS THE DEMONS OF YSMAULT AND THE HORDES OF SINESTRO WANT YOU TO.
YOU REMEMBER THE PROPHECY WELL, BROTHER GANTHET. YOU MUST HAVE READ IT OFTEN...
SO THE NAME OF SODAM YAT WILL ALSO BE FAMILIAR TO YOU.
SODAM YAT?
YES. EVEN NOW A NEW LANTERN WITH THAT NAME IS FIGHTING IN THE BATTLE BETWEEN RANX AND MOGO.
IT IS NOT WE WHO SPEAK FROM FEAR, GANTHET. IT IS YOU AND SAYD.
DON'T YOU SEE, GANTHET? THEY TOLD THE TRUTH.
HOW THE DEMONS OF YSMAULT MUST BE LAUGHING NOW.
WE ARE DOOMED BY FEAR. BY OUR INABILITY TO ACT. WHAT COULD DELIGHT THEM MORE?
SO WE MUST CONFOUND THEM.
WE MUST ACT NOW.
ACT WITH THE SAME BOLDNESS AND COURAGE THAT OUR LANTERN CORPS DISPLAYS.
WE MUST REWRITE THE BOOK OF OA ITSELF.

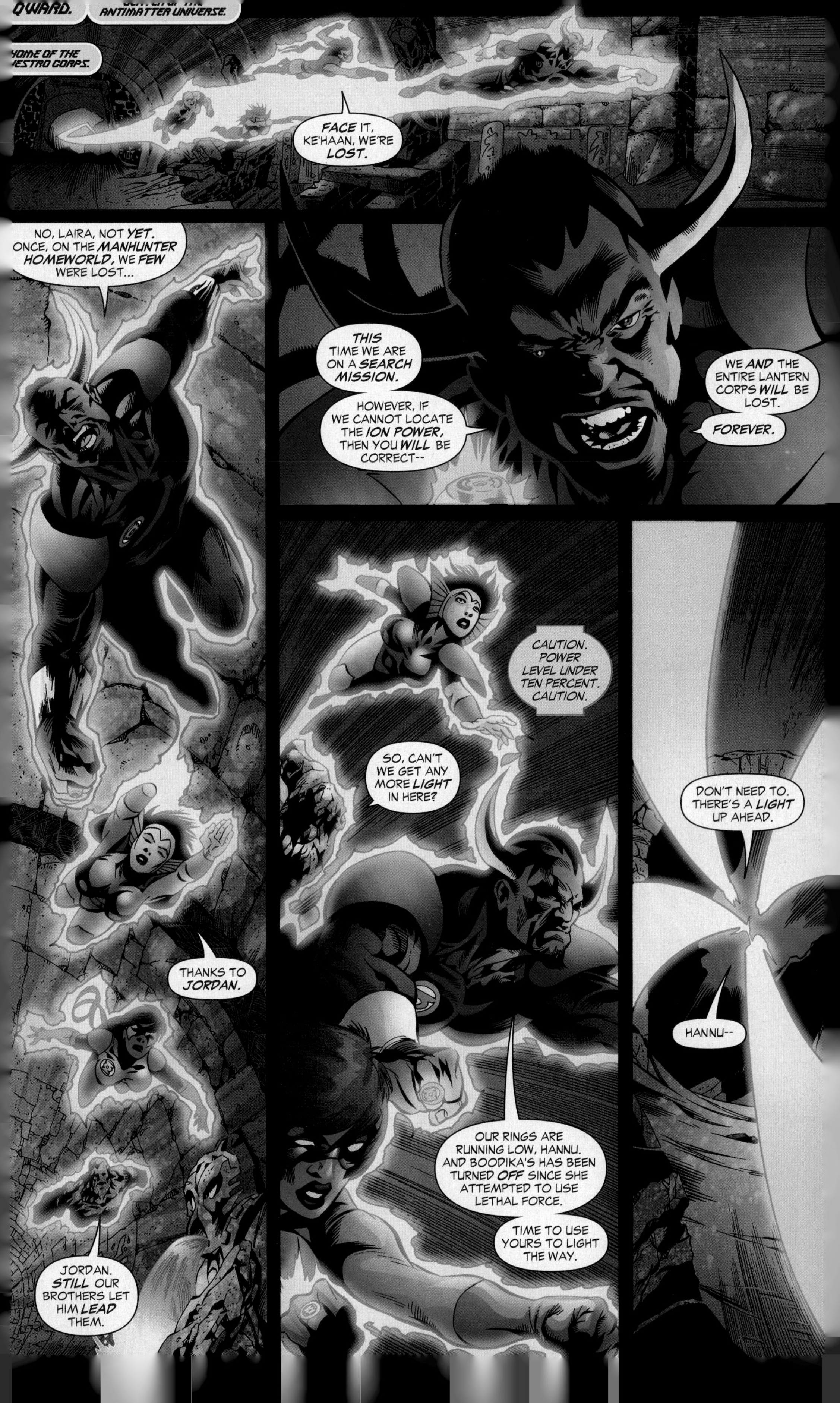
QWARD.
ANTIMATTER UNIVERSE.
HOME OF THE
ESTRO CORPS.
FACE IT, KE'HAAN, WE'RE LOST.
NO, LAIRA, NOT YET. ONCE, ON THE MANHUNTER HOMEWORLD, WE FEW WERE LOST...
THIS TIME WE ARE ON A SEARCH MISSION.
HOWEVER, IF WE CANNOT LOCATE THE ION POWER, THEN YOU WILL BE CORRECT--
WE AND THE ENTIRE LANTERN CORPS WILL BE LOST.
FOREVER.
THANKS TO JORDAN.
JORDAN. STILL OUR BROTHERS LET HIM LEAD THEM.
CAUTION. POWER LEVEL UNDER TEN PERCENT. CAUTION.
SO, CAN'T WE GET ANY MORE LIGHT IN HERE?
OUR RINGS ARE RUNNING LOW, HANNU. AND BOODIKA'S HAS BEEN TURNED OFF SINCE SHE ATTEMPTED TO USE LETHAL FORCE.
TIME TO USE YOURS TO LIGHT THE WAY.
DON'T NEED TO. THERE'S A LIGHT UP AHEAD.
HANNU--

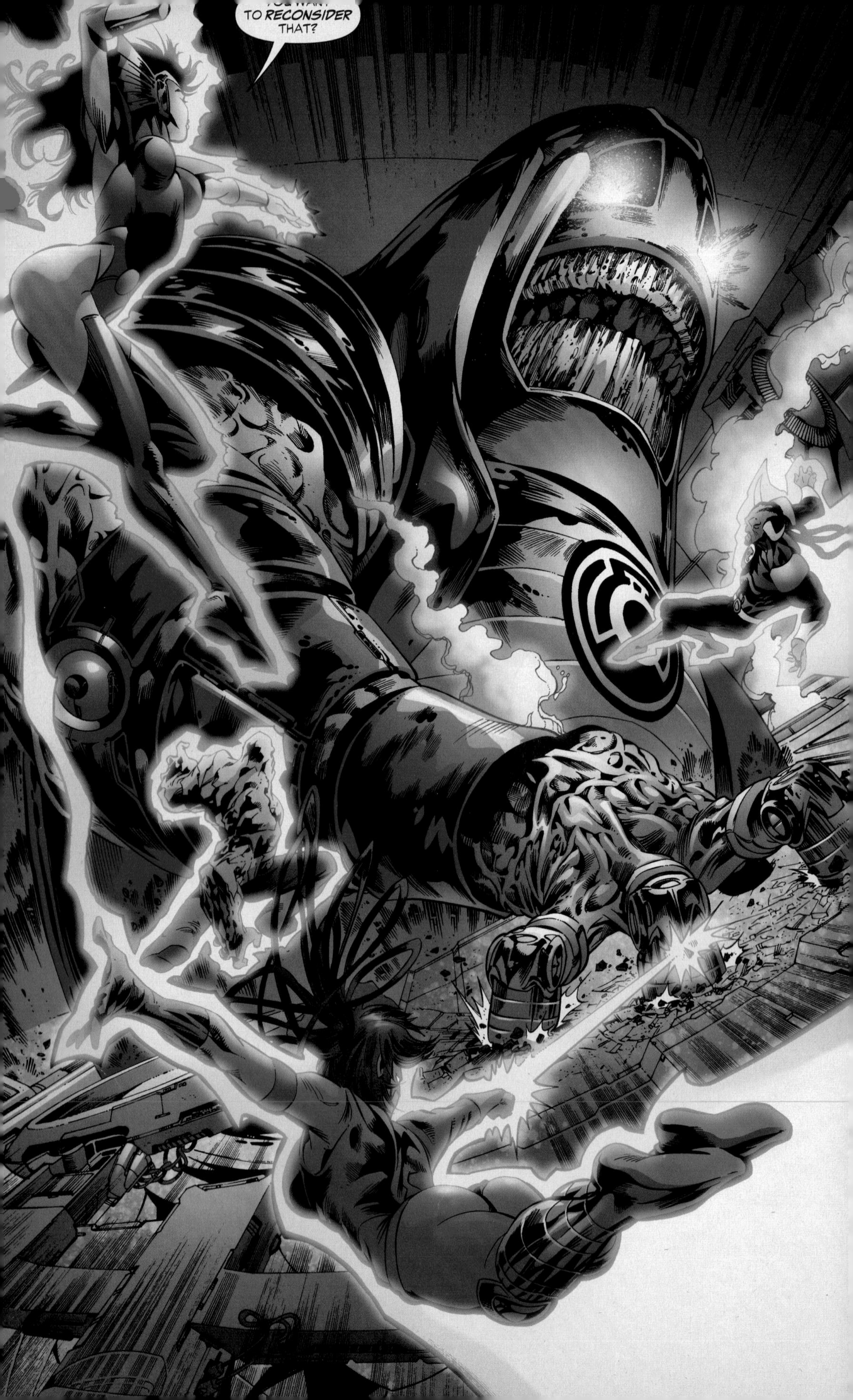
TO RECONSIDER THAT?

GREEN LANTERN 23
Ivan Reis
Oclair Albert
Moose Bauman

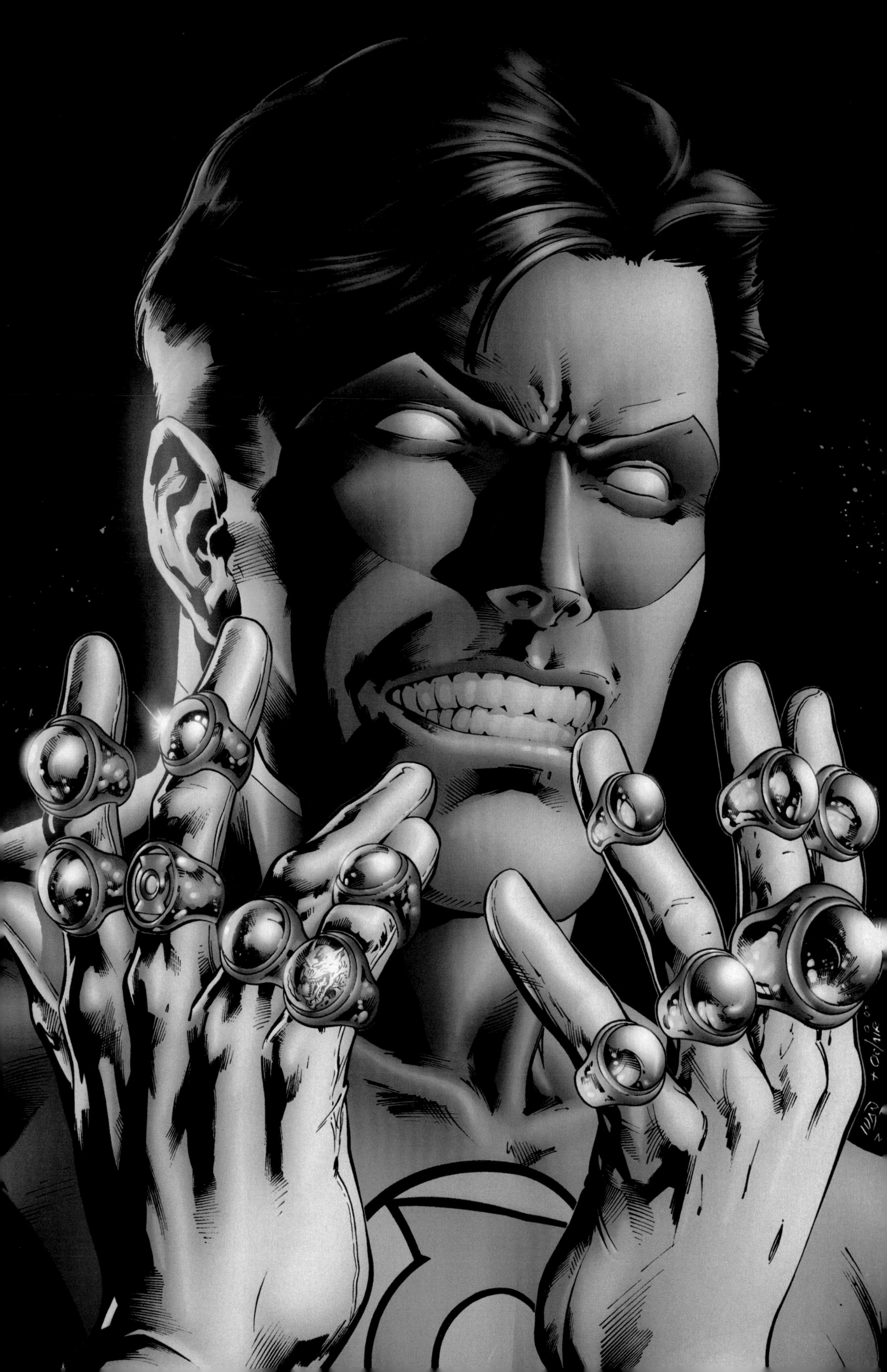

THE SINESTRO CORPS WAR
Chapter Five
BROKEN LAWS
Writer: **Geoff Johns**
Penciller: **Ivan Reis**
Inker: **Oclair Albert**
Colorist: **Moose Baumann**
Letterer: **Rob Leigh**

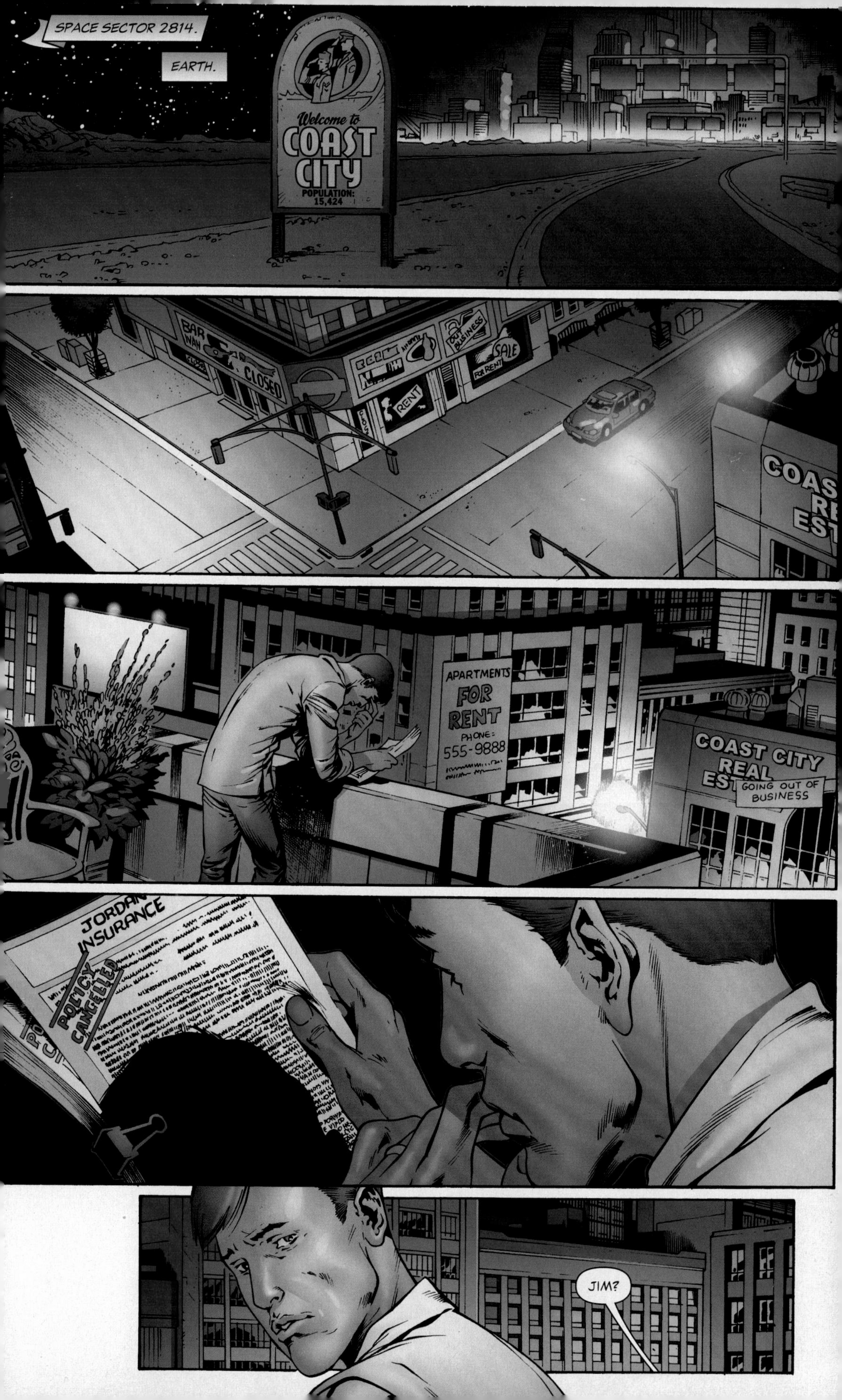

SPACE SECTOR 2814.
EARTH.
Welcome to COAST CITY
POPULATION: 15,424
BAR
CLOSED
RENT
SALE
FOR RENT
APARTMENTS FOR RENT
PHONE: 555-9888
COAST CITY REAL
GOING OUT OF BUSINESS
INSURANCE
POLICY CANCELLED
JIM?

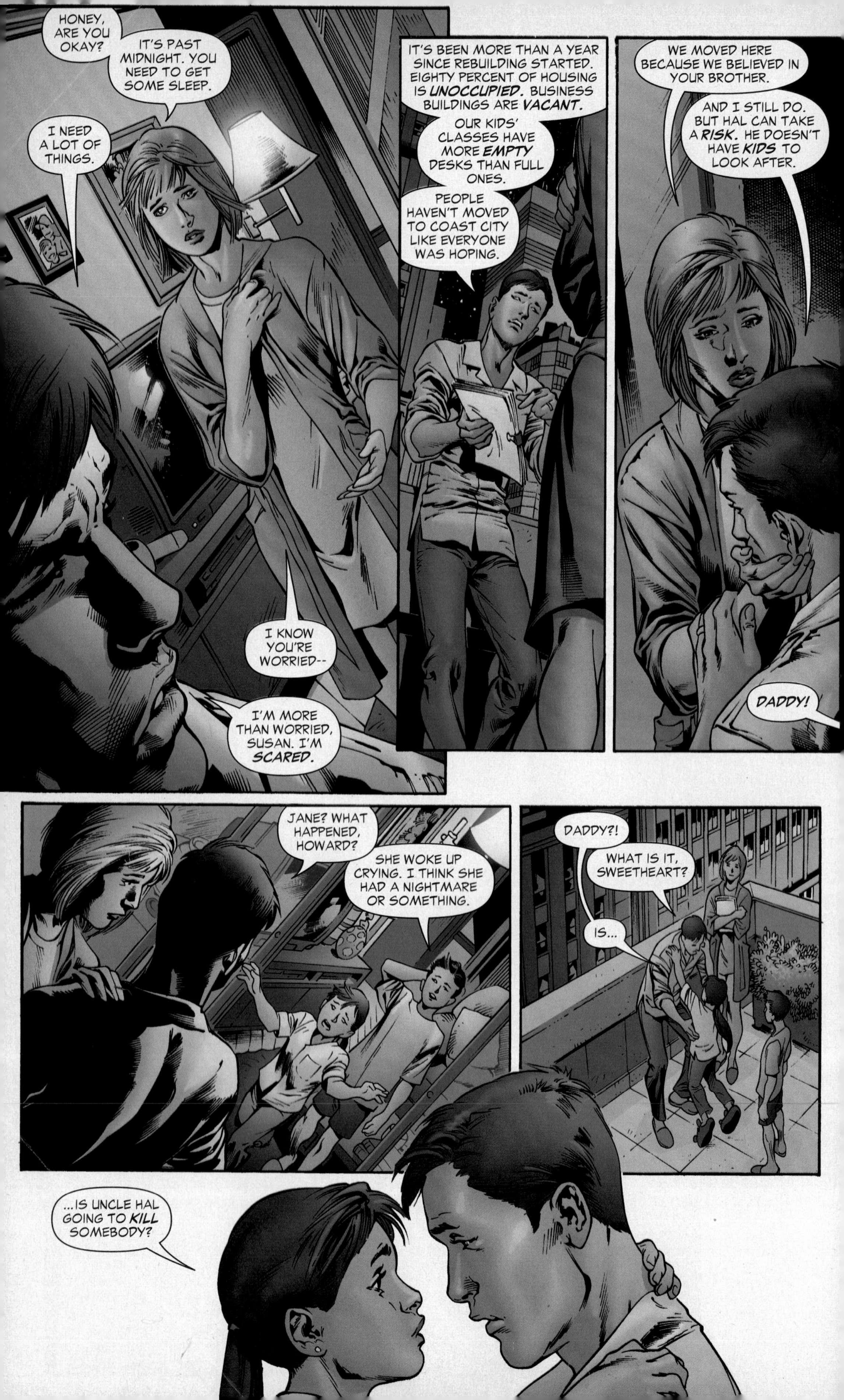

HONEY, ARE YOU OKAY?
IT'S PAST MIDNIGHT. YOU NEED TO GET SOME SLEEP.
I NEED A LOT OF THINGS.
I KNOW YOU'RE WORRIED--
I'M MORE THAN WORRIED, SUSAN. I'M SCARED.
IT'S BEEN MORE THAN A YEAR SINCE REBUILDING STARTED. EIGHTY PERCENT OF HOUSING IS UNOCCUPIED. BUSINESS BUILDINGS ARE VACANT.
OUR KIDS' CLASSES HAVE MORE EMPTY DESKS THAN FULL ONES.
PEOPLE HAVEN'T MOVED TO COAST CITY LIKE EVERYONE WAS HOPING.
WE MOVED HERE BECAUSE WE BELIEVED IN YOUR BROTHER.
AND I STILL DO. BUT HAL CAN TAKE A RISK. HE DOESN'T HAVE KIDS TO LOOK AFTER.
DADDY!
JANE? WHAT HAPPENED, HOWARD?
SHE WOKE UP CRYING. I THINK SHE HAD A NIGHTMARE OR SOMETHING.
DADDY?!
WHAT IS IT, SWEETHEART?
IS...
...IS UNCLE HAL GOING TO KILL SOMEBODY?

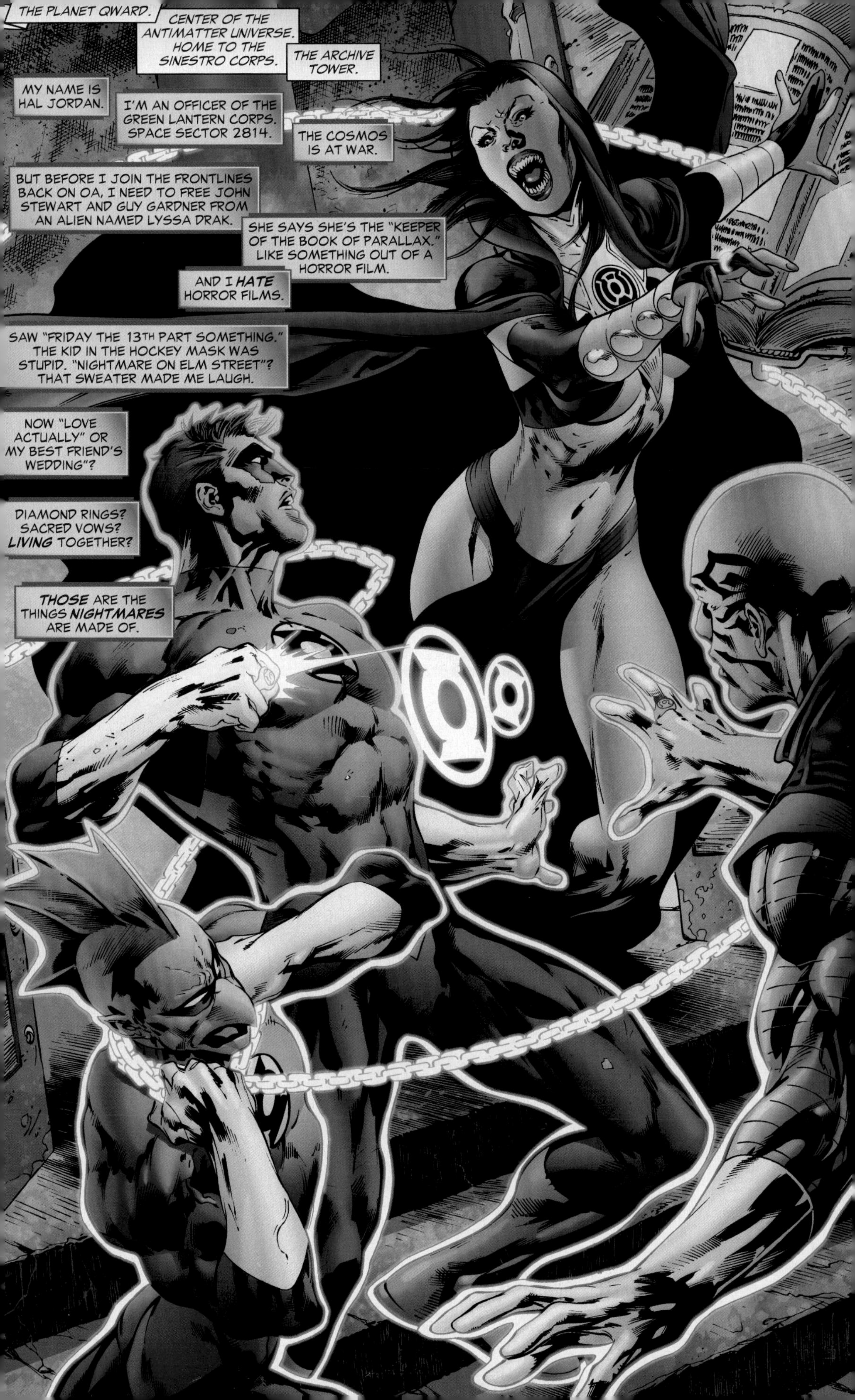
THE PLANET QWARD.
CENTER OF THE ANTIMATTER UNIVERSE. HOME TO THE SINESTRO CORPS.
THE ARCHIVE TOWER.
MY NAME IS HAL JORDAN.
I'M AN OFFICER OF THE GREEN LANTERN CORPS. SPACE SECTOR 2814.
THE COSMOS IS AT WAR.
BUT BEFORE I JOIN THE FRONTLINES BACK ON OA, I NEED TO FREE JOHN STEWART AND GUY GARDNER FROM AN ALIEN NAMED LYSSA DRAK.
SHE SAYS SHE'S THE "KEEPER OF THE BOOK OF PARALLAX." LIKE SOMETHING OUT OF A HORROR FILM.
AND I HATE HORROR FILMS.
SAW "FRIDAY THE 13TH PART SOMETHING." THE KID IN THE HOCKEY MASK WAS STUPID. "NIGHTMARE ON ELM STREET"? THAT SWEATER MADE ME LAUGH.
NOW "LOVE ACTUALLY" OR MY BEST FRIEND'S WEDDING"?
DIAMOND RINGS? SACRED VOWS? LIVING TOGETHER?
THOSE ARE THE THINGS NIGHTMARES ARE MADE OF.

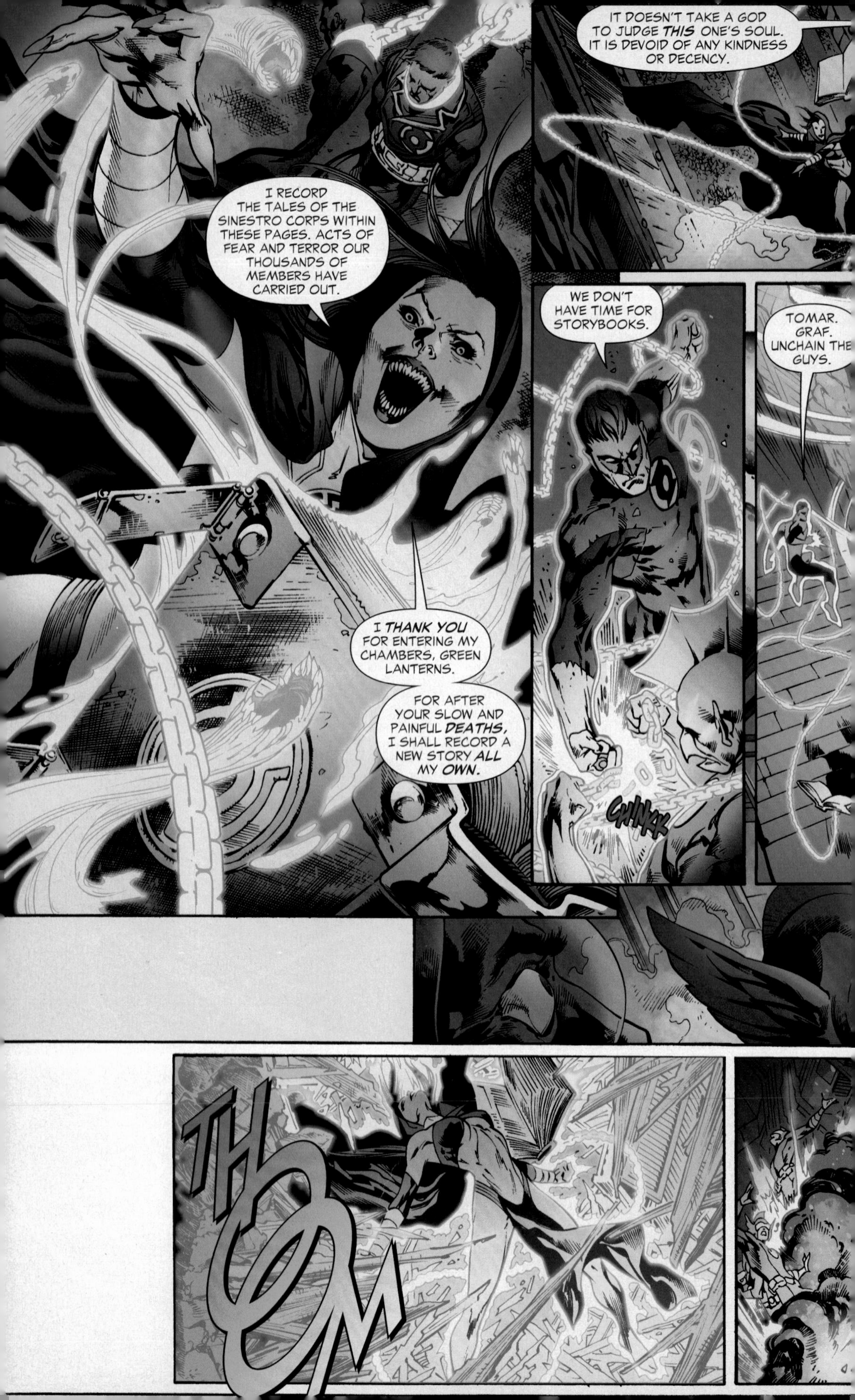
I RECORD THE TALES OF THE SINESTRO CORPS WITHIN THESE PAGES. ACTS OF FEAR AND TERROR OUR THOUSANDS OF MEMBERS HAVE CARRIED OUT.
I THANK YOU FOR ENTERING MY CHAMBERS, GREEN LANTERNS.
FOR AFTER YOUR SLOW AND PAINFUL DEATHS, I SHALL RECORD A NEW STORY ALL MY OWN.
IT DOESN'T TAKE A GOD TO JUDGE THIS ONE'S SOUL. IT IS DEVOID OF ANY KINDNESS OR DECENCY.
WE DON'T HAVE TIME FOR STORYBOOKS.
CHINKK
TOMAR. GRAF. UNCHAIN THE GUYS.
THOOM

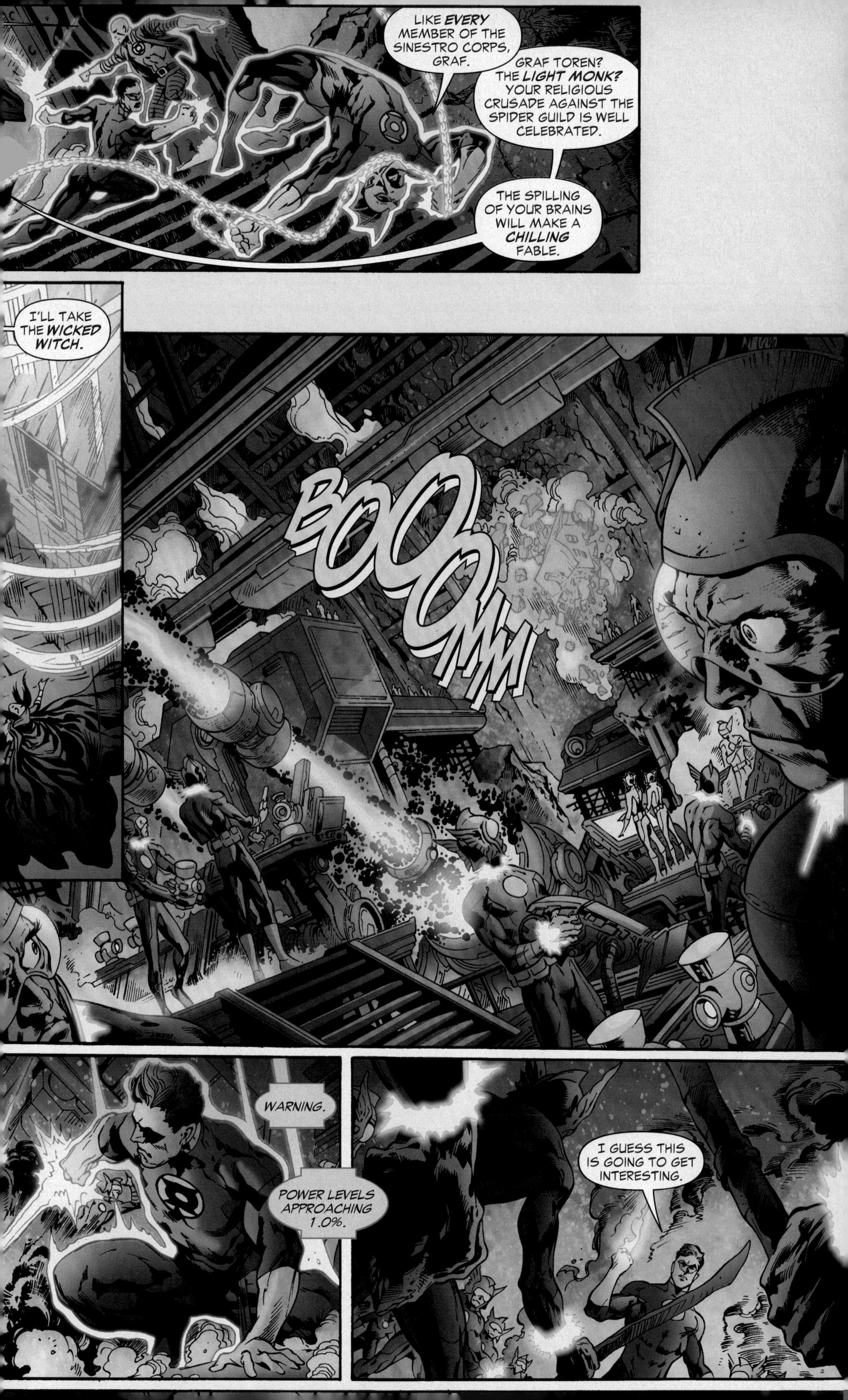
LIKE EVERY MEMBER OF THE SINESTRO CORPS, GRAF.
GRAF TOREN? THE LIGHT MONK? YOUR RELIGIOUS CRUSADE AGAINST THE SPIDER GUILD IS WELL CELEBRATED.
THE SPILLING OF YOUR BRAINS WILL MAKE A CHILLING FABLE.
I'LL TAKE THE WICKED WITCH.
BOOOMM
WARNING.
POWER LEVELS APPROACHING 1.0%.
I GUESS THIS IS GOING TO GET INTERESTING.

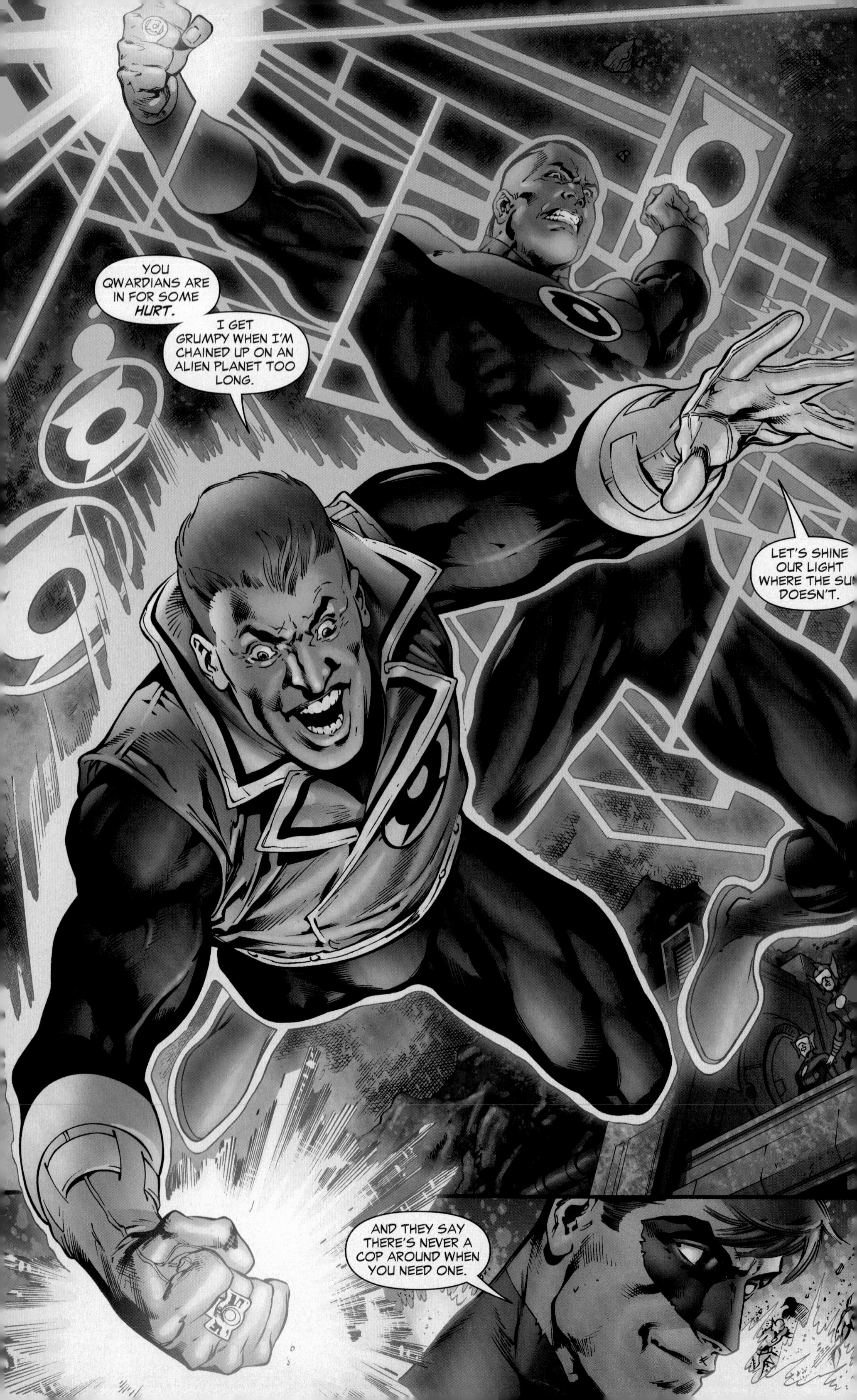
YOU QWARDIANS ARE IN FOR SOME HURT.
I GET GRUMPY WHEN I'M CHAINED UP ON AN ALIEN PLANET TOO LONG.
LET'S SHINE OUR LIGHT WHERE THE SU DOESN'T.
AND THEY SAY THERE'S NEVER A COP AROUND WHEN YOU NEED ONE.

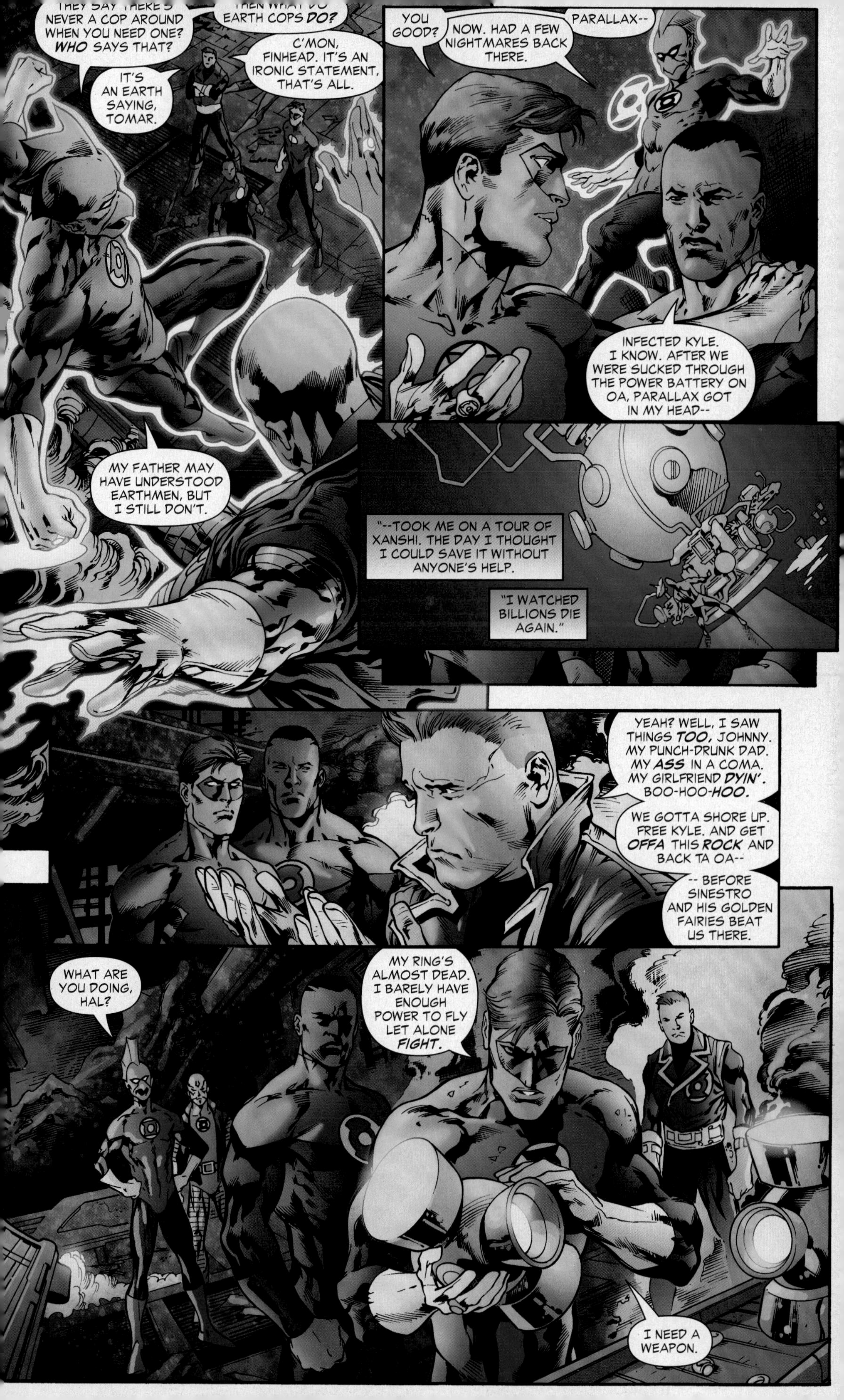
THEY SAY THERE'S NEVER A COP AROUND WHEN YOU NEED ONE? WHO SAYS THAT?
THEN WHAT DO EARTH COPS DO?
IT'S AN EARTH SAYING, TOMAR.
C'MON, FINHEAD. IT'S AN IRONIC STATEMENT, THAT'S ALL.
YOU GOOD?
NOW. HAD A FEW NIGHTMARES BACK THERE.
PARALLAX--
INFECTED KYLE. I KNOW. AFTER WE WERE SUCKED THROUGH THE POWER BATTERY ON OA, PARALLAX GOT IN MY HEAD--
MY FATHER MAY HAVE UNDERSTOOD EARTHMEN, BUT I STILL DON'T.
"--TOOK ME ON A TOUR OF XANSHI. THE DAY I THOUGHT I COULD SAVE IT WITHOUT ANYONE'S HELP.
"I WATCHED BILLIONS DIE AGAIN."
YEAH? WELL, I SAW THINGS TOO, JOHNNY. MY PUNCH-DRUNK DAD. MY ASS IN A COMA. MY GIRLFRIEND DYIN'. BOO-HOO-HOO.
WE GOTTA SHORE UP. FREE KYLE. AND GET OFFA THIS ROCK AND BACK TA OA--
-- BEFORE SINESTRO AND HIS GOLDEN FAIRIES BEAT US THERE.
WHAT ARE YOU DOING, HAL?
MY RING'S ALMOST DEAD. I BARELY HAVE ENOUGH POWER TO FLY LET ALONE FIGHT.
I NEED A WEAPON.

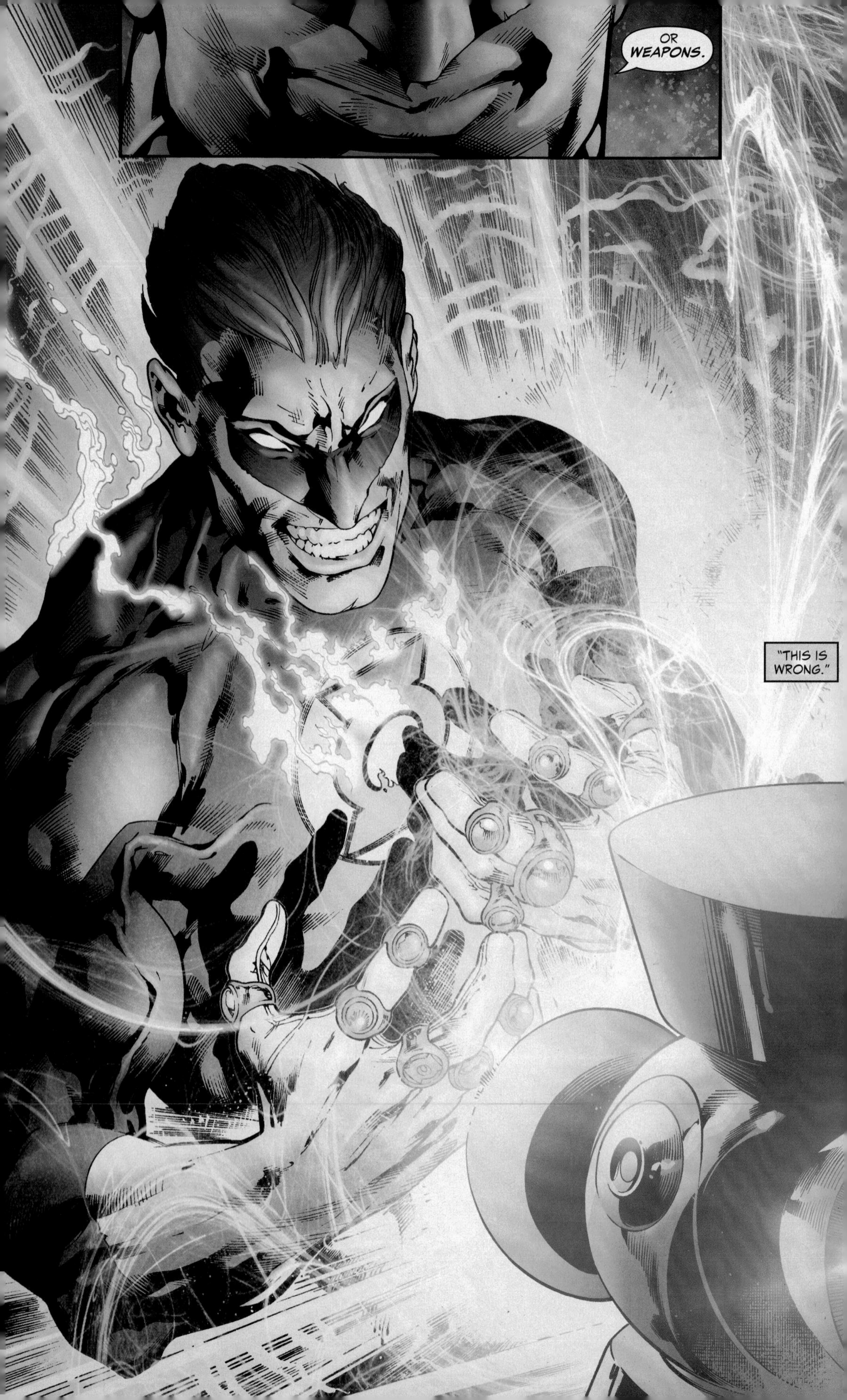
OR WEAPONS.
"THIS IS WRONG."

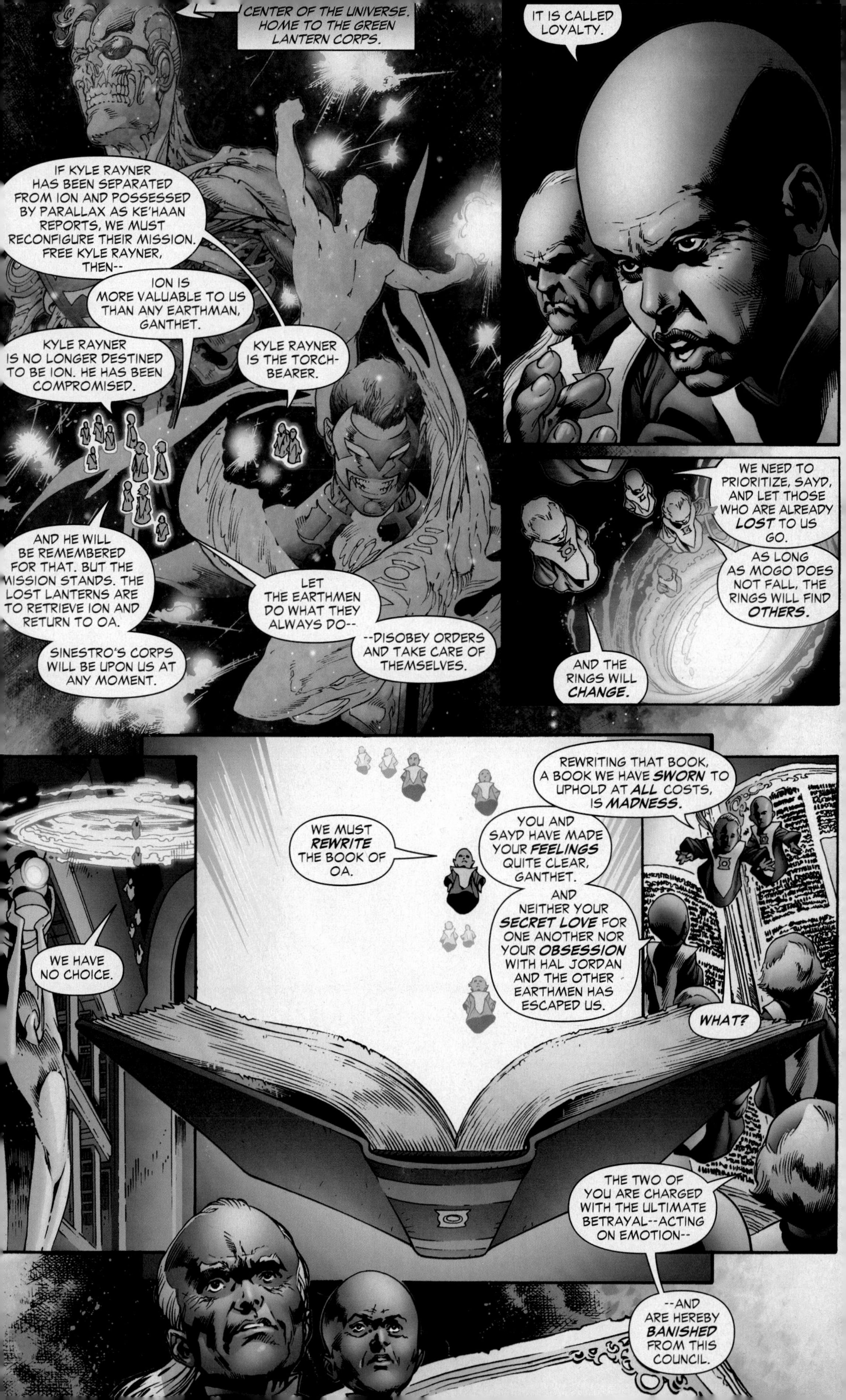
CENTER OF THE UNIVERSE. HOME TO THE GREEN LANTERN CORPS.
IT IS CALLED LOYALTY.
IF KYLE RAYNER HAS BEEN SEPARATED FROM ION AND POSSESSED BY PARALLAX AS KE'HAAN REPORTS, WE MUST RECONFIGURE THEIR MISSION. FREE KYLE RAYNER, THEN--
ION IS MORE VALUABLE TO US THAN ANY EARTHMAN, GANTHET.
KYLE RAYNER IS NO LONGER DESTINED TO BE ION. HE HAS BEEN COMPROMISED.
KYLE RAYNER IS THE TORCH-BEARER.
AND HE WILL BE REMEMBERED FOR THAT. BUT THE MISSION STANDS. THE LOST LANTERNS ARE TO RETRIEVE ION AND RETURN TO OA.
SINESTRO'S CORPS WILL BE UPON US AT ANY MOMENT.
LET THE EARTHMEN DO WHAT THEY ALWAYS DO--
--DISOBEY ORDERS AND TAKE CARE OF THEMSELVES.
WE NEED TO PRIORITIZE, SAYD, AND LET THOSE WHO ARE ALREADY LOST TO US GO.
AS LONG AS MOGO DOES NOT FALL, THE RINGS WILL FIND OTHERS.
AND THE RINGS WILL CHANGE.
WE HAVE NO CHOICE.
WE MUST REWRITE THE BOOK OF OA.
REWRITING THAT BOOK, A BOOK WE HAVE SWORN TO UPHOLD AT ALL COSTS, IS MADNESS.
YOU AND SAYD HAVE MADE YOUR FEELINGS QUITE CLEAR, GANTHET.
AND NEITHER YOUR SECRET LOVE FOR ONE ANOTHER NOR YOUR OBSESSION WITH HAL JORDAN AND THE OTHER EARTHMEN HAS ESCAPED US.
WHAT?
THE TWO OF YOU ARE CHARGED WITH THE ULTIMATE BETRAYAL--ACTING ON EMOTION--
--AND ARE HEREBY BANISHED FROM THIS COUNCIL.

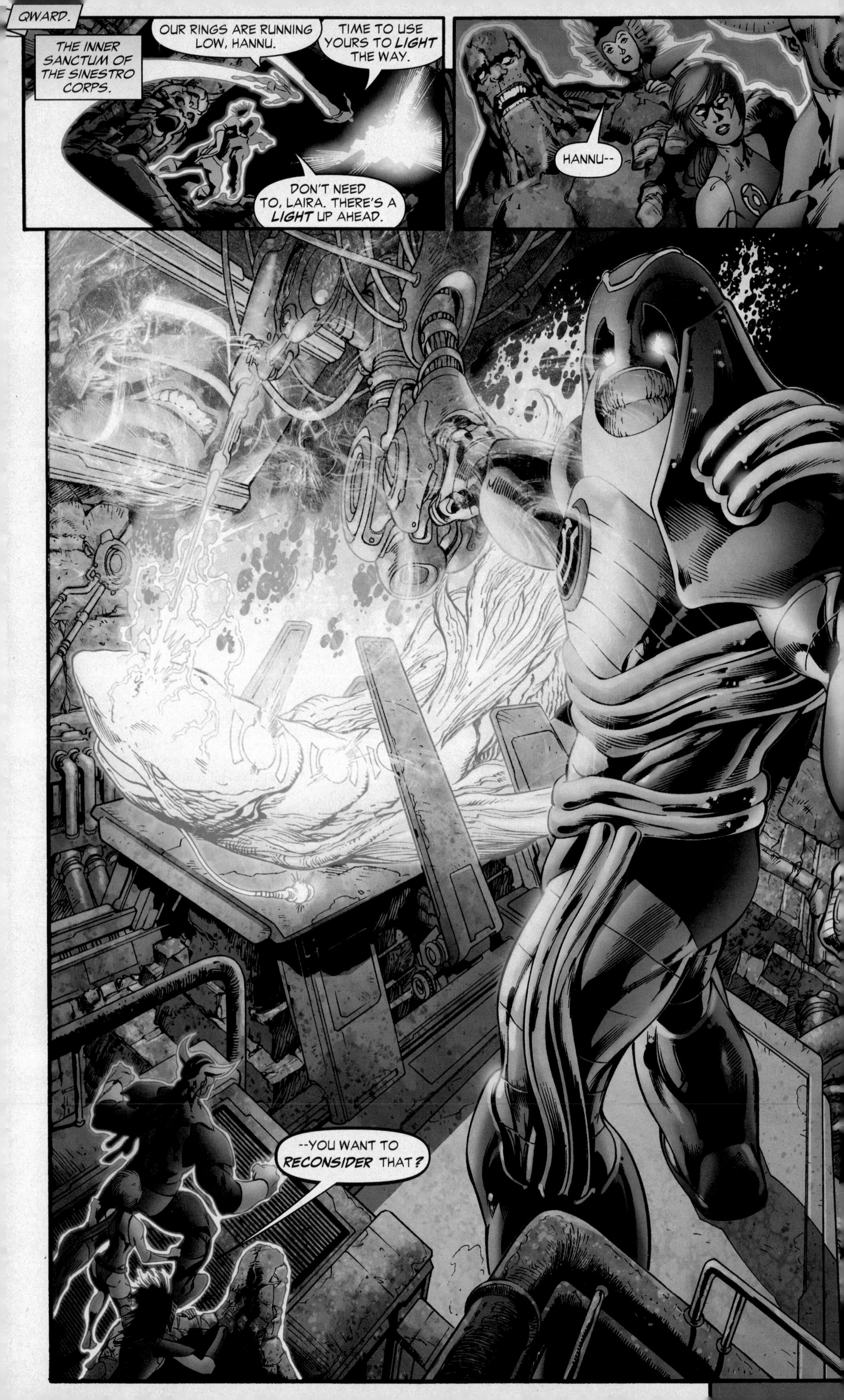
QWARD.
THE INNER SANCTUM OF THE SINESTRO CORPS.
OUR RINGS ARE RUNNING LOW, HANNU.
TIME TO USE YOURS TO LIGHT THE WAY.
DON'T NEED TO, LAIRA. THERE'S A LIGHT UP AHEAD.
HANNU--
--YOU WANT TO RECONSIDER THAT?

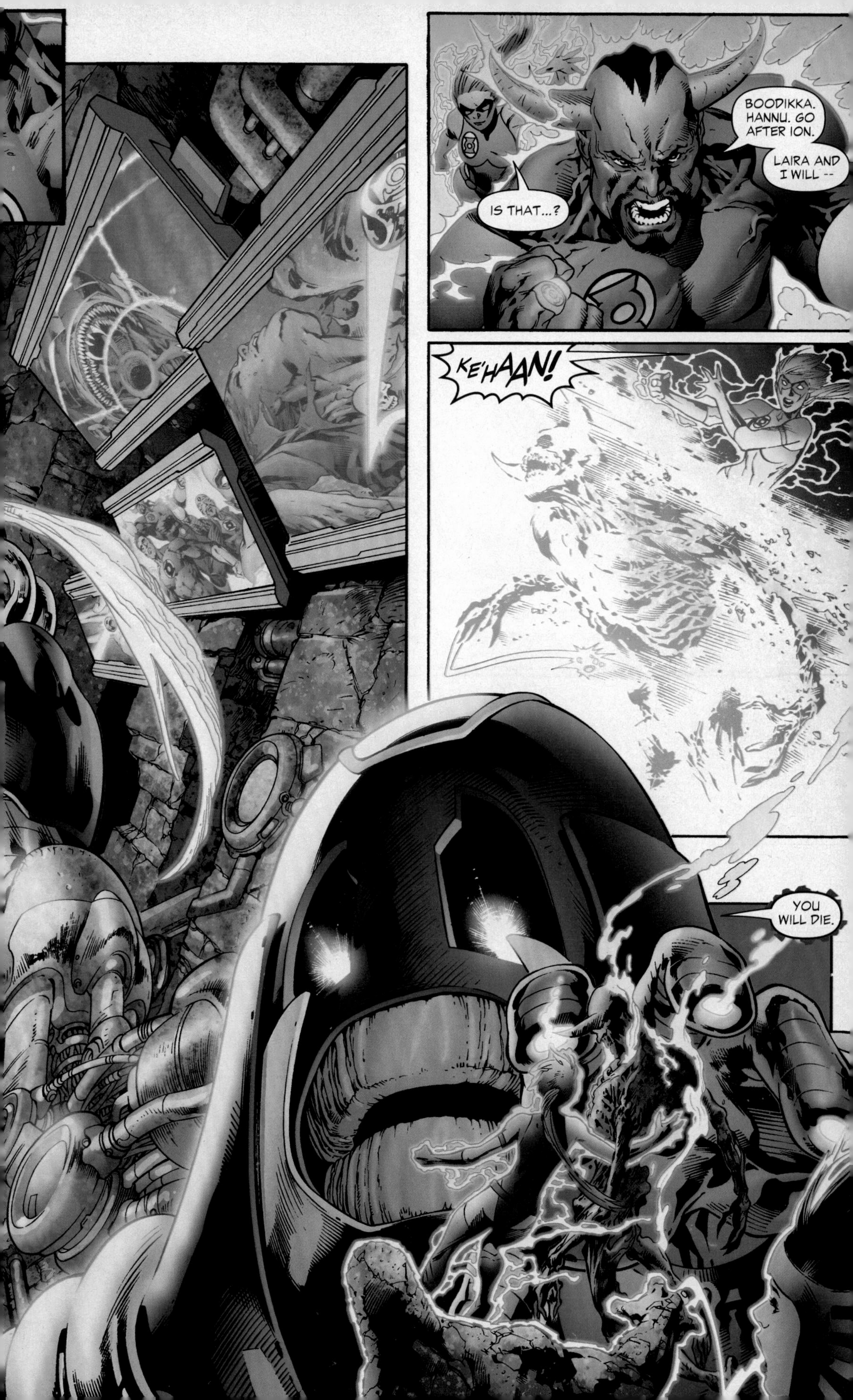
BOODIKKA. HANNU. GO AFTER ION.
LAIRA AND I WILL --
IS THAT...?
KE'HAAN!
YOU WILL DIE.

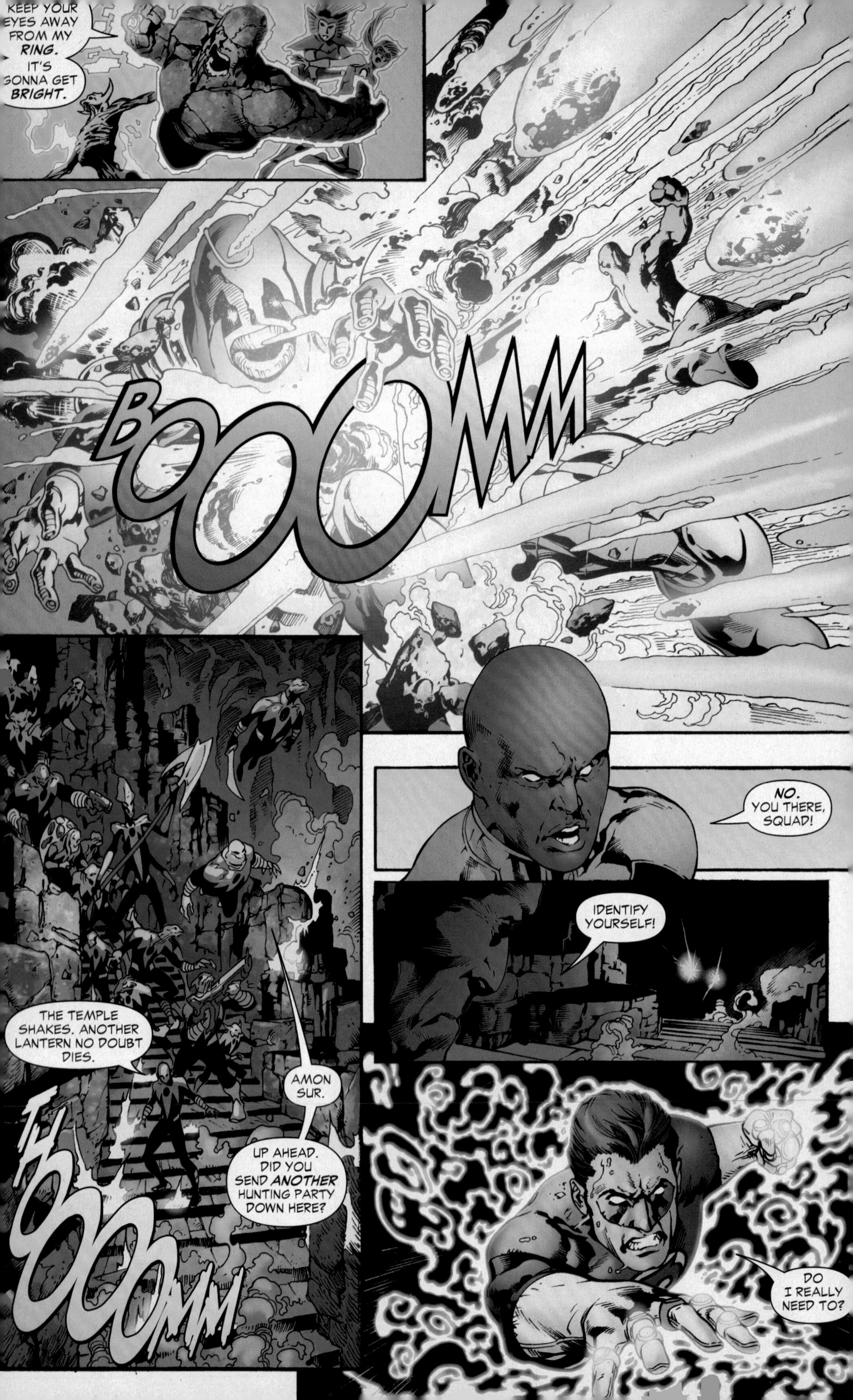
KEEP YOUR EYES AWAY FROM MY RING. IT'S GONNA GET BRIGHT.
BOOOMMM
NO. YOU THERE, SQUAD!
IDENTIFY YOURSELF!
THE TEMPLE SHAKES. ANOTHER LANTERN NO DOUBT DIES.
AMON SUR.
UP AHEAD. DID YOU SEND ANOTHER HUNTING PARTY DOWN HERE?
THOOOMM
DO I REALLY NEED TO?

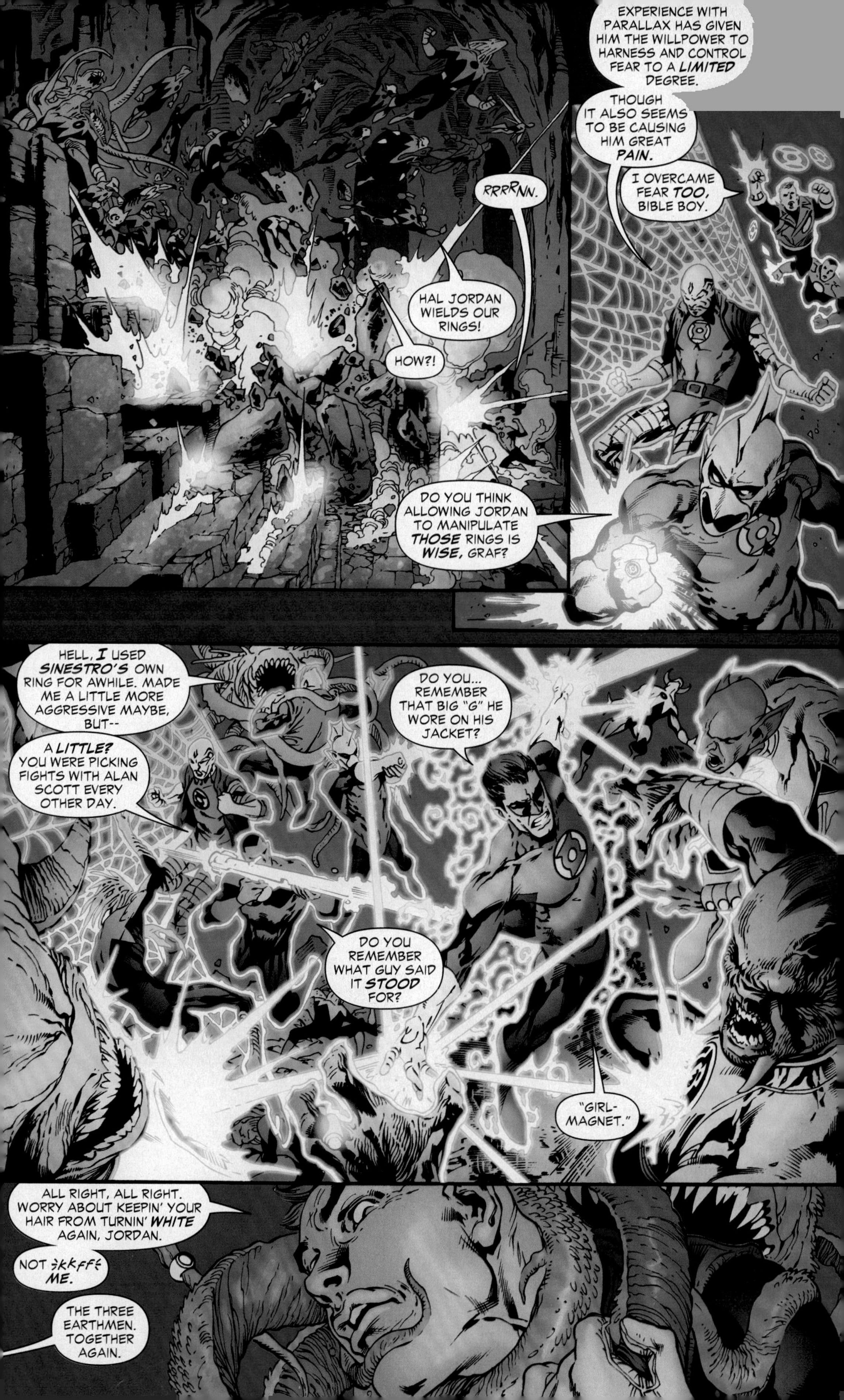
EXPERIENCE WITH PARALLAX HAS GIVEN HIM THE WILLPOWER TO HARNESS AND CONTROL FEAR TO A LIMITED DEGREE.
THOUGH IT ALSO SEEMS TO BE CAUSING HIM GREAT PAIN.
I OVERCAME FEAR TOO, BIBLE BOY.
RRRRNN.
HAL JORDAN WIELDS OUR RINGS!
HOW?!
DO YOU THINK ALLOWING JORDAN TO MANIPULATE THOSE RINGS IS WISE, GRAF?
HELL, I USED SINESTRO'S OWN RING FOR AWHILE. MADE ME A LITTLE MORE AGGRESSIVE MAYBE, BUT--
A LITTLE? YOU WERE PICKING FIGHTS WITH ALAN SCOTT EVERY OTHER DAY.
DO YOU... REMEMBER THAT BIG "G" HE WORE ON HIS JACKET?
DO YOU REMEMBER WHAT GUY SAID IT STOOD FOR?
"GIRL-MAGNET."
ALL RIGHT, ALL RIGHT. WORRY ABOUT KEEPIN' YOUR HAIR FROM TURNIN' WHITE AGAIN, JORDAN.
NOT SKKFF ME.
THE THREE EARTHMEN. TOGETHER AGAIN.

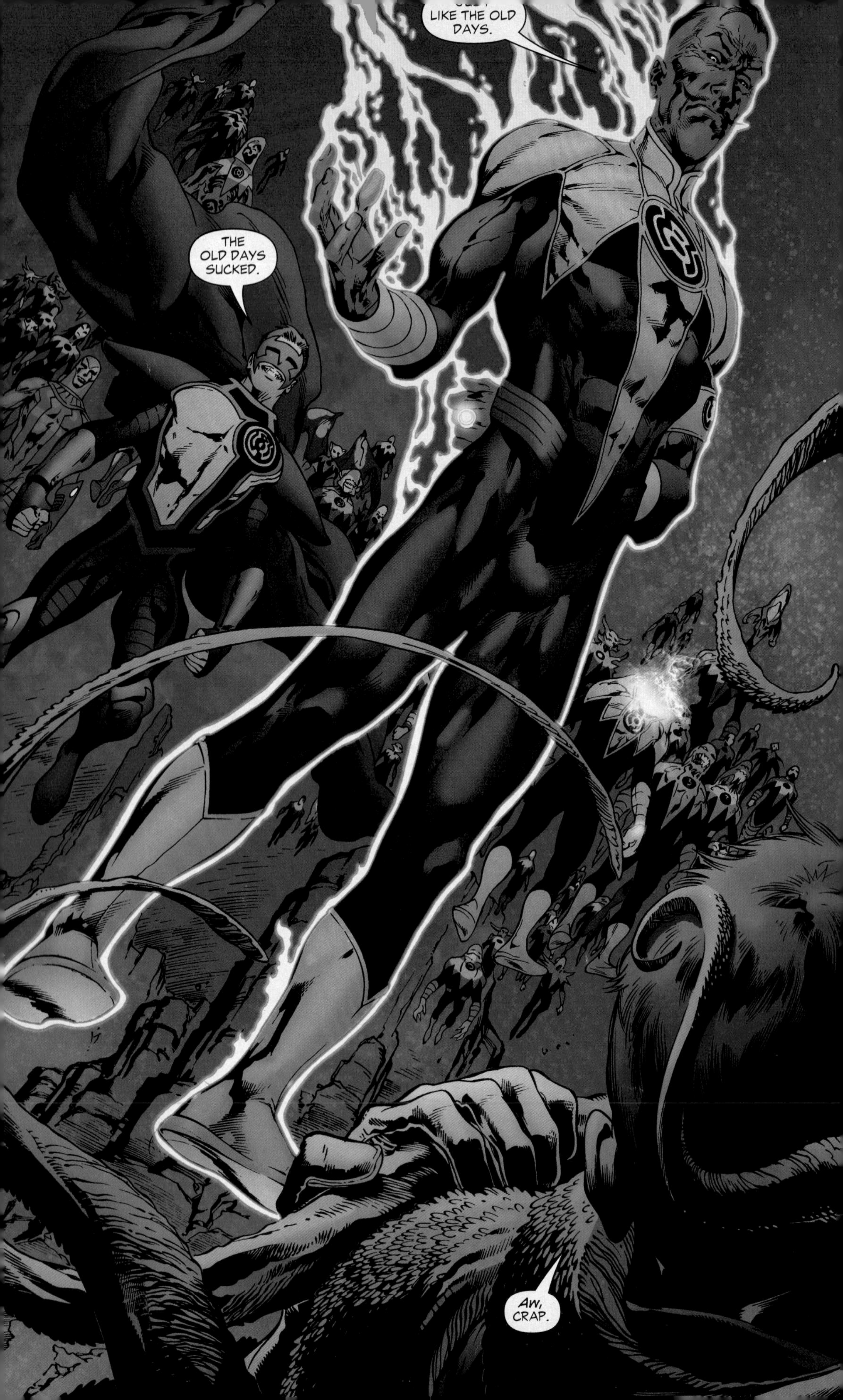
LIKE THE OLD DAYS.
THE OLD DAYS SUCKED.
AW, CRAP.

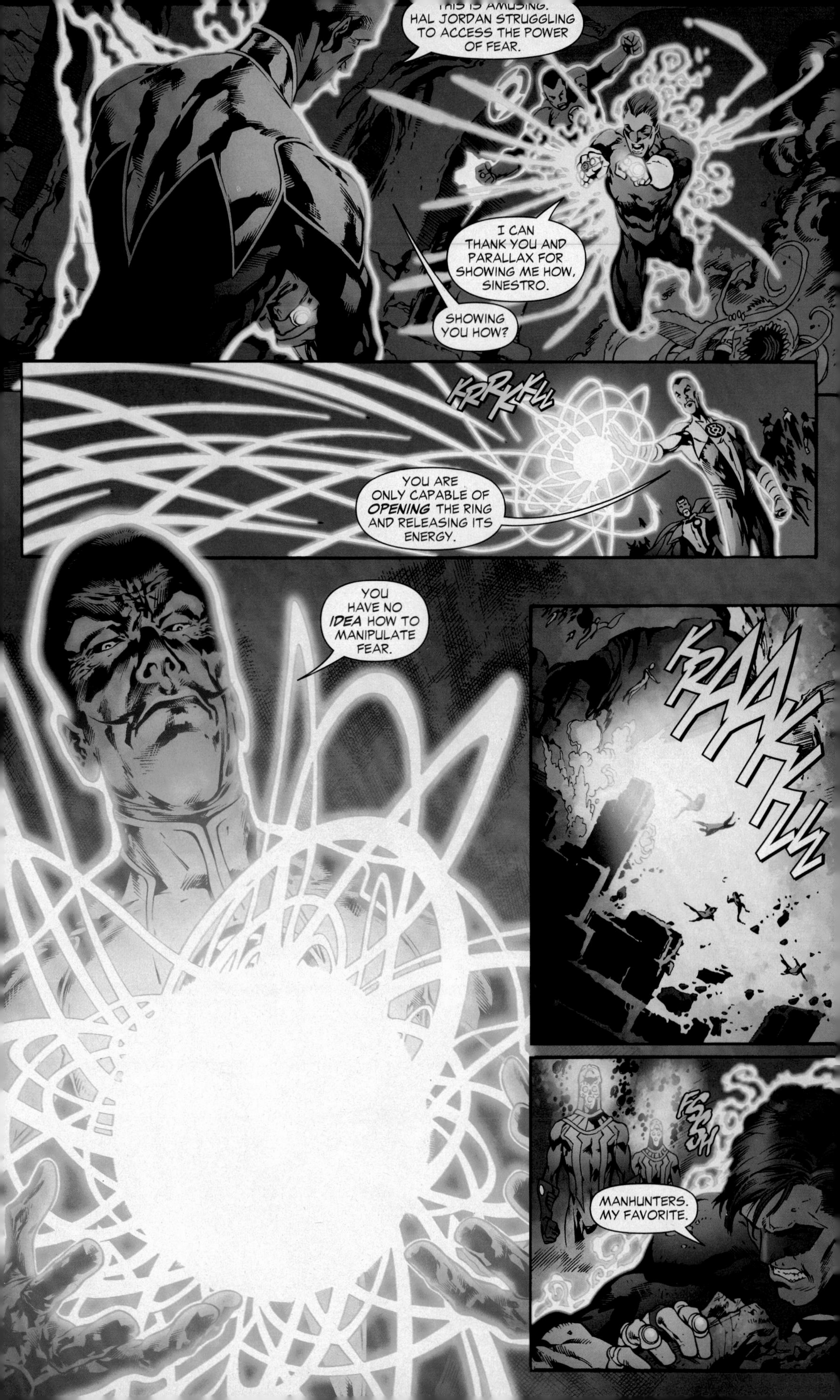
THIS IS AMUSING. HAL JORDAN STRUGGLING TO ACCESS THE POWER OF FEAR.
I CAN THANK YOU AND PARALLAX FOR SHOWING ME HOW, SINESTRO.
SHOWING YOU HOW?
KRRKKU
YOU ARE ONLY CAPABLE OF OPENING THE RING AND RELEASING ITS ENERGY.
YOU HAVE NO IDEA HOW TO MANIPULATE FEAR.
KRAAKKOW
FSSSH
MANHUNTERS. MY FAVORITE.

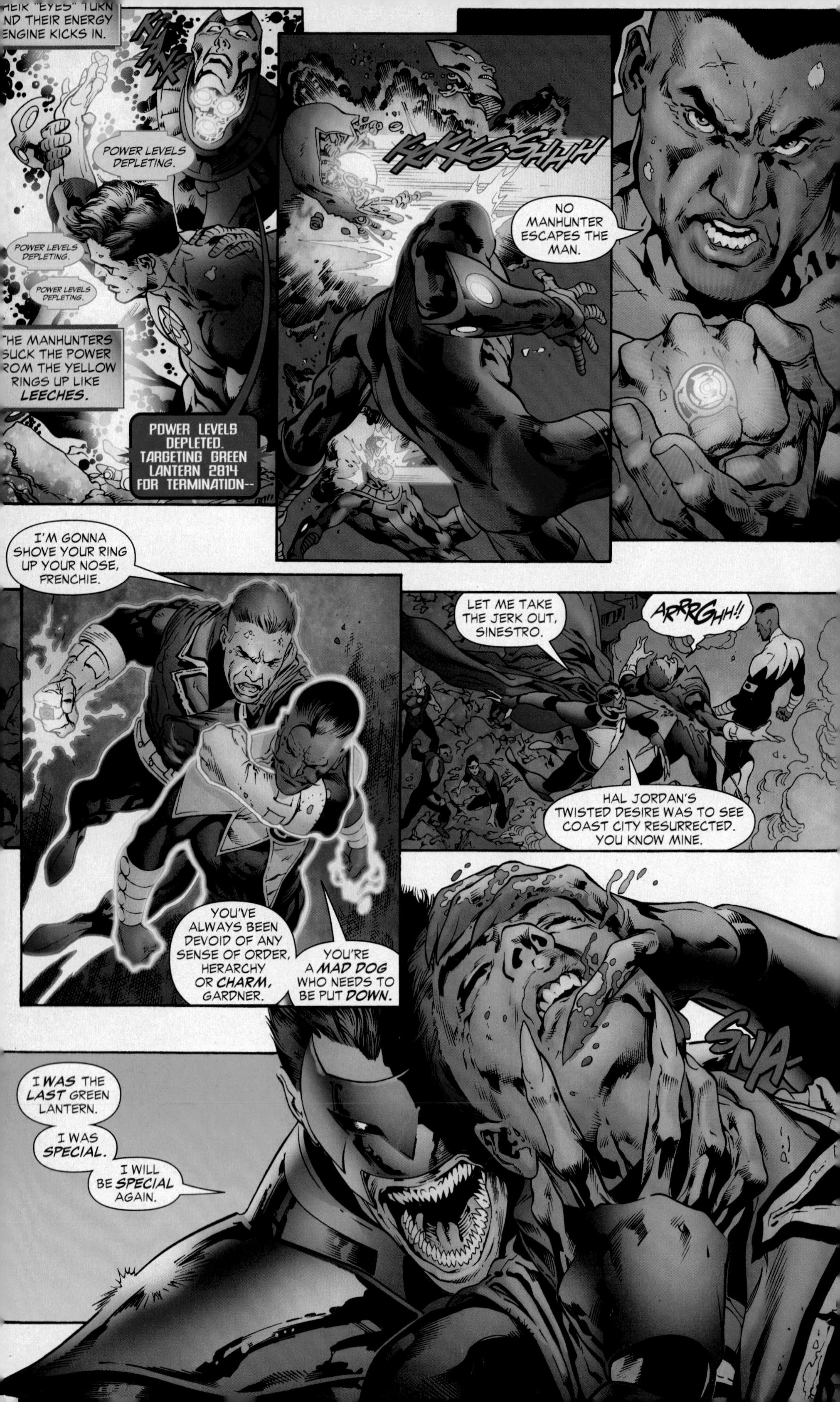

HEIR "EYES" TURN
ND THEIR ENERGY
ENGINE KICKS IN.
KLANK
POWER LEVELS DEPLETING.
POWER LEVELS DEPLETING.
POWER LEVELS DEPLETING.
THE MANHUNTERS SUCK THE POWER ROM THE YELLOW RINGS UP LIKE LEECHES.
POWER LEVELS DEPLETED. TARGETING GREEN LANTERN 2814 FOR TERMINATION--
KKKSSHHH
NO MANHUNTER ESCAPES THE MAN.
I'M GONNA SHOVE YOUR RING UP YOUR NOSE, FRENCHIE.
LET ME TAKE THE JERK OUT, SINESTRO.
ARRRGHH!!
HAL JORDAN'S TWISTED DESIRE WAS TO SEE COAST CITY RESURRECTED. YOU KNOW MINE.
YOU'VE ALWAYS BEEN DEVOID OF ANY SENSE OF ORDER, HERARCHY OR CHARM, GARDNER.
YOU'RE A MAD DOG WHO NEEDS TO BE PUT DOWN.
I WAS THE LAST GREEN LANTERN.
I WAS SPECIAL.
I WILL BE SPECIAL AGAIN.
SNA

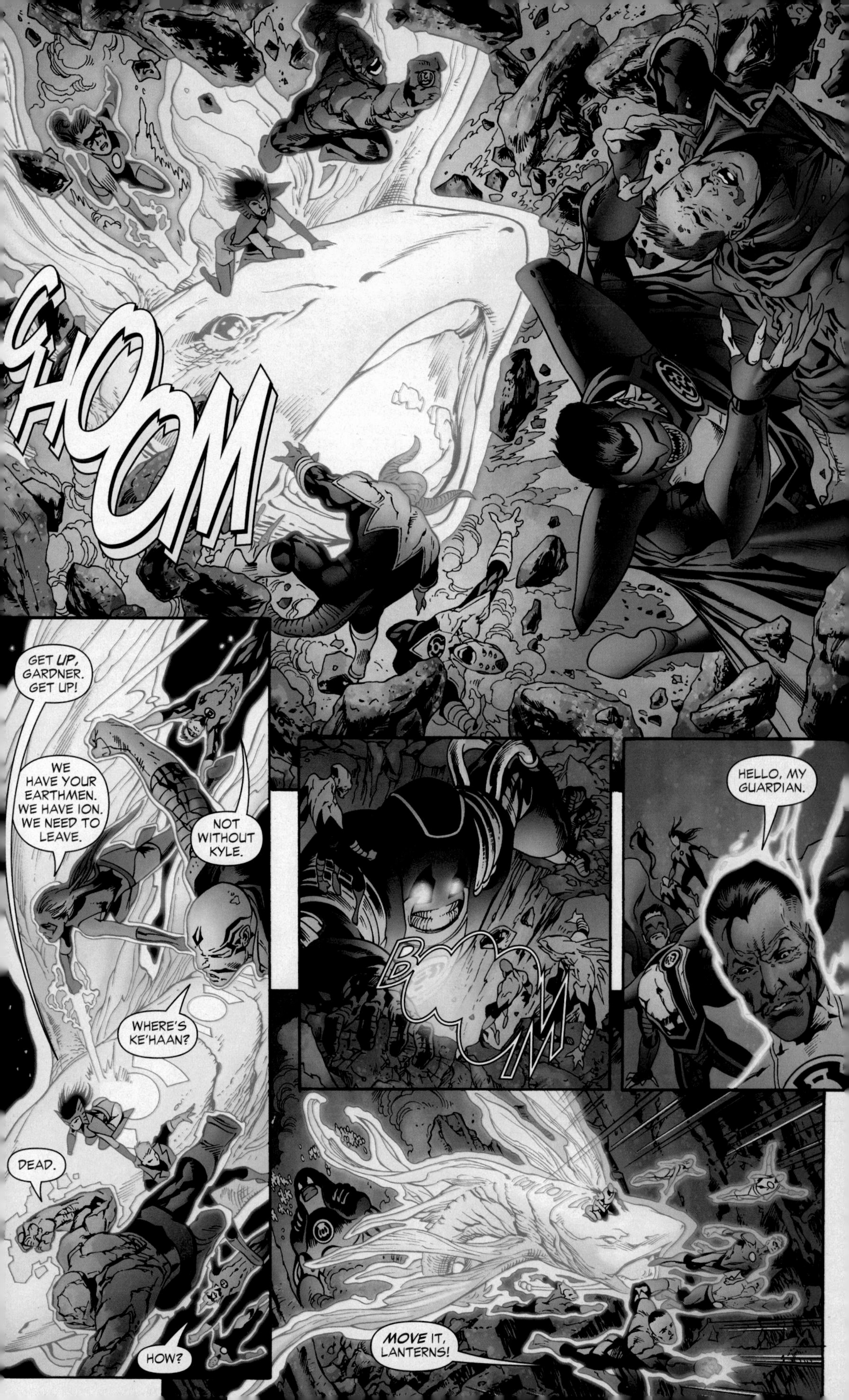
CHOOM
GET UP, GARDNER. GET UP!
WE HAVE YOUR EARTHMEN. WE HAVE ION. WE NEED TO LEAVE.
NOT WITHOUT KYLE.
WHERE'S KE'HAAN?
DEAD.
HOW?
BOOM
HELLO, MY GUARDIAN.
MOVE IT, LANTERNS!

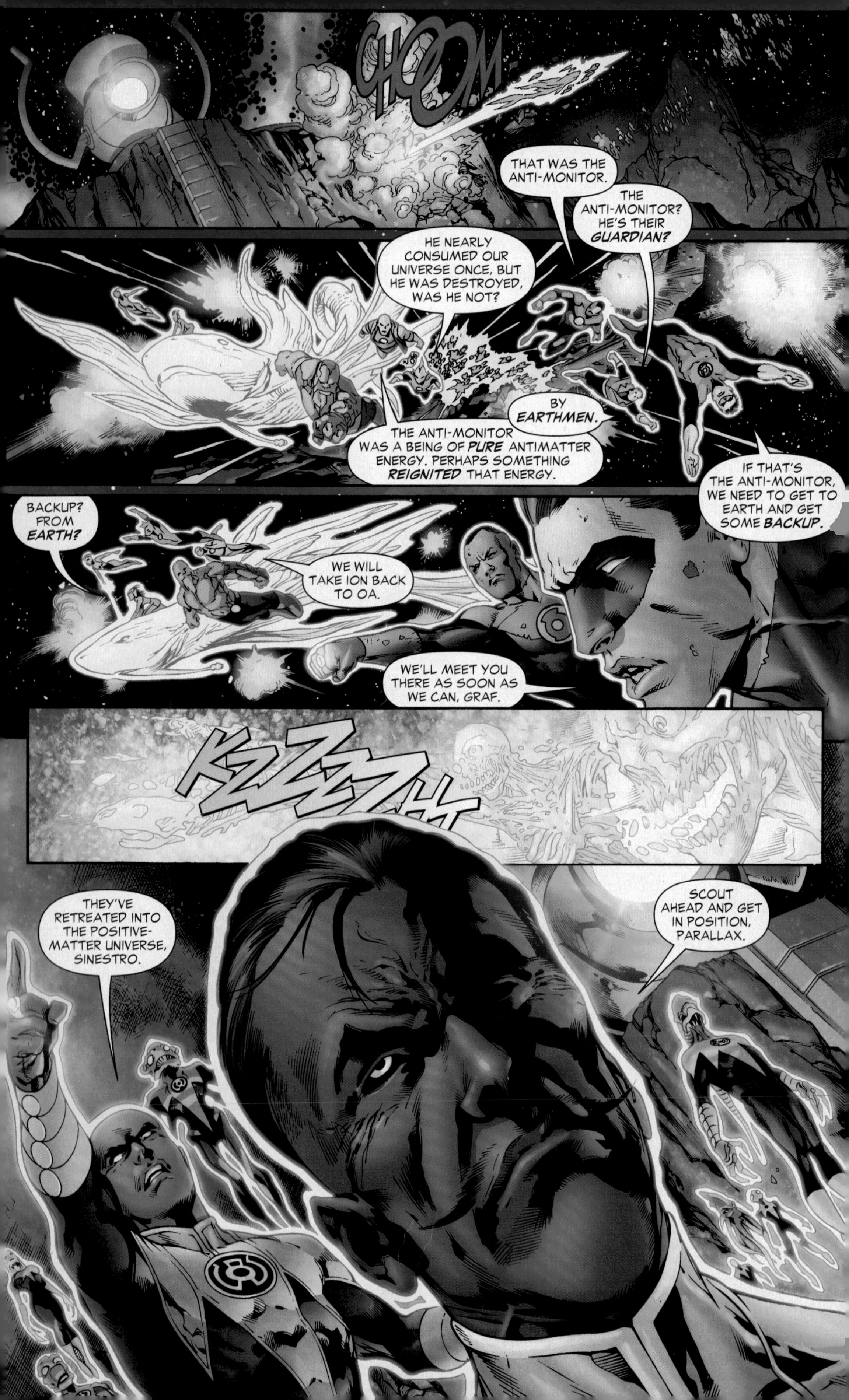
CHOOM
THAT WAS THE ANTI-MONITOR.
THE ANTI-MONITOR? HE'S THEIR GUARDIAN?
HE NEARLY CONSUMED OUR UNIVERSE ONCE, BUT HE WAS DESTROYED, WAS HE NOT?
BY EARTHMEN.
THE ANTI-MONITOR WAS A BEING OF PURE ANTIMATTER ENERGY. PERHAPS SOMETHING REIGNITED THAT ENERGY.
IF THAT'S THE ANTI-MONITOR, WE NEED TO GET TO EARTH AND GET SOME BACKUP.
BACKUP? FROM EARTH?
WE WILL TAKE ION BACK TO OA.
WE'LL MEET YOU THERE AS SOON AS WE CAN, GRAF.
KZZZZMMHH
THEY'VE RETREATED INTO THE POSITIVE-MATTER UNIVERSE, SINESTRO.
SCOUT AHEAD AND GET IN POSITION, PARALLAX.

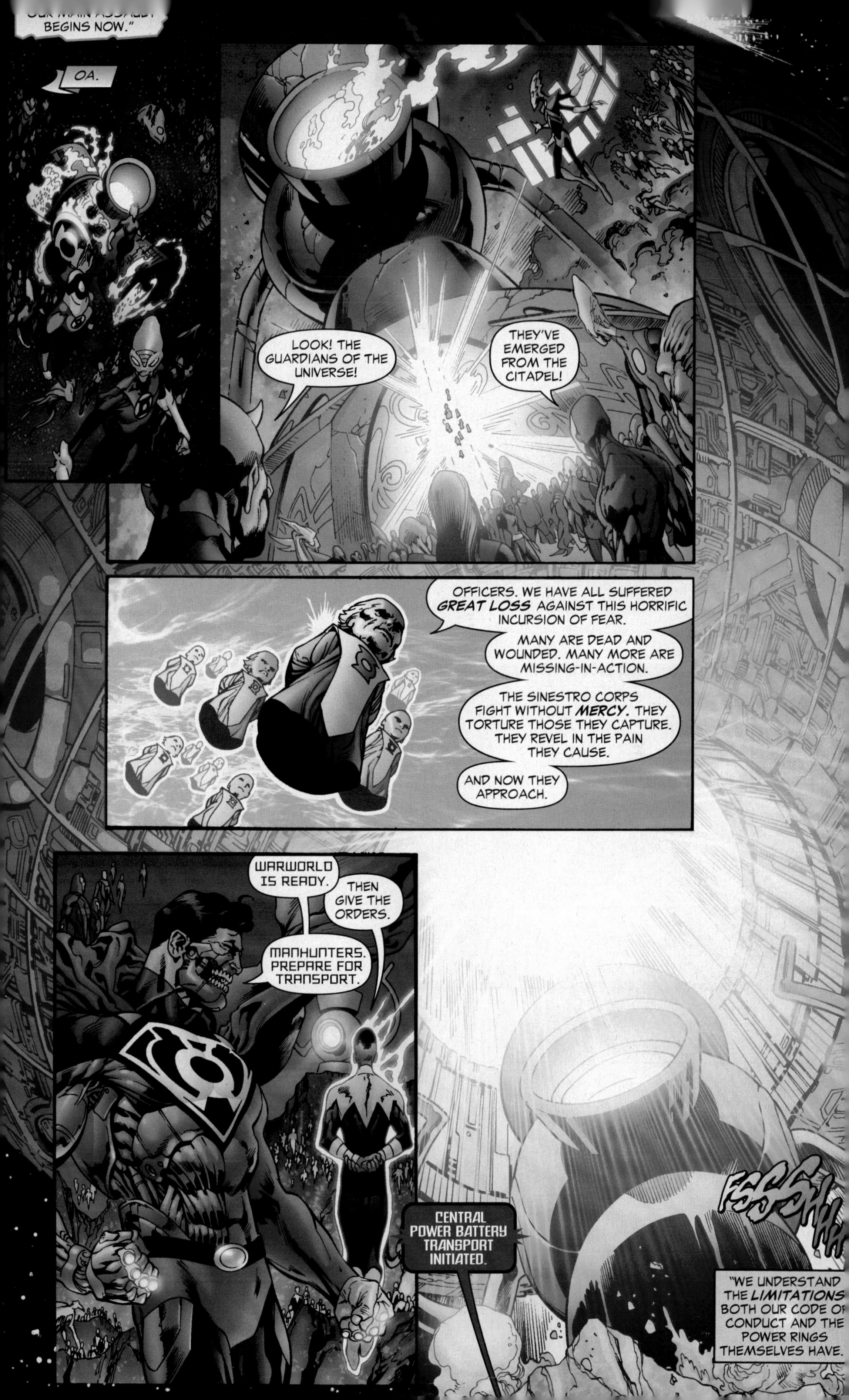
BEGINS NOW."
OA.
LOOK! THE GUARDIANS OF THE UNIVERSE!
THEY'VE EMERGED FROM THE CITADEL!
OFFICERS. WE HAVE ALL SUFFERED GREAT LOSS AGAINST THIS HORRIFIC INCURSION OF FEAR.
MANY ARE DEAD AND WOUNDED. MANY MORE ARE MISSING-IN-ACTION.
THE SINESTRO CORPS FIGHT WITHOUT MERCY. THEY TORTURE THOSE THEY CAPTURE. THEY REVEL IN THE PAIN THEY CAUSE.
AND NOW THEY APPROACH.
WARWORLD IS READY.
THEN GIVE THE ORDERS.
MANHUNTERS. PREPARE FOR TRANSPORT.
CENTRAL POWER BATTERY TRANSPORT INITIATED.
"WE UNDERSTAND THE LIMITATIONS BOTH OUR CODE OF CONDUCT AND THE POWER RINGS THEMSELVES HAVE.

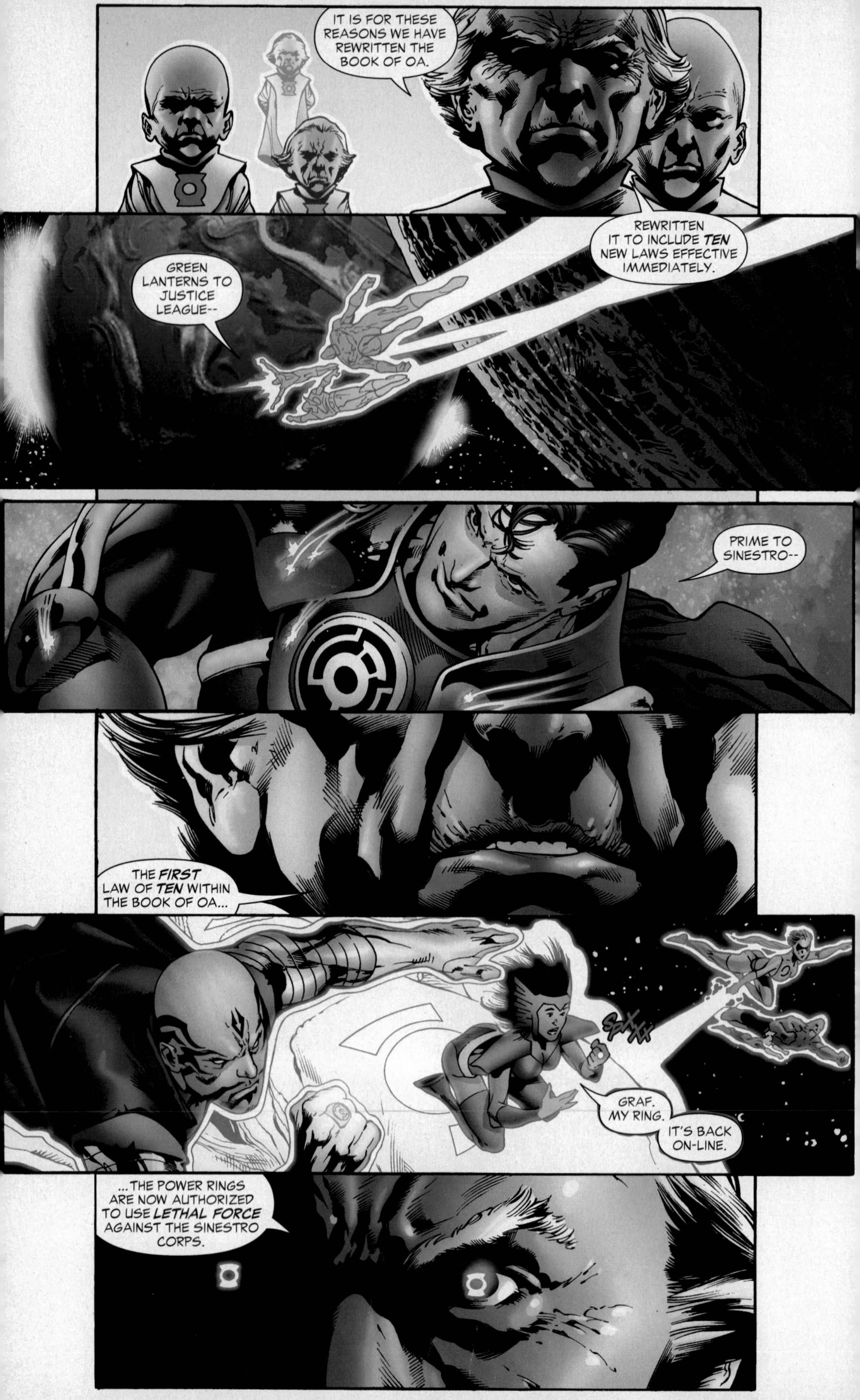
IT IS FOR THESE REASONS WE HAVE REWRITTEN THE BOOK OF OA.
REWRITTEN IT TO INCLUDE TEN NEW LAWS EFFECTIVE IMMEDIATELY.
GREEN LANTERNS TO JUSTICE LEAGUE--
PRIME TO SINESTRO--
THE FIRST LAW OF TEN WITHIN THE BOOK OF OA...
GRAF. MY RING.
IT'S BACK ON-LINE.
...THE POWER RINGS ARE NOW AUTHORIZED TO USE LETHAL FORCE AGAINST THE SINESTRO CORPS.

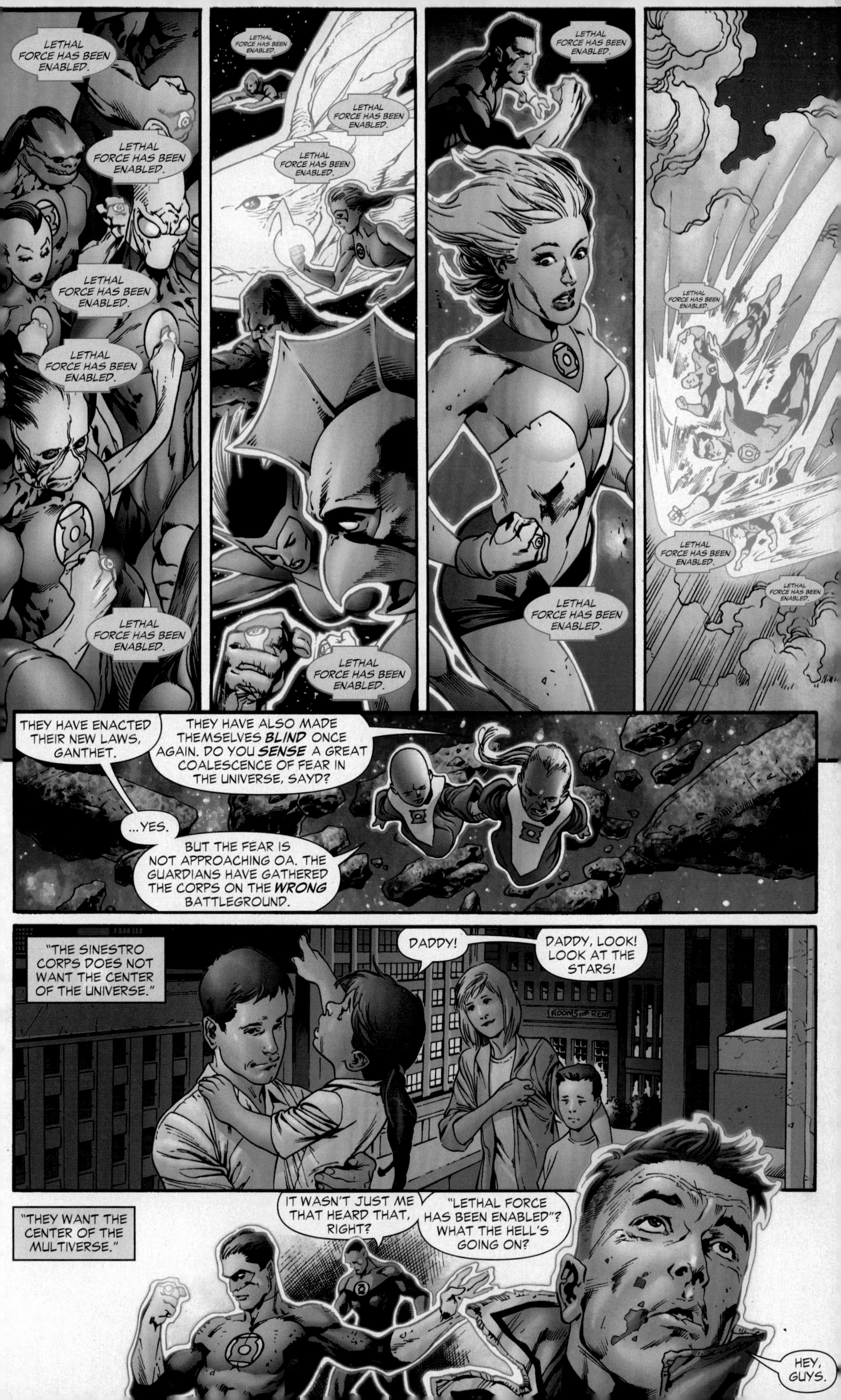
LETHAL FORCE HAS BEEN ENABLED.
LETHAL FORCE HAS BEEN ENABLED.
LETHAL FORCE HAS BEEN ENABLED.
LETHAL FORCE HAS BEEN ENABLED.
LETHAL FORCE HAS BEEN ENABLED.
LETHAL FORCE HAS BEEN ENABLED.
LETHAL FORCE HAS BEEN ENABLED.
LETHAL FORCE HAS BEEN ENABLED.
LETHAL FORCE HAS BEEN ENABLED.
LETHAL FORCE HAS BEEN ENABLED.
LETHAL FORCE HAS BEEN ENABLED.
LETHAL FORCE HAS BEEN ENABLED.
LETHAL FORCE HAS BEEN ENABLED.
LETHAL FORCE HAS BEEN ENABLED.
THEY HAVE ENACTED THEIR NEW LAWS, GANTHET.
THEY HAVE ALSO MADE THEMSELVES BLIND ONCE AGAIN. DO YOU SENSE A GREAT COALESCENCE OF FEAR IN THE UNIVERSE, SAYD?
...YES.
BUT THE FEAR IS NOT APPROACHING OA. THE GUARDIANS HAVE GATHERED THE CORPS ON THE WRONG BATTLEGROUND.
"THE SINESTRO CORPS DOES NOT WANT THE CENTER OF THE UNIVERSE."
DADDY!
DADDY, LOOK! LOOK AT THE STARS!
ROOMS FOR RENT
"THEY WANT THE CENTER OF THE MULTIVERSE."
IT WASN'T JUST ME THAT HEARD THAT, RIGHT?
"LETHAL FORCE HAS BEEN ENABLED"? WHAT THE HELL'S GOING ON?
HEY, GUYS.

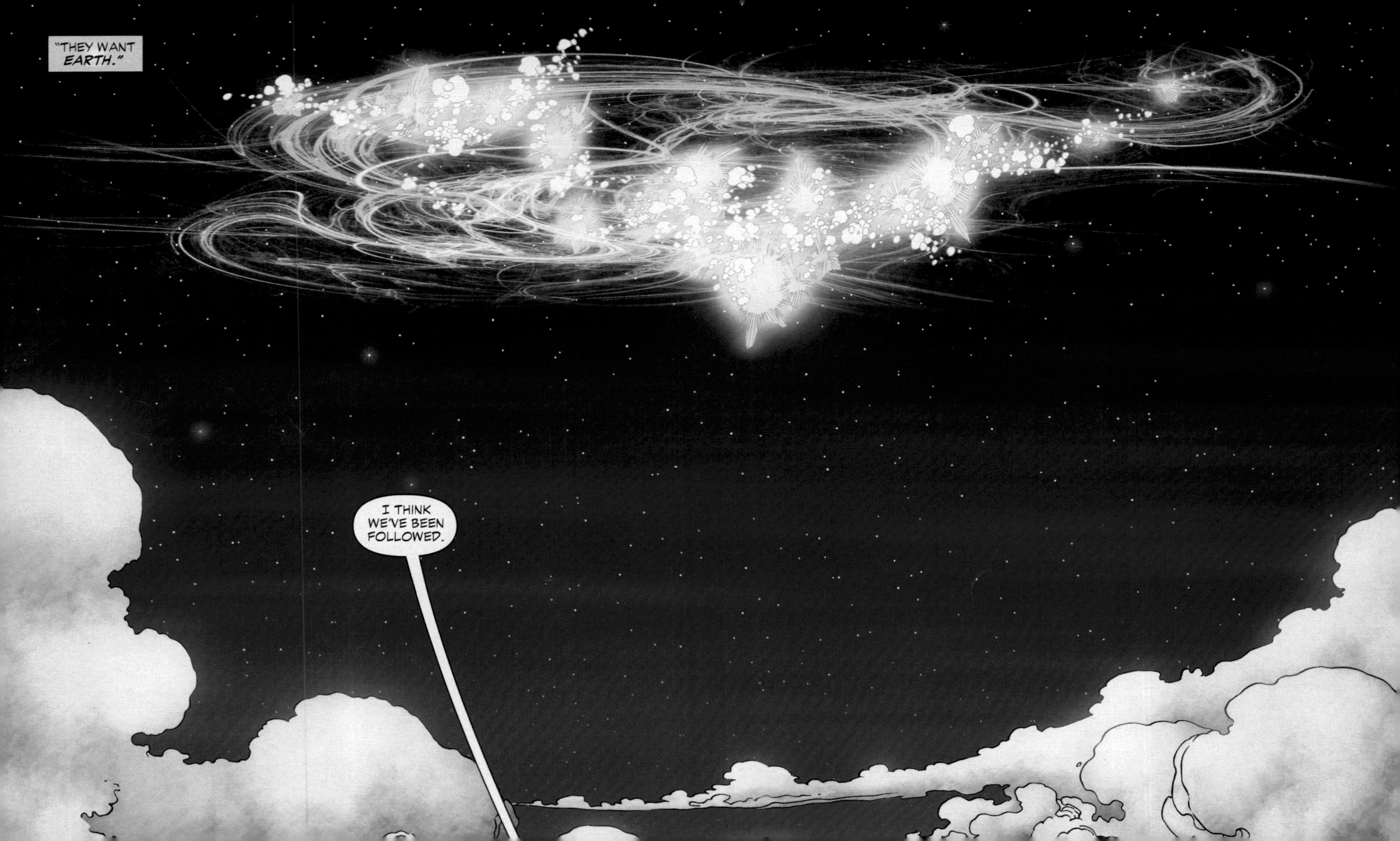
"THEY WANT EARTH."
I THINK WE'VE BEEN FOLLOWED.

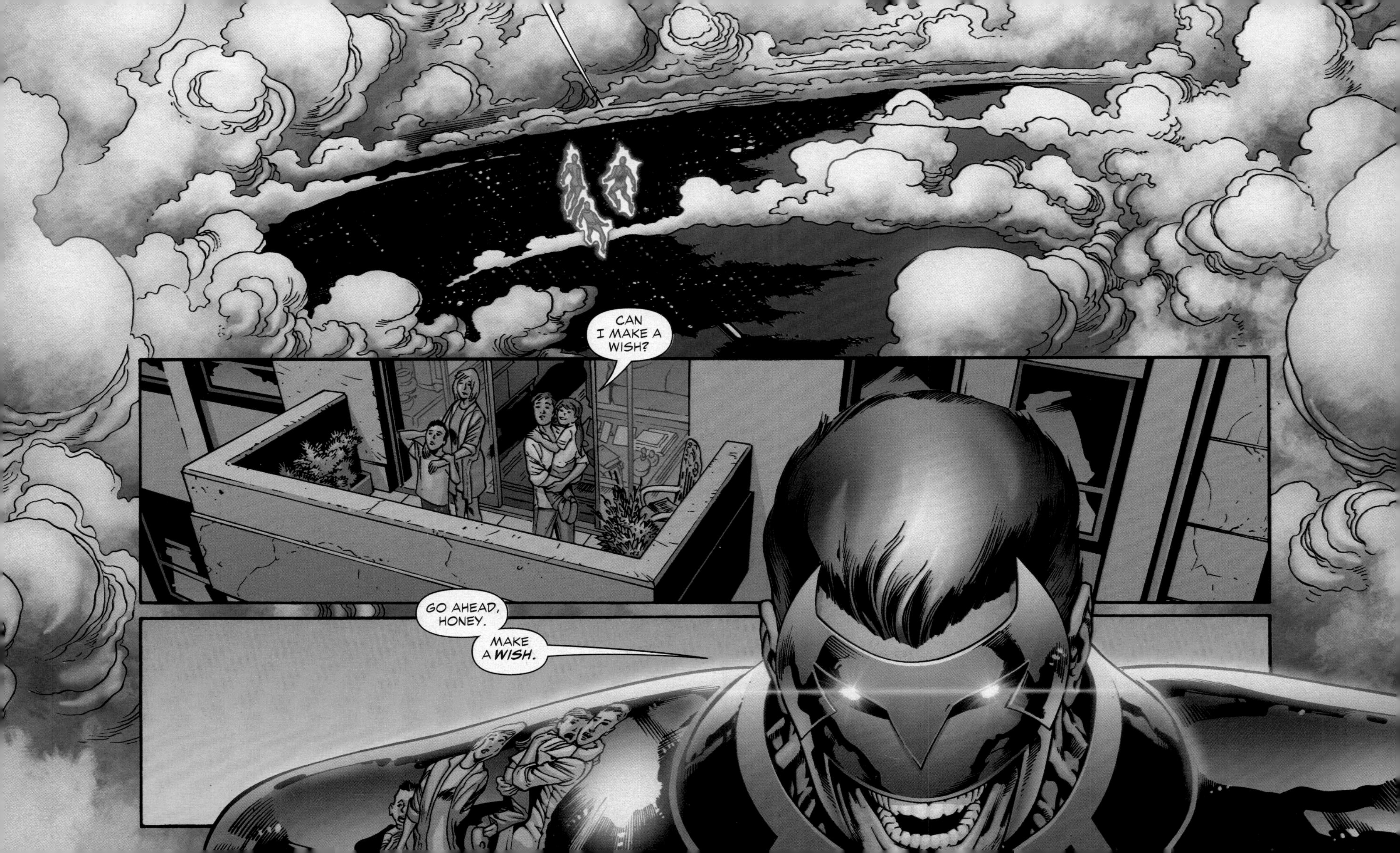
CAN I MAKE A WISH?
GO AHEAD, HONEY.
MAKE A WISH.

THOSE WHO WORSHIP EVIL'S MIGHT

The Green Lantern Corps was formed to maintain order in the universe. Only the most strong-willed and fearless beings in the universe could wield their power ring — able to create whatever the wearer can imagine.

Once one of the most honored members, Sinestro of Korugar fell to the corrupting influence of the ring's nearly limitless power and was banished from the known universe for his crimes.

Now, together with some of the most powerful villains from across the cosmos — the Anti-Monitor, a being who once destroyed the Multiverse; Parallax, a malevolent force that once decimated the Green Lantern Corps; Superman-Prime, the young Kal-El turned mad killer from a doomed dimension; and the Cyborg-Superman, a savage being bent on destroying all around him — Sinestro builds a new Corps.

Their mission: Rid the cosmos of Green Lanterns and establish a new universal order in the galaxy — under the merciless shadow of the Sinestro Corps!

Critically acclaimed storytellers Geoff Johns (JUSTICE SOCIETY OF AMERICA, ACTION COMICS, 52) and Dave Gibbons (THE ORIGINALS, WATCHMEN) team with superstar artist Ivan Reis (ACTION COMICS, RANN-THANAGAR WAR) Patrick Gleason (AQUAMAN, ROBIN) and Ethan Van Sciver (SUPERMAN/ BATMAN, FLASH: IRON HEIGHTS) will tear apart a universe to tell the most tragic tale in the Book of Oa.

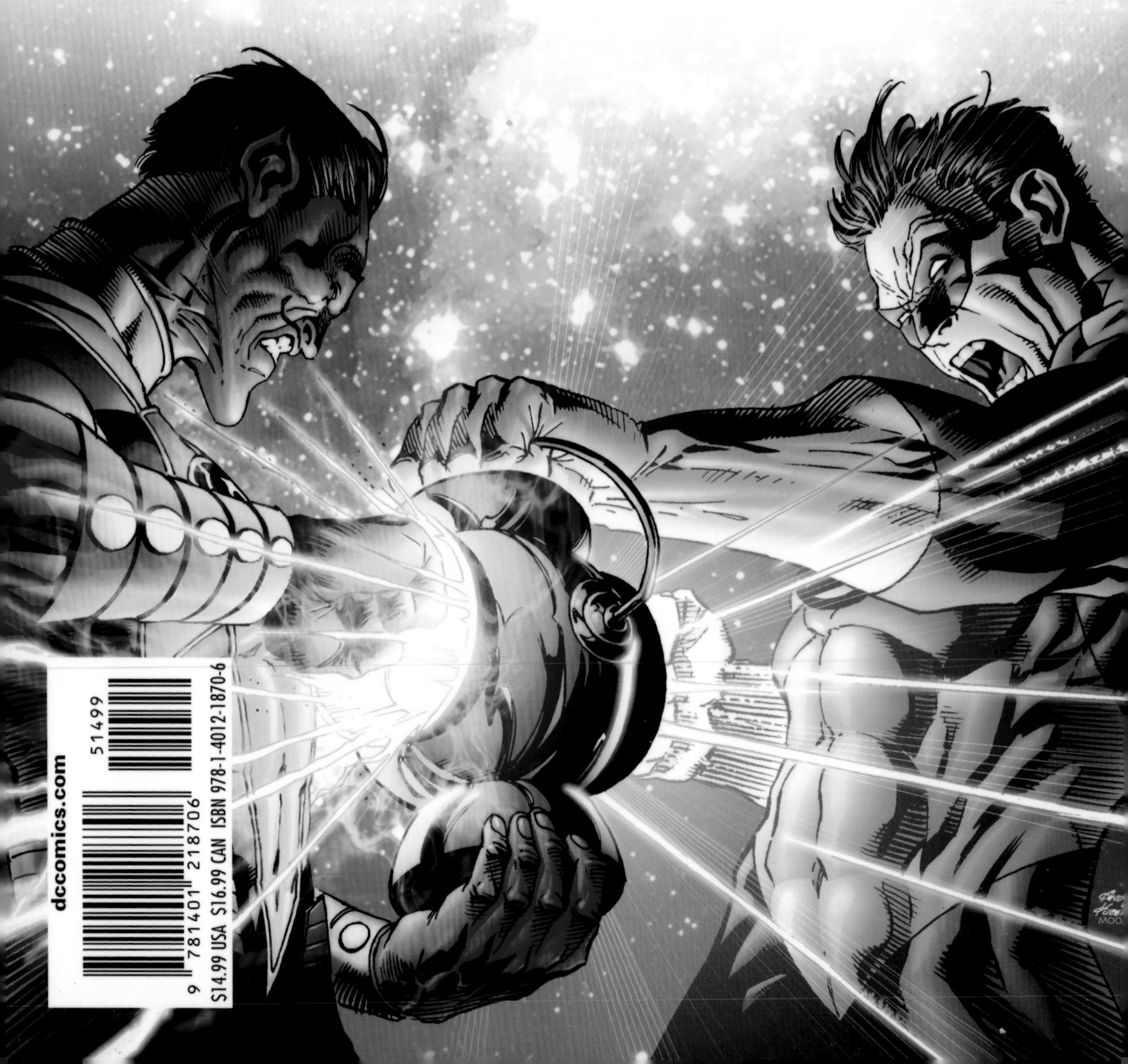

dccomics.com
$14.99 USA $16.99 CAN ISBN 978-1-4012-1870-6